Designing for the Circular Economy

The Circular Economy (CE) describes a world where product life extension through repair, refurbishment and remanufcaturing is the prevailing social and economic model. The goal of product circularity is to maximise value in products, materials and components in economic and social systems to the highest level over the longest time. The business opportunities are huge but developing product and service offerings and achieving competitive advantage means rethinking your business model from early creativity and design stages, through marketing and communication to supply and reverse logistics. *Designing for the Circular Economy* highlights and explores 'state of the art' research and industrial practice, highlighting CE as a source of: new business opportunities, radical business models, disruptive innovation, social change and new consumer attitudes.

The 34 chapters provide a comprehensive overview of issues related to product circularity from policy through to design and development. Chapters are designed to be easy to digest and include numerous examples. An important feature of the book is the case studies section that covers a diverse range of topics related to CE, business models and design and development in sectors ranging from construction to retail, clothing, technology and manufacturing.

Designing for the Circular Economy will inform and educate any companies seeking to move their business models towards sustainability; organizations already working in the CE can benchmark their current activities and draw inspiration from new applications and an understanding of the changing social and political context. This book will appeal to both academia and business with an interest in CE issues related to products, innovation and new business models.

Martin Charter has worked as a manager and trainer on sustainable innovation and product sustainability for 30 years in academia, business and consultancy. He is a Professor of Innovation & Sustainability and is the Founding Director of The Centre for Sustainable Design® and Senior Associate of the Business School for the Creative Industries at the University for the Creative Arts (UCA). Martin is a recognised international expert in innovation and sustainability and is the author or co-author of *Greener Marketing 1 & 2: Sustainable Solutions and System Innovation for Sustainability.*

Designing for the Circular Economy

Edited by
Martin Charter

Routledge
Taylor & Francis Group

LONDON AND NEW YORK

First published 2019
by Routledge
2 Park Square, Milton Park, Abingdon, Oxon OX14 4RN

and by Routledge
711 Third Avenue, New York, NY 10017

Routledge is an imprint of the Taylor & Francis Group, an informa business

British Library Cataloguing-in-Publication Data
A catalogue record for this book is available from the British Library

Library of Congress Cataloging-in-Publication Data
Names: Charter, Martin, editor.
Title: Designing for the circular economy / edited by Martin Charter.
Description: Abingdon, Oxon ; New York, NY : Routledge, 2018. | Includes bibliographical references and index.
Identifiers: LCCN 2018014824 (print) | LCCN 2018018179 (ebook) | ISBN 9781315113067 (eBook) | ISBN 9781138081017 (hardback : alk. paper)
Subjects: LCSH: Product design—Environmental aspects. | Recycled products. | Green products. | Sustainable development. | Environmentalism—Economic aspects.
Classification: LCC TS171.4 (ebook) | LCC TS171.4 .D492 2018 (print) | DDC 658.5/752—dc23
LC record available at https://lccn.loc.gov/2018014824

ISBN: 978-1-138-08101-7 (hbk)
ISBN: 978-1-315-11306-7 (ebk)

Typeset in New Baskerville
by Apex CoVantage, LLC
Printed and bound by CPI Group (UK) Ltd, Croydon, CR0 4YY

Contents

About the editor

Professor Martin Charter co-founded The Centre for Sustainable Design ® at University for the Creative Arts (UCA) in 1995 and has directed it since 1996. He is Professor of Innovation and Sustainability and Senior Associate at the Business School for the Creative Industries at UCA. Martin previously held the roles of Visiting Professor of Sustainable Product Design at UCA, Visiting Fellow at University of Southampton and is presently an External Examiner for the University of Mauritius.

Martin has worked at Director level in business sustainability issues in consultancy, leisure, publishing, training, events and academia for 29 years. Prior to this, he held management positions in strategy, research and marketing for gardening, building products, trade exhibitions and financial services.

Martin was the Launch Director of Greenleaf Publishing, Marketing Director at the Earth Centre and former Director of Business Networks focused on sustainable business, green electronics and eco-innovation. He is currently a member of the editorial boards of the *International Journal of Sustainable Engineering* and the *International Journal of Sustainable Design*.

Martin has been a member of advisory boards covering green electronics, environmental technology, sustainability reporting and sustainable innovation for brands such as P&G and InterfaceFlor. He has sat on expert boards of the EC Eco-Innovation Observatory, ResponseAbility Alliance, One Earth Innovation and World Resources Forum. Martin is the convenor of ISO 14006 (eco-design), UK expert to ISO/IEC 62959 (eco-design), member of BS8001 (Circular Economy) core group and was previously UK expert to ISO TR 14062 (eco-design).

Martin is the founder of the 'Sustainable Innovation' international conference series that reached its 21st year in 2016. He is a regular international conference speaker, author and editor of various books about sustainable design, and is the pioneer of the GreenThink training programme that uses applied creativity techniques to develop sustainable solutions.

Martin has an MBA from Aston Business School (UK), was a delegate at The Earth Summit in 1992 and is Chairman of the Board of Trustees and Founder of Farnham Repair Café.

About the contributors

Dr Deborah Andrews is Associate Professor of Design, School of Engineering, London South Bank University. Deborah has 20 years' experience in the field of sustainable design and manufacture, which she incorporates into research, enterprise and teaching activities. Her specialism is the development of the Circular Economy and the inter-relationship between embodied and operational impacts, and projects range in scale from data centres to programmable thermostatic radiator valves. In addition to TSB/Innovate, Knowledge Transfer Partnerships and EPSRC-supported projects, Deborah regularly collaborates with industry and has been involved in the development of sustainable design tools and services for a design consultancy and new product development tools for a commercial refrigeration manufacturer. Ongoing research includes an exploration of the influence of user behaviours on a Circular Economy in the commercial refrigeration, construction and IT sectors productivity and thermal comfort in the built environment and tools to facilitate design for Circularity.

Duncan Baker-Brown has practised, researched and taught around issues of sustainable development for over 25 years. He has worked on projects as diverse as 'The Greenwich Millennium Village' with Ralph Erskine and HTA, and more recently the multi-award-winning New Country House at Hadlow Down. Author of *The Re-Use Atlas: A Designer's Guide Towards a Circular Economy* published by RIBA, he is perhaps best known for a series of thought-provoking 'house' projects including 'The House that Kevin Built' in 2008 and 'The Brighton Waste House' in 2014. Baker-Brown's research tests the viability of a number of practices and materials, recognising the potential of discarded 'waste' as a valuable resource in the future of building, as well as live projects as valuable teaching aides. Through his projects, he fosters community development and regeneration, working with apprentice builders and students, informing young people of all ages as to their role in sustainable living. Baker-Brown creates examples of community practice that, through the use of innovative techniques such as 'resource mapping' can redefine what local materials are and match them with local skills and trades.

Conny Bakker is Professor of Design Methodology for Sustainability and Circular Economy at TU Delft, Faculty of Industrial Design Engineering. She explores strategies such as product life extension, reuse, remanufacturing and recycling, and the business models that enable these strategies. A second research interest is the field of sustainable consumption, which focuses on exploring the relationships between consumer behaviour, sustainability and design. Conny Bakker coordinates and teaches several courses in Sustainable Design and Circular Product Design, as well as an edX MOOC on the Circular Economy.

Professor Ruud Balkenende is Professor of Circular Product Design at TU Delft, Faculty of Industrial Design Engineering since 2015. His research, projects and teaching concentrate on the connection between product design and Circular Economy, especially addressing product lifetime extension through reuse, repair, refurbishment and material recovery through recycling. A core aspect of his work is relating engineering aspects to business aspects and user behavior to achieve solutions that allow for implementation. He joined TU Delft after 25 years of experience at Philips Electronics, where he has been active in materials related research for devices ranging from magnetic tapes and steam irons, to televisions, laser diodes and LEDs, also exploring design for sustainability. He published about 40 papers and holds 30 patents.

Anne-Marie Benoy is a Research and Partnership Associate in the Hoffmann Centre for Sustainable Resource Economy at Chatham House. Anne-Marie joined Chatham House in 2017 and works on a variety of topics including waste, Circular Economy, agricultural supply chains and diets. Before joining Chatham House, Anne-Marie was manager of the All-Party Parliamentary Sustainable Resources Group (APSRG) and the Sustainable Resource Forum based at Policy Connect. In this role, Anne-Marie brought together stakeholders from a variety of industries and sectors to inform UK policy on waste and Circular Economy and raise the profile of these policy areas in Parliament. Anne-Marie was also lead author of the APSRG's inquiry into UK remanufacturing (published in 2014) and edited an essay collection on supply chain sustainability (published in 2016). She has a Bachelor of Science in Geography and Masters of Arts in Environment, Politics and Globalisation both from King's College London.

Dr Fenna Blomsma is a post-doc researcher at the Technical University of Denmark. With this, she continues a journey towards making sustainable business practices accessible and relevant for all businesses. Fenna has a Bachelor's in Industrial Design Engineering and a Master's in Design for Interaction, both from Delft University of Technology. She furthermore has a Master's in Sustainable Manufacturing from Cranfield University and has recently completed a PhD at Imperial College London into how practitioners interpret and use the Circular Economy concept when innovating.

Dr Geraldine Brennan is a post-doc researcher at Middlesex University Business School, UK, and part of the ESRC Centre for the Understanding of Sustainable Prosperity (CUSP). As part of her current work, she is exploring the roles of alternative models of enterprise and alternative investment strategies in contributing to sustainable prosperity. Previously, Geraldine completed a PhD at Imperial College London into how organizational influence shapes sustainable value creation opportunities in value network relationships. Before this, she worked as a sustainability consultant as well as completed a Master's at Imperial College into Environmental Technology: Business & Environment.

Louis Brimacombe is a thought leader in sustainable development and Life Cycle Assessment, working across a wide network of industry and academic partners. In 2015, he became Chair of the Product Sustainability Committee of the World Steel Association and presented his work to steel industry leaders in Japan, Europe, China, USA and Latin America. He is Chairman of the IOM3's Sustainable Development Group, with membership representing all materials, industry sectors, supply chains and markets. He was awarded the IOM3, Sir Robert Hadfield Medal and he delivered the Bessemer Master Class in 2014. From 2001 up to July 2016, Louis was Head of Environmental Technology, leading a 50-person research team at Tata Steel. He is a Fellow of IOM3 and a chartered Chemical Engineer. In 2016, he became a Visiting Fellow in the Faculty of Engineering at the University of Sheffield.

Dave Bush owns and runs and Hallmark Blinds, commercial shading specialist; in 2017-18 he is also honorary president of the BBSA and a Director of the European Solar Shading Organisation (ES-SO). As a key member of BBSA and ES-SO, Dave has worked tirelessly to promote the significance and value of passive shading products in the built environment.

James D. Burgon is a researcher in the University of Glasgow's Institute of Biodiversity, Animal Health and Comparative Medicine (IBAHCM). He has a background in zoology and ecology, with a PhD in Evolutionary Biology. In 2016, he was a Postgraduate Fellow at the Parliamentary Office of Science and Technology (POST; UK), where he produced an information briefing document for Parliamentarians on the opportunities of, and barriers to, transitioning to a Circular Economy. This involved an extensive review of current literature and legislations, as well as interviews with experts from academia, government bodies, NGOs, business and professional organisations.

Konstantinos Chalaris is an architecture educator, design researcher and practitioner, whose work bridges academic research and industry practice with a particular interest in sustainable design. Konstantinos has been practising architecture and design since his graduation from the Royal College of Art, working with prominent clients including: The Design Council, British Gas, L'Oréal, as well as start-ups in the field of the Internet of Things, which has resulted in his work being widely published. He is currently a Senior Lecturer in Interior Design at Kingston University, as well as a Research Fellow for The Body Shop Innovation Catalyst.

Andrew Chalk is Director of Operations at the British Blind and Shutter Association (BBSA). As a key member of BBSA and ES-SO, Andrew has worked tirelessly to promote the significance and value of passive shading products in the built environment.

Dr Jonathan Chapman is Professor and Director of Doctoral Studies at Carnegie Mellon University's School of Design. His research shapes future design paradigms for longer-lasting materials, products and user experiences – an approach he defines as 'emotionally durable design'. He has developed this research with over 100 global businesses and governmental bodies – from Sony, Puma, The Body Shop and Philips to the House of Lords and the United Nations – advancing the social and ecological relevance of their products, technologies and systems. Chapman's work in sustainable design has generated international attention from media such as the *New York Times*, the *Guardian*, the *Independent*, CNN International and BBC Radio 4. *New Scientist* described him as 'a mover and shaker' and a 'new breed of sustainable design thinker'.

Ichin Cheng is director and co-founder of Sustainable Innovation Lab, a consultancy which helps governments and businesses to innovate and become more sustainable. Ichin has over 25 years of international professional experience in the field of environment related to green business, climate change policy mitigation and adaption, clean technology and Circular Economy. She has been involved in many international expert committees and advisory boards including Climate KIC, EC Horizon 2020 (Industrial Leadership and International Cooperation), EC foresight panels on European Industrial Landscape Vision (2025) and Systemic Eco-innovation and Eco-industries 2035. Ichin co-authored eight books and more than 250 reports and research papers. She holds a Master's degree in Geography and Environmental Engineering from the John Hopkins University in the US and an EMBA fellowship from Cambridge University in the UK.

Phil Cumming is a senior member of Marks and Spencer plc's Plan A team. Phil has over 18 years' experience supporting a wide range of organisations in the UK and globally on sustainability, including the London 2012 Olympic Games and Paralympic Games, Kingfisher plc and the World Economic Forum. He chaired the British Standards Institution (BSI) Technical Committee on Sustainable Resource Management which was responsible for developing BS 8001 believed to be the world's first Circular Economy business standard. He also sits on the boards of Julie's Bicycle (a leading sustainability charity working with the music, theatre and creative industries) and Resource Futures (a Certified B Corp with a 25-year heritage of promoting sustainable resource management).

Dr Elma Durmišević is head of EU research group Reversible Buildings at University of Twente, founder of Centre for Green Transformable Buildings in the Netherlands, and International Green Design Foundation, head of 4D Architects office in Amsterdam, executive board member of Dutch Building Innovation Platform Boosting and jury member for the Dutch Building Award 2016 and 2017. Elma Durmišević holds a PhD from the Delft University of Technology on Transformable Building Structures, and Design for Disassembly. As Associate Professor at the University of Twente, Durmišević developed a Master's programme for dynamic and sustainable buildings that introduced green engineering in industrial design of architecture. Durmišević initiated a consortium for the development and construction of a Green Transformable Building Laboratory in the Netherlands, is a member of a number of juries and scientific committees, reviewer of scientific books and journals, was a project leader of a number of innovation projects and has developed innovative building systems and measurement tools for sustainable architecture and construction.

Professor Rebecca Earley has been a design researcher at Textiles Environment Design (TED) since 2000 and was Director of the Textile Futures Research Centre (TFRC) from 2010–2017. In 2017, she co-founded Centre for Circular Design at UAL. She researches sustainable design strategy, curates exhibitions, and creates original materials, models and prototypes. In 2007, she was nominated as a Morgan Stanley Great Briton for her contribution to sustainable fashion textiles in the UK. Becky now works with organisations to embed sustainable design research within the academic and corporate culture. Clients include H&M, Filippa K and VF Corporation. She currently works on two Swedish-based projects with Research Institutes of Sweden (RISE) – MISTRA Future Fashion and Trash-2-Cash. Between 2015 and 2017 Becky was a judge for the Global Change Award – a visionary programme for entrepreneurs funded by the H&M Foundation.

Dr Kate Goldsworthy is a designer and academic working to bridge science, industry and design through multidisciplinary and practice-led research. Projects currently include Mistra Future Fashion (2015–2019), the EU Horizon 2020 project, Trash-2-Cash (2015–2018) and a longstanding working relationship with Worn Again, a revolutionary new recycling-tech company based in the UK. She first began her research with Textiles Environment Design (TED) and the Textile Futures research Centre (TFRC) at the University of the Arts London in 2005 with the first UK practice-based doctorate focused on 'designing for the Circular Economy'. Her Laser Finishing process, developed in 2008, enables fully closed-loop recycling of polyester fibres at end of life, and has been exhibited internationally. She is currently a member of the EPSRC Forum in Manufacturing Research, and was named by the *Guardian* as one of their top 10 Circular Economy experts in 2015.

Zoe De Grussa graduated from London South Bank University with a first-class honours degree in Engineering Product Design in 2015. During the course, she developed an active interest in sustainable design and manufacture. Since graduation she has been studying for a PhD investigating the sustainability of solar shading products in the built environment. In addition to environmental and economic benefits (by saving energy), she is investigating their impact on health, wellbeing, and productivity.

Mark Hilton is an aeronautical and environmental engineer with 14 years' experience in the aerospace industry, developing future project concepts, and over 20 years in environmental consultancy, currently as Head of Circular Economy and Sustainable Business at Eunomia Research and Consulting in the UK. Mark has worked extensively with the UK's Waste and Resources Action Programme (WRAP) and with companies of all sizes in most sectors, from leading corporates such as Airbus, Vodafone and Dell to innovative start-ups and SMEs, helping to deliver resource efficiency and eco-design solutions and to develop pragmatic and profitable circular business models.

Rhiannon Hunt is an accomplished designer and researcher specialising in sustainable design concepts for a Circular Economy. She holds a BSc Environmental Science from the University of Southampton and completed an MA Textile Design at the University of the Arts London in 2014. Rhiannon has since worked in the private sector developing sustainability experience across both the construction and fashion industries. She is currently completing a PhD with The Centre for Sustainable Design® at the University for the Creative Arts where she is researching Industry 4.0, design and the Circular Economy.

Scott Keiller is Sustainability Officer at the University for the Creative Arts, UK and a researcher in Sustainable Innovation at the Centre for Sustainable Design®. Previously, Scott worked for over 16 years leading the sustainability and communications programmes for companies in the retail and financial services sectors and holds degrees in Ecology and Mathematics. Scott was involved in the research and development of Farnham Repair Café, was an early volunteer and is a keen amateur fixer.

Jon Khoo is an Innovation Partner at Interface with a focus on sustainability, inclusive business and intrapreneurship. Following a former career as a city lawyer, Jon joined Interface in 2012 having chosen to reapply his skills to tackle the global challenges of marine plastics, inequality and climate change. Jon's own decision to switch careers was itself inspired by the oceans, in particular, surfing trips and a marine conservation sabbatical with Blue Ventures monitoring coral reefs and engaging with a local community in Fiji. Jon is a trustee of environmental charity Surfers Against Sewage. Jon works on Interface and the Zoological Society of London's (ZSL) *Net-Works*™ partnership, a community-based supply chain for discarded fishing nets that provides access to finance and seeks to provide long-term conservation benefits.

Dr Cindy Kohtala is a Design-for-Sustainability researcher in Aalto University School of Arts, Design and Architecture, Helsinki, Finland. Her research focuses on grassroots communities that explore digital fabrication technologies and processes in devoted spaces – Fab Labs – and how these communities address sustainability issues in their ideologies and practices. She also lectures and writes about sustainable Product Service System design, open design, distributed economies and design activism, and she has been involved in several urban activism initiatives in Helsinki.

Johanna Lehne is a Research Associate in the Energy, Environment and Resources Department at Chatham House. Johanna joined Chatham House in 2015. She has published on issues spanning Circular Economy and developing countries, energy access for refugees and displaced populations and chokepoints and infrastructure vulnerabilities in global food trade. Her research includes Circular Economy, low-carbon innovation in the built environment, green innovation, resource governance, low-carbon development and low-carbon transition in China. She has a Bachelor of Arts in European Social and Political Studies from University College London and a Master of Philosophy in International Relations from the University of Oxford, where her dissertation research focused on the relationship between interstate conflicts and national oil and water endowments in the Middle East.

Professor Mattias Lindahl has worked at Linkoping University in Sweden since 2003, and is among the top internationally-recognized scholars in the areas of EcoDesign and Product Service Systems (PSS). He is currently running several large projects, e.g. about design and business aspects related to PSS, e.g. Mistra REES – Resource-Efficient and Effective Solutions based on Circular Economy thinking. He is the EcoDesign and PSS subject editor for the reputable *Journal of Cleaner Production*.

Lars Luscuere is Scientific Project Manager at EPEA Nederland B.V. He is Project Manager and Co-Developer of the Horizon 2020 Buildings as Material Banks (BAMB) project. In this project, he leads the development of Materials Passports as a tool to move towards a Circular Economy. Lars has a background in Human Technology and Industrial Ecology, studying the application of circularity to sociotechnical systems.

Professor Tim C. McAloone is Professor of Sustainable Product/Service-Systems at the Technical University of Denmark (DTU). He has a strong collaboration with industry, and has been creating methods and models for innovation issues such as sustainable product/service-systems, sustainable design and product innovation since 1993. He is currently engaged in a number of projects to support the transition to Circular Economy in industry. He is also the Vice-President of the Design Society and co-founder of essensus. Tim received his PhD from Cranfield University, where he studied the integration of EcoDesign strategies into industry. He has also served as guest professor at Stanford University, working with sustainable product/service innovation.

Dr Kirstie McIntyre is Global Director for HP Inc's sustainability operations. Her remit covers all product and service-related environmental laws and market access agreements on energy efficiency, chemical/material restrictions and end-of-life considerations. Her teams manage takeback and recycling, IT system support for reporting and disclosure and WW product compliance programmes. She liaises with government, industry associates and peers, supply chain partners as well as HP's customers and channel sales on environmental regulations, recycling and other sustainability aspects of HP's products. Kirstie also co-leads HP's Circular Economy programme and has worked for a number of years in the strategic development of sustainability and supply chain programmes for various companies in the electronics sector. She has an engineering doctorate in environmental technology and has published widely on sustainability and supply chain issues. Please see hp.com/sustainability for more information.

Dr Stuart McLanaghan is a business sustainability professional and IEMA Fellow. Founder and director of business consultancy – eden21; he works with clients to reposition their business towards more sustainable operating practices. Stuart played a major role in developing the world's first circular economy standard – BS 8001. A BBC Food Hero, he founded and operationally directed a multi-award winning wild food business, providing 'fells to plate' traceability for Waitrose. Stuart has advised the UK Prime Minister's Cabinet Office, other government departments, Environment Agency, British Army and major private/public sector clients. He has jointly developed and delivered training courses for BSI on behalf of the Welsh Government and businesses to progress circular economy thinking and its implementation. Through sister company fish21, and as a Global Ghost Gear Initiative partner, he is working to develop solutions to the problem of lost recreational fishing/angling gear worldwide.

Douglas Mulhall has co-developed buildings for the Circular Economy (CE), led CE studies for the government of Luxembourg and the European Investment Bank, and trained the leadership of the Ellen MacArthur Foundation. He is a business developer consulting with EPEA Umweltforschung GmbH and an associate researcher at TUDelft

Faculty of Architecture in the Netherlands and Technical University of Munich School of Architecture in Germany. He consults to the Horizon 2020 Buildings as Material Banks (BAMB) project. He co-authored *Cradle to Cradle Criteria for the Built Environment* and many other publications that form the basis for CE principles and practices.

Dr Frank O'Connor is an award-winning values-led Irish designer, activist, poet and artist focused on environmental and social responsibility. He began his first environmental research project in 1988. Since then, he has been fortunate to experience design from many perspectives including as in-house designer, mentor, coach, writer, advisor, consultant, strategist, teacher, lecturer, researcher, speaker, founder/entrepreneur and director. Working all over the globe, he has inputted into design and business strategies for hundreds of start-ups, SMEs and multinationals in a wide range of industrial sectors. He has also worked with many other institutes including governments on policy and delivery, inter-government organisations on capacity building and evaluation and universities on curriculum and research programmes. In doing so, he has stuck to his stubborn belief that environmental and social responsibility should be at the core of all design and organisational strategy and delivery.

David Parker is a Chartered Environmentalist and Chemical Engineer. Having worked for ICI and DuPont in a number of roles, he joined sustainability consultancy Oakdene Hollins in 2001. Since then, he has been involved in diverse activities related to waste and resources working with the UK's Innovate UK, Department for Food and Rural Affairs (Defra) and the Waste & Resources Action Programme (WRAP). A running theme has been remanufacturing which was his first project at Oakdene Hollins, and this escalated into running the Defra-funded Centre for Remanufacturing & Reuse in the period 2006–2010. Over that period, the Centre delivered actions to address barriers to adoption of product reuse by businesses and purchasers, including standards; carbon benefits; government buying specifications; remediation technologies; learning and skills modules; collaborative supply chain initiatives; product re-design sponsorship and others. Having completed a Horizon 2020 project on the same topic, his focus is products loops in the Circular Economy. He now operates his own circular economy consultancy, getsetera.uk.

Dr Daniela C. A. Pigosso is Senior Researcher at the Technical University of Denmark (DTU). She has been actively researching into the area of Sustainable Innovation since 2006, with strong industrial collaboration.

Daniela's current research activities include projects related to supporting companies to make a transition to Circular Economy, focusing on
readiness assessment, business model innovation, design & innovation
processes and value chain collaboration. She is also co-founder of essensus, a spin-out from DTU that supports companies in integrating sustainability into their business processes. Daniela received her PhD from
the University of São Paulo, where she developed a maturity model for
EcoDesign implementation and management.

Flora Poppelaars is a PhD candidate in the Design for a Circular Economy research group at TU Delft University of Technology. Her PhD
focuses on the shift towards a circular economy from a consumer perspective. She researches how consumer participation in collection and
access-based consumption can be improved and how social change can
be encouraged. Flora has a bachelor in Industrial Design Engineering
and a master in Integrated Product Design from the TU Delft, and is a
Schmidt-MacArthur Fellowship alumna.

Dr Anne Prahl is a research and design consultant with over 20 years of
experience in the international fashion and sportswear industry. She
specialises in sustainable design innovation, working on a diverse range
of projects, which contribute to resource efficiency and the development of a Circular Economy. Projects include the re-use and recycling
of obsolete stock and developing brand-specific sustainable design strategies, as well as motivating industry professionals through talks, collaborative design projects, interactive workshops and tailor-made tools (such
as the WRAP Clothing Knowledge Hub). Anne is a regular speaker at
international conferences and industry events and contributes to various industry publications, including Greenpeace's 'Fashion at the
Crossroads' report (2017). Anne holds a Master's degree in Design for
Textile Futures from Central Saint Martins College of Art & Design and
was awarded the PhD degree for her research *Designing Wearable Sensors
for Preventative Health: An Exploration of Material, Form & Function* at London College of Fashion in 2015.

Professor Walter R. Stahel has been founder-director of the Product-Life
Institute (Switzerland), the oldest established consultancy in Europe
devoted to developing sustainable strategies and policies, since 1983.
From 1986 to 2014, he was also Director of Risk Management Research
of the Geneva Association. In 1971, he graduated from ETH Zurich
with an MA in architecture; he has been a full member of the Club
of Rome since 2013. Walter has been Visiting Professor at the Faculty

of Engineering and Physical Sciences of the University of Surrey since 2005, and of l'Institut EDDEC de Université, HEC et Polytechnique de Montréal in 2016. He was awarded degrees of Doctor honoris causa by the University of Surrey (2013) and l'Université de Montréal (2016). In 1982, with 'The Product-Life Factor', he won a Mitchell Prize in Houston, TX; In 1978, together with Peter Perutz, he won a first prize in the competition of the German Future's Society, Berlin, with a paper on unemployment, occupation and profession. His 'corner' books are *Jobs for Tomorrow, the Potential for Substituting Manpower for Energy* (1981) and *The Performance Economy* (2010).

Professor Ab Stevels has university degrees in chemistry and physics. He worked for 40 years at Philips in a variety of jobs in research, product development, production and business management. As of 1993 he became an Environmental Advisor at the Philips Consumer Electronics Division. His activities there include environmental design of products, environmental management and the organization of recycle systems for discarded consumer electronics products. The same fields were addressed as a part-time professor at Delft University of Technology between 1996–2008. Currently, Ab is still active as a 'professional volunteer'.

Dr Erik Sundin works as an Associate Professor at the Division of Manufacturing Engineering, Department of Management and Engineering at Linköping University, Sweden. He conducted his PhD in the area of remanufacturing at Linköping University and his thesis was entitled: *Product and Process Design for Successful Remanufacturing.* Currently, he is performing research within *remanufacturing, Circular Economy, product-service systems (PSS)* and *sustainable manufacturing.* He has been working in EU-projects including *ERN, CIRC€UIT, L4IDS, CAN-Reman* and *CarE-Service* as well as many national projects. Since 2012 he is acting associated editor for *Journal of Remanufacturing* (Springer). All in all, he has written 111 papers and 11 book chapters. According to Google Scholar, Erik has 3,068 citations with an h-index of 27. More information can be found at: https://liu.se/en/employee/erisu71.

Dr Nazli Terzioglu is a researcher and designer who challenges people to think differently about products, repair and obsolescence. In 2017, Nazli completed her PhD at Royal College of Art during which she developed Do-Fix repair kits that combine new technologies such as 3D printing with traditional repair methods such as kintsugi, darning and patching, focused on making repairs both visible and engaging to carry out. She has a BID in Industrial Design and a BA in Sociology from Middle East Technical University. She graduated with a M.Sc.

in Industrial Design in 2013, during which she explored the means of extending the lifespan of kitchen appliances, mainly focusing on the reasons for breakdown and repair problems. Nazli's expertise includes Circular Economy, sustainable product design, product longevity and visible product repair. Through designing workshops, objects and writing, Nazli investigates the ways to inspire and encourage people to change the current economic and social system

Sigurd Sagen Vildåsen is Research Fellow, Department of Industrial Economics and Technology Management, NTNU. Sigurd works in the field of corporate sustainability, which refers to social and environmental concerns in business operations. His research activities at NTNU, the largest university in Norway, are part of the project 'Sustainable Innovation and Shared Value Creation in Norwegian Industry' (SISVI). SISVI is a four-year industry-academia collaboration that runs in the period of June 2014 to June 2018. His empirical work deals with a longitudinal case study on the development of a circular business model in the plastic industry. The case study focuses on how networks and third-party actors can help a small company to overcome barriers such as quality of secondary material. Besides research and teaching, Sigurd is heavily involved in administrative roles at the university along with volunteer work in external organizations. He has in recent years years become active in the 'International Sustainable Development Research Society' (ISDRS) where he focuses on career development for young scholars.

Jonathan Wentworth has a background in plant ecology with a PhD in Plant Ecological Genetics. He worked as a British civil servant in the Ministry of Agriculture, Fisheries and Food (MAFF) and the Department for Environment, Food and Rural Affairs (Defra) before joining the Parliamentary Office of Science and Technology (POST) in 2007. His current role as Environmental Adviser includes the production of information briefings for Parliamentarians (POSTnotes and POST-briefs) and providing support for evidence-based scrutiny of government policies by Parliamentary select committees.

Kyle Wiens is the CEO of iFixit, the free repair manual. He has dedicated his life to defeating the second law of thermodynamics, a battle fought in the courtroom as often as in the workshop. The Right to Repair campaign has, so far, successfully legalized cell phone unlocking and tractor repair. Kyle regularly speaks on design for repair, service documentation and the environmental impact of manufacturing. His writing has appeared in *The Atlantic, Harvard Business Review, Wired, Popular Mechanics* and the *Wall Street Journal.*

Acknowledgements

The Editor would like to thank all the contributors for their hard work and dedication in producing their chapters for this volume. Thanks also goes to Routledge and Apex CoVantage in bringing the book through production. My appreciation also goes to Ichin, Jessica, Stephen, John and other family, friends and colleagues for their support and encouragement. Finally, thanks go to Trustees, volunteers and visitors to Farnham Repair Cafe for showing how product circularity can become a reality.

In memory of John and Diana.

Martin Charter
Farnham, UK
May 2018

Preface

Five mega trends (PWC, 2017) will affect the world as we move towards 2030: urbanisation; shifts in global economic power; demographic change; technological breakthroughs; and climate change and resource scarcity. Growth in the global population will mean growing pressures on energy and resources. As a result, preventing and designing out waste will become a key focus of a new resource-efficient, low carbon paradigm. Circular Economy is increasingly being used around the world to describe the transition away from existing linear systems that take-make-waste. Leading companies are recognising the need to understand the implications of Circular Economy for business models, processes and product-services. *Designing for the Circular Economy* requires thinking about how to enable product circularity at both a systems level and at the early creativity, design and development stages, where 80% of product's environmental impacts are determined. Product circularity means taking an extended lifecycle perspective that focuses on maximising value in economic and social systems for the longest time; the focus is on the (re)use of products, and the materials and components within them rather than on the 'end of life'. To enable this, systems design and designing for loops to maximise value will be increasingly needed. Many of the elements of Circular Economy are not new but the emphasis on design and the need for systemic, systematic and coordinated approaches is new

Designing for the Circular Economy was conceived as a book to bring together a range of expert thinkers, researchers and practitioners to comprehensively fill the gap in understanding and knowledge around product circularity and related issues. Chapters have been designed to be concise and digestible to give "time poor" readers a means to develop a clearer world view on product sustainability. In the "Age of Acceleration", with the world moving faster and faster, Circular Economy thinking will become ever more important and understanding the implications for business models, innovation and product-services will be essential. A transition towards Circular Economy will be a key part of achieving the United Nations seventeen Sustainable Development

Goals (SDGs) by 2030; but a focus Circular Economy alone is not a "magic bullet". Achieving a more sustainable future will require integrated, systemic thinking, creativity, hard work and change.

My personal journey into business sustainability over the last thirty years has taught me several lessons that are perhaps relevant to enabling product circularity: recognise that there are change makers and change inhibitors – try and work with them both; try and think about other people's perspectives; think and think creatively; do what you can do to change something – however small or large; do what you say you will do; and trust in yourself.

BIBLIOGRAPHY

PWC (2017). Megatrends. [Online] http://www.pwc.co.uk/issues/megatrends. html [Accessed: 3rd February 2018]

1 Introduction

Martin Charter

> *The global economic model of value creation is wasteful and – for all practical purposes – continues to operate in a linear (take-make-dispose) system. Adopting Circular Economy principles could generate $4.5 trillion of additional economic output by 2030 whilst decoupling economic growth and natural resource consumption*
> *(Lacy and Rutqvist, 2015)*

BACKGROUND

Since the late 2000s, after the global economic crash, there has been growing discussion over Circular Economy (CE) at economic, societal and business levels. This followed on from longstanding – and sometimes forgotten – initiatives focused on resource efficiency and resource productivity that emerged in the 1990s in Japan, Germany and other European countries. The 1990s saw the publication of the influential *Factor Four* book (von Weizsäcker et al., 1998) focused on adding value through resource and energy efficiency, and increased policy, research and industry activity related topics such as 'extended producer responsibility', recycling and eco-design (including design for disassembly). Other catalysts to increased CE awareness emerged in the 2000s and included the publication of *Cradle to Cradle* in 2002 (Branungart and McDonough, 2002) and the emergence of the Ellen McArthur Foundation in the early 2010s.

At a high level, CE can be seen as part of sustainable development and touches on a number of the United Nations Sustainable Development

Goals (SDGs), in particular Responsible Consumption and Production. However, research has indicated that there is no universally accepted definition of CE (Kirchherr et al., 2017), with few explicitly linking the concept to sustainable development. This is a challenge for stakeholders in that with no common context and perspective on CE this means that policy makers, business and civil society may be talking at cross purposes. This may also be true in some countries that are taking a very broad definition of CE that seemingly includes renewable energy. There will be an increasing need for agreement over the terms and boundaries of CE if substantial progress is to be made in policy, business and civil society. For example, is waste management and recycling in or out of the scope of CE?

CE describes a world where maximising material use to its highest value over time in biological and technical systems is the prevailing economic and social model. The business opportunities that will emerge from CE are potentially huge, but developing more circular product-service solutions will mean rethinking business models from design through (re)manufacturing, supply chain, (reverse) logistics to marketing and communications. Increased circularity will see design for maintenance, repairability, reconditioning, refurbishment, upgradability, remanufacturing, recyclability and compostability being fully integrated into business models, and product-service design and development processes.

However, it is important to recognise that the concept of CE is still evolving and may mean different things to different people at different levels in different countries. It is also important to remember that in many parts of the world there aren't even basic waste management systems in place. A key topic then is how to design and implement new systems that focus on maximising materials value in the system for the longest time period, where waste is 'designed out' from the beginning. This will mean that radical new policy frameworks will need to be developed to enable the extension of the life cycle of product-services and packaging and the components and materials within them.

Despite the evolutionary nature of CE, we may be moving towards a tipping point where there is a growing consensus in the global community about starting the transition away from the linear economy toward a more circular one. This is being driven by a range of issues including increasing global population, resource constraints and risks, policy changes, raising awareness, social and technological innovation, new materials and recognition of business opportunities.

CE activity is emerging at European Commission (EC) policy and standards levels, with new initiatives also emerging in the Netherlands and Finland, that go well beyond sector-based extended producer responsibility initiatives and increased recycling targets. For example, a CE policy package was launched by the EC in December 2015 which has resulted in new standardisation activity related to repair, durability, remanufacturing and re-use. In 2018, China is revising its Circular Economy Promotion Law and Japan will move into the 3rd phase of its movement towards a Circular Society.

CE is moving into the boardroom – however, implementation is still at an early stage – and there is much to learn in relation to the implications for business models and product-service design and development. Against this backdrop, BS8001:2017 (BSI, 2017) was published in May 2017 to provide guidance on the implementation of CE in organisations. Whilst many of the components of CE have been in place in companies for many decades, what is new is the focus on retaining materials' value in systems over time, eliminating waste at the design stage, and the need to take a systemic and coordinated approach to CE within organisations and value networks. Even companies taking a leadership position on CE have not yet developed comprehensive approaches. For most organisations, CE is likely to lead to a re-engineering or adaption of existing business models rather than development of new business models – unless there are major threats, risks or opportunities. Disruptive innovation is more likely to occur from start-ups and/or from new technologies or in response to societal change, e.g. the 'Right to Repair' movement that started in the US is moving across to Europe.

CE thinking at a 'product level' or product circularly is focused on the use or *re-use* stage of the life cycle and is fundamentally *not* about end-of-life. It is about proactively building into the design and development phase of products-services, strategies to enable maintenance, repair, refurbishment, reconditioning, upgrading, remanufacturing, parts harvesting and finally recycling. In CE terms, recycling should be thought of, as much further down the line, than in traditional Life Cycle Thinking. CE thinking should lead to an extended life cycle perspective where materials are kept in the system to the highest value over the longest time period. However, a key issue is not to lose the life cycle perspective and to become myopic, e.g. trade-offs with other environmental aspects need to be considered. CE does not operate in a vacuum and is not a panacea.

CONCEPT

The focus of *Designing for the Circular Economy* is not on CE at a macro-economic or materials flow level (e.g. global steel consumption and production), but at the company level and more specifically at business model and product-service level; although, inevitably they are inextricably linked.

Designing for the Circular Economy explores 'state-of-the-art' research and industrial practice, highlighting CE as a source of: new business opportunities, radical business change, disruptive innovation, social change and new consumer attitudes. The target audience for the book is academia and business with an interest in CE issues related to products, innovation and new business models.

The 34 chapters provide a comprehensive overview of issues related to product circularity from policy through to design and development. All the chapters are designed to be easy to digest and include numerous examples. An important feature of the book is the case studies section that covers a diverse range of topics related to CE, business models and design and development in sectors ranging from construction to retail, clothing, technology and manufacturing.

The authors highlight innovative examples from a variety of practice in industries and businesses. Contributors illustrate the business, and design and development capabilities, thinking and skills that will be required to realise the potential opportunities resulting from a transition towards a more circular way of thinking. *Designing for the Circular Economy* aims to inform and educate companies, entrepreneurs and designers that are seeking to shift their business models, product-services and processes to align with the new paradigm. Organisations already working on CE, and those new to CE, will be able to benchmark their thinking and activities, gain improved understanding of emerging business practice and draw inspiration from innovative leaders, and new applications.

Designing for a Circular Economy is divided into five sections: Overview, Business Models, Design and Development, Technological and Social Innovation, and Case studies.

SECTION I: OVERVIEW

In Chapter 2, Stahel argues that a transition towards a Circular Industrial Economy (CIE) requires a paradigm shift from: consumers being motivated to be *consumers of products* to consumers becoming motivated to be *users of materials*; and companies shifting business models to sell *utilisation* rather than ownership. The chapter highlights emerging trends that support the premise that a movement has started from a Linear Industrial Economy (LIE) towards a CIE that includes: intelligent decentralisation, longer-life technologies, and re-usable high-technology. It is argued that central to the transition to the CIE will be a shift from the 'era of R' e.g. reuse, repair, etc., to the 'era of D' e.g. de-linking assemblies, de-polymerisation, etc. Design will play a key role in the shift.

In Chapter 3, Charter highlights that CE is not a totally new topic and that it emerged from longstanding discussions over resource efficiency and productivity that started in Japan and Germany in the 1990s. The chapter highlights that there are many definitions of CE with no one universally agreed and that CE should be viewed as part of a sustainable development. At product level, design for circularity should be considered within a broader eco-design approach and integrates an extended life cycle perspective that focuses on (re)use rather than end of life. The chapter includes discussion on a range of current and emerging future issues that will impact on product circularity, including policy, infrastructure, technology, the role of designers and materials.

In Chapter 4, Cumming references a number of 'schools of thought' that have fed into the emerging concept of CE and highlights where they differ. The practicalities of implementing CE within business are also discussed, as well as the key challenges. The chapter highlights that many companies are still at an early stage in their CE thinking and implementation, and there is a need for guidance, as there is still confusion even over the terminology and language of CE.

In Chapter 5, Benoy and Lehne give an overview over emerging developments in CE policy worldwide. The chapter highlights that CE-type policies have existed for decades but the explicit use of the term in policy is relatively new with a lack of definitive approaches. A CE policy toolkit is presented and the chapter concludes with some thoughts about future development.

In Chapter 6, Cheng gives an overview of CE policy development in three Asian countries: Japan is the front runner of CE with comprehensive legislative and recycling systems; China is the second biggest economy and has an ambitious CE strategy; and Taiwan has transformed itself into a recycling powerhouse. In addition, the chapter presents a series of examples of innovative circular products and technologies from each of the countries.

In Chapter 7, Burgon and Wentworth give an overview of key issues associated with transitioning towards CE that includes improved product design, extended producer responsibility and new business models. An introduction to selected national CE policies is given with a specific example of the UK highlighted. Key challenges to achieving CE are illustrated with discussion over what needs to happen to achieve increased circularity.

In Chapter 8, O'Connor reflects on 25 years of experience related to circularity in design in the electronics sector. A case study is presented that compares activities in the 1990s to 2017 and questions whether substantial progress has been made.

SECTION II: BUSINESS MODELS

In Chapter 9, Charter and McLanaghan discuss CE-related business models. The development of new circular business models has been closely aligned to many CE discussions; however, it is argued that for many organisations, CE may lead to the adaption of existing business models rather than significant change unless there are major opportunities, risks or threats. Disruptive start-ups are likely to be those that will drive new circular business models. Circular business model groupings are described and illustrated with examples related to the potential re-use and recycling of polymer-based fishing nets.

In Chapter 10, McAloone and Pigosso present a framework to support the design and development of Product Service Systems (PSS) that consider CE. The components of the framework are illustrated followed by a discussion of the development of PSS in a CE context.

In Chapter 11, Lindahl describes the issues surrounding CE-focused product-service solutions based on an extended life cycle perspective. An example of a CE-focused product-service approach is given from a Swedish company that has shifted to re-using cores from paper rolls that had not previously been considered in the sector.

In Charter 12, Parker highlights market, business model and design issues associated with remanufacturing in the laser printing market. The case of Kyocera is presented, highlighting the company's approach to design for remanufacturing.

In Charter 13, Blomsma and Brennan describe two systems-thinking tools that have been developed to support circular business modelling and product development. The Circular Compass identifies where waste is generated in systems and highlights three states of existence: particles, parts and products. The Circular Grid defines CE-related relationships in systems in terms of cost, risk, dependency, infrastructure and knowledge. The authors suggest that applying Circularity Thinking will provide a better understanding of what CE strategies, business models or product developers might pursue.

SECTION III: DESIGN AND DEVELOPMENT

In Chapter 14, Bakker, Balkenede and Poppelaars put forward the concept of product integrity in the context of CE. In a CE, a product repeatedly cycles through the economy in different states of integrity. Two scenarios are presented that have very different implications for product integrity within a CE. 'Open-loop, open-source' focuses on the individual and collective role of citizens and consumers in CE, and 'closed-loop, closed-source' emphasises Original Equipment Manufactuer (OEM) control through access through CE business models. Lessons are drawn from these scenarios for designers.

In Chapter 15, Brimacombe introduces the importance of integrating Life Cycle Thinking (LCT) into product circularity. There are illustrations of, for example, energy implications of CE decisions, trade-offs and the potential for unintended consequences if LCT is not considered. The concept of Social Value is introduced that highlights the importance of considering customer-focused product use over time. The chapter also explores the challenges associated with short-term costs and investment required for product circularity versus the longer-term benefits.

In Chapter 16, Stevels discusses the evolution of eco-design that was initially focused on recycling and chemicals, and then became particularly targeted at energy reduction in the 2000s. In the late 2000s, there was re-emergence of concerns over the economics and supply risks associated with materials that led to a growing interest in CE issues. The concept of Design for Resource Value (DfRV) is introduced as a mechanism to incorporate CE considerations into eco-design and the need for new metrics is discussed.

In Chapter 17, Earley and Goldsworthy discuss emerging approaches to circular design in the textiles and clothing sector. Lessons from four practised-based research projects utilising circular design approaches are discussed. Finally, some insights into principles of circularity for designers are put forward.

In Chapter 18, Sundin introduces issues associated with design for remanufacturing. The chapter postulates the idea that products have three life stages – beginning, middle and end – and that CE places a greater focus on the *use* phase of the product. Design-related experience is also highlighted from four Japanese photocopier manufacturers that both manufacture and remanufacture.

In Chapter 19, Keiller and Charter highlight recent repair-related policy developments and the emergence of community repair organisations, including repair cafés. Lessons are drawn from data derived from the repair activity of a repair café and the implications for design and development are discussed.

In Chapter 20, Chapman and Chalaris highlight the growing interest in design for CE in business but that few design schools have taken this on board. The chapter particularly focuses on collaboration between researchers from a design school and an international retailer that covered CE-related topics. Experience from the project illustrates, for example, that academia and business operate in different time frames and that hybrid approaches need to be developed if such collaborations are to be successful.

SECTION IV: TECHNOLOGICAL AND SOCIAL INNOVATION

In Chapter 21, Hunt provides an introduction to Industry 4.0 (I4.0) – cyber-physical-systems – and highlights the implications for CE. The future impact of I4.0 enabling technologies on CE and the implications for designers are explored and are illustrated with a series of examples.

In Chapter 22, Terizioglu illustrates how 3D printing (3DP) can be used to repair products and shows the potential for the technology to support product life extension. The chapter is based on the lessons learnt from 20 experiments with different products that illustrate the key issues and challenges related to 3DP and repair.

In Chapter 23, Prahl gives an overview of textile-based wearable technologies and emerging CE challenges including potentially short product lives and that the category falls outside of present 'producer responsibility' legislation. The need to bring in circularity into the design and development of wearable technologies is discussed and practical steps are proposed.

In Chapter 24, Kohtala highlights that at present, the development of makerspaces is weakly aligned to CE and broader sustainability issues, and that designers and non-designers involved in makerspaces are often more interested in 'cool' new technologies and materials. There is discussion over how makerspaces might become more circular.

In Chapter 25, Charter and Keiller discuss the emergence of repair cafés – community-led workshops – focused on repairing products, particularly consumer electronics and clothing. Results of a global survey highlight the high levels of repair being completed by skilled volunteers at repair cafés worldwide, the likely future growth of community repair and the implications for urban repair eco-systems.

SECTION V: CASE STUDIES

In Chapter 26, Hilton discusses the implications of the growth in returns of consumer electronics in the UK retail sector that are predicted to continue due to the increase in online sales. The chapter highlights a series of strategies that both manufacturers and retailers could pursue to improve product circularity of electrical and electronic equipment (EEE).

In Chapter 27, McIntyre describes how HP is driving CE into its core strategies and its supply chain. Three key areas are highlighted: closed-loop recycling, product as a service, and 3D printing. Finally, a series of recommendations for progressing CE in organisations are introduced.

In Chapter 28, Wiens gives an overview of the issues and challenges associated with the repair of electrical and electronic equipment (EEE). The background to the development of iFixit – a US-based open-source repair company – is discussed and how the firm has adapted its business model to the EEE market that is generally not implementing circularity in product design. This is illustrated by how iFixit has had to innovate to access spare parts and develop its own tooling to enable repair.

In Chapter 29, Vildåsen discusses a case study on Plasto – a Norwegian plastics products company – who set up a pilot project to use recycled plastic in a product working with a customer in the aquaculture sector. The case illustrates a range of issues including: the need for senior management commitment, importance of external feedback, perceptual challenges amongst internal and external stakeholders related to use of recycled materials, and the technical challenges of using recycled plastics in existing production equipment.

In Chapter 30, Khoo describes Interface's journey and lessons learnt in relation to circular materials innovation in its carpet tiling products. The set-up, implementation and learning from the NetWorks project – using waste nylon from fishing nets – is discussed in detail. Finally, a series of recommendations for CE innovators are proposed.

In Chapter 31, Baker-Brown reviews a number of CE cases from both the product and building worlds and highlights common issues such as the need for materials innovation. Examples are given of how architects are developing new approaches to the re-use of buildings, products, materials and components which is also leading to, in some instances, the development of new business models.

In Chapter 32, Durmišević highlights that most building and construction is still focused on 'design for demolition'. The chapter discusses the need for and practical implications of implementing reversible building design highlighting that 'design for disassembly' and reuse of buildings, systems, products, materials and components is new for this sector.

In Chapter 33, Andrews, Grussa, Chalk and Bush provide a case study on the blind and shutter sector in the UK. The chapter highlights that there is evidence of existing repair and refurbishment of these products in the UK market but that circularity needs to be improved substantially if fewer products are not going to end up in landfill. The chapter highlights a number of design improvements that the sector could take to improve product circularity.

In Chapter 34, Luscuere and Mulhall discuss the evolving concept of materials passports in the buildings sector. The chapter illustrates the need for improved product circularity information systems that are accessible to stakeholders through the life cycle of buildings. The chapter emphasises that if circularity is to be accelerated in the building sector that new systems need to be developed to collect and disseminate CE data and information throughout the life cycle.

FUTURE ISSUES

The concept and application of CE will continue to evolve worldwide. Policy tools will be deployed to stimulate circularity in Europe, Japan and China. There is an increasing global population and urbanisation worldwide, and cities will play a key role in driving CE. Companies will respond to external drivers and CE will increasingly drive innovation in product-services, technologies and materials. Large companies will adapt business models, processes and product-services, and CE will act as stimulus for a number of disruptive start-ups. Technology will be increasingly integrated into products and will create growing problems at end-of-life if circularity is not considered at the design and development stage. A range of social issues surrounding product circularity will emerge such as growing discussion over the 'right to repair' and built-in product obsolescence. There will be continued growth in places and spaces to enable collaboration in making (makerspaces), modifying (hackerspaces) and fixing (repair cafés). Community and self-repair of products will be increasingly enabled by collaboration, online video content and 3D printing utilising open data access to design files of spare parts. Industry 4.0 enabling technologies will move from discussion into application and will enable product life extension through smarter maintenance via embedded sensors and increased disassembly, repair and remanufacturing through new types of robots. The precise vision for 2030 and 2050 is unclear, but it is clear that CE has a role to play in a more sustainable future.

BIBLIOGRAPHY

Branungart, M. and McDonough, W. (2002). *Cradle to Cradle: Remaking the Way We Make Things*. New York: North Point Press.

BSI. (2017). *BS 8001:2017 'Framework for Implementing the Principles of the Circular Economy in Organizations: Guide'*. London, UK: British Standards Institution.

Kirchherr, J., Reike, D., and Hekkert, M. (2017). Conceptualizing the circular economy: An analysis of 114 definitions. *Resources, Conservation and Recycling* 127: 221–232.

Lacy, P. and Rutqvist, J. (2015). *Waste to Wealth*. London, UK: Palgrave Macmillan, ISBN 978-1-137-53068-4.

von Weizsäcker, E., Lovins, A., and Lovins, H. (1998). *Factor Four: Doubling Wealth, Halving Resource Use*. Abingdon, UK: Routledge, ISBN 978–1853834066.

2 Circular Industrial Economy

Walter R. Stahel

CIRCULARITY, CIRCULAR ECONOMY AND CIRCULAR INDUSTRIAL ECONOMY (CIE)

Circularity has been the base of life on planet Earth; water, carbon dioxide (CO_2) and matter circulate in chaotic self-organised systems, which do not know time or money constraints, nor waste. Early man had to cope with whatever resources were available and could be used as, or transformed into, shelter, food, products or tools. This was a Circular Economy based on scarcity, as expressed by settlers in an old New England maxim: *use it up, wear it out, make it do or do without.* Circularity was a necessity for most; only the rich and mighty lived in relative comfort. This situation can still be found in less industrialised countries.

The Industrial Revolution enabled society to overcome scarcities of shelter, food and objects; mass-production turned scarcities first into plenty, then abundance and a plethora of waste.

The post-industrial 'economy in loops' is a Circular Industrial Economy (CIE) based on saturated markets. It needs the personal motivation of economic actors and consumers to renounce excessive consumption in order to reduce environmental impairment both at the beginning and at the end of the pipe; sometimes social factors play a role: the Amish are an extreme example based on religious conviction. The CIE is by design a substitution of manpower for energy (Wijkman and Skanberg, 2016) – job creation is inherent in the CIE and overlooked by many policymakers.

The CIE's objective is to manage stocks (assets, capitals) and to maintain their value. The value of objects now depends on their use value, no longer on newness; economic growth in the CIE is measured as an increase in quality and quantity of all stocks, be they natural, human, cultural, manufactured or financial assets. The CIE is sustainable because it decouples wealth (value) creation from resource consumption and substitutes manpower for energy, material and water (Stahel and Reday, 1976).

Sustainable Development and the CIE are two sides of a coin, the former representing a qualitative world with happiness as its objective, the latter a material world with the objective to decouple wealth creation and resource consumption, to achieve more from less by managing existing capitals, assets (see Figure 2.1).

If nature is a self-organised system of virtuous cycles, then the economy is a system driven by entrepreneurship, regulations, human desires and policymaking. The competitiveness of managing stocks in the CIE over managing flows in the Linear Industrial Economy (LIE) has been blurred by subsidies on the production and consumption of natural resources, on transportation and waste elimination as well as by high taxes on labour. Alternatives such as 'economics as if people mattered' are traditionally ignored (Schumacher, 1973); 'sustainable taxation' starts to be timidly discussed (Stahel, 2013).

But this no longer slows a shift to a CIE, which is fuelled by a broad set of trends. One is intelligent decentralisation, visible in additive manufacturing (3D printing), micro-production in medicine and food, teleworking and manufacturing processes using local robots instead of

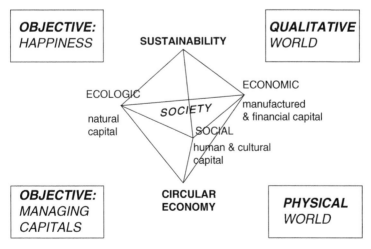

Figure 2.1 Situating society, sustainable development and a Circular Industrial Economy

Source: Stahel, Walter (2016) Preserving value my managing stocks in the circular industrial economy, lecture at the SINTEF CE conference, Mo I Rana, 10 May 2017.

the cheapest labour globally. A second trend supporting the CIE is lon-ger-life technologies: electric motors with a technical life of 100 years are set to replace combustion engines with a life of 30 years; electronic equipment not subjected to wear and tear replaces mechanical objects. A further trend is reusable high-technology objects, such as Falcon rockets and Dragon capsules by Space X and the USAF's unmanned X-378B spaceplane, which are cheaper to run than disposables. The CIE also grows as part of the growing Performance Economy (PE) (Sta-hel, 2010), when manufacturers become fleet managers selling perfor-mance, function and goods as a service instead of selling goods. Finally, social trends of a 'sharing society' strengthen circularity: repair cafés, barter trades and other self-help forms of circularity are gaining popu-larity in industrialised countries.

Throughout the chapter a number of terms will be used:

- 'Objects' embrace infrastructure, buildings, equipment, products, goods, components, food.
- 'Tools' are objects destined for productive tasks, to make money, such as machine tools.
- 'Toys' are objects destined for personal aims, to represent the owner and carry his/her (fashion or status) message, such as handbags, smartphones and cars; 'teddy bears' are toys to which the owner has a personal relationship, typically collectors' items.
- 'Sustainable use' replaces sustainable consumption for all objects, with the exception of food, fuel and water; sustainable consumption is an oxymoron for manufactured objects.
- 'Waste' is defined as objects without value and without liable owner.

CIE CYCLES OF BIOECONOMY AND FOOD, MANUFACTURED OBJECTS, INFRASTRUCTURE

Several cycles – with different characteristics but the same objective of managing stocks and maintaining values – make up the CIE: food, manu-factured mobile objects, and built environment. The strategies to increase resource efficiency and prevent waste are different for each cycle.

Bioeconomy life-cycles including food are subject to the annual fluctuations of natural cycles: extreme climate and weather events like droughts and the intensity of sunshine can destroy harvests and create famines. In the northern hemisphere, 1816 was a 'year without summer', when harvests were minimal and hunger forced people to eat roots and leaves. The cause was the eruption in 1815 of Tambora, a volcano in Indonesia, polluting the atmosphere and greatly reducing solar radiation in 1816. Food waste can be greatly reduced by consumers and retailers through changes in consumption patterns and supply chain management, but the reuse of food is limited to cascading: food waste can be used to feed pigs or produce biogas. Water consumption can be reduced through systems solutions. Timber and other bioeconomy resources adopt the life cycles of the host objects when integrated into such objects as buildings, furniture, paper or garments.

The life cycles of manufactured mobile objects, such as machinery and equipment, vehicles, furniture, clothing and packaging, are influenced by changes in technology, function and fashion as well as legislation. Waste prevention depends on design, the availability of spare parts, services to extend the service-life of goods and services to recover materials through recycling. Owner-users have a substantial influence on extending the service-life of goods through an intelligent and caring use (Pirsig, 1974) and a differentiation between *tools* and *toys*. However, natural disasters regularly terminate the service life of manufactured objects prematurely.

The life-cycle management of infrastructure – also referred to as built environment, comprising roads and railways, tunnels and bridges, buildings and technical infrastructure – is a given because service-lives are long, often longer than a human life. As infrastructure is the biggest resource consumer and waste producer, local operation and maintenance activities to extend their service-life are key waste prevention strategies and will gain in importance in combatting the phenomenon of aging infrastructure. The impact of natural disasters, such as floods and earthquakes, can be mitigated in the design phase, if buildings and the manufactured objects inside are designed as systems. When hurricane Sandy flooded lower Manhattan in the United States, critical electrical and information technology (IT) equipment, which are heavy and therefore traditionally placed in basements, were destroyed. An extensive strengthening of existing tall structures and changes in the design of new buildings became necessary to house these equipment in the future on upper floors.

Policymakers in the past were preoccupied with waste management policies instead of efficient resource use and waste prevention. Designers who in the past designed sexy products will increasingly have to consider the duration, mobility and systems-relevance of objects in the CIE, focussing on designing *tools*, not *toys*; function, not fashion.

THE LINEAR INDUSTRIAL ECONOMY (LIE)

The objective of the LIE is to manage manufacturing flows in added value chains from mines to products. Competitiveness comes from higher economies of scale – bigger volumes enabling lower unit costs – and a process optimisation up to the point of sale, where ownership and liability for the costs of risk and waste are passed on to the buyer. Growth in the LIE is measured as increase in annual monetary flows at the point of sale: gross domestic product (GDP) for countries and annual turnover for corporations. Economic growth is thus directly coupled with resource throughput, and the diseconomy of risk that comes with economy of scale is largely ignored.

The LIE is further ruled by depreciation value: fiscal legislation, not use value, determines the exchange value of objects. Computers are depreciated and thus reach zero-value after three years, cars after seven. If repair costs are higher than the depreciated value, economics demand that goods are scrapped rather than repaired. In the CIE, by contrast, the use value reigns; fully depreciated *objects* may increase even above the original sales price, witness antiques, historic buildings, vintage cars, paintings and other cultural assets that still have a 'use', and teddy bears, if the owner still has an emotional attachment.

These rules of the LIE have started to change: recent policy developments like extended producer responsibility (EPR) tried 'closing the waste liability loop' by making manufacturers responsible to take products back at the end of life, but have missed their objective because manufacturers can delegate this responsibility to third parties; recent consumer actions to fight 'planned obsolescence' by extending the mandatory warranty period beyond the point of sale have failed. Some waste managers have successfully transformed themselves into resource managers but lack the authority to maximise profits by remarketing used components and objects for the highest profit. The most successful change comes from economic actors, which are changing their business models from selling toys to selling tools.

FROM TOOLS AND TOYS: BUSINESS MODELS IN THE LIE AND THE CIE

In business-to-business (B2B) transactions, the buyer at the point of sale is an economic actor, and the *object* is treated as a *tool* to create revenue: the longer its service-life, the lower the buyer's investment and the higher their profit. Function dominates over fashion and maintenance skills are available in-house – some (machine) tools live for ever.

If the buyer at the point of sale is a consumer, the *object* is regarded as a *toy* to increase satisfaction and status value. When sexier new products become available for the same function, peer pressure may force the owner to dump the 'old' one in working order for the fashionable new one. The service-life of most *toys* is thus shorter than their technical life; the exception is owners who develop a caring stewardship, giving the *object* a 'teddy-bear' status.

Many electrical and electronic equipment and cars are used by professionals (as *tools*, such as taxis) and by individuals (as *toys*); what differs is their demand on the CIE. A broken refrigerator at home may be a problem, in a shop it leads to economic loss. Design may be identical, but services are different: fast in the latter case, slow in the former.

The present trend towards business models of functional services – selling goods as a service (shared utilisation, rental and leasing) – turns all *objects* into *tools*. Economic actors now retain the ownership of, and liability for, goods and internalise the costs of risk and waste. For designers, designing 'stock optimisation' into *objects* becomes an economic imperative: loss and waste prevention over the full service-life of *objects*, ease of repair and remanufacture, and designing *objects* so that later changes in fashion and technology can be integrated through component upgrades or exchange.

Owner-consumers become users, gaining high flexibility at known cost-per-use but waiving any capital gains, for example in real estate.

THE TWO MAIN ERAS OF THE CIE – *R* AS IN *RE-USE* AND *D* AS IN *DE-LINK*

To optimise the material, energy and water resources embodied in *objects*, the CIE develops techno-commercial strategies in the 'era of R' for goods, and opportunities of scientific and technologic innovation in the 'era of D' for materials (see Figure 2.2).

In addition, the CIE knowledge, both technical and economic, needs to spread to classrooms and boardrooms, to academia and vocational training institutions. New professions of 'holistic skills' will be created, such as restorers of vintage technical *objects*, antique furniture and other collection items, in order to preserve society's cultural capital.

The 'era of R' comprises techno-commercial strategies to re-use, repair, restore, remarket, remanufacture and reprogramme objects as well as to re-refine and recycle catalytic chemicals, such as lubrication

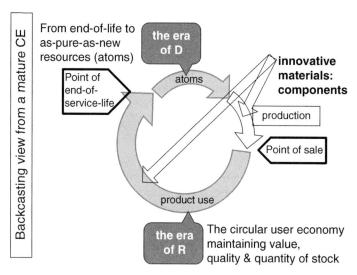

Figure 2.2 The structure of a mature Circular Industrial Economy

Source: Stahel, Walter (2016) Opportunity and Risk – two sides of systems solutions, lecture at MPI Magdeburg, 17 November 2016.

oils. Also needed is related innovation in marketing, policymaking and R-technologies: reuse options lead to innovation in manufacturing, as used banknotes or bottles, for instance, do not come in identical batches and need tolerant equipment (cashpoints or ATMs, bottling plants) to cope with qualitative variations.

At some point, the options of the 'era of R' come to an end. A few *objects* may become part of national heritage, but the majority will enter the 'era of D'.

The 'era of D' comprises technologies and policies to de-link assemblies, de-polymerize, de-alloy, de-laminate, de-vulcanize, de-coat materials in order to recover atoms for reuse; and to de-construct infrastructure and high-rise buildings in order to reuse materials and related innovation in D-technologies.

Waste and secondary resources are a thing of the past if atoms or molecules can be recycled to the quality and purity of virgin material, such as self-reinforcing PET (sr-PET), which can be re-melted and reused indefinitely.

The highest competitiveness and profit potential of CIE innovation may lie in the 'Era of D'. Many new technologies and processes in chemical engineering and material sciences can be patented; corporate income then comes from licensing knowledge instead of selling materials. Mining countries are looking at these options – whoever is first wins. The Ana

Intercontinental hotel in Tokyo was the first high-rise building to be sustainably deconstructed, disassembled top down in a closed room with minimal noise and dust emissions. How is this done? Imagine a dome at the top of the building which encloses the floor that is hydraulically lowered as each floor is dismantled. Bringing items down efficiently from the top of a high-rise building enables recovering the energy spent on hoisting them up in construction, making deconstruction a low-carbon activity.

The biggest societal benefits potential of CIE innovation is the 'era of R' – re-use, repair and remanufacture offer ample techno-economic opportunities in a skilled-labour intensive regional economy. Society therefore needs policy innovation: labour is the only renewable resource, which in addition can be educated but will deteriorate if unused. Stop taxing labour and tax things you do not want: emissions, consumption of non-renewable resources, waste (Stahel, 2013).

SHARING ECONOMY AND SHARING SOCIETY: THE ROLE OF OWNERSHIP AND CONTROL

A Sharing Economy involves owners making goods available as a service and users using them responsibly: rights (value and liability) and duties (ownership and stewardship) are clearly defined. Typical examples are shipping containers, hotels, taxis, public transport, libraries and airlines (see Figure 2.3). The point of sale has now become a point of service, ownership and liability remain with a fleet manager – the manufacturer or an independent service company.

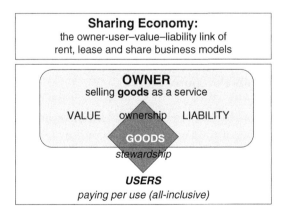

Figure 2.3 The structure of a Sharing Economy

Source: Stahel, Walter R. (2016) The Circular Economy, its environmental and social impacts and opportunities, lecture at *Université de Montréal*, May 5, 2016.

We have moved into the realm of the Performance Economy (Stahel, 2010), the objective of which is to produce, sell and maintain performance over longer periods of time.

A sharing society can be a group of people with common vital interests, sharing ownership and stewardship for a common good: historic examples include water supply infrastructure in arid zones, and state forests and highways open to the public. A sharing society with unrestricted access, no ownership, no control and undefined responsibility, such as the global commons (the atmosphere, space and the oceans), can easily become victim of the 'tragedy of the commons': assets will be lost (through CO_2 emissions, overfishing, waste accumulation) without punishment or remedy.

Platform Economies (witness UBER) are sharing economies with a go-between that takes no responsibility for the quality of results ('we are computer platforms where demand and supply meet') but retains a quarter of the payment as monopoly rent and commercially exploits the data created by owners and users.

The Internet of Things (IoT), which includes smartphones, smart fridges and wearable information technology (IT), marries the LIE with the sharing society: manufacturers sell the ownership and liability of goods to buyers (LIE) but retain an undeclared control over the use of the goods – blocking remarketing – and commercially exploit the data created by the owners of the goods – violating buyers' ownership and intellectual property rights. After the point of sale, manufacturers thus play the role of platform economies in competition with network operators, while the (cyber)risks are carried exclusively by the owner-user.

THE SOURCES OF INNOVATION IN THE CIE

An analysis of the above shows that innovation for sustainable solutions comes from a number of sources:

- Economic actors in the 'era of R' and 'era of D' of the CIE
- Economic actors of the Performance Economy (PE), which are manufacturers retaining the ownership of objects and internalising the costs and liability for use and waste by selling performance, goods and molecules as a service, or manufacturers that sell function guarantees
- Social innovators, such as repair cafés, barter trades and other self-help forms of circularity, which are rapidly gaining popularity in industrialised countries

- Designers who conceive business models, which link the necessary with the enjoyable, such as combining laundromats with such 'fun' activities as a dancing or Internet café, packaging the sustainability of shared use of washing machines with the opportunity of meeting people.

Yet policymakers may face the biggest challenges, such as closing the liability loop of used goods from manufacturer back to manufacturer, shifting taxation from labour to non-renewable resource consumption, safeguarding users' rights in platform economies – in short, creating the framework conditions which will promote and reward the emergence of sustainable, ethical and competitive solutions.

DESIGN FOR WHICH E?

In the LIE, designers work for manufacturers of objects and try to optimise the manufacturing process and the marketing at the point of sale, where ownership and liability pass to the buyer–consumer. Design focuses on reducing the costs of manufacturing (cars) and logistics (IKEA); after 1981 increasingly on Design for Emotions (Sottsass, Memphis group) and even inbuilt-obsolescence to accelerate replacement sales.

In the CIE, designers work for manufacturers of *objects* but try to reach beyond the point of sale through eco-design, such as ease of repair, remanufacturing and recycling. But designers have no direct influence on the use of the *objects* by the consumer. Eco-design is driven by waste legislation, corporate social responsibility (CSR) and lower point-of-sale costs (such as design for zero packaging).

In the PE, designers work for manufacturers or fleet managers of technical systems with a view to optimise the full service-life of systems. Design for functional efficiency reduces the costs of operation and maintenance as well as of liability for end-of-life objects; one objective is the standardisation of components and their reuse across product lines and generations (Xerox). Designing sustainable solutions becomes the new challenge (Stahel, 2001).

BIBLIOGRAPHY

Pirsig, R. (1974). *Zen and the Art of Motorcycle Maintenance.* New York: William Morrow & Co.
Schumacher, F. (1973). *Small Is Beautiful.* London: Blond & Briggs.

Stahel, W.R. and Reday-Mulvey, G. (1976). *The Potential for Substituting Manpower for Energy*, a report to the Commission of the European Communities, Brussels; and (1981) *Jobs for tomorrow*, New York, NY: Vantage Press.

Stahel, W.R. (2001). From 'design for environment' to 'designing sustainable solutions'. In: M.K. Tolba (ed.) *Our Fragile World: Challenges and Opportunities for Sustainable Development.* Cambridge, UK: UNESCO and EOLSS (editors) (Encyclopedia of Life Support Systems), pp. 1553–1568.

Stahel, W.R. (2010). *The Performance Economy* (2nd edition). Houndmills: Palgrave-Macmillan.

Stahel, W.R. (2013). Policy for material efficiency: Sustainable taxation as a departure from the throwaway society. *Philosophical Transactions A of the Royal Society, London* 371(1986): 20110567. DOI: 10.1098/rsta.2011.0567.

Wijkman, A. and Skanberg, K. (2016). *The Circular Economy and Benefits for Society*. Retrieved from: www.clubofrome.org/wp-content/uploads/2016/03/The-Circular-Economy-and-Benefits-for-Society.pdf.

3 Circular Economy innovation and design
Setting the scene

Martin Charter

INTRODUCTION

Since the late 2000s, there has been increasing discussion and usage of the term 'Circular Economy' (CE). However, there are many definitions and a lack of consensus over the term (Kirchherr et al., 2017). Discussion over CE has emerged from the growing recognition of the need to transition away from the current linear 'take, make and waste' models of production and consumption towards more circular models that maximise value in systems over time. Some consider CE to be a re-badging of existing concepts related to resource efficiency and resource productivity, whilst others consider it to be a different model with more of a focus on value retention over time and others consider it to be a paradigm shift in thinking. Another perspective is that CE turns the traditional 'waste hierarchy' on its head as the focus is on resource consumption over time rather than waste management.

A number of countries are taking forward the CE concept explicitly and strategically – at a policy level-notably China, Netherlands and Finland. Whilst other countries, notably Japan and Germany, continue to progress long-term commitments towards resource efficiency without using the term 'CE'. The European Commission (EC) launched the Circular Economy Action Plan in December 2015 (European Commission, 2015), which, for example, initiated a new European standardisation process focused on materials-efficiency aspects of energy-related products that include separate standards on durability, repair, re-use of components and remanufacturing. BS8001 – a guidance standard on CE implementation in organisations – was launched in May 2017 after a two-year development process including piloting with a number of companies (BSI, 2017). In companies, many specific aspects of circularity of course are not new, e.g. maintenance, repair, refurbishment, remanufacturing, etc. But what is new is bringing CE considerations together in a systemic and coordinated manner that is then integrated into the business. On the ground, a number of companies are starting to develop more thought-through approaches to product circularity. Product circularity is about taking an extended life cycle perspective with a greater focus on the (re)use phase of the life cycle rather than on end of life.

This chapter highlights a series of emerging topics from a company, and particularly a product-service, perspective.

PRODUCT-SERVICE DESIGN AND DEVELOPMENT

Let's first consider design and development. An estimated 80 percent of a product's environmental impact is determined at the design and development stage. Therefore, if circularity is not considered at this stage there is little opportunity for change. This affects both new product development and the redesign of existing products. Therefore, consideration of an organisation's CE objectives (e.g. repair, refurbishment, reconditioning, remanufacturing, recycling, etc.) in the design and development phase is essential to extend the life of products and the sub-assemblies, components, parts and the materials within the product. Some organisations create, design and manufacture their own products or services, whereas others act as 'system integrators', sourcing sub-assemblies and components procured via networks of suppliers and then assembling and delivering them as a final solution to customers. Others outsource product design and development to third parties, including contract manufacturers. However, the world has got a lot more complicated over recent decades with the increased integration and diffusion of information and communication technologies (ICT) into products. This means that many solutions on the market are product–service combinations; and in practice many organisations are now creating, producing and/or delivering integrated product–service solutions or product–service-systems (PSS).

At a product-level, designing-in circularity forms part of a process which is variously known as eco-design, environmental-conscious design, 'design for environment' or green design. 'Eco-design' is used as an equivalent for the other terms in this chapter. Eco-design is the process – within design and development – of integrating environmental considerations into product design and development with aim of reducing environmental impacts of products through the life cycle. The organisation's CE objectives should be incorporated into each phase of the design and development process from product planning, idea generation, concept development, and design to production, launch and after-sales service. This includes specific product circularity considerations such as the consideration of the types of materials to be used at each stage of the life cycle, from extraction through to end of life. The precise circularity considerations that are relevant to a product, service or PSS will be dependent on the type of product, e.g. active (energy-using) or non-active (non-energy-using), its place in the value chain and markets addressed.

DESIGNERS

Historically, some have argued the most important actors in product design and development have been designers. Classically, designers (design engineers, product designers, architects, packaging designers, chemists, etc.) have been the focus of product design and development; however, other internal and external stakeholders are playing an increasingly important role in the process, e.g. procurement and contract management. There are often different business functions that are involved in product (*hardware*) and service (*software*) dimensions of a PSS solution. For example, marketing, customer services and legal may be involved in 'service design' elements of a PSS solution. It is also important to recognise designers or more precisely *those performing design tasks* (whatever their job title) in design and development may be in-house and/or ex-house, and/or partially in-house and ex-house. Therefore it is important to ensure that relevant CE considerations are communicated to and addressed by designers within eco-design process wherever they sit. CE will need to be considered at each life cycle stage within an extended life cycle perspective and balanced against market, technical and cost aspects.

Eco-design (including circularity considerations) requires a team approach and the engagement and involvement of a range of internal business functions and external stakeholders as indicated above. At a design level, a number of design options are available to improve product circularity at different life cycle stages.

Table 1 highlights a series of design options that can be used to improve product circularity. The options highlighted are generic and the appropriateness will be depend on each situation.

Table 1 Generic eco-design checklist highlighting product circularity considerations (non exhaustive)

Design Focus Area	Options for Design Improvement
Design for Material Sourcing	*Reduce weight and volume of product*
	Increase use of recycled materials to replace virgin materials
	Increase use of renewable materials
	Increase incorporation of used components
	Use materials with lower embodied energy and/or water
Design for Manufacture	Reduce energy consumption
	Reduce water consumption
	Reduce process waste
	Use internally recovered or recycled materials from process waste
	Reduce emissions to air, water and soil during manufacture
	Reduce number of parts
Design for Transport and Distribution	*Minimise product size and weight*
	Optimise shape and volume for maximum packaging density
	Optimise transport and distribution in relation to fuel use and emissions
	Optimise packaging to comply with regulation
	Reduce embodied energy and water in packaging
	Increase use of recycled materials in packaging
	Eliminate hazardous substances in packaging
Design for Use (Including installation, maintenance and repair)	Reduce energy in use
	Reduce water in use
	Increase access to spare parts
	Maximise ease of maintenance
	Maximize ease of reuse and disassembly
	Avoid design aspects detrimental to reuse
	Reduce energy used in disassembly
	Reduce water used in disassembly
	Reduce emissions to air, water and soil
	Maximize ease of materials recycling
Design for End of Life	*Avoid design aspects detrimental to materials recycling*
	Reduce amount of residual waste generated
	Reduce energy used in materials recycling
	Reduce water used in materials recycling

Note: The options highlighted in italics support product circularity.

Incorporating circularity into eco-design means considering how value can be maximised over time using an extended life cycle perspective which will mean, depending on the context, designing for durability, longevity, or multiple uses or lives.

SYSTEMS

Systemic thinking is fundamental to CE. A mechanism to interpret CE is to think about the different types of materials (or nutrients) that are utilised within PSSs that operate within biological systems and technical systems. The goal of CE is to maximise the value over time of renewable materials (e.g. natural fibres) within biological systems and to extend the life of non-renewable materials (e.g. plastics and metals) within technical systems. However, in some product categories there is a cross-over between both systems. For example, in clothing, the mixing of biological and technical materials in individual products needs to be carefully thought about at the design stage to enable disassembly and separation of mixed fibres and materials at 'end of (1st) life' to enable product and/or material life extension.

CONTEXT

There is a need to consider the 'big picture' when thinking about CE. The concept builds on longstanding discussions over resource efficiency and resource productivity that have been led by Japan, Germany and others since the 1990s. CE is one aspect of sustainable development, and whilst not explicitly highlighted in the United Nations Sustainable Development Goals (SDGs), CE is relevant to a number of the 17 goals e.g. Responsible Consumption and Production (Goal 12). As indicated above, there are some emerging 'schools of thought' that believe CE is a fundamentally different concept that might replace sustainable development. However, these schools often ignore the broader environmental, economic and social dimensions of sustainable development, and the complex inter-relationships e.g. between CE, climate change, energy and carbon. From an organisational perspective, CE should be part of an organisation's broader sustainability approach that impacts on business models, processes and product-services. CE should not be viewed as a 'magic bullet'. The tendency for some organisations is to develop myopic approaches related to sustainability waves, where the current hot topic becomes the prime focus and organisations lose a holistic and longer-term perspective. For example, in very broad terms, one could argue that the 2000s was the 'decade of climate change', that we are now in the 'decade of CE' and the 2020s maybe the 'decade of water'. Keeping the 'big picture' in mind is important if one is not going to get 'locked in' to decisions and miss increasingly fast moving trends, risks and opportunities. Transitioning towards more circular approaches in organisations – from current linear patterns – will mean that top management will need to demonstrate leadership, complete two-way communications and gain organisational buy-in, and have change management plans in place to enable a transition; CE is not 'business as usual'.

POLICY

At an international policy level, there needs to be improved clarity over the relationship between emerging goals, initiatives and approaches e.g. green growth, low carbon transition, CE and the SDGs. To transition to economies that are more circular (and less linear), there is a need for smart policy development that covers both the demand and supply side. Various instruments are available to policy makers to stimulate increased circularity, e.g. Sweden is providing tax breaks to increase repair levels (Orange, 2016). The combination and sequence of the implementation of policy instruments to support the transition towards CE needs to be carefully considered and there is a need to think medium- to long-term to predict and avoid unintended consequences. There needs to be further thought about what can be done and what can't be done at international, national, regional and local levels. Lessons for CE policy development can be drawn from the EC's Integrated Product Policy (IPP), a holistic approach aimed at greening markets/ products that emerged in the late 1990s (DG Environment, Undated); and Japan's product policy approach that has included, for example, demand-side instruments such as the Green Purchasing Law and the development of a Green Purchasing Network (Ministry of Environment – Government of Japan, 2000).

CONSUMERS

To transition towards CE, there needs to be more engagement with consumers and users of products (and more awareness of the materials and components within them). Most consumers and users will not recognise the term 'CE'; however, they recognise terms like 'waste', 'repair' and 'built-in obsolescence'. The authenticity, transparency and provenance of data and information related to materials will be of increasing concern. There will be growing scrutiny amongst consumers and NGOs over circularity claims and green washing, and increased pressure for improved data and information-based product-related environmental communications, e.g. labelling, on-line information, posters, point-of-sale, advertising, etc.

BUSINESS MODELS

Business models are 'all organization' approaches aimed at delivering (more) value to customers and there has been considerable discussion over CE and (new) business models. However, many large and complex organisations will not be interested in changing existing (successful) business models unless they see major opportunities, threats or risks driven by CE considerations. For many organisations, it will be more about re-engineering existing business models, product-services and/or processes to take account of circularity. New business models driven by CE are more likely to come from start-ups and SMEs that are more agile and not 'locked-in' to existing systems. Some maybe disruptive – iFixit (iFixit, 2017) and bio-bean (bio-bean, 2017) – and others may be just cool products/businesses, e.g. Bureo (2017). Some existing incumbents may see the emergence of disruptive innovators as a threat to the 'established order' whilst others see opportunities for partnership and to move with the times, e.g. HP are now collaborating with iFixit.

INFRASTRUCTURE

To transition towards CE (from linear systems), new physical infrastructure will need to be developed and built, and this will need investment. A key issue will be the relationship between private and public sector in developing new structures and systems to enable CE and retrofitting existing infrastructure to enable circularity. A focus on 'zero waste' and maximising value in the system over time will mean significant process re-engineering; for example, requiring product and behavioural changes on a major scale. Much will depend on government and company commitment, priorities and focus. For example, recycling factories implemented in the Japanese electronics sector (DTI Global Watch Mission, 2005) resulted from consensus-based, legislative change whereas remanufacturing factories developed by Xerox and Caterpillar resulted from changes in individual business models (Gray and Charter, 2006). At a company level, developing take-back and reverse logistics systems or reverse supply networks (either legislative driven or voluntary) to capture products (and the materials within them) will be increasingly important.

LANGUAGE

There is no universally agreed definition of CE; and the terminology used around CE can be fluid and used interchangeably, which is often confusing outside of specialist networks (BSI, 2017). For example, there are clear differences between maintenance, repair, refurbishment, remanufacturing and recycling in terms of focus, scale and complexity. In an expert meeting attended by the author, the founder of an established white goods refurbisher described his business as being in the recycling business. There are other terms that might not necessarily thought to be part of CE discussion but are also important. For example, maintenance is a key part of CE – as it is part of waste prevention or more appropriately, product life extension – as it shifts the focus to the use phase of the life cycle and hence the user.

TECHNOLOGY

Technology will play a key role in the transition to CE. This will mean adapting old technologies and industrial processes to enable product life extension as well as the development of new Industry 4.0 (Wikipedia, 2017) enabling technologies that can potentially foster circularity, e.g. robotics, Big Data, sensors, machine learning, artificial intelligence, blockchain, etc. A number of leading companies have now developed hierarchies of product circularity, e.g. Philips (De Burin, Undated) and HP (HP, 2017) that have various technological implications. Existing and new technologies need to be re-engineered and developed to address those hierarchies, and a growing issue will be whether the companies' CE approaches are closed- or open-loop. For example, Apple's Liam I-Phone disassembly robots (Whitwam, 2016) are organised within Apple's network ('closed-loop') whereas Veolia uses robots to disassemble various brands of television (Cellan-Jones, 2016) within their facilities ('open-loop'). 3D printing or additive manufacturing is creating opportunities to produce products using filaments from recycled polymers, e.g. Fishy Filaments (Fishy Filaments, 2017) and bio-polymers, and also to print components using open-sourced designs to enable repair and product life extension. In addition, there is the emergence of new DIY machines that enable the production of products at a local level that use waste plastics as feedstock. For example, the Dutch designer, Dave Hakken's Precious Plastic (Precious Plastics, 2017) blueprint of open-sourced plastic recycling machines that can be built locally at low cost.

MATERIALS

Materials are at the heart of the CE discussion and there is likely to be increased research and development (R&D), innovation, process and infrastructures changes, and possible public policy shifts. For example, in the technical system there will be discussion over the legacy of materials that come back in the second life, third life, etc. through increased circularity. For example, older steels may be weaker and have higher carbon content than ones used today and older plastics may off-gas chemicals. Materials scientists and chemical engineers will have an increasingly important role in the R&D of new smart(er) materials that can be un-zipped, easier to separate and are more recyclable. For example, Aquafil have developed a process that de-polymerises and re-polymerises nylon into a second-life nylon – Econyl ® – which the company claims has the same properties as the first-life nylon (Econyl, 2017). There may well be increasing trust issues associated with circularity claims of existing and new products and materials, and an emerging discussion over a potential need for improved standards and better information systems.

'END OF LIFE'

In an extended life cycle perspective, materials recycling should be thought of as a distant 'end of life' strategy prior to final disposal. As part of this thinking, companies designing for circularity should plan for materials re-use in later lives of products and consider re-use in other sectors, e.g. rubber from Nike training shoes is now incorporated into playgrounds. Original equipment manufacturers (OEM) that sell product's business-to-business (B2B) will increasingly need to consider their final customer(s) and what happens to their products at the 'end of life' and build-in circularity, e.g. reparability. To enable increased circularity, there will need for more engagement with final customers prior to the 'end of life', e.g. increased access to spare parts as part of customer service. What sort of incentives could be put in place to increase the return of products (and the materials within them) to the

OEM or intermediaries even if products are sold B2B through distribution channels? Bureo offer a free replacement service for broken skateboards made from second-life polymers, e.g. new products are supplied at no charge to replace broken products.

IMPLEMENTATION

CE implementation poses a range of technical and people-oriented challenges. Technical challenges include engineering, chemistry and material science issues related to, for example, the dis- and re-assembly of products and de- and re-polymerisation of plastics. People challenges include softer aspects, e.g. awareness, (re)education, (re)skilling, etc. A key issue for many organisations is where and how to start to engage in the CE discussion, e.g. some may use pilot projects to learn lessons and may focus initially on product(s) or process(es) rather than existing or new business model(s) for the reasons discussed earlier. At an organisational level, it is essential to gain buy-in and there is a need to develop and build a common vision of CE with both internal and external stakeholders.

FUTURE

There is a need to learn lessons from Japanese and German approaches to circularity that started in the early 1990s and transfer to those that are making new commitments, e.g. China, Netherlands and Finland. Common visions of CE need to be developed through engaging policy makers, business and civil society – which means that new stakeholder platforms need to be created at international, national, regional and local levels, e.g. European CE Stakeholder Platform established in 2017. There will be growing drive to 'design-out' waste, enable product life extension and move away from built-in product obsolescence. Cities will play a key role in CE due to increased urbanisation worldwide and the proximity of key stakeholders in the urban innovation system. However, we will need to design systems to enable CE innovation in urban areas, as they are presently not established. In a smarter and more connected world, there is a need for better understanding of the potential relationship between CE and the implementation of Industry 4.0 strategies. In parallel to 'top down' developments, there is need to harness 'bottom-up' grassroots innovation – driven by a new movement of 'makers, modifiers and fixers' – to help deliver more decentralised, circular and low-carbon solutions.

BIBLIOGRAPHY

bio-bean. (2017). [Online]. Available at: www.bio-bean.com/ [Accessed 25 November 2017].

BSI. (2017). *BS 8001:2017 'Framework for Implementing the Principles of the Circular Economy in Organizations: Guide'*. London, UK: British Standards Institution.

Bureo. (2017). [Online]. Available at: https://bureo.co/ [Accessed 25 November 2017].

Cellan-Jones, R. (11 November 2016). *Robot Recycling: Extracting Value from Old TVs* [Online]. Available at: www.bbc.co.uk/news/technology-37944502 [Accessed 25 November 2017].

De Burin, H. (Undated). *How Circular Thinking Could Improve People's Lives* [Online]. Available at: www.philips.com/a-w/innovationmatters/blog/how-circular-thinking-could-improve-people-lives.html [Accessed 25 November 2017].

DG Environment. (Undated). *Integrated Product Policy (IPP)* [Online]. Available at: http://ec.europa.eu/environment/ipp/index_en.htm [Accessed 25 November 2017].

DTI Global Watch Mission. (2005). *Waste Electrical and Electronic Equipment (WEEE): Innovating Novel Recovery and Recycling Technologies in Japan* [Online]. Available at: http://cfsd.org.uk/aede/downloads/JapaneseWEE. PDF (Pera on behalf of the Department of Trade and Industry) [Accessed 25 November 2017].

Econyl. (2017). [Online]. Available at: www.econyl.com/ [Accessed 25 November 2017].

European Commission. (December 2015). *Closing the Loop: An EU Action Plan for the Circular Economy*. COM(2015) 614 final. Retrieved from: http://eur-lex.europa.eu/legal-content/EN/TXT/?uri=CELEX:52015DC0614.

Fishy Filaments. (2017). [Online]. Available at: https://fishyfilaments.com/ [Accessed 25 November 2017].

Gray, C. and Charter, M. (2006). *Remanufacturing and Product Design* [Online]. Available at: http://cfsd.org.uk/Remanufacturing%20and%20Product%20Design. pdf, The Centre for Sustainable Design, UCA [Accessed 25 November 2017].

HP. (2017). *Building a Circular Economy* [Online]. Available at: http://www8. hp.com/us/en/hp-information/environment/productsandsolutions.html [Accessed 25 November 2017].

iFixit. (2017). [Online]. Available at: www.ifixit.com/ [Accessed 25 November 2017].

Kirchherr, J., Reike, D., and Hekkert, M. (2017). Conceptualizing the circular economy: An analysis of 114 definitions. *Resources, Conservation and Recycling* 127: 221–232.

Ministry of Environment – Government of Japan. (2000). *Act on Promotion of Procurement of Eco-Friendly Goods and Services by the State and Other Entities* [Online]. Available at: www.japaneselawtranslation.go.jp/law/detail/?ft=5&re=01&dn=1&gn=4&sy=&ht=A&no=100&ia=03&x=49&y=9&ky=&page=1 [Accessed 25 November 2017].

Orange, R. (2016). *Waste Not Want Not: Sweden to Give Tax Breaks for Repairs* [Online]. Available at: www.theguardian.com/world/2016/sep/19/waste-not-want-not-sweden-tax-breaks-repairs [Accessed 25 November 2017].

Precious Plastics. (2017). [Online]. Available at: https://preciousplastic.com/en/ [Accessed 25 November 2017].

Whitwam, R. (22 March 2016). *Apple Unveils 29-Armed Robot Designed to Disassemble Old iPhones* [Online]. Available at: www.extremetech.com/mobile/225337-apple-unveils-29-armed-robot-designed-to-disassemble-old-iphones [Accessed 25 November 2017].

Wikipedia. (2017). [Online]. Available at: https://en.wikipedia.org/wiki/Industry_4.0 [Accessed 25 November 2017].

4 Framing circularity at an organisational level

Phil Cumming

INTRODUCTION

Most people would agree that the Circular Economy (CE) stands in contrast to our current linear economic model where we take materials, use them to make products and then dispose of them. It has its origins in several schools of thought, some of which date back to the 1960s. These include Cradle to Cradle (McDonough and Braungart, 2008), regenerative design (Lyle, 1996), natural capitalism (Hawken et al., 2010), blue economy (Pauli, 2010), industrial ecology (Graedel and Allenby, 2002), Performance Economy (Stahel and Redray, 1976; Stahel, 2006) and biomimicry (Benyus, 1997). Resource efficiency and sustainability in a broader sense have also been linked to the CE concept (Geisendorf and Pietrulla, 2017). Geisendorf and Pietrulla (2017) argue that whilst these concepts have overlapping ideas and similar goals, they also differ in certain characteristics and can even be competing priorities. Indeed, making something more circular does not automatically mean that it is also more sustainable. As a result, while research and interest has increased in recent years, various interpretations of the CE have emerged across organisations and sectors.

Conceptually, it could be argued that the CE is well understood, at least at a macro level. Increasingly, organisations seem to be recognising that the traditional 'take, make, dispose' model could be reaching its limits and the availability of cheap, easily accessible materials and energy can no longer be taken for granted. The UN Sustainable Development Goals recognise this trend, providing a context to enable a global response via Goal 12 (Responsible consumption and production), which aims to change the way products and resources are consumed and produced (DSD, n.d.). In 2015, the Ellen MacArthur Foundation (EMF) and the McKinsey Center for Business and Environment identified a net economic benefit from the CE in Europe of €1.8 trillion by 2030 (Ellen MacArthur Foundation and McKinsey & Company, 2015). These reported economic benefits are leading to the emergence of policy interventions by governments such as the EU Action Plan for the Circular Economy (European Commission, 2015). That said, the CE is not without its critics. In recent years there has been a decline in some commodity prices contrary to arguments that resource prices are increasing ever upwards. Some argue that European companies are already capturing the economically attractive opportunities to reuse, remanufacture and recycle – to achieve higher levels would incur substantial costs (Howard and Galloway, 2017).

This should, however, be viewed and planned as a long game. Global demand for products and services will rise as the world's population grows and the number of middle-income consumers increases. This will increase demand for natural resources. In Europe, security of supply is already an issue where internal resources are limited and import dependency high. Reducing the world's population is unlikely to be a quick solution to this. More immediate results are likely from policies and technologies that aim to reverse the rising consumption of natural resources (Bradshaw and Brook, 2014).

FROM CONCEPT TO REALITY

There is no doubt that the CE is gaining traction in business. EMF has been widely credited with engaging the business, policy and education communities, focusing on pressure points and levers that accelerate the transition to a CE. Yet research and stakeholder engagement conducted by the British Standards Institution (BSI) found that organisations still needed guidance on how to identify the relevance of the CE to them and what were the practical implications (Suff, 2015). Organisations also wanted clarity on factors which might affect their ability to become more circular. These findings are borne out by the author's own personal experience of progressing circular thinking within a business context.

The CE represents a paradigm shift in thinking. In a CE, 'by design' the value of products and materials is maintained, waste is avoided and resources are kept within the economy at end of life (Geisendorf and Pietrulla, 2017). This is a systemic approach. It requires organisations to understand how they create value and how they can influence more sustainable outcomes in the wider economic system. This requires greater transparency and collaboration and more consideration of the role of the end user. The design and innovation of processes and products and services (e.g. for repair, reuse, recyclability, etc.) can be complemented by business model design and innovation (e.g. servitisation – shifting from selling products to selling services) to manage how products and materials circulate within the economic system. This is no easy task for any organisation no matter their size. The policy and legislative landscape, changing economics and emerging technologies play a major part in determining how far organisations can go to become more circular and more sustainable.

Organisations looking to embark on this journey will need to be mindful of a number of issues and considerations, several of which are highlighted below.

Lost in translation

Firstly, despite it gaining traction in business, there is still confusion surrounding the CE concept. One of the challenges is the lack of a common definition. The definition offered by EMF: 'an economy that is restorative and regenerative by design, and which aims to keep products, components and materials at their highest utility and value at all times, distinguishing between technical and biological cycles' is seen by many as the reference point (BSI, 2017a). Yet, research by Kirchherr et al. (2017) found 114 CE definitions in use with few explicitly linking CE to sustainable development.

There is also an abundance of terminology, often misused or used interchangeably. Take, for example, the term 'closed-loop' (i.e. the product is recycled by an organisation or co-operating group of organisations at the end of its life into the same product system). This is often used as a vernacular term for the CE or used incorrectly to describe an 'open-loop' system (i.e. the product is recycled into a different product system).

There also appears to be a lack of a shared understanding of how renewable materials and products fit into the CE concept. For example, it has been argued that the bioeconomy is circular by nature and is fully aligned with the biological cycle (Carrez and van Leeuwen, 2015). In reality, the management of biological materials can be quite linear in practice even if circular in principle and biological materials can also be managed within the technical cycle – paper being a case in point.

Semantics aside, this confused vocabulary is likely to be hindering the development of clear guidelines on the CE. Two specific issues are marketing and collaboration. For example, organisations wishing to market items based on their circularity credentials (e.g. 'closed-loop') will need to ensure that all claims and declarations are legal, fair, honest and transparent. With regards collaboration, it is unlikely that any organisation can achieve substantial progress without collaborating with others in their value chain/network. In this context, it is essential for all parties to have a common understanding so they can work towards common goals – otherwise the collaboration could fail.

The importance of framing and scoping

It is important that organisations spend time determining how the CE is relevant to their long-term business success and resilience. An organisation should not embark on this journey without a full appreciation of this and what their role might be. In one case, a chief executive of a large multinational company set a CE target but then left the business without bestowing a clear vision on what this entailed and why. The business ended up with different pockets of interest and varying perspectives and failed to move forward (Suff, 2016).

The CE is often framed as a new model for a sustainable economy and healthy society. However, there are limits to the impact the CE can have on specific sustainability issues such as climate change, species extinction, human rights, health and wellbeing, etc. In fact, Geisendorf and Pietrulla (2017) argue that whilst factors such as profitability and social criteria (e.g. employment creation) are desirable outcomes, they are not intrinsically part of the criteria for assessing circularity. The CE should be seen as one possible approach for progressing sustainability rather than as an end in itself.

Sustainable development should, however, be an underlying principle of the CE. Becoming more circular does not inevitably create a more sustainable outcome (see the hierarchy dogma below). Indeed, an organisation may on careful consideration of environmental, social and economic factors decide that the CE is not right for them – or at least not at this time. This would be a perfectly acceptable conclusion.

The hierarchy dogma

For years the 'waste hierarchy' has been the basic principle used by many countries to prioritise waste management options according to their environmental desirability (Tjell, 2005). Of course, the CE turns this on its head – the goal is not how to best manage waste but to eliminate it altogether. Materials should not be discarded as wastes but treated as raw materials with inherent value.

The 'Butterfly Diagram', EMF's widely reproduced visual CE system diagram, essentially sets out a new hierarchy. This should not, however, be treated as dogma without having a full appreciation of the impacts (positive or negative). For example, designing a product to be modular and easily disassembled and upgraded will influence materials selection. Yet certain decisions here could result in producing something that actually has a greater negative environmental and social impact than if there had not been any attempt to prolong the products life in the first place.

There is potential for conflicts between resource efficiency and the CE. For example, reducing product packaging might save on materials usage and waste but lead to an increase in greenhouse gases and air quality impacts if it makes the distribution process inefficient. Companies may find it challenging to simultaneously pursue strategies for dematerialisation (modularity, miniaturisation, light-weighting, etc.) and up-weighting for durability.

In recent years, the fall in commodity prices has undermined the economics of recycling certain materials (e.g. virgin polymer prices have undercut those of recycled plastics) (Howard and Galloway, 2017). Within the systemic context of the CE, to what extent should business be prepared to intervene to improve secondary materials supply and demand? Designing something to be recycled is good but unlikely to be sufficient. The saga of recycling black plastic in the UK is a case in point (WRAP, n.d.) – whose role is it to make this happen and ensure end markets are available? The companies placing it on the market, the plastics recyclers or both?

Of course, there should be a presumption against the use of any disposal method, be it landfill or incineration. Use of waste to energy technology should ideally never compete with or compromise prevention, reuse and recycling opportunities (European Commission, 2017).

This is all likely to present a real measurement challenge for business. For example, whilst a Material Circularity Indicator has been created to assess the 'circularity' of a product or organization, this only really looks at how restorative or linear the flow of materials is (Ellen MacArthur Foundation and Granta Design, 2015). Important factors such as energy costs and usage, avoided greenhouse gas emissions, chemical ingredients/toxicity, natural capital and air quality are not considered.

Systems thinking should be seen as a key tool for avoiding unintended consequences and identifying a range of opportunities for redesigning ways of working, products and services and business models.

MORE CIRCULAR BUSINESS MODELS

The term 'circular business model' has to some become synonymous with applying the CE in an organisational context.

There are various viewpoints on what a business model is and what components it should include. In general terms, it describes the rationale of how an organisation creates, delivers and captures value (Osterwalder and Pigneur, 2010). The underlying dimensions are threefold: resource structure (the core resources leveraged to serve customers), transactional structure (the configuration that determines key transactions with partners and stakeholders) and value structure (the system of rules, expectations and mechanisms that determine the organisation's value creation and capture activities) (George and Bock, 2011).

Business model innovation for the CE needs to go beyond advances in ways of working (processes) and/or products and services. Innovation in these areas might well lead to something better, without necessarily challenging how resources are managed. For example, the introduction of a range of recycled products as part of a wider product offering is unlikely to be a 'circular business model'.

Indeed, the term 'circular business model' is misleading. More correctly, there are business models which have the potential to 'fit' within a circular economic system. Unless the wider systemic context is considered, then they are simply new or reimagined business models operating within the linear economy.

This would be a bold move for an organisation to take. It is likely to require organisations to challenge assumptions and make considerable changes to the business structure to enable a mode of operation which is both more circular and more sustainable. If the prevailing business model is predicated on excessive consumption and short-term profit maximization, it is questionable whether it can ever be sustainable. For example, if profits are dependent on sales of products with linear life cycles, planned product obsolescence is presumably inevitable. The design challenge is therefore to create a financially viable business model which fully addresses the challenges of sustainability and circularity.

OTHER ORGANISATIONAL ISSUES
AND CONSIDERATIONS

The transition to a mode of operation which is both more circular and more sustainable is complex. There are a huge range of factors which may enable or impede progress. It is a case of needing to be prepared for all eventualities – to 'expect the unexpected'. Existing infrastructure and business models, existing market priorities, policy and regulatory landscape, behaviour and consumer habits can all conspire to keep the organisation 'locked in' to the linear model.

For example, existing regulation has, in general, been developed for a linear economy. As such, rules (e.g. how discarded items are managed, how organisations collaborate or how business is financed) are not always supportive of the CE.

Other areas of potential challenge range from accounting and finance, chemicals transparency, through to logistics, marketing and having a good appreciation of materials markets. For example, should a product be designed for disassembly if take-back mechanisms and viable materials markets are yet to exist?

Many of the emerging business models which have the potential to 'fit' within a circular economic model are still at pilot scale and it may be difficult to secure traditional forms of finance, particularly if profitability is yet to be demonstrated. This is one of the biggest challenges facing business. As long as there continues to be a focus on short-term profits and dividends, it will be difficult to take a long-term view on the investment required to become more circular. Prices paid for products and services typically do not take into account the economic value of environmental damage caused or avoided. Progress towards a CE may be accelerated if this were to happen (e.g. as a result of changes in policy or market forces) (Wallace et al., 2015).

CONCLUSION

Implementing the CE within an organisational context should be viewed first and foremost as a design challenge – be it about ways of working, products and services or business models. The prevailing linear economic model stacks the odds against us. There is likely to be a limit for the foreseeable future on how far organisations can progress in this regard – be it organisationally or systemically. While taking a more sustainable approach can lead to higher costs, it needs to be looked at in terms of net overall value creation to the business and society. This can after all spur innovation and help protect against supply chain shocks and reputational risks. However, you need to be clear why circularity is being pursued, what your organisation's particular role is and whether change is likely to bring a more sustainable outcome. Your organisation needs to be willing and able to challenge its underlying value structure.

An Internet search will yield myriad publications and resources on the CE. Yet few help organisations take practical action. One recent development is the advent of BS 8001 – the world's first CE standard – in 2017 (BSI, 2017b). It is the culmination of over two years' work, involving 60 technical experts from a variety of fields. Many elements have been informed by lessons learned by first-mover organisations, small and large, attempting to become more circular. The standard takes a principles-based approach and organisations are free to determine how aligned they want to be. It will not provide all the answers but offers a shared understanding of how to get started and to work towards common goals.

BIBLIOGRAPHY

Benyus, J. (1997). *Biomimicry: Innovation Inspired by Nature*. London, UK: Harper Collins.

Bradshaw, C.J.A. and Brook, B.W. (2014). Human population reduction is not a quick fix for environmental problems. *Proceedings of the National Academy of Sciences of the United States of America* 111(46): 16610–16615.

BSI. (2017a). *BS 8001:2017 Draft for Public Comment Consultation Responses Review*. BSI, Unpublished.

BSI. (2017b). *BS 8001:2017 'Framework for Implementing the Principles of the Circular Economy in Organizations: Guide'*. London, UK: British Standards Institution.

Carrez, D. and van Leeuwen, P. (September 2015). Bioeconomy: Circular by nature. *The European Files*. (38): 34–35.

DSD. (n.d.). *Sustainable Development Goals*. UN Division for Sustainable Development. Retrieved from: https://sustainabledevelopment.un.org/sdgs.

Ellen MacArthur Foundation and Granta Design. (2015). *Circularity Indicators: An Approach to Measuring Circularity: Methodology*. Retrieved from: www.ellenmacarthurfoundation.org/programmes/insight/circularity-indicators.

Ellen MacArthur Foundation and McKinsey & Company. (2015). *Growth Within: A Circular Economy Vision for a Competitive Europe*. Retrieved from: www.mckinsey.com/business-functions/sustainability-and-resource-productivity/our-insights/europes-circular-economy-opportunity.

European Commission. (December 2015). *Closing the Loop: An EU Action Plan for the Circular Economy*. COM(2015) 614 final. Retrieved from: http://eur-lex.europa.eu/legal-content/EN/TXT/?uri=CELEX:52015DC0614.

European Commission. (2017). *The Role of Waste-to-Energy in the Circular Economy*. COM(2017) 34 final. Retrieved from: http://ec.europa.eu/environment/waste/waste-to-energy.pdf.

Geisendorf, S. and Pietrulla, F. (2017). The circular economy and circular economic concepts: A literature analysis and redefinition. *Thunderbird*

International Business Review: 1–12. Retrieved from: https://doi.org/10.1002/tie.21924.

George, G. and Bock, A.J. (2011). The business model in practice and its implications for entrepreneurship research. *Entrepreneurship Theory and Practice* 35(1): 83–111.

Graedel, T. and Allenby, R. (2002). *Industrial Ecology.* London, UK: Pearson.

Hawken, P., Lovins, A.B., and Lovins, L.H. (2010). *Natural Capitalism: Creating the Next Industrial Revolution.* London, UK: Routledge.

Howard, R. and Galloway, T. (2017). *Going Round in Circles: Developing a New Approach to Waste Policy Following Brexit.* London, UK: Policy Exchange. Retrieved from: https://policyexchange.org.uk/publication/going-round-in-circles/.

Kirchherr, J., Reike, D., and Hekkert, M. (2017). Conceptualizing the circular economy: An analysis of 114 definitions. *Resources, Conservation and Recycling* 127: 221–232.

Lyle, J.T. (1996). *Regenerative Design for Sustainable Development.* Hoboken, NJ: John Wiley & Sons.

McDonough, W. and Braungart, M. (2008). *Cradle to Cradle: Remaking the Way We Make Things.* London, UK: Vintage.

Osterwalder, A. and Pigneur, Y. (2010). *Business Model Generation: A Handbook for Visionaries, Game Changers and Challengers.* Hoboken, NJ: John Wiley & Sons.

Pauli, G. (2010). *The Blue Economy: 10 Years, 100 Innovations, 100 Million Jobs.* Taos, NM: Paradigm Publications.

Stahel, W. (2006). *The Performance Economy.* London, UK: Palgrave Macmillan.

Stahel, W. and Redray, G. (1976). *The Potential for Substituting Manpower for Energy.* Report to the European Commission.

Suff, P. (June 2015). Framing circularity. *The Environmentalist*, 20–21.

Suff, P. (December 2016). Coming full circle. *The Environmentalist*, 30–33.

Tjell, J.C. (2005). Is the 'waste hierarchy' sustainable? *Waste Management & Research* 23(3): 173–174.

Wallace, S., Fleming-Williams, V., and De Leon, J.M. (2015). *Resource Efficient Business Models: The Roadmap to Resilience and Prosperity.* London, UK: Aldersgate Group. Retrieved from: www.aldersgategroup.org.uk/events/resource-efficient-business-models-the-roadmap-to-resilience-and-prosperity.

WRAP. (n.d). *Recyclability of Black Plastic Packaging.* Waste and Resources Action Programme. Retrieved from: www.wrap.org.uk/content/recyclability-black-plastic-packaging-0.

5 Circular Economy policy

Anne-Marie Benoy and Johanna Lehne

INTRODUCTION

In recent years, the concept of a Circular Economy (CE) has gained traction as a new model of sustainable economic development. Notwithstanding the proliferation of private sector initiatives and the accelerated push for appropriate policy interventions at different levels, what constitutes definitive CE policies remains in question. This is in part because a number of different philosophies of environmental thinking, such as industrial ecology, waste management, resource and energy efficiency and eco-design have been around for many decades and shaped what we now understand as the CE.

The 'closed-loop'-type thinking associated with CE, for example, has roots in industrial ecology (IE), which emerged as an academic field around 30 years ago and focuses on embedding 'resource cycling' through material and energy flows in industrial systems (Preston, 2011). Modern solid waste management practices date back to nineteenth-century 'dust-yards' (Velis et al., 2009), and twentieth-century efforts of phasing out landfills (e.g. Denmark introduced a landfill tax in 1987, Kjær, 2013), applying the waste hierarchy and life-cycle thinking, and concerns around hazardous wastes and environmental pollution (e.g. Clean Air Act, 1956 in the UK and Clean Water Act, 1972 in the United States) to name but a few.

Alongside these, energy and resource efficiency has shaped CE thinking as efficiency processes were incorporated in industrial and resource management, not only due to environmental concerns but also because of recurring resource scarcity, oil price volatility (particularly in the

1970s) or geopolitical challenges. Cradle to Cradle (C2C) design philosophy, developed by Michael Braungart and William McDonough, has also inspired many CE proponents. This framework emphasises that waste as a concept could be eliminated if products and systems were designed with nature's processes in mind, viewing materials as biological nutrients. According to its founders, if C2C design thinking was applied accurately, 'waste' would become 'food' (Braungart and McDonough, 2002).

Although CE-type thinking has been around for many decades, it was not until the 2000s that policies explicitly referring to the Circular Economy were introduced (McDowall et al., 2017). This chapter outlines the diversity of CE policy globally and explores the range of policy interventions that could support the shift to more circular practices.

POLICIES

The implementation of CE-interpreted policies has followed different patterns worldwide, varying in application and terminology depending on region and country (see Figure 5.1) The EU, Japan and China already have major legislative frameworks on the CE, but there are also activities in these and other regions which are driven from the community and city-level (Ghisellini et al., 2016).

In Japan, 3R (Reduce, Reuse, Recycle) has been used to promote bottom-up environment and waste management policies. Historically, a critical shortage in natural capital availability, high density living and low land space have made recycling activities (from household waste to industrial waste processing) more attractive for both businesses and individuals (Benton and Hazell, 2015). There has been a considerable investment in recycling infrastructure and close cooperation between civil society, public sector and manufacturers to improve recovery processes. As a result, Japan has some of the most impressive recycling rates globally and, in contrast to many recycling systems around the world, its policies stand out for focusing on recovering value rather than recycling volumes (techUK, 2015). Japan was also an early proponent of using specific towns as testing grounds for environmental strategies, policies and concepts: 26 eco-towns were created in Japan in the late 1990s.

China adopted legislation using the CE terminology in 2002. Although the concept has featured prominently in its 12th and 13th Five-Year Plans, the main policy framework for pursuing CE has been the Circular Economy Promotion Law. Introduced in 2009, it calls for specific improvements in recycling and resource recovery in production, distribution and consumption (NPC, 2008). Since then, a number

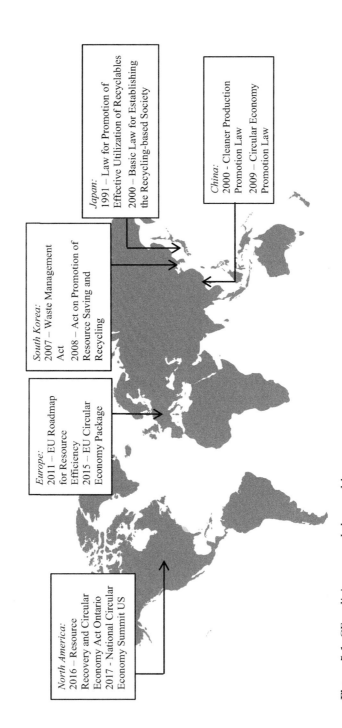

Figure 5.1 CE policies around the world

Source: Authors' own analysis based on diagram in Preston and Lehne (2017).

of supplementary action plans have been introduced, adding additional details for specific sectors and directives on the implementation of certain provisions of the CE Promotion Law (McDowall et al., 2017). China's CE policy framework stands out for its emphasis on geographic zones, e.g. cities and industrial parks, as pilot projects and areas for demonstration of circular activities. Three-quarters of China's industrial parks, for example, are being asked to adopt CE practices under the government's current Five-Year Plan (NDRC, 2016).

By comparison, North America has seen no legislation that specifically speaks to the CE. Since the 1980s, most US states have adopted a solid waste management hierarchy but the US lacks any relevant federal policy on CE (Park and Chertow, 2014). In Canada, CE is similarly promoted at the sub-national level, with leadership from cities like Ontario which enacted a Resource Recovery and Circular Economy Act in 2016 (Government of Ontario, 2017).

The launch of the EU Circular Economy Package in 2015 marked the growing significance of CE policy in the European Union. Prior to this launch, the EU's primary focus was on 'resource efficiency', identifying this as one of its seven flagship initiatives in 2010 and launching a Roadmap to a Resource Efficient Europe in 2011 (European Commission, 2011). The EU Circular Economy Package is one of the more ambitious and cross-sectorial legislative packages on the CE agenda (European Commission, 2015). The EU has emphasised CE as a means to 'boost global competitiveness, foster sustainable economic growth and generate new jobs' (European Commission, 2017a). This is reflected in the EU's broader-than-waste-management CE approaches, progressing from earlier policies in the 1990s.

The EU first highlighted the importance of the waste hierarchy in a Waste Strategy Communication in 1996 which also identified priority waste streams and policy around the 'polluter pays' principle. This evolved into product specific Extended Producer Responsibility (EPR) concept core to the Waste of Electrical and Electronic Equipment (WEEE) Directive, End-of-life vehicles Directive and Batteries Directive, all of which were implemented in the early 2000s. EPR was the first European policy mechanism which began to encourage producers to take environmental implications of their products into account already at the design and manufacture phases, a move which has become an increasing focus in EU CE policy.

'Closing the loop – An EU action plan for the Circular Economy', the action plan for EU member states to achieve a CE, aims to cover 'the whole cycle' – production, consumption, waste management and the market for secondary raw materials (European Commission,

2017a). The EU has raised recycling targets for a number of materials as well as focused on implementing material and product specific strategies for priority areas such as plastics, chemicals and food. This includes establishing product requirements around durability, repairability, upgradeability, design for disassembly, information and ease of reuse and recycling (European Commission, 2017b). The Action Plan also aims to update a number of existing directives on waste, packaging waste, landfill, and WEEE, which may highlight that the EU's CE policies continue to be heavily focussed on waste management policies (Ghisellini et al., 2016; Haass et al., 2015). However, the EU has extensively communicated that product design will be key to drive CE and is working towards updating the 2005 and 2009 EcoDesign Directives as well (Legco, 2016).

Within the EU, a few particular countries are taking leadership in CE policy, including the Netherlands, Finland and Scotland. The Netherlands presented an ambitious goal of achieving a CE in the country by 2050, also aiming to reduce primary raw material consumption by 50 percent by 2030 (Government of the Netherlands, 2016). Finland published a CE roadmap off the back of the European CE Action Plan (Sitra, 2016). Not unlike the EU, both countries highlight that a mixed focus on procedures (e.g. design, consumption, reuse, repair, business models, product life extension) and prioritisation of specifically problematic sectors (e.g. food, plastics and other raw materials, manufacturing, logistics) will increase the circularity of their economies.

AN EVOLVING TOOLKIT

As shown in Figure 5.1, the global CE policy landscape is diverse; reflecting local infrastructure, geography, capabilities and politics. Furthermore, the variety in approaches reflects the complexity of trying to shift whole economies and societies onto more circular and sustainable development pathways. A number of regulatory and financial factors maintain the status quo. For example, without appropriate price incentives, it is often cheaper for firms to use virgin materials than to use recycled materials or re-use existing products (The Recycler, 2017). The transition towards a CE will incur transaction costs and may not always be compatible with current legislation (Kennis Kaarten, 2017).

Despite growing momentum around CE approaches, there is, therefore, a long way to go before the concept is scaled up. A successful transition towards a more CE will rely on policy tools and financial instruments to align incentives along the whole supply chain, creating the right enabling conditions, removing regulatory barriers and changing behaviour.

In many instances, policies could be designed in a way that aligns environmental and economic policy objectives. For example, around:

- Fostering innovation and encouraging private sector investment in resource-efficient design, technologies and new business models
- Shaping behaviour of actors in the economy to encourage more resource-efficient behavior around consumption, waste management, reuse and recycling
- Directing waste streams to be captured at a higher stage of the 'waste hierarchy'
- Creating markets for the use of secondary materials and products

To realise these wide-ranging objectives, policymakers will need to utilise a variety of policy tools (see Table 5.1) across entire material and product value chains and life cycles.

DISCUSSION

CE policy to date has been fragmented, embedded in different government departments and policy areas, reflecting different interpretation and priorities around the issue. The gap between these different policies and the rhetoric embraced by advocates also means that CE practitioners do not necessarily share one set of vocabulary, nor the same priorities. In spite of this diversity, two common lessons are emerging from existing CE policy initiatives. Governments looking to accelerate the shift towards a CE over the coming years could use these lessons to inform new policy developments both domestically and internationally.

Trade-offs and expectations will have to be managed

Countries and actors have different, sometimes competing, motives and implementation pathways for CE, which need to be considered in international policy discussions. CE policies can also conflict with other regulatory objectives and can be costly to implement. Moreover, CE approaches and technologies are not always going to be the most environmentally and socially beneficial. These trade-offs need to be managed by policy makers, and will rely on extensive cooperation along the supply chain and between governmental departments.

Table 5.1 Circular Economy policy toolkit

Type	Policy	Description	Example
Regulatory	Design directives and product standards	Standards that seek to increase the energy – and resource – efficiency (i.e. durability and reparability) of products	EU's Eco-Design Directive
	Directives and legislation	Regulations to encourage use of waste, remanufacturing and reuse	Taskforce on Resource Efficiency in Denmark set up to remove regulatory barriers to CE practices in existing regulation
	Targets and indicators	Resource consumption and waste management targets, and indicators to measure progress towards those targets	EU's recycling targets – 65% municipal waste, 75% packaging waste–should be recycled by 2030
	Product labelling and certification	Labelling to give consumers information about the energy and resource-efficiency of a given product or service	EU Ecolabel; Der Grüne Punkt in Germany
Financial	Fiscal incentives	Shifts via taxes, charges and levies; removal of subsidies on resources, and energy, e.g. removing VAT on repair of or use of recyclates	Landfill tax in the UK, Denmark and the Netherlands
	Research, development and demonstration (RD&D)	Public sector funding to build innovation capacity in resource-efficient technologies and business models	EU Circular Economy Finance Support Platform; EU InnovFin backed by Horizon 2020; Innovate UK

Category	Instrument	Description	Examples
	Infrastructure investment	Public sector investment in recycling, remanufacturing infrastructure and reverse logistics	UK Recycling and Waste LP fund for smaller-scale recycling and waste infrastructure
	Extended producer responsibility (EPR)	Transfer of costs of recovery, treatment and/or disposal of post-consumer products to producers.	India 2016 E-Waste Management Rules.
	Container deposit legislation	Legislation that requires the collection of a monetary deposit on containers at the point of sale	AB Svenska Returpak in Sweden
Institutional	Public procurement	Obligations on public-sector agencies and government departments to purchase resource-efficient CE products	Dutch Government's Green Deal
	Pilot zones	New approaches to industrial processes trialled in special zones; Lessons are used to inform future policy making	CE industrial parks in China; Eco-industrial parks in Scandinavia
	Public awareness campaigns	Information dissemination about impacts of resource consumption and better waste management practices	EU public information campaign on environmental damage caused by plastic waste
	Skills and training	Public sector investment in skills and training for remanufacturing, repair and better waste recovery and management approaches	Scotland Skills Investment Plan
Private-sector led	Voluntary agreements	Commitments by industry to meet specific objectives setting out measurable targets	European PVC industry voluntary agreement; WRAP's Courtauld Commitment to reduce private sector food waste

Source:: Authors' own analysis.[1]

Policies will have to be flexible and diverse

As outlined previously, there are many different ways that CE policies and approaches can be implemented, and this often depends on specific local or national geographies. Technology and business model innovation will only add to the need for flexibility. There is a role for policy in guiding technology pathways. The challenge will be how to incentivise innovation without being overly prescriptive. The continued focus on waste management in CE policy suggests that policymakers need to continue reviewing how to link this policy area with design and manufacturing as well as other stages of the supply chain.

NOTE

1 *Regulatory policies = law and administrative rules; Financial instruments = include fees, taxes and subsidies; Institutional instruments = the provision of public services and other direct actions by government; Private-sector led = any policies, targets, commitments set by private-sector actors.*

BIBLIOGRAPHY

Benton, D. and Hazell, J. (April 2015). *The Circular Economy in Japan.* London: The Institution of Environmental Sciences.

Braungart, M. and McDonough, W. (2002). *Cradle to Cradle: Re-Making the Way We Make Things.* London: Vintage.

European Commission. (20 October 2011). *The Roadmap to a Resource Efficient Europe.* Luxembourg: Publications Office of the European Union.

European Commission. (12 December 2015). *Closing the Loop – An EU Action Plan for the Circular Economy.* Luxembourg: Publications Office of the European Union.

European Commission (2017a). *Circular Economy, European Commission* [Online]. Available at: http://ec.europa.eu/environment/circular-economy/index_en.htm [Accessed 7 November 2017].

European Commission (2017b). *Report from the Commission on the Implementation of the Circular Economy Action Plan.* Luxembourg: Publications Office of the European Union.

Ghisellini, P., Cialini, C., and Ulgiati, S. (2016). A review on circular economy: The expected transition to a balanced interplay of environmental and economic systems. *Journal of Cleaner Production* 114(7): 11–21.

Government of the Netherlands (2016). *A Circular Economy in the Netherlands by 2050.* The Ministry of Infrastructure and the Environment, the Ministry of Economic Affairs, the Ministry of Foreign Affairs and the Ministry of the Interior and Kingdom Relations.

Government of Ontario. (2017). *Strategy for a Waste-free Ontario: Building the Circular Economy*. Toronto: Government of Ontario.

Haass, W., Krausmann, F., Wiedenhofer, D., and Heinz, M. (2015). How circular is the global economy? An assessment of material flows, waste production and recycling in the European Union and the world in 2005. *Journal of Industrial Ecology* 19(5): 765–777.

Kennis Kaarten. (2017). *Barriers in the Current Economic System?* [Online]. Available at: https://kenniskaarten.hetgroenebrein.nl/en/knowledge-map-circular-economy/the-current-economic-system/ [Accessed 9 November 2017].

Kjær, B. (2013). *Municipal Waste Management in Denmark*. Copenhagen: European Environment Agency.

Legco. (2016). *Designing a Circular Economy*. Postnote, Number 536. The Parliamentary Office of Science and Technology.

McDowall, W., Geng, Y., Huang, B., Bartekova, E., Bleischwitz, R., Tuerkeli, R., Kemp, R., and Domenech, T. (2017). Circular economy policies in China and Europe. *Journal of Industrial Ecology* 21(3): 651–661.

NDRC. (2016). *The 13th Five-Year Plan for Economic and Social Development of the People's Republic of China (2016–2020)* [Online]. National Development and Reform Commission. Available at: http://en.ndrc.gov.cn/newsrelease/201612/P020161207645765233498.pdf [Accessed 11 September 2017].

NPC. (29 August 2008). *Circular Economy Promotion Law of the People's Republic of China* [Online]. Promulgation Department: The Standing Committee of the National People's Congress. Available at: www.fdi.gov.cn/1800000121_39_597_0_7.html (Accessed 8 November 2017).

Park, J.Y. and Chertow, M.R. (2014). Establishing and testing the "reuse potential" indicator for managing wastes as a resource. *Journal of Environmental Management* 137: 45–53.

Preston, F. (2011). *A Global Redesign? Shaping the Circular Economy*. London: Chatham House, The Royal Institute of International Affairs.

Preston, F. and Lehne, J. (2017). *A Wider Circle? The Circular Economy in Developing Countries*. London: Chatham House, The Royal Institute of International Affairs.

Sitra (2016). *Leading the Cycle: Finnish Road Map to a Circular Economy 2016–2015*. Sitra, Helsinki: The Finnish Innovation Fund.

techUK. (2015). *The Circular Economy: A Perspective from the Technology Sector* [Online]. techUK. Available at: www.techuk.org/circulareconomy [Accessed 8 November 2017].

The Recycler. (21 September 2017). Giant corporations seek to push circular economy. *The Recycler* [Online]. Available at: www.therecycler.com/posts/giant-corporations-seek-to-push-circular-economy/ [Accessed 9 November 2017].

Velis, C.A., Wilson, D.C., and Cheeseman, C.R. (2009). 19th century London dust-yards: A case study in closed-loop resource efficiency. *Waste Management* 29(4): 1282–1290.

Why Asia matters

6 Circular Economy in Japan, China and Taiwan

Ichin Cheng

INTRODUCTION

The Circular Economy (CE) concept is not new for many Asian countries with the roots in traditional values. This chapter gives an overview of the Asian context to CE, and CE policy development and best practice in Japan, China and Taiwan. In summary: Japan is the front runner of CE in Asia with comprehensive CE legislative and recycling systems; China is the second biggest economy and has an ambitious CE strategy; Taiwan has transformed itself into a recycling powerhouse.

Japan has established some of the most comprehensive CE legislative and recycling systems in the world and its approach has had a significant impact on China and Taiwan. China passed its Circular Economy Promotion Law in 2009 and has now established CE as a core part of its strategy to realise a Chinese 2050 ecological civilization (Wang et al., 2014).

Why Asia matters

Asia will play a key role in future global resource consumption due to its population and economic growth. In 2017, Asia accounted for 60 percent of current global population (7.6 billion) and by 2050, it is predicted to represent 53.5 percent of the world population of 9.8 billion (UN, 2017). Asian nations generate about 2.5 billion tonnes per annum of municipal solid waste and this is expected to increase twofold by 2050 adding more pressure on global resource management (Switch-Asia, 2016).

In recent decades, Asia has become the global manufacturing hub and is predicted to continue to be the world's economic centre. A map developed by McKinsey shows how the global economic centre of gravity has shifted to Asia (McKinsey, 2012), mainly due to China's economic growth which is predicted to account for 30 percent of global economy by 2040.

Currently, China consumes a huge amount of resources annually (Figure 6.1) and produces significant waste and pollution. In 2014, China generated 3.2 billion tonnes of industrial solid waste, only 2 billion tonnes of which were recovered for recycling, incineration and reuse. In 2011, China produced 46 percent of global aluminium, 50 percent of steel and 60 percent of the world's cement, which means it consumed more raw materials than the 34 countries of the Organisation for Economic Co-operation and Development (OECD) combined: 25.2 billion tonnes (Mathews and Tan, 2016). In addition, China used more cement between 2011 and 2013 than the US used in the entire twentieth century (USGS, 2014).

Many Asian countries are newly industrialising and their waste management was poorly regulated in the past. Pollution and waste issues are now becoming environmental challenges. For example, the growing concern over plastic waste in the ocean illustrates the mismanagement of waste and resource challenges. There are estimated to be 165 million tonnes of plastic in the ocean, and research shows 58 percent of ocean plastic waste is from six Asian countries: China (28 percent), Indonesia (10 percent), Philippines (6 percent), Vietnam (6 percent), Sri Lanka (5 percent) Thailand (3 percent) (Jambeck et al., 2015).

Managing waste is the starting point in relation to CE in Asia. The second step is implementing 3R principles (reduce, reuse and recycle) and is the strategy for many Asian countries now. However, some more advanced CE countries have set up small scale 'industrial symbiosis' projects – in which waste of one firm becomes the raw materials of another, e.g. Yokohama (Japan) and Ulsan (South Korea).

JAPAN: SYSTEMIC DRIVEN APPROACH

In Japanese culture, there is a deeper meaning to elements of CE. *Kintsugi* which means 'golden repair' is the art of repairing broken pottery with a special lacquer using powdered gold, silver or platinum which dates back to fifteenth century. This gives a unique appearance to the repaired piece and celebrates a second life. *Mottainai*

Resource flows equal to or greater than $1 billion in 2014, equalling 98.3% of all resource flows into China

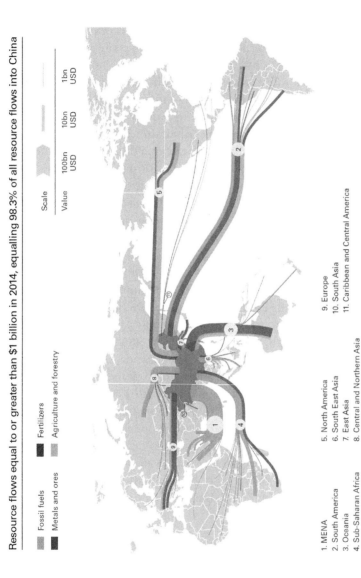

| Fossil fuels | Fertilizers |
| Metals and ores | Agriculture and forestry |

Scale

Value   100bn USD   10bn USD   1bn USD

1. MENA
2. South America
3. Oceania
4. Sub-Saharan Africa
5. North America
6. South East Asia
7. East Asia
8. Central and Northern Asia
9. Europe
10. South Asia
11. Caribbean and Central America

Figure 6.1 China consumes a huge amount of global resources

Resource flows equal to or greater than $1billion in 2014, equalling 98.3 percent of all resource flows into China.

Source: Preston et al., Navigating the New Normal: A Joint DRC and Chatham House report, China and Global Resource Governance, Chatham House Resource Trade Database, COMTRADE Circular Economy overview in Asia, p. 18, 2016.

means a sense of regret related to the production of waste and is frequently spoken by Japanese people in relation to the recycling of food, material and energy.

Japan is the front-runner in the development of CE and has already set up one of the most comprehensive legislative and recycling systems in the world with 98 percent of metals in 2014 (Itoh, 2014) and 74 percent to 89 percent of the materials from home appliances recovered. Most significantly, many of these materials go back into the manufacture of the same type of product (Benton and Hazell, 2015). In comparison, the EU had a 32.2 percent of e-waste recycling rate in 2015 (De Groene Zaak 2015). Japan also has the highest number (28 percent) of CE technology patents globally (Welfens, 2017).

Japan passed its first waste management laws in 1970 and have progressed resource efficiency activities since then. Japan has used other terms to describe its approach to CE and is using the concept of circulatory system of the heart to describe activities: the CE manufacturing cycle is described as an arterial industry and recycling and remanufacturing industry as a venous industry.

In 2000, Japan announced the year 2000 was 'the first year of Japanese Circular Society' and the Fundamental Law for Sound Material-Cycle Society (MCS) was passed in 2001. This approach was underpinned by legislation related to resource efficiency, waste and several sector-specific initiatives. For example, the Law for Promotion of Effective Utilisation of Resources (2001) formed a legal framework covering a wide range of products from plastics, electronics and electrical, paper, packaging, automobile and raw material processing industries. It set basic requirements for producers: obligations to use recycled materials and reusable parts in the production of new products; guidelines to ensure products are designed to be easy to recycle; and requirements for 'voluntarily' take back (Charter, 2006). In 2012, 32 of Japan's industries produced 74.8 percent less waste than in 2000 (compared to 92.2 percent reduction in 1990) (Yagai, 2015).The second wave of MCS started in 2008 and the third wave of MCS plan starts in 2018 (Japan Ministry of the Environment. 2010, 2017).

The success of Japan's CE strategy comes from its comprehensive, collaborative and systemic approach.

• Japan is a major industrial producer but has very limited natural resources (metal and minerals), which has made materials recycling attractive – e.g. 50 recycling factories for EEE including white goods were launched in early 2000s. Japan has systemically

Japan	China	Taiwan
• The Container and Packaging Recycling Law (1997)	• Circular of the Ministry of Finance and State Administration of Taxation on Preferential Policies in Respect of Enterprise Income Tax (1994)	• Taiwan National Extended Producer Responsibility (EPR) system (1998)
• The Construction Material Recycling Law (2000)		• Environmental Basic Law (2002)
• The Food Recycling Law (2000)		• Resource Recycling and Reuse Act (2002)
• Green Purchasing Law (2000)		
• Fundamental Law for Sound Material-Cycle Society (2001)	• The Administrative Measures on Pollution Prevention of Waste Electrical and Electronic Products officially (2008)	• Responsible Enterprise Regulated Recyclable Waste Management Regulations (2002)
• The Law for Promotion of Effective Utilization of Resources (2001)		• Renewable Resource Reuse Management Regulations (2003)
• The Home Appliance Recycling Law (2001)	• The Regulation on the Recovery and Disposal of Waste Electrical and Electronic Products (2009)	• Waste Disposal Act (2004)
• The End-of-Life Vehicle Recycling Law (2002)		• Management Regulations for the Import and Export of Industrial Waste (2013)
• Japanese RoHS (2006)	• The Circular Economy Promotion Law (2009)	
• Small Electrical and Electronic Equipment Recycling Law (2012)	• Investment and Financing Polices and Measures Supporting Circular Economy Development (2010)	• Standards for Defining Hazardous Industrial Waste (2017)
• Second and Third of Action Plan for Sound Material-Cycle Society (2008, 2017)	• Special Funds for Circular Economy Development (2012)	

Figure 6.2 Main CE-related legal framework in Japan, China and Taiwan

Source: Charter, Clark (2006); Japan Ministry of the Environment. (2010, 2017); Taiwan EPA (2017); Qi et al. (2016).

developed and invested in recycling infrastructure with close cooperation between civil society, government and manufacturers.
• The Green Purchasing Law (GPL) was passed in 2000 to provide economic incentives for green product development and stimulate the use of recycled materials and reusable parts. Prior to establishing GPL, the Green Purchasing Network was established in 1996.

- The government promotes research and development (R&D) activities, urban mining (reusing and recycling critical metal from e-waste), provide financial incentives (e.g. tax reduction) and completes educational and public awareness programmes.
  After four decades of regulations and R&D effort, Japanese companies have developed some unique CE business models and products/services.

Sekisui chemical: modular re-used housing system

Sekisui Chemical launched a CE Product Service System (PSS) for reusing houses in 2002. The aim of reused housing system is to recycle 100 percent of waste enabled through modular design, and reverse manufacturing and logistics. The company produces modular housing and units are transported to the housing site. The house is designed for disassembly and up to 70 percent of the products, components and materials can be reused. It is claimed that the buildings can be rebuilt and completed within only 60 days; and on-site building takes just one day (Sekisui, 2017).

Teijin eco circle: re-cycle and re-used polyester technology

Teijin have developed a closed-loop chemical recycling technology that makes it possible to recycle waste polyester into new polyester. Teijin's technology de- and re-polymerises waste polyester back into new material equivalent to that made from petroleum (Teijin, 2017).

Epson: paperlab prints waste paper into white paper

In 2016, Epson launched the world first office papermaking system: PaperLab that turns waste paper into new paper in three minutes. PaperLab Epson has developed 'dry fibre technology' that (1) fiberizes, (2) binds and (3) forms waste paper into new paper (Epson, 2016).

CHINA: TOP-DOWN AND SCALING-UP APPROACH

Chinese CE policy was inspired and influenced by Germany and Japan, and has now started to develop its own CE policy and strategy. The manufacturing industry is the major contributor to China's economic growth but also a major source of waste and pollution. In the past 10–15 years, China focused on establishing a sound industrial system and is now focusing on remanufacturing and materials reuse. The Chinese government aims to address environmental problems in parallel to maintaining economic growth. China's Circular Economy Promotion Law came into force in 2009 and CE has become one of China's key national strategies to build China's ecological civilization (Qi et al., 2016; Zhu, 2016).

The Chinese government has focused on a top-down approach and scaling up through massive demonstration programmes. The evolution of China's CE approach has gone through three stages over the last 20 years.

> **Stage 1:** Concept and regulation development (1998–2008): CE policy discussion among Chinese scholars and government. Following that a series of laws, regulations and policies were formulated and the State Council officially announced an acceleration of CE development in 2005.
>
> **Stage 2:** Implementation of the Circular Economy Law and related policies (2008–2011) that included: Administrative Measures on Pollution Prevention of Waste Electrical and Electronic Products (2008); Regulation on the Recovery and Disposal of Waste Electrical and Electronic Products (2009); and the Circular Economy Promotion Law (2009).
>
> **Stage 3:** Accelerating the national strategy and action plan (2012–present): guided by China's 12th (2011–2015) and 13th Five-Year-Plan (2016–2020) and Made in China 2025 Strategy (2015), China is now promoting CE as national strategy related to greening of industry and reducing waste. The State Council officially issued the CE Development Strategy and Immediate Action Plan in 2013 and during the 12th Five-Year-Plan, China established CE as national strategy that includes setting up several sub-systems, e.g. circular agricultural system, resource recycling system and finance system to facilitate CE in society.

Since 2011, the major '10–100–1,000' pilot programmes have been implemented through central and local governments and industries. The '10–100–1000' covers: 10 CE demonstration programmes; 100 CE demonstration cities; 1,000 CE demonstration enterprises (Industrial Parks). The scope of the CE 10 demonstration programmes includes: 60 demonstration projects of comprehensive resource utilisation, 100 CE-oriented upgrading of Industrial Parks, 200 demonstration projects of resource recovery, 50 'urban mining' demonstration projects, industrialisation of remanufacturing and resource recovery, establishing an agricultural CE system, etc. By the end 2016, China has achieved over 6,000 demonstration enterprises (Zhu, 2016) and materials recycling and remanufacturing industries have been accelerated. China is now a top 3 global remanufacturing market (Figure 6.3) and is expected to overtake US and EU in the near future (Wang and Fitzsimons, 2017). After two decades of regulations and top-down policy, Chinese companies have developed fast growing CE companies.

Tianjin Beijiang thermal power plant's resource efficiency 'five-in-one' model via industrial symbiosis concept

Tianjin Beijiang thermal power plant has established a 'five-in-one' CE model to implement an industry symbiosis approach. The thermal power plant has utilised the waste heat from power generation to desalinate seawater, while the concentrated seawater generated from the

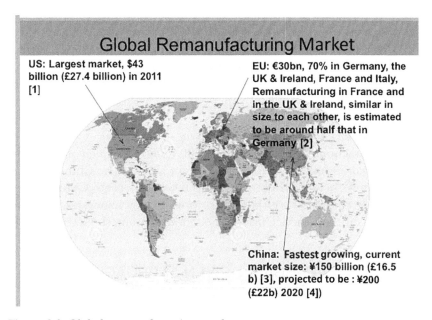

Figure 6.3 Global remanufacturing market

Source: Wang and Fitzsimons, 2017.

Notes: The detailed data in the figure came from various references shown in the figure. As following:

[1] The UK's All-Party Parliamentary Manufacturing and Sustainable Resource Groups, "Triple Win - The Social, Economic and Environmental case for Remanufacturing", 2014.

[2] The European Remanufacturing Network, "European Remanufacturing market study", 2016.

[3] Construction Shows (2014) 4th China International Remanufacturing Summit, 2014.

[4] MIIT governmental plan, "High end intelligent Remanufacturing act plan(2018–2020)

process has been used as the raw material to make salt and develop salt chemical industries. The fresh water has been used by the power plant as cooling water, and then transferred to neighbouring enterprises to be used for production and domestic life. The fly ash and desulfurized gypsum from burning coal has been used as the raw materials to produce building materials (Qi et al., 2016).

Green Eco Manufacture's full-scale e-waste reverse manufacturing

Green Eco Manufacture (GEM) is one of the biggest 'urban mining technology' enterprises in the world and specialised in e-waste resource recovery and recycling. Since it was founded in 2002, GEM has focused on recycling e-waste, used batteries and waste scrap back into materials and other new products. GEM's material recycling and products includes cobalt and nickel powder and salts, wood-plastic-composites, etc. GEM is based on an 800-acre industrial scale urban mine (closed-loop industrial park) and has set up many recycling points in China (GEM, 2017).

Sharing economy

In 2016, China's sharing economy accounted for more than $500 billion in transactions involving roughly 600 million people compared to an estimated 55 million in the US (Larmer, 2017). The Chinese 'sharing economy' includes those providing bikes, cars (Didi Chuxing, the ride-sharing company), refrigerators, tools, luxury handbags, etc. and indicates a shift to a service-oriented economy among some consumers.

TAIWAN: SUPPLY-CHAIN DRIVEN APPROACH

Taiwan holds an important position in the global manufacturing supply chain for textiles and electronics and a key driver for CE activities was from European Union regulations (e.g. WEEE Directive).

Historically, Taiwan had major waste management challenges and its regulatory system dates back to 1974 (Figure 6.2). But over the past two decades Taiwan has transformed itself into a recycling leader with an overall recycling rate of 55-percent municipal solid waste in 2015. Taiwan's recycling firms have grown from about 100 in the 1980s–1990s to more than 2,000 in 2013. Some pilot programmes provided tax and financial incentives, technical assistance and information related to industrial waste recycling. The Industrial Waste Exchange Information Center and Environmental Technology Park Development Program also been developed in Taiwan to promote CE. A Circular Economy Promotion Law was submitted to Taiwan government in late 2016 (Taiwan EPA, 2017).

The domestic recycling collection system is one of the keys to Taiwan's success. In Taipei, 'musical' garbage trucks come to more than 4,000 pickup spots in communities, five nights a week. In addition, the Tzu Chi Foundation, a Buddhist non-governmental organisation with more than 6 million members, operates more than 4,500 additional recycling stations in Taiwan. That combined effort helps Taiwan achieve more than 96-percent recycling of polyethylene terephthalate (PET) bottles in 2012 compared to 72.1 percent in Japan, 59 percent in Europe and 28.4 percent in the US (NAPCOR, 2016). The Tzu Chi Foundation and its business members (e.g. Far Eastern New Century) have further developed PET recycling technology. In the 2014 football World Cup, there were 10 teams wearing Nike branded sports shirts incorporating Taiwanese recycled PET textiles.

Some examples of Taiwanese companies that have developed industrial scale CE solutions and innovative business are highlighted below:

SJ Group: bio-based material vegetable leather

SJ Group's main business is selling materials and products from plastics and rubber that are used in various consumer products. SJ Group started their CE business from recycling plastics and rubber and have moved up the value chain to develop various new bio-based materials that are used in their products, e.g. sportswear. Some examples are: (1) TAIFOAM™ is a vegetable-based leather that is now used in shoes; and (2) TAIFOAM™ NROL is leather-like material that is derived from natural plant fibres and can substitute traditional synthetic materials in a variety of products (SJ group, 2017).

Industrial Technology Research Institute (ITRI): LCD waste recycling system

ITRI developed the liquid-crystal display (LCD) waste recycling system to recycle scrap LCDs and separate the liquid crystal, indium, and glass for reuse. The LCD waste recycling system recently received an R&D 100 Special Recognition Award in Green Tech (ITRI, 2017).

Miniwiz: upcycle from waste to building materials

The Taiwanese architectural firm Miniwiz have designed and built what could be the largest structure in the world clad in recycled plastic. A nine-story exhibition hall in Taipei called the EcoArk, has walls made of 1.5 million PET bottles. The company has also made several recycled plastic products for the construction industry, including Polli-Bricks, a curtain wall system for buildings made from 100-percent recycled PET; Polli-Ber, a composite made from recycled polymers and agricultural waste; and Natrilon, a fibre made from 100-percent recycled PET and silicon dioxide from rice husks. In addition, Miniwiz has also designed high street shops for Nike in London and Paris, and a beer bar in Taiwan all using reused materials (Miniwiz, 2017).

ANALYSIS: ASIAN CE BEST PRACTICE AND THEIR BUSINESS MODEL

In Asia, traditional business models have relied on large quantities of cheap and easily accessible materials and energy. However, physical and environmental limits are now being reached and a number of Asian companies are now starting to transition to new CE business models, products and services.

There are five CE business models (Figure 6.4) that have been identified by Accenture. Examination of best practice in Japan, China and Taiwan found the majority of the Asian companies identified focused on 'waste-as-a-resource', e.g. (1) circular supplies, (2) resource recovery (3) product life-extension. Fewer companies focused on (4) sharing platform and (5) products as a service. However, some front-runner companies have started to develop disruptive technologies, advanced materials or advanced manufacturing processes, e.g. Sekisui Chemical's modular re-used housing system and Epson's PaperLab (Figure 6.4).

To transition towards CE and a Circular Society in Asia, the current 3Rs approach needs to be expanded to (1) take account of the life cycle perspective that considers repair, refurbish and repurposing; and then to (2) move up the value-chain towards the 12Rs that includes re-design of products, services, business models and systems; remanufacturing; R&D into new materials, processes and technologies; re-skilling people; reverse supply chain management and logistics (Figure 6.5).

CONCLUSION

Lessons learnt

- To achieve CE, there is a need to balance economic, environmental and social goals. Both Japan's and China's CE policies have very strong regulations, comprehensive links to industrial strategy as well as environmental protection goals.

Five CE Business Model	Japan	China	Taiwan
1. **Circular supplies:** Use renewable energy and bio-based or fully recyclable inputs	Sekisui Chemical	GEM Tianjin Beijiang Thermal Power Plant	SJ Group
2. **Resource recovery:** Recover useful resources out of materials, by-products or waste	Sekisui Chemical Teijin Eco Cir Epson, PaperLab	GEM Tianjin Beijiang Thermal Power Plant	Miniwiz ITRI
3. **Product life-extension:** Extend product life cycles by repairing, upgrading and reselling, as well as through innovation and product design	Sekisui Chemical Teijin Eco Cir Epson, PaperLab	GEM	Miniwiz ITRI
4. **Sharing platform:** Connect product users to one another and encourage shared use, access or ownership to increase product use		600 million users of Chinese 'sharing economy' business	
5. **Products as a service:** Move away from product ownership and offer customers paid access to products, allowing companies to retain the benefits of circular resource productivity or ownership to increase product use	Epson, PaperLab	'Sharing economy' businesses	

Figure 6.4 Asian CE best practice and their business model

Source: Accenture, WBCSD (2015); this research analysis.

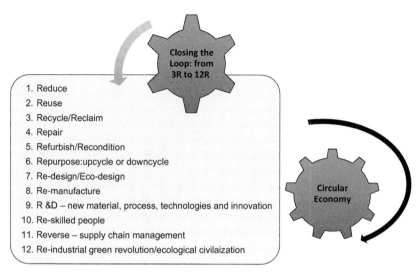

Figure 6.5 CE from 3Rs to 12Rs
Source: Cheng, 2016.

- Japan has developed systemic infrastructure for recycling. To transition towards CE, governments need to design circular systems, so that businesses can design circular products and services.
- There are indications that China's top-down approach and its economic scale could play major role in its transition towards CE.
- Taiwan's businesses may further develop CE technologies and products through early adaption to supply chain pressures and innovation.

The way forward
- In Asia, the CE's staring point is waste management and the 3Rs (reduce, reuse and recycle). Further development of 12Rs will help transition towards more circular production and consumption in Asia.
- EU and Asia have started cooperation on CE and this could be very important for a global transition towards CE. For example, China still holds a dominant position in global manufacturing, which means that it has led to it being the largest importer of materials including recyclables. In 2016, Chinese manufacturers imported 7.3 million tonnes of waste plastics from developed countries including EU, US and Japan; in the EU, 87 percent of the

recycled plastics were exported directly or indirectly to China in 2016 (Anon, 2017). In early 2017, China announced that it would ban imports of 24 categories of recyclables and solid waste by the end of the 2017 creating a headache for many countries. China's Belt and Road Initiative (BRI) (Chinese State Council, 2017) will initiate potentially new trade and infrastructure projects among China, Central Asia and Europe. This will result in added pressure on global resources. In 2017, the EU and China agreed to continue to promote further cooperation on integrating CE into BRI through EU/China experts dialogue and a CE memorandum of understanding signed in 2017 (Cheng, 2017).

BIBLIOGRAPHY

Accenture. (2015). *Circular Advantage Innovative Business Models and Technologies to Create Value in a World without Limits to Growth* [Online]. Available at: https://www.accenture.com/t20150523T053139__w__/us-en/_acnmedia/Accenture/Conversion-Assets/DotCom/Documents/Global/PDF/Strategy_6/Accenture-Circular-Advantage-Innovative-Business-Models-Technologies-Value-Growth.pdf [Accessed 13 April 2018].

Anon. (20 October 2017). *China Bans Foreign Waste: But What Will Happen to the World's Recycling?* [Online]. Available at: https://theconversation.com/china-bans-foreign-waste-but-what-will-happen-to-the-worlds-recycling-85924 [Accessed 4 Dec. 2017].

Benton, D. and Hazell, J. (March 2015). The Circular Economy in Japan: new materials and the Circular Economy. The Institution of Environmental Sciences [Online]. Available at: https://www.the-ies.org/analysis/circular-economy-japan. [Accessed 13 April 2018].

Charter and Clark. (2006). Issues and capacity-building needs of the Asian electronics sector in complying with international product-related environmental regulations and other requirements, The Centre for Sustainable Design, European Aid Asia ProECo: Asia Eco-design Electronic [Online]. Available at: http://cfsd.org.uk/aede/ [Accessed 13 April 2018].

Cheng, I. (2017). *EU Expert's Delegation to China: Climate Change Round Table Presentation*, EU DRAGON-STAR Plus 'Climate Change Expert Workshop', May 15th, 2017, Zhejiang University, Hangzhou, PR China Chinese State Council, 2017.

Chinese State Council. (2017). *China Policies Watch* [Online]. Available at: http://english.gov.cn/policies/policywatch/#, PR China Chinese State Council [Accessed 13 April 2018].

Dajian, Z. (2016). *Circular Economy Speaker Series 2016: Circular Economy & China* [Online]. Available at: https://www.youtube.com/watch?v=Cd45z8q8va4 [Accessed 14 Dec. 2017].

De Groene Zaak. (2015). *Governments Going Circular: A Global Scan by De Groene Zaak.* Dutch Sustainability Business Association [Online]. Available at: http://www.govsgocircular.com/ [Accessed 14 Dec. 2017].

Epson. (2016). *PaperLab* [Online]. Available at: https://www.epson.co.uk/ insights/article/paper-from-waste-with-paperlab [Accessed 14 Dec. 2017].

GEM. (2017). [Online]. Available at: http://www.gemchina.com/ [Accessed 14 Dec. 2017].

Itoh, H. (2014). The recent trend of e-waste recycling and rare metal recovery in Japan. *WIT Transactions on Ecology and The Environment* 180 [Online]. Available at: www.witpress.com, ISSN 1743–3541 [Accessed 14 Dec. 2017].

ITRI. (2017). *LCDs Waste Recycling System* [Online]. Available at: www.itri.org.tw/

Jambeck, J., Geyer, R., Wilcox, C., Siegler, T., Perryman, M., Andrady, A., Narayan, R., and Law, K. (2015). Plastic waste inputs from land into the ocean. *Science* 347(6223): 768–771.

Larmer, B. (2017). *China's Revealing Spin on the 'Sharing Economy'* [Online]. Available at: nytimes.com [Accessed 14 Dec. 2017].

Mathews, J. and Tan, H. (24 March 2016). Circular Economy: Lessons from China. *Nature* 531: 440–442 [Online]. Available at: https://www.nature.com/polopoly_fs/1.19593!/menu/main/topColumns/topLeftColumn/pdf/531440a.pdf

McKinsey. (2012). By far the most rapid shift in the world's economic center of gravity happened in 2000–10, reversing previous decades of development evolution of the earth's economic center of gravity 1 AD 1 to 2025, *McKinsey Global Institute Analysis, Using Data from Angus Maddison.* University of Groningen [Online]. Available at: https://globaltrends2030.files.wordpress.com/2012/07/nic-blog-mgi-shifting-economic-center-of-gravity.pdf [Accessed 14 Dec. 2017].

Preston, F. Bailey, R. Bradley, S., Wei, J. and, Zhao, C. (2016). *Navigating the New Normal: A Joint DRC and Chatham House report, China and Global Resource Governance, Chatham House Resource Trade Database,* COMTRADE [Online]. Available at: https://www.chathamhouse.org/sites/files/chathamhouse/publications/research/2016-01-27-china-global-resource-governance-preston-bailey-bradley-wei-zhao-final.pdf [Accessed 13 April 2018]. pp. 18.

Japan Ministry of the Environment. (2010, 2017). *Establishing a Sound Material-Cycle Society: Milestone Toward a Sound Material-Cycle Society* [Online]. Available at: www.env.go.jp/en/recycle/ smcs/a-rep/2010gs_full.pdf [Accessed 20 Dec. 2017].

MINIWIZ. (2017). [Online]. Available at: www.miniwiz.com/ [Accessed 20 Dec. 2017].

NAPCOR. (2016). *The National Association for PET Container Resources (NAPCOR): Report on Postconsumer PET Container Recycling Activity in 2016* [Online]. Available at: https://napcor.com/wp-content/uploads/2017/10/NAPCOR-APR_2016RateReport_FINAL.pdf [Accessed 20 Dec. 2017].

Qi, J. et al. (2016). Development of circular economy in China. *Research Series on the Chinese Dream and China's Development Path.* DOI: 10.1007/978-981-10-2466-5_2, Springer, 2016, 21–53.

Sekisui chemical. (2017). *Reuse System House* [Online]. Available at: Sekisuichemical.com.

SJ Group. (2017). [Online]. Available at: www.seegreen.com.tw

Switch-Asia Mag. (Winter 2016/17). *Advancing the Circular Economy in Asia* [Online]. Available at: http://www.switch-asia.eu/fileadmin/user_upload/ SWITCH-Asia_Briefing_No6_-_Waste_Management_-_Screen_FINAL.pdf [Accessed 18 Dec. 2017].

Taiwan EPA. (2017). *Environmental Law of Taiwan* [Online]. Available at: https://oaout.epa.gov.tw/law/EngLawQuery.aspx [Accessed 4 Dec. 2017]. [Accessed 18 Dec. 2017].

Teijin. (2017). [Onine]. Available at: www.teijinfiber.com.

UN. (2017). *The 2017 Revision of The UN's World Population Projections Population and Development Review* [Online]. Available at: https://esa.un.org/unpd/ wpp/ [Accessed 18 Dec. 2017].

USGS. (2014). 1900–2000, & Mineral industry of China, 2011–2013 USGS, Bill Gates: how China used more cement in 3 years than the U.S. did in the entire 20th century [Online]. Available at: https://www.washingtonpost. com/news/wonk/wp/2015/03/24/how-china-used-more-cement-in-3- years-than-the-u-s-did-in-the-entire-20th-century/?utm_term=.1c0d38caf3df [Accessed 18 Dec. 2017].

Welfens, P. (2017). The Circular Economy in China and Europe: latest insights and future perspectives, EU/China Circular Economy Expert Workshop Presentation, Chatham House.

Wang, Y. and Fitzsimons, D. (2017). Remanufacturing in China and EU/UK, EU/China Circular Economy Expert Workshop Presentation, Chatham House, the detailed data in the figure came from various references shown in the figure.

Yagai, Y. (2015). *Recycling Scheme of a WEEE in Japan, 2015* [Online]. Available at: www.env.go.jp/en/focus/docs/files/20151112-96.pdf

Yi, W. et al. (2014). Policy Frame Work and Key Mechanisms for Ecological Civilization, *China Sustainable Development Report* 2014—*Building Institutions for Ecological Civilization*, Chinese Science Publisher, (C7) pp. 228–251.

Circular businesses

7 Benefits, approaches and challenges

James D. Burgon and Jonathan Wentworth

INTRODUCTION

Many current approaches to product manufacture and use are considered linear: make, use and dispose. This results in valuable materials being wasted. In contrast, a circular approach uses restoration and recovery processes to increase the lifespan of products, components and materials to keep them at their most useful and valuable. This goes beyond present recycling practices, which largely focus on 'easy wins' in waste streams like paper, as circular products (or their components) are designed for repair and reuse. Circular products are also made in a way that allows them to be disassembled and used as a materials input for new industry at end-of-life. These practices seek to decouple economic growth from resource consumption, which could help overcome pressures on natural resources. For example, the European Commission has identified 20 critical raw materials, which have both high economic importance to the European Union (EU) and high supply risk. While this list includes the rare earth elements used in modern technologies, less than 1 percent of these are currently recycled (Binnemans et al., 2013). Moving to a Circular Economy (CE) could also create new economic and employment opportunities, and provide environmental benefits through improved materials and energy use. However, such changes can only arise through a combination of voluntary action by individual businesses, government intervention and international co-operation.

This chapter will outline what a CE approach is before summarising how one may be achieved. First, important changes required to product design, producer responsibility and business models will be outlined. Examples of policy-led strategies will then be used to show how legislative processes may be used to encourage and facilitate businesses when transitioning to a circular model, including a detailed case study of the United Kingdom (UK). Finally, barriers to achieving a CE will be highlighted, along with potential approaches for overcoming them.

WHAT IS A CIRCULAR ECONOMY (CE) APPROACH?

Circular systems are either technical (restorative) or biological (regenerative). Both incorporate a range of activities that reduce the demand for material inputs and recover/reuse materials already in the system. As a result, the World Economic Forum (2014) estimates that the CE could contribute $1 trillion a year to the global economy through reduced material use by 2025, with the largest benefits seen in Europe (which relies on imports) and materials-intensive sectors like the automotive industry. For example, in a technical cycle a car can first be fixed, then components reused, and finally materials like alloys recovered. This extracts the highest quality and value at each stage in the products' life cycles and preserves the energy invested during production, known as 'embedded energy'.

Biological cycles focus on 'renewable' materials, such as bio-waste, timber and plant-based textiles like cotton. These resources also cascade down a value chain, but with the ultimate aim of returning nutrients to the soil. This can be achieved through composting or approaches like anaerobic digestion, where opportunities exist for chemical production (like biofuels and fertilisers) and energy generation; the London Waste Recycling Board (2015) estimate that London's food waste alone could generate £11m worth of savings a year though energy capture or extraction. Technical and biological cycles can also overlap; for example, high quality timber can be reused or remanufactured into multiple products before being returned to the nutrient cycle.

ACHIEVING A CE

Although there is broad consensus that a CE is desirable, there is debate over how it can be achieved. Transitioning to such a model will require changes to product design, product ownership and business models.

This would likely result in an increased service economy, with a focus on access to product use rather than ownership; for example, Philips' selling of 'lighting as a service' instead of selling light fixings.

Product design

One of the most important steps in developing a CE will be changing the approach to product design. Around 80 percent of a product's environmental impact is determined at the design stage (Environmental Change Institute, 2005). For example, gluing together smartphone cases makes them thinner and more attractive to consumers, but harder to repair and reuse compared to using screws. However, by focusing on eco-design, businesses can make their products more resource efficient over whole life cycles. This approach seeks to integrate all environmental aspects of a product into its design, with the aim of improving its environmental performance throughout its whole life cycle. This includes the consumption of resources like materials, energy and water, but also externalities like pollution. Various eco-design strategies exist that fit a circular model, for example building modular products and designing for more efficient disassembly and reuse.

A lot of current product-related environmental legislation focuses on making products more energy efficient. For example, the EU's Ecodesign Directive (2009/125/EC) set rules on a product's environmental performance. However, areas like durability are also important, and within Europe the Committee for Standardization (CEN) and the European Committee for Electrotechnical Standardization (CENELEC) are now working to expand materials efficiency aspects considerations. In addition, other policy developments might include the introduction of regulatory reuse requirements or market incentives for secondary material use, like variable VAT based on recycled content or pricing externalities (like emissions) into raw materials.

Extended producer responsibility (EPR)

Within a traditional waste management system, the costs associated with end-of-life product disposal are not borne by producers. This approach can lead to wasteful linear supply chains, as there is little incentive to design for disassembly and reuse. EPR can change this as it shifts the practical or economic burden of end-of-life goods, partly or fully, from local authorities to producers (Green Alliance, 2013). There are two approaches, collective (CPR) and individual (IPR) producer responsibility. Within the EU, both CPR and IPR approaches are included in the Waste Electrical and Electronic Equipment (WEEE; 2002/96/EC), End-of-Life Vehicles (ELV; 2000/53/EC) and Battery directives (2006/66/

EC). Broadly, these set targets for the collection, recycling and recovery of products, and restrict the use of hazardous materials. However, specific EPR obligations currently vary considerably across product categories and legislations.

While CPR spreads costs and responsibilities between brands, IPR makes producers responsible for their own products, which could directly encourage more circular designs. IPR could also benefit producers if combined with a 'closed-loop' business model. For example, Apple's Liam robot can disassemble and sort the components of an iPhone 6S in 11 seconds, and when combined with take-back schemes this would allow Apple to retain control of all aspects of its products, from hardware to intellectual property. However, IPR has proven difficult to enact compared to CPR, with no legislative body having fully implemented it to date.

New business models

New service-based businesses could arise through changes to product ownership and the emergence of a more sharing economy. For example, in the UK, recent Office for National Statistics (ONS) data shows more spending on renting and services than on buying to own (Whalen, 2016), indicating that desired customer benefits come from use not ownership. Businesses focusing on access over sales could gain from longer relationships with customers, consumers could access products they could not afford to own, and inefficient products could be taken out of circulation. Product Service Systems, where customers pay for performance not products, is a proven model (Mont and Tukker, 2006). Examples include Rolls Royce's 'Power by the Hour' aircraft engine maintenance, Michelin's 'pay-per-km' tyres and Xerox take-back scheme; by selling 'copies' not printers, more than 90 percent of Xerox equipment is reused or recycled (Xerox, 2010).

CE STRATEGIES

Dedicated national strategies have helped industry increase resource efficiency in some countries. This is largely because markets cannot deliver a CE through 'business as usual' and government help or intervention is often required. For example, due to its high resource use, China has promoted circular tax, fiscal, pricing and industrial policies in its 11th, 12th and 13th Five-Year Plans (2006–2020), and its State Council's National Strategy for Achieving a Circular Economy (2013) was the first of its kind in the world. A lack of natural resources has also led to many 3R (reduce, reuse, recycle) policies in Japan: its Law Promotion of Effective Utilization of Resources (2000) covers 10 industries and 69 product categories, outlining requirements and voluntary actions for businesses, consumers and government to improve resource use. Germany took similar actions with its Closed Substance Cycle and Waste Management Act (1996), which promotes multi-use, low-waste, long-life and repair-friendly products. It also makes industry responsible for product recovery and disposal – the 'polluter pays principle'. However, with global supply chains there is a need to coordinate strategy internationally as production is likely to be at a different point from consumption.

In 2015 the EU adopted a Circular Economy (CE) Package (COM (2015) 614, final), which seeks to enable the transition to a more CE through a range of measures aimed at increasing resource efficiency and minimising waste across all member states. The package contains an action plan and updates to six directives: waste framework, packaging, landfill, WEEE, ELV and batteries. Key proposals include increased funding for CE-related initiatives; common 2030 targets for the recycling and landfilling of municipal waste; and the harmonisation of calculations, terminology and definitions relating to waste management across legislations and member states. Importantly, it also seeks to work with industry to develop quality standards for secondary materials and promote industrial symbiosis and eco-design.

Case study: CE within the UK

In recent decades, EU membership has shaped much of the UK's waste, resource use and industrial policies. However, Brexit has thrown the continued enforcement of these into doubt, even though the European Union (Withdrawal) Bill (2017–2019) will initially adopt all EU law into UK domestic law through the mechanism of 'retained direct EU legislation'. Some companies – for example, Unilever, Kingfisher plc and Marks and Spencer plc – have voluntarily integrated circular concepts into their business models. In addition, the British Standards Institution published a guide (BS 8001:2017) to help companies, the *Framework for Implementing the Principles of the Circular Economy in Organizations*. However, resource management organizations like SUEZ (Baddeley and Vergunst, 2016) and CIWM (Moore, 2017) have called for the CE to be integrated into the Department for Business, Energy and Industrial Strategy's (BEIS) new industrial strategy.

While the UK's government has recognised the need for intervention to achieve a CE, no formal strategy has been implemented. This is despite estimates that a more circular UK economy could potentially be worth £29 billion a year and create around 175,000 jobs (Voulvoulis, 2015). While there are many reasons for this, it is largely due to key policy areas being divided between government departments, devolved administrations and local authorities. Brexit will further complicate this, as the European Union Withdrawal Bill will revert devolved areas of EU environmental competence to the UK national government (Department for Exiting the European Union, 2017). This situation has resulted in different approaches to the CE emerging across the UK:

England: While there is no formal strategy, supporting measures have been implemented, including: funding for research and businesses; waste prevention and reuse criteria within central government procurement; and the Built Environment Commitment (WRAP, 2014) for low-carbon, resource-efficient construction. The London Assembly has also developed a CE strategy with the London Waste and Recycling Board, outlined in their document: *Towards a Circular Economy – Context and Opportunities* (2016).

Northern Ireland: While there is no formal strategy, prosperity agreements have supported businesses to move beyond minimum compliance in energy use and resource management.

Scotland: A comprehensive strategy has been adopted: *Making Things Last: A Circular Economy Strategy for Scotland* (2016). There is also a Scottish Materials Brokerage Service for recycled materials and the Scottish Institute of Remanufacture.

Wales: In a written statement, *Achieving a More Circular Economy for Wales* (2016), the Welsh government committed to greater collaboration with academia and WRAP Cymru; recycling; and funding opportunities for small and medium enterprises (SMEs).

CHALLENGES FOR THE CE

Barriers to the CE have been identified at the level of government, industry and individuals. While some are likely to be overcome in time, such as skills training and technological research, others may require intervention.

Achieving economies of scale

Resources circulate at different geographic scales depending on the sector, meaning that care must be taken to ensure there is both a sufficient quantity of material collected for an economically viable supply chain and that it is handled appropriately. For example, glass has to be recycled within 200 miles of its collection point for it to have lower carbon emissions than new production (British Glass, 2004), while materials used in small quantities, or that require special infrastructure to recover, may need international supply chains. However, this raises questions about the need for internationally recognised standards for secondary materials, especially after China announced its intention to ban the import of all recyclable materials by the end of 2017 over concerns arising from the presence of hazardous contaminants (World Trade Organisation, notification G/TBT/N/CHN/1211).

Cooperation and competition law

Standardisation within a sector is required for mass resource recovery, for example, UK dairy producers standardising the materials used in milk bottles. This also helps create more stable secondary material markets – by making the quality and quantity of resources in them more predictable – and could create the infrastructure necessary to track EPR obligations. However, this requires data sharing between supply chains, with commercial sensitivity and a lack of clarity over competition laws potentially making businesses hesitant to disclose information (Green Alliance, 2013). As a result, oversight by neutral bodies may be required, like The Ellen MacArthur Foundation's 'Circular Economy 100', which encourages global collaboration by bringing together international companies, governments, academics, SMEs and other stakeholders. Business support schemes like the Netherlands' 'Green Deals' could also be valuable, as they facilitate eco-innovation by removing barriers like ambiguous or restrictive legislation, legal confusion or a lack of partners. A recent international Green Deal between the Netherlands, France, Flanders and the UK (the North Sea Resources Roundabout) aims to improve the trade of secondary resources. For example, incinerator bottom ash, from which the Dutch firm Inashco can recover metals.

Infrastructure and investment

Product recovery, transport and reprocessing require dedicated infrastructure. Some existing installations can be repurposed, although any transition will incur short-term costs. For example, turning the Port Talbot Steelworks in Wales from a producer of new steel into a producer of high-quality recycled steel was estimated at £1–2 billion, similar to that of closing the site or a government subsidised purchase (Allwood, 2016). However, significant investment and planning is needed in many sectors, with needs varying by industry and product. For example, while over 86 percent of non-hazardous construction waste is recovered in the UK (Defra, 2016), value is lost because of a geographic mismatch between areas of supply and demand, transport costs and challenges with multi-material product recovery (Knowledge Transfer Network, 2016).

Some government-level support has been made available to help off-set the short-term costs incurred by transitioning to a circular business model. For example, Scotland's 'Circular Economy Investment Fund' (£18 million; open until 2018) and Wales's 'Circular Economy Capital Investment Fund' (£6.5 million; beginning in 2019), both target SMEs. The European Commission also committed over €725 million of Horizon 2020 funding for CE-related calls in 2016–2017. However, most investment will likely be private. Market incentives or legislative requirements could encourage bigger firms to invest, while the Centre for European Policy Studies (Rizos et al., 2015) suggests that SMEs would benefit from increased funding and help understanding already available opportunities.

Consumer behaviour

Moving to a CE will require changes in how people consume products. This is challenging, as attitudes towards products are complex. However, the growth of platforms like eBay and initiatives like repair cafés suggests an acceptance of reuse by some segments of the population. Businesses providing greater information to buyers can also alter their decision making and encourage better eco-design. For example, a study by the European Economic and Social Committee (2016) found that people would pay more for items labelled 'long-lasting'. While such activities may result in higher buy-to-own prices, they combine circular objectives with consumer-desired benefits.

SUMMARY

Circular Economies recover resources at their highest value and keep them in circulation. This is not only good for the environment but also offers substantial business benefits through reduced waste and materials use. However, a CE cannot be delivered through business-as-usual or government policy alone. It will require both domestic and international cooperation between industry and governments, and a mix of voluntary and legislative action. Companies must put greater consideration into the circularity of their products at the design stage, where its environmental impact and reusability is largely determined, and policymakers must be willing to alter and provide legislation to facilitate such a transition. In particular, businesses must approach product development with eco-design in mind, which can be encouraged through greater IPR requirements or market incentives. An increased focus on product access over ownership and product take-back is also essential to delivering new circular business models. However, barriers to such an economic transition do exist, like achieving economies of scale in recovery processes, short-term business costs, and even fractured and inconsistent legislation within and between nation states. Only through a business-led dialogue involving all stakeholders can the full potential of the circular economic model be realised.

BIBLIOGRAPHY

Allwood, J.M. (2016). *A Bright Future for UK Steel: A Strategy for Innovation and Leadership Through Up-Cycling and Integration.* Cambridge, UK: University of Cambridge.

Baddeley, A. and Vergunst, T. (2016). *A Resourceful Future: Expanding the UK Economy.* London, UK: SUEZ and Eunomia.

Binnemans, K., Jones, P.T., Blanpain, B., Van Gerven, T., Yang, Y., Walton, A., and Buchert, M. (2013). Recycling of rare earths: A critical review. *Journal of Cleaner Production* 51: 1–22.

British Glass. (2004). *Glass Recycling: Life Cycle Carbon Dioxide Emissions.* Wokingham, UK: Enviros Consulting Ltd.

Rizos, V., Behrens, A., Kafyeke, T., Hirschnitz-Garbers, M. and Ioannou, A. (2015). *The Circular Economy: Barriers and Opportunities for SMEs.* Brussels, Belgium: Centre for European Policy Studies.

Defra. (2016). *UK Statistics on Waste.* London, UK: Defra and Government Statistical Service.

Department for Exiting the European Union. (2017). *Legislating for the United Kingdom's withdrawal from the European Unions.* London, UK: Department for Exiting the European Union.

Environmental Change Institute. (2005). *40% House.* Oxford, UK: Environmental Change Institute.

European Economic and Social Committee. (2016). *The Influence of Lifespan Labelling on Consumers.* Brussels, Belgium: European Economic and Social Committee.

Green Alliance. (2013). *Resource Resilient UK: A Report from the Circular Economy Task Force.* London, UK: Green Alliance.

Knowledge Transfer Network. (2016). *Innovation Opportunities from Industrial Waste.* London, UK: Knowledge Transfer Network.

London Waste and Recycling Board. (2015). *Towards a Circular Economy: Context and Opportunities.* London, UK: London Waste and Recycling Board.

Mont, O. and Tukker, A. (2006). Product-service systems: Reviewing achievements and refining the research agenda. *Journal of Cleaner Production* 14: 1451–1454.

Moore, D. (19 April 2017). Circular economy should be "pillar" of UK industrial strategy. *CIWM Journal* [Online]. Available at: https://ciwm-journal.co.uk/circular-economy-pillar-uk-industrial-strategy/ [Accessed 16 April 2018].

Voulvoulis, N. (2015). *The Circular Revolution.* Imperial College London report, Commissioned by Veolia.

Whalen, C. (24 February 2016). *"Peak Stuff": Households Now Spend More on Services than Physical Goods.* Carbon Commentary [Online]. Available at https://www.carboncommentary.com/blog/2016/2/24/peak-stuff-households-now-spent-more-on-services-than-physical-goods [Accessed 16 April 2018].

World Economic Forum. (2014). *Towards the Circular Economy: Accelerating the Scale-Up Across Global Supply Chains.* Joint report with the Ellen MacArthur Foundation and McKinsey & Company.

WRAP. (2014). The Built Environment Commitment: Delivering low carbon and resource efficiency. WRAP [Online]. Available at: http://www.wrap.org.uk/sites/files/wrap/Built%20Environment%20Commitment%20v2%2019.12.2014.pdf [Accessed 16 April 2018].

Xerox. (2010). *Report on Global Citizenship.* Norwalk, Connecticut, USA: Xerox Corporation.

Circular thinking in design

8 Reflections over 25 years' experience

Frank O'Connor

PREFACE

While the author did not realise it at the time, he first experienced the Circular Economy (CE) in the early 1980s. Working in his dad's small construction company in Ireland, waste made no sense as everything had value and a potential use. The company would dismantle sections of buildings to recover bricks, wood, fasteners, slate, iron and whatever was deemed reusable. Scrap metal was sent for recycling, unusable wood was chopped for firewood, while other materials were down-cycled to aggregate. Little did the author know that 35 years later (2017) he would be participating in an invite-only stakeholder work-shop in Amsterdam, surrounded by CE professionals, enthused about the prospect of and perceived novelty of 'urban mining', construction disassembly and repurposing. So is the CE new, the radical step forward that so many are suggesting or is it just the emperor in new clothes? This chapter explores these questions through an industry eco-design case study of the electronics sector from 25 years ago of which the author was a member of the in-house design team.

A CIRCULAR ECONOMY (CE)

A CE has been proposed as the solution to our wasteful and inefficient linear economy. Over the past few years, numerous companies have made claim to be embracing the CE, through modifying their product designs, innovating their business models and offering new services to their customers. However the CE is not just the sole domain of the business community. The CE philosophy is also being embedded in many government policies, international forums, academic institutes and consultancies.

While there is a lot of time and money being spent on promoting the perception that companies are going circular, it is unclear how much change is happening. Many solutions proposed involve ideas that are far from unique to this circular movement while countless propositions are merely conceptual in nature or a logical progression leading on from existing business strategy and efficiency measures. Unfortunately, in many cases the supporting communication can feel like 'circular wash' to deflect from 'business as usual'.

DESIGNING THE WAY TO A CE

The generally-accepted premise is that to go circular, businesses should implement a new business model and embrace circular design. While several circular business models have been proposed by academics, consultancies and government organisations these models will be recognisable by anyone who has worked in the field of eco-design. While it can be argued that there are slight variations in semantics, the only notable differences are in the terminology and the emphasis on the role of technologies such as 3D printing, digitisation and data processing. These business models are dependent on the way goods and services are designed.

The CE design approach being promoted is termed 'circular design', which is a sub-category of eco-design. Both approaches aim to close resource loops through strategies such as design for maintenance, repair, reuse, remanufacture and recycling. The communication around circular design places a greater emphasis on maintaining the value of products, components and materials. However unlike eco-design there is insufficient evidence to suggest that circular design adequately considers energy or carbon issues or full life cycle impacts. Circular design also inadequately tackles the more challenging issue of real citizen need. They both have failed to sufficiently confront the global widespread culture of built-in obsolescence, largely ignoring unsustainable consumption patterns, with sharing and servitization frequently offered as the only tangible solutions to counteract.

CASE STUDY: IN-HOUSE DESIGN

Alps Electric (Ireland) Ltd. (herein known as Alps) is a Japanese electronic components manufacturer based in Ireland. At the time of the
case study, Alps specialised in manufacturing computer peripheral
devices for brands such as Apple, Dell and Microsoft. When the author
joined their in-house design team in 1992, they were in the initial stages
of developing a new computer keyboard product range. Shortly after-
wards they set up a cross-departmental electronic waste-recycling group
as a means of pre-empting future producer responsibility legislation and
as a response to rising levels of obsolete computer equipment (O'Connor et al., 1998). This created a new mandate for eco-design of which
the author led. Alps decided to focus their eco-design efforts on strategies that would support dismantling, repair and recycling of the keyboards. Warranties and in-house repair were already key Alps customer
service strategies.

The author and an electronic waste-recycling group developed an
eco-design checklist, which was built into the design review process for
all new product development. Alps then collaborated closely with their
customers, suppliers and sub-contractors to implement the checklist. In
parallel, Alps instigated initiatives around waste minimisation, energy
management and wider environmental management systems.

The eco-design principles the company applied included:

- Component and material minimisation
- Use of recycled and recyclable materials
- Product life extension through warranties, disassembly and repair
- Component and material recovery through disassembly, reuse and
  recycling

Some of the key innovations were around housing redesign for snap
fit assembly and material selection where Alps targeted recycled content from post-process waste such as regrind. Alps achieved 25-percent
post-process waste on external plastics and up to 100-percent post-process waste on internal parts such as the switch frames. Being able to
demonstrate 25-percent recycled-content in a cosmetic application
was a major milestone. Alps had a goal to use recycled plastics from
post-consumer waste, but it was not commercially available at the time.
The company also switched to 100-percent recycled paper in their
packaging.

ANALYSING THE CASE STUDY

Given current CE conversations and communication it may seem hard to believe that Alps implemented circular design (i.e. design for disassembly, repair and recycling) strategies in the early 1990s. However, Alps were not unique. Many global giants such as Philips and Hewlett-Packard were also taking similar journeys. In fact, Life Cycle Thinking and end-of-life asset management were fast becoming the norm in the electronics sector by the late 1990s, with environmental responsibility being viewed as a potential source of competitive advantage. This global push was supported by significant academic research on topics such as disassembly, recycling, remanufacture and eco-design, as well as new university curricula and government policies.

In 1997 during his PhD research into environmentally conscious design approaches (O'Connor and Hawkes, 2001), the author realised that Alps had made one crucial mistake. While visiting a recycling company, he came across some obsolete Alps keyboards. The recycling company was not carefully taking the keyboards apart and separating the materials and components. Instead they were shredding them to a fluff for export and further processing. There was no obvious means for the recycling company to know that the products were designed with disassembly in mind, aside from the recycling coding on materials. Alps had not conversed with any recyclers during the design process and thus a mutually beneficial recovery system had not been explored, e.g. material and component harvesting for reuse. Disassembly did not make financial sense.

In hindsight it was something the author should have foreseen if he had reflected back on an earlier experience. In 1989 the author had worked at a precious metal recycling company, Eagle Metals Ltd. One of his roles was to manually dismantle computer products to remove the components containing the most valuable materials, such as the circuit boards and cabling. There were no instructions on how to take any of the products apart, no bill of materials and it was unclear whether some parts of the products were ever intended to be taken apart, without getting destroyed in the process. It was a slow, labour intensive process, which only made financial sense due to the products being considered as waste, low operational costs (e.g. wages, overheads) and the high percentage of gold and silver used in earlier computer equipment.

WHAT HAS CHANGED IN 25 YEARS?

When Alps made their 'paradigm shift' to product life cycle responsibility, one of their main customers was Apple. It is worth looking at this relationship in more detail, as well as Apple's current CE policies, to try and understand what has changed. In the early 1990s, while Alps were exploring design for repair and end-of-life strategies, Apple was also exploring ways to integrate environmental considerations in their new product development process. This resulted in a number of innovations to their desktop products, including modular design to simplify reconfiguration, facilitate servicing and speed up disassembly (Fiksel et al., 1996). The author developed a close working relationship with their environmental team sharing insight, checklists and strategies. Like Alps, Apple shared key findings in research publications.

Fast-forward to 2017, Apple is a member of the Ellen McArthur Foundation CE100, a programme established to enable organisations to develop new opportunities and realise their CE ambitions faster (Ellen MacArthur Foundation, 2017). Apple products can be returned to the company for recycling and refurbishment as part of their Renew program that operates in 19 countries. An online gift card or credit towards a purchase in-store is offered for certain products that are assigned a trade-in value. Returned devices are either refurbished for resale as 'Apple Certified Refurbished' with a one-year warranty, or the materials are recycled (Apple, 2017). While this is positive, recent research uncovered that Apple only takes back a small percentage of what they sell and the trade-in value is far below what the products are worth on the open second-hand market (Koebler, 2017). This research also discovered that Apple rejects current industry best practices by forcing recyclers to shred their products so they cannot be repaired or reused. These findings raise key questions around CE-related progress, as one would expect Apple to prioritize maintaining product integrity through reuse over energy intensive recycling.

A recent report by Greenpeace and iFixit found Apple products to be some of the most difficult electronic products to repair and upgrade (Greenpeace, 2017). It highlighted that their products were designed to make it difficult for users to fix, as Apple frequently glue separate pieces together as well as provide no spare parts or repair manuals, thus shortening the product lifespan and hence increasing electronic waste. These findings are in stark contrast to discussions the author had with his Apple counterparts in the early 1990s. Additionally, it does not seem a sensible environmental life cycle strategy given one would expect Apple to be repairing products during their production process, as well as servicing customer returns. The strategy also does not seem to fit with their refurbishment policy mentioned earlier. Apple may be closing resource loops; however, it would seem that they do not want to do so in an open, collaborative manner. This is evident through the aforementioned strategies as well as their custom screws, special tools and their authorised repair centres. It is worth noting that Apple has been lobbying to contest the right to repair based on arguments around intellectual property (The Guardian, 2017).

In 2016 Apple announced their iPhones would be robotically disassembled for recycling (Prindle, 2016). The robots are only capable of disassembling a total of 2.4 million iPhones per year, nowhere near the capacity required, given sales in 2016 alone were 215.3 million (Koebler, 2017). This demonstrates that Apple's focus is on energy intensive recycling and not product life extension. On a more positive note, Apple has a long-term aim of making all their electronic products from 100-percent recycled materials in the future. However, not having a plan or concrete targets for meeting this goal is concerning and creates opportunities for their ambitions to be doubted (Holder, 2017).

SO WHAT CAN BE LEARNT?

Clearly there was progress in the 1990s when businesses started to respond to global environmental pressures through waste minimisation, eco-design, recycling, take-back and related initiatives. Business opportunities and external pressures were the main drivers then with predominantly small, incremental steps taken towards achieving greater business efficiency. Twenty-five years later, advocates for a CE would argue that there is also a lot more happening and the changes in the 1990s were not the game-changing business models of today.

However a closer examination of one of the more prominent CE players and global brands, Apple, has suggested differently. It is hard to see how Apple's CE strategies are advancements from the 1990s. And their drivers, other than generating positive PR and maximizing their financial return, are less clear. It seems that the widespread business mentality of profit at all costs has not changed with the advent of the CE. If it does not make financial sense (to the company) in terms of bottom line profit, it is not going to happen, irrespective of the consequences on the planet and its inhabitants. Coupled to this, tools such as Life Cycle Assessments (LCA) are still largely ignored and the true whole-life cycle costs of production and consumption habits are still not being accounted for.

A key lesson learnt in the 1990s was to involve all actors in a life cycle design process. Yet it can be argued that as one of the 'CE leaders', Apple is not taking this lesson on board through largely ignoring real user needs such as ease of disassembly for repair. Apple is not alone in terms of this type of behaviour. Samsung and Microsoft products were also among the least easy to repair and upgrade according to the Greenpeace and iFixit study in 2017 (The Guardian, 2017). In fact, the study found a trend in electronic products away from repairability with limited or no access to repair manuals or spare parts and a trend towards the use of non-replaceable batteries and non-standard tools (Greenpeace, 2017). Added to this a report, commissioned by Repair.org, found hardware manufacturers were watering down green standards for their own benefits to drive sales at the expense of the environment (Kingsley, 2017).

So it seems that there is an unwillingness to learn from history and worryingly CE may be just painting over some of the cracks. Of course, an argument can also be made around the lack of external drivers such as legislation and wider customer demand. But given the excellent progress made by industry in the 1990s, this is not a convincing line of reasoning. On a positive note, the CE has caught global attention. Some argue it has also generated more constructive debate; however, that is difficult to verify. Industry and government targets seem more widespread and ambitious than those being set than in the 1990s, but they clearly do not go far enough given what has been learnt from this study. Yes, there are some good CE-branded activities happening, such as innovative start-ups up recycling waste into responsible products, but given the greater scheme of things these are just a relatively few cases. In most situations there is a very narrow circular approach, with the main focus being on waste recovery, recycling and in many cases incineration for heat recovery. Hardly game changing approaches – far more like 'business as usual' supported by misinformed and/or dishonest communications and widespread 'circular wash'. Of course, some of this may relate to not comprehending the subject or be caused by inadvertently 'jumping on the bandwagon' without understanding the wider consequences.

CONCLUSION

The findings from this research indicate that eco-design practice in the electronics sector remains largely the same as in the 1990s, or in the case of some companies it may have regressed. While CE thinking has not disrupted this behavior, it can be argued that it has done a great job in recycling already established ideas and concepts to mask over 'business as usual' – thus the emperor's new clothes. The findings suggest that there is a grave danger that many companies are just hiding behind CE rhetoric without making any significant changes, and promoting 'circular wash' to deflect from irresponsible business practices. Yes, there are innovative technologies and materials, greater access to renewable energy, improved data and communication tools and a move towards a service-based economy. However these 'CE innovations' are largely a logical progression from earlier work in the fields of eco-design. The main differences seem to be in the terminology being used.

While this chapter only focuses on one industry sector, and just explores a few scenarios in detail, the evidence to suggest that the CE is a radical step forward is weak. It is worth noting that these findings reflect the author's experience of working with industry over the past 25 years, including the period where he ran the award-winning International Centre of Excellence, the Ecodesign Centre.

Given the astonishing profitability and reserves of many high-profile companies that have joined the CE100, it is difficult to justify why they cannot invest in infrastructure, business models and eco-design strategies to make the CE happen even quicker. Particularly given that many CE solutions exist and are just waiting to be applied and the eco-design tools and methodologies have long been available. Surely these companies are missing a fantastic opportunity, particularly given rising global concerns on resource depletion, pollution and climate change.

Moving forward, companies need to move beyond eco-design and circular design to a more sustainable design philosophy and practice, one that adopts a collaborative systems approach to satisfying real societal needs in an environmentally, socially, ethically and economically responsible way. This will require confronting the global widespread culture of built-in obsolescence and unsustainable consumption patterns. This radical shift is not up to business alone. Full stakeholder collaboration and widespread behaviourial change is required. Citizens need to act now and influence through their purchasing decisions, while educational institutes and governments need to immediately put the right mechanisms in place to enable a truly responsible, fair and just economy to be created. Time will tell if all the actors are brave enough to take this radical leap and ensure the next 25 years bring truly sustainable outcomes.

Note

The author has had no professional involvement with either Alps or Apple since the late 1990s.

BIBLIOGRAPHY

Apple. (2017). [Online]. Available at: www.apple.com/iphone/trade-up/ [Accessed 12 September 2017].

Ellen MacArthur Foundation. (2017). [Online]. Available at: www.ellenmacar thurfoundation.org/ce100 [Accessed 12 September 2017].

Fiksel, J., Cook, K., Roberts, S., and Tsuda, D. (1996). Design for environment at Apple computer: A case study of the new PowerMacintosh 7200. Proceedings of IEEE International Symposium on Electronics and the Environment, May 6–8, Dallas, TX: pp. 218–223.

Greenpeace. (27 June 2017). *Apple, Samsung Products Among Least Repairable in New Greenpeace Assessment of Tech Brands* [Online]. Available at: www. greenpeace.org/international/en/press/releases/2017/Apple-Samsung-products-among-least-repairable-Greenpeace-assessment-of-tech-brands/ [Accessed 12 September 2017].

Holder, M. (24 April 2017). *Greenbiz, Can Apple Close the Loop? Tech Giant Targets 100% Recycled Material* [Online]. Available at: www.greenbiz.com/article/can-apple-close-loop-tech-giant-targets-100-recycled-material [Accessed 12 September 2017].

Kingsley Hughes, A. (3 August 2017). *Hardware 2.0, Tech Companies Using Green Standards 'to Greenwash Products,' Claims Report* [Online]. Available at://www-zdnet-com.cdn.ampproject.org/c/www.zdnet.com/google-amp/article/tech-companies-using-green-standards-to-greenwash-products-that-have-a-devastating-environmental/ [Accessed 12 September 2017].

Koebler, J. (20 April 2017). *Apple Forces Recyclers to Shred All iPhones and Mac-Books, Motherboard* [Online]. Available at: https://motherboard.vice.com/en_us/article/yp73jw/apple-recycling-iphones-macbooks [Accessed 12 September 2017].

O'Connor, F., Blythe, D., O'Sullivan, J., and Phelan, P. (1998). Initialisation of an environmental philosophy: A case study of Alps Electric (Ireland) Ltd. *Proceedings of Business Strategy & the Environment Conference*, University of Leeds, UK, pp. 168–173.

O'Connor, F. and Hawkes, D. (2001). A multi-stakeholder abridged environmentally conscious design approach. *The Journal of Sustainable Product Design* 1: 247–262.

Prindle, D. (21 March 2016). *Digital Trends, Apple's New Recycling Robot Rips Old Iphones Apart in Search of Gold, and More* [Online]. Available at: www.digi taltrends.com/cool-tech/apple-liam-phone-recycling-robot/ [Accessed 12 September 2017].

The Guardian. (2017). *Under Pressure from Tech Companies, 'Fair Repair' Bill Stalls in Nebraska* [Online]. Available at: www.theguardian.com/us-news/2017/mar/11/nebraska-farmers-right-to-repair-bill-stalls-apple [Accessed 12 September 2017].

9 Business models for a Circular Economy

Martin Charter and Stuart McLanaghan

INTRODUCTION

This chapter introduces principles related to business models with broad applicability to the Circular Economy (CE), as well as providing some specific thoughts in relation to their potential applicability to waste polymer fishing nets and ropes (FNRs). The chapter treats CE as one important aspect of a broader approach to 'triple bottom line' sustainability (economic, environmental and social). The content draws on research and thinking completed in relation to Clause 6 ('Guidance on enabling mechanisms and business models') of British Standard BS8001:2017 – a pioneering new guidance standard focusing on implementing the principles of the CE in organisations (BSI, 2017).

In recent years, there has been increasing discussion over green business models (Charter, 2013), sustainable business models (Clinton et al., 2014), and more recently, CE business models (Bocken et al., 2016; van Renswoude et al, 2015). In the case of the latter, the literature has rapidly expanded over the last few years. However, the emergence of national and academic approaches reflects diverse terminology, with the result that similar business models might be defined differently.

BUSINESS MODELS AND CIRCULARITY

A business model should reflect an organisation's chosen system of interconnected and interdependent decisions and activities that determines how it creates, delivers and captures value over the short-, medium- and long-term. However, to be applicable to the CE thinking, business model innovation needs to progress beyond advances in processes, products or services. Whilst innovation in products, processes or services might result in business benefits (e.g. product light-weighting), it doesn't necessarily address sustainable resource management in a systemic way within an organisation's central value proposition.

Some existing business models deliver clear environmental and societal benefits, although these might be secondary to the organisation's main value proposition. As outlined above, whilst the term 'circular business model' is increasingly being used, this is misleading because it may suggest something that might not be the case. Implementing any one business model does not necessarily equate to a shift to a more circular mode of operation. More correctly, there are business models which have the potential to 'fit' within a more circular economic system. However, unless the wider systems context is considered at the same time, then they are simply new business models operating within the prevailing linear economy.

An established organisation is unlikely to change a (commercially) successful business model(s) unless it sufficiently understands the long-term opportunities and threats associated with moving to a more circular mode of operation. Where a strong business case exists, established organisations (e.g. a manufacturer of car components) are more likely to re-engineer existing business model(s) to simultaneously deliver their main value proposition and chosen CE objectives. Both internally and across the organisation's value chain, this will require an effective process of change management, where staff are proactively engaged to develop a supportive culture across all business functions, championed at senior executive and/or board level. For new more disruptive start-up companies – where their value proposition is underpinned by the principles of the CE from the outset – this may lead to a more rapid transition to a more circular mode of operation.

ENABLING MECHANISMS

Central to the implementation of CE (or circularity) thinking in organisations is the need to distinguish between business models and 'enabling mechanisms'. An enabling mechanism(s) can assist an organisation to capture and deliver value, together with more sustainable resource management. For example, financing mechanisms (e.g. crowd-funding) can aid value proposition delivery. However, there are exceptions where one (or more) enabling mechanism(s) capture or deliver an organisation's entire value proposition where 3D printing (or additive manufacturing) is the focus of the business, e.g. Fishy Filaments, who are producing filaments for 3D printing from recycled polymers from waste fishing nets.

The selection of enabling mechanism(s) should also form part of a systemic approach to implementing principles of the CE. Otherwise, they could potentially run contrary to a more circular mode of operation (e.g. if 3D printing resulted in mass production of disposable products for convenience, rather than to produce replacement parts extending product-life).

BUSINESS MODEL DESIGN

The value proposition is central to any business model, as it defines the products and services that create value for the organisation's existing and/or new customer base. It is also central to the viability of the business; more traditionally, the value proposition identified how the organisation proposed to make money (e.g. revenue mechanism employed). However, for organisations transitioning to a more circular mode of operation, the value proposition might not be solely financial in nature and instead reflect delivery of wider environmental and social benefits.

Key decision makers should be aware of both the business model(s) design and their organisation's specific approach. Identifying associated business opportunities and risks is a prerequisite to determining which business model would be best suited to simultaneously deliver an organisation's value proposition and CE objectives. An organisation's ability to continuously innovate around circularity is likely to be increasingly key to its long-term economic competitiveness.

Business model methodologies typically comprise four interconnected elements: *Who, What, How* and *When*. These elements are introduced in Figure 9.1 and all support the development of the organisation's value proposition. In effect, a business model defines the organisation's market and customers; its products and services; its activities, processes and infrastructure; and the value it creates, captures and

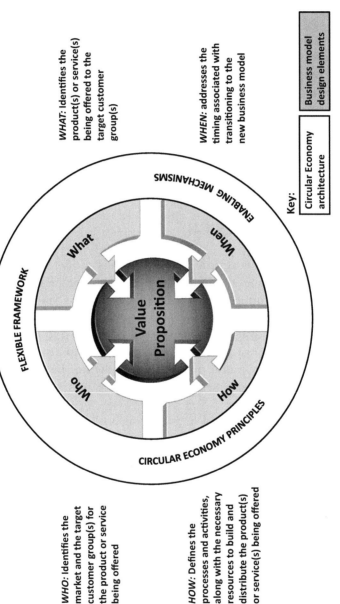

WHAT: Identifies the product(s) or service(s) being offered to the target customer group(s)

WHEN: addresses the timing associated with transitioning to the new business model

WHO: Identifies the market and the target customer group(s) for the product or service being offered

HOW: Defines the processes and activities, along with the necessary resources to build and distribute the product(s) or service(s) being offered

Key:

| Circular Economy architecture |
| Business model design elements |

Figure 9.1 Overview of business model methodology

Source: Modified from Clause 6, BS 8001:2017 (BSI, 2017).

delivers which includes its financial viability. In a non-commercial context, organisations might not have the same motivations as a for-profit organisation, but fundamentally they still create, capture, deliver and return value. For example, they create public benefits, programmes and services rather than products and services in the classic for-profit sense.

NO ONE-SIZE-FITS-ALL

This chapter is not prescriptive on business model selection, as there is no one-size-fits-all approach for an organisation to deliver its defined CE objectives. This is due to the highly organisation-specific nature of the underlying decision-making; difficulties in determining a clear 'ranking' rationale; and the different levels at which business models can operate (e.g. division/group and/or individual product or service). The way in which the principles of the CE are implemented is also heavily dependent on such factors as leadership, organisational maturity and culture. However, systemic approaches to business model design should promote sustainable resource management by, for example, optimising how resources are managed, including: the reuse, repair, refurbishing, remanufacture and recycling of materials and products.

For an established business, with many years' trading experience, innovation around the existing business model might be more focused on adaption (e.g. re-engineering) of a more linear approach, towards more circular modes of operation. For example, an organisation might shift from the extension in the lifetime of ink cartridges by offering a refill service. Product manufacturers will most likely commence their CE journey by focusing on a single product as a pilot; where new concepts can be tested (e.g. prototypes) and lessons learnt (e.g. scalability). Once the business case has been demonstrated, the organisation can then assess wider roll-out across its entire product range.

BUSINESS MODEL GROUPINGS

As indicated above, there are numerous references to CE business models in the literature. In Table 9.1, six business model categories are introduced which have the potential to be compatible with circular

economic systems; however, these are not mutually exclusive or definitive. In practice, larger more complex organisations might concurrently
have different business models operating across their divisions and for
different products/markets.

In the following table, there is a brief description of each category,
together with generic benefits/advantages and potential applications in
relation to waste polymer FNRs – see Circular Ocean project www.circu-
larocean.eu. Whilst not repeated for each business model grouping, all
examples have potential to help reduce raw material and (carbon-based)
energy consumption and therefore have associated sustainable resource
management benefits.

The six categories are:

1. On-demand
2. Dematerialization
3. Product life cycle extension/reuse
4. Recovery of secondary raw materials/by-products
5. Product as a service/product – service system (PSS)
6. Sharing economy and collaborative consumption

CONCLUSIONS

Discussion over the applicability of business models for circularity
purposes are at an early stage, but rapidly evolving. There are viewpoints that to transition towards circularity always means a change
in business model. However, for many organisations moving towards
circularity will mean, at least early on, a focus on processes, products or services, without a fundamental change in their business
model(s), unless there are major new identified opportunities or
threats. Some companies may start to adapt existing business models
for circularity purposes; whereas fundamentally new business models, which systematically address sustainable resource management
within an organisation's value proposition(s), may emerge from the
outset for disruptive start-ups. Whether a company is existing or new,
(re-)examining business model types applicable for circularity may
generate new insights, leading to more profitable and sustainable
business.

Table 9.1 illustrates the application of six business model categories
to waste polymer fishing nets and ropes (FNRs) and highlights a range
of potential new business opportunities.

Table 9.1 Circular Economy business models and potential applicability to waste polymer fishing nets and ropes (FNRs)

Business Models	Brief Description	General Comments and Specific Applications to Waste Polymer Fishing Nets and Ropes (FNRs)	Illustrative Circular Economy Benefits/Advantages
On Demand			
Produce on demand (made to order)	Producing a product or providing a service only when customer demand has been quantified and confirmed	FNRs: production based 'on demand', with assembly in ports and/or fishing communities	Minimises raw material demand and avoids over-stocking. Can enhance 'personalisation' via delivery of a better fit to customers' requirements, leading to less product redundancy and improved material utilisation
Dematerialisation			
Digitisation	Replacing physical infrastructure and assets with digital/virtual services	FNRs: N/A	Reduced product manufacture
Product Life-Cycle Extension/Re-Use			
Product life-extension	New products designed to be durable for a long lifetime (durability). Design improvements might be needed to also facilitate easier repair, particularly by third parties	Specifications with an extended design-life. FNRs: using more durable materials ('design for longevity')	Increased product-life

(*Continued*)

Table 9.1 (Continued)

Business Models	Brief Description	General Comments and Specific Applications to Waste Polymer Fishing Nets and Ropes (FNRs)	Illustrative Circular Economy Benefits/Advantages
Facilitated re-use	Reuse with or without repair/upgrade and supplied either free of charge, or resold	Enable re-use through: • Free of Charge: FNR reuse networks • Resale: e.g. online via 'for sale' websites specialising in FNR	Reduces the demand for new products
Product modular design	Products designed to be modular so that parts can be replaced to update/upgrade a product, but not replace the whole item	Modular construction: design FNRs to be more modular to enable repair, but maybe limited due to structural integrity issues; other applications might relate to FNR handling plant and equipment (e.g. winches) where electronic modules might be designed to be repaired/upgradable	Replacement at a part(s) level e.g. sections of damaged FNRs rather than product level e.g. complete FNR. Can also encourage cost-effective product repairs and reduce need for replacement of integrated components, thereby reducing resource consumption
Refurbish, repair, remanufacture and recondition	Product gets a next life (e.g. after remanufacturing – the process of restoring the product or part functionality to 'as-new' quality; facilitated by design for disassembly). Enables the producer to put the products back into the market to earn a second, or subsequent income, from a second or subsequent user	Implement new strategies: • Remanufactured products and components provided with 'as-new' performance and reliability at reduced cost compared with new • Manufacturers offer to exchange parts remanufactured from returned used ones which are inspected and rebuilt to meet the same quality standards and performance as new, and carry the same warranty	Reduces demand for new products

	• Implementing take-back systems to enable FNRs to be returned by fishermen to manufacturers or recyclers locally to remanufacturing sites. This will enable product life extension (incorporates localised mechanical or chemical recycling processes). Remanufacture more suited to FNR handling plant and equipment (e.g. winches)	Reduces material and energy use, and minimises waste
Recovery of Secondary Raw Materials/By-Products		
Recovery of secondary materials/by-products (including recycling)	Value optimization by creating products from secondary raw materials/by-products and recycling (e.g. depolymerization), whether open- or closed-loop	Closed-loop: • FNRs collected, followed by chemical depolymerisation and new FNR product manufacture Open-loop: • Used FNR nylon used in carpet and skateboard manufacture (produced via injection-moulding, e.g. www.bureoskateboards.com/) • Potentially produce waste bins etc. using waste FNRs through DIY recycling machines (e.g. https://preciousplastic.com/en/)

(*Continued*)

Table 9.1 (Continued)

Business Models	Brief Description	General Comments and Specific Applications to Waste Polymer Fishing Nets and Ropes (FNRs)	Illustrative Circular Economy Benefits/Advantages
Incentivized return/ extended producer responsibility	Incentivizes customers to return used/unwanted items back to the producer via a convenient system. Producer then repairs or refurbishes or remanufactures the product and/or recycles materials. Incentives are usually in the form of a discount offered on a new product for surrendering the old one	Scope to implement at scale via national take-back schemes (extended producer responsibility) organised between FNR manufacturers and fishermen – as part of manufacturers' contractual repairs and/or re-utilise polymers into 2nd-life nets and/or other products. Financial or alternative incentives may be offered for the return of used or unwanted FNRs (e.g. credit against new purchases)	Facilitates recovery of used/ unwanted products (and embodied materials and energy) through a controlled and auditable system. Minimises raw material consumption
Product Service Systems – Including Product as a Service			
Lease agreement	Leasing access to and not selling ownership of a product or service. This can be on a Business to Business (B2B) or Business to Consumer (B2C) basis. In general, an 'operating lease' model is likely to be best suited for Product Service System (PSS) models in the context of a Circular Economy, as ownership of the asset is retained by the lessor and can	Fishermen lease FNRs from the manufacturers and pay a regular fee for their use, repair and replacement	The lessee's capital outlay is typically lower when compared to outright purchase when taking depreciation, maintenance and disposal/replacement costs into account. The lessor typically benefits from higher overall profitability during the lease period and retains ownership

(Continued)

	be combined with service or performance-based business models	Customer purchases a solution delivering the desired level of performance
Performance-based (pay for success)	Company delivers product performance or defined results rather than the product or service itself. The customer purchases a defined level of performance, where the company's primary revenue stream comes from payments for performance delivered or demand-fulfilment. Ownership remains with the operating company	Re-focus the FNR business model on providing efficient fish catching solutions (by volume, by quality, etc.) rather than fishing nets per se; new payment systems need to be developed; fishing net manufacturers ensure 100% availability of fish catching solutions
Sharing Economy/Platforms and Collaborative Consumption		
Sharing Economy	No direct financial transaction occurs. More socially driven, rather than commercial, where access might strengthen community relationships. For B2B lending, business benefits might include reduced costs over directly sourcing the products/services concerned	More traditionally dependent on the participation and generosity of community members to share goods/services. Can be more formalised. Increasing interest in community-based lending of skills/know-how. Facilitates the sharing of over-capacity or underutilisation. Fishing communities purchase or lease FNRs based on a 'shared value' and 'shared use' model. Strengthens local/neighbour engagement. Reduces need for ownership and storage of goods. Sharing can be extended to skills/know-how

Table 9.1 (Continued)

Business Models	Brief Description	General Comments and Specific Applications to Waste Polymer Fishing Nets and Ropes (FNRs)	Illustrative Circular Economy Benefits/Advantages
Sharing platforms/ resources (collaborative consumption)	Peer-to-peer (P2P) lending or 'collaborative consumption' amongst users, either individuals or organizations, but where some form of transactional arrangement (which could be financial) is provided	Owners of FNRs rent out these assets to other fishermen to improve utilisation rates. FNRs designed to be more durable	Enable increased utilisation rate of products and services by making possible shared use/ownership among consumers. Enables customers to access a product, rather than owning it outright, and use it only as needed

Source: Adapted from Clause 6, BS 8001 (BSI, 2017).

Note: The terms used both above and below – repair, refurbish, recondition, remanufacture, recycling and recovery – are consistent with those used in BS8001 (BSI, 2017).

BIBLIOGRAPHY

Bocken, M.P., de Pauw, I., Bakker, C., and van der Grinten, B. (2016). Product design and business model strategies for a circular economy. *Journal of Industrial and Production Engineering* 33(5): 308–320. DOI: 10.1080/21681015.2016.1172124.

BSI. (2017). *BS8001: 2017: 'Framework for Implementing the Principles of Circular Economy in Organisations: Guide'* [Online]. Available at: www.bsigroup.com/en-GB/standards/benefits-of-using-standards/becoming-more-sustainable-with-standards/Circular-Economy/

Charter, M. (4–5 November 2013). *Editor, Collaboration, Co-creation & New Business Models, Sustainable Innovation 2013* [Online]. Epsom, Surrey, UK: University for the Creative Arts, ISBN 978-0-9543950-6-3. Available at: http://cfsd.org.uk/Sustainable%20Innovation/cfsd_si-proceedings.html

Clinton, L. and Whisnant, R. (February 2014). *Model Behavior: 20 Business Model Innovations for Sustainability, SustainAbility* [Online]. Available at: http://sustainability.com/our-work/reports/model-behavior/

van Renswoude, K., ten Wolde, A., and Joustra, D.J. (April 2015). *Circular Business Models: Part 1 and Part 2: An introduction to IMSA's Circular Business Model Scan, IMSA Amsterdam* [Online]. Available at: https://groenomstilling.erhvervsstyrelsen.dk/sites/default/files/media/imsa_circular_business_models_-_april_2015_-_part_1.pdf

Designing Product Service Systems for a Circular Economy

10

Tim C. McAloone and Daniela C. A. Pigosso

INTRODUCTION

Circular Economy (CE) is increasingly seen as a key approach to supporting the transition to a more sustainable society by enhancing competitiveness and economic growth. When properly planned and implemented, CE can lead to improved sustainability, improved innovation ability, decreased costs and thus improved competitiveness (Ellen MacArthur Foundation, 2015). This also leads to the ability to turn challenges related to currently experienced increases in raw material costs and price volatility (which are projected to continue) into opportunities for companies that systematically engage CE in their business and asset management strategies (Ellen MacArthur Foundation, 2013).

Creating a CE requires fundamental changes throughout the value chain, from innovation, product design and production processes to the end of life, new business models and shifts in consumption patterns (EEA, 2016). Large and established, as well as small and start-up, companies are increasingly recognising the need to develop and commercialise solutions that go beyond traditional product manufacture and sales, and instead focus upon the delivery of so-called Product Service Systems (PSS), defined as 'a marketable set of products and services, capable of jointly fulfilling a user's need' (Goedkoop et al., 1999). Among the PSS strategies being addressed are: expansion of high value-added services, focus on total cost of ownership over the product lifetime, outsourcing agreements and rental offerings, technical leadership and optimised product quality (Baines et al., 2009). The activities and knowledge associated with PSS lead to the need for more holistic design processes, which includes the design of both products and services and which takes a much broader life cycle perspective. Such design processes are also key for the establishment of a CE. The question is, how to organise the design of combined products and services, over expanded time periods and new stakeholder boundaries within a CE context?

This chapter presents a systematic framework to support the design and development of PSS that takes account of circularity. Its main elements, stages and characteristics are presented in the following sections, followed by a discussion on the development of PSS in a CE context.

PSS DEVELOPMENT

PSS expands product development considerations in a number of ways (Figure 10.1). This brings a number of possibilities in a CE context: closing material loops (e.g. through take-back systems and end-of-use strategies), achieving resource efficiency (e.g. through enhanced product utilisation and lifetime extension) and dematerialisation (by activating users to fulfil their functional and value needs with less products).

A number of PSS design frameworks exist. In this chapter, we choose one of these frameworks, which is based on an extensive study of PSS frameworks and research activities into the design and development of PSS solutions (Matzen, 2009). The framework includes four fundamental PSS dimensions (key elements that should be considered when designing a PSS) and four PSS design stages (steps from conceptualisation to implementation).

Fundamental PSS dimensions
PSS design and development involves the consideration of four fundamental PSS dimensions (Figure 10. 1)

Value proposition
The starting point for the conceptualisation of PSS solutions is the value proposition, which encapsulates value for different stakeholders. The value proposition can range from product-dominant to service-dominant, with many blends and flavours in between. The key goal when designing PSS for CE is to attempt to ensure that the value proposition is delivered as effectively as possible, aiming at a maximization of the value creation to the key stakeholders. The basic questions when

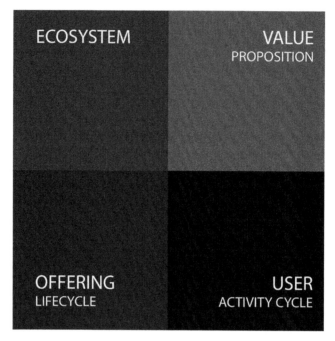

Figure 10.1 Fundamental PSS dimensions (Finken et al., 2013)

considering the value proposition should be 'What is the customer's actual need? How can this need best be fulfilled and in as resource-efficient a manner as possible? Which stakeholder has the best-suited competencies to solve the customer's needs? Why should the customer change from their current mode of needs satisfaction to the new value proposition? What potential 'rebound effects' can the value proposition bring? How can circular strategies integrate into the value proposition?'

Offering life cycle
When developing PSS, it is important to take a broader view of the opportunities that lie in the product life cycle, so that any type of 'offering' can be considered (including tangible/intangible products or services). In a PSS-based business, the producing company often assumes greater responsibility for the product, away from a traditional 'cradle-to-gate' over to a 'cradle-to-grave' (or Cradle to Cradle) responsibility, which brings the biggest opportunities in a CE context due to the high potential for decoupling value creation from the consumption of physical products. Furthermore, supporting a longer life cycle requires new competencies (e.g. customer support, maintenance/upgrade services, advice/consultancy for the use phase), but could give new benefits for the provider of the PSS solution (e.g. steady income streams, customer retention).

The activity of mapping and designing the solution's life cycle (this could be the product life cycle, or a combination of physical products and other ancillary products) facilitates the necessary collection of in-depth knowledge of the whole life cycle of the PSS, spanning from the production of the related products through to all further interactions with the customer, users, and other stakeholders, during and after any use-related interaction with the PSS. The mapping is especially important in a CE context, where several use phases must be taken into account and properly planned.

User activity cycle

The third dimension is the user activity cycle – a mapping of the key stakeholders' needs, in the sequences of activities carried out 'before', 'during' and 'after' needs fulfilment. The 'after' phase is especially relevant in a CE context, as this is the phase in which strategies like remanufacturing, reuse, recycling, etc. will traditionally take place. Subsequently, the related product- or service-elements are mapped onto the users' activities, in a process that starts to design the PSS solution to the users' activities. The user activity cycle prompts the designer to consider the sequence of activities of the stakeholders connected to the PSS under development, hereby contributing to the knowledge of the designed solution's use phase. It is often when considering the user activity cycle that stakeholders and their activities are uncovered that had not previously been considered.

Ecosystem (actor network)

The fourth and final PSS design dimension is the understanding, mapping and actual integrated design of relationships among relevant stakeholders. In order to function and to create value, PSS closely intertwines with customers, actual users, partners and many other stakeholders. The identification of all the active stakeholders around the PSS and the map of the flows of value, material, energy, information, service and transport, where appropriate, among the relevant stakeholders defines the actor network. By drawing the ecosystem, important characteristics of the circular value chain are established, which are important for ensuring an enhanced sustainability performance of the chain. In PSS design, the roles and relationships of the stakeholders are designed to be more rewarding for all, bringing a number of win-win situations. In a CE context, new actors may appear that can facilitate reuse, refurbishing, remanufacturing, recycling the physical parts of a PSS. An example of this could be a company that purchases used electronic equipment, refurbishes it and the resells it as quality second-life products.

PSS design process

The PSS design process is iterative, generally moving through steps which have been identified as *analysis, definition, conceptualisation* and *evaluation* (Figure 10. 2).

ANALYSE

There is a need to understand the impacts of products and services in relation to the value that they provide before attempting to change and improve existing systems. CE can often bring a new perspective when analysing the current market and can generate new and innovative solutions (e.g. sharing platforms, performance-based contracts, activity management relationships, upcycling of end-of-use products). Some of the understanding may already exist in the company, whereas specific data about the market and the required capabilities to provide solutions are typically not available. Frequently, additional data will be required related to consumer behaviour, digital technology enablers and cultural aspects when CE is considered in solutions development. Developers of both products and services exercise a dominant influence on a number of aspects, ranging from performance, through customer satisfaction and to profitability. By coupling this influence to an understanding of offerings throughout their lifetime, the needs of the user and the full ecosystem around them, there is a great potential to identify solutions that better meet the needs of the user (e.g. through the delivery of

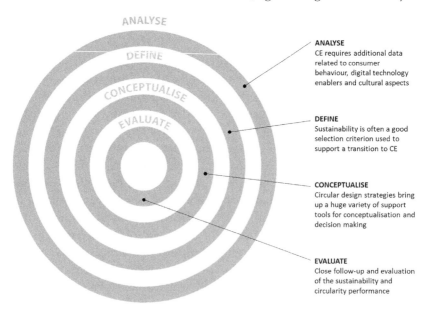

Figure 10.2 PSS development phases and link to CE (Finken et al., 2013)

functionality instead of product ownership). *This phase should result in a clear overview of the market, the need, the current ecosystem and the PSS providing company's own capabilities, relevant to solving the need.*

DEFINE

At an early stage, it is necessary to prioritise actions from the many possible routes that the PSS may take. Resulting from the *analysis of the market and company capabilities*, the potential of alternative PSS ideas is identified. Following this, the focus and goals (or requirements) can be defined to guide both the conceptualisation and the selection of ideas. The objective is to focus on the key elements in the value proposition, the user needs that should be addressed and the key stakeholders to involve. Feasible goals should be established related to, for example, customer segment(s) (e.g. business-to-business or business-to-consumer), expected market share, dimensions of the value proposition (e.g. mix between service and product offerings) and a clear definition of which measureable elements will lead to customer need satisfaction. In a CE context, it is also important to define goals related to the circularity of the PSS solution (e.g. enhanced value creation, lifetime extension) combined with sustainability goals (including environmental, social and economic dimensions). *This phase should result in a focused PSS description, sufficiently delimited to fulfil the needs of the customer and a basic specification for the emerging PSS, including tangible goals for the final PSS design that includes both enhanced circularity and broader sustainability performance.*

CONCEPTUALISE

PSS concepts are an integrated chain of product and service offerings, which describe a holistic solution to the user's needs, where the combination of product and service elements is chosen on the basis of the best way to meet the goals. The PSS concept describes the most important features and requirements of the final solution. In this step, all relevant dimensions should be sufficiently described and unknown risks investigated (i.e. risks arising from the PSS provision, which might include lack of market readiness, legislative barriers, consumer behaviour change, etc.). By developing multiple concepts, the possibility of identifying the best solution is increased, whether it appears from one concept alone or as a combination of numerous ideas and concepts. Conceptualisation involves the development of prototypes, in order to test out the many ways in which the identified customer need can be satisfied. Circular design strategies (e.g. design for product lifetime extension, reuse, remanufacturing, upcycling) play a key role in this step, and there are various potential design options that might be considered in the conceptualisation process (e.g. facilitate disassembly, enable material separation, allow for easy access to parts/components, etc.). *This step should result in a number of PSS concepts, ideally described to the same level of detail, prototyped to an extent where they can be tested, and prioritised by means of a systematic selection process, through a set of business, circularity and sustainability criteria.*

EVALUATE

An existing baseline should be established that consists of the most relevant current product and/or service offered by the company. This is important in the development the PSS, as it should be used to compare and evaluate new ideas and concepts. A particular challenge with PSS solutions is that they are difficult to test. Unlike typical products, PSS solutions do not simply reach a final design, ready for launch on the market. By very nature, one needs to 'connect the power' to the PSS concept to bring it alive, and this means involving a select few lead-users in a closely monitored pilot implementation of the concept. All PSS solutions depend on collecting and processing customer- and usage-intelligence. Co-development partnerships are often ventured – either together with the customer of the emerging PSS (this is common in business-to-business cases) or by creating a consortium of investors and service providers. Furthermore, the PSS product performance during operation (e.g. damage of components and parts, energy efficiency), which entails multiple use cycles and intensified use, is difficult to predict due to technical barriers and potential consumer behaviour changes triggered by the provision of the PSS. Digital technologies, the Internet of Things and Big Data are increasingly being seen as important enablers for CE, as they potentially enable more effective management of the product's lifetime and support the decision-making related to end-of-use strategies (e.g. reuse/remanufacturing/recycling).

This step should result in the chosen PSS solution being implemented by the customer. A close follow-up and evaluation is necessary in order to test and adjust the PSS solution when experienced in use, where the evaluation cycles should be short and flexible in the early implementation. The advantage of the producer being present whilst the PSS is in operation (as opposed to a traditional product scenario) is that close improvement cycles can be achieved. Furthermore, PSS enables enhanced control over the product life cycle, which enables the implementation of circular strategies and approaches (e.g. extended life time through predictive maintenance or take back solutions that enable repair/ remanufacturing/recycling).

PSS METHODOLOGICAL REFERENCE MODEL

Figure 10.3 illustrates the methodological reference model for PSS, including a synthesis of the four PSS development steps, the four fundamental PSS dimensions and the iterative nature of PSS design.

Within the model, the four development phases: *analyse, define, conceptualise,* and *evaluate* form the concentric rings focusing on the result, whereas the four fundamental PSS dimensions: *value proposition, user activity cycle, offering life cycle, ecosystem,* occur as segments of each concentric ring. The implicit recommendation, built into the model, is to follow a process from outside-in and in a clockwise direction. It is, however, a general understanding that the activities and nature of any PSS design team in any given company may differ, for which reason the reference model is flexible and non-normative in its form. While it is important to move from analyse and define to conceptualise and evaluate, in this order, the four dimensions can be completed in a number of sequences. As an overarching concept, CE must be taken into account

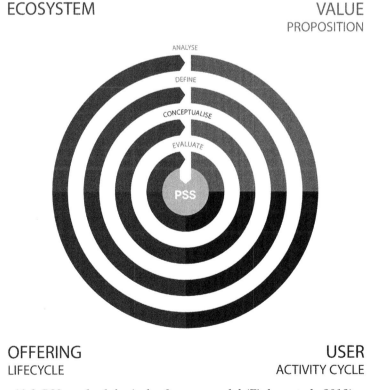

Figure 10.3 PSS methodological reference model (Finken et al., 2013)

in all development phases and for all PSS dimensions. CE brings a set of new considerations that have an important role in shaping the PSS, including the partnerships, customer segments, new solutions (offerings) and infrastructure.

Creative design processes are always threatened by the rigid format of following a linear process. The PSS methodological reference model provides a flexible approach that can be tailored to the individual user's needs and process. Such a process is likely to evolve over time and adapt to the company's changing situation.

DISCUSSION: DOES PSS ALWAYS LEAD TO CE AND SUSTAINABILITY?

It is, of course, important to note that CE approaches based on PSS are not intrinsically sustainable. For example, product leasing is not automatically 'greener' (Agrawal et al., 2012), but might in contrast inspire more frequent replacements of products. Furthermore, in the case of sharing systems such as car-sharing, these systems often lead to more people getting easier access to products (Madsen, 2015), which ultimately can result in increased consumption, even though car-sharing in itself is more resource-efficient than private car ownership. Take-back services, which may also entail that ownership stays with the provider, have a circularity potential within PSS, as they may entail product redistribution (e.g. transportation from one customer to the other) and remanufacturing. However, second-hand products often supplement, rather than replace new products (Eichner and Runkel, 2003) and when sold at lower prices, the result is often an overall increase in consumption. From a business perspective, this behaviour is positive, as it avoids the cannibalisation of the current market for new products, but it does not necessarily lead to resource decoupling. Studies have shown that historically, incremental efficiency improvements have not succeeded in outpacing increases in the quantity of goods and services consumed (Dahmus, 2014). These effects are termed 'rebound effects' and without mitigation, efficiency improvements will at best lead to reductions in resource consumption that are smaller than expected; at worst, they will lead to larger overall resource consumption (Dahmus, 2014). Finally, it is also worth noting that CE strategies are not always desirable (e.g. recycling of certain contaminated materials might lead to the recirculation of hazardous substances), which might also lead to a number of rebound effects.

FINAL REMARKS

A successful transition to CE requires a systemic change in the way companies understand and do business, with sustainability as a strong foundation for the development of new PSS solutions and the transition from selling products to providing services. In many industries, production is in the midst of a shift, away from a mass production paradigm over to mass customisation, serving a highly globalised and diversified customer base.

The PSS methodological reference model provides a simplified overview of the main elements of PSS development, both in terms of generic PSS contents (the four PSS dimensions) and also of process (the four PSS design phases). PSS design attempts to identify not only changes to the product but also which changes can be made to the entire production and consumption system and how stakeholders' motivations and incentives can be aligned – therefore, its high potential to contribute to a transition towards CE (e.g. through incentives for more efficient operation, extended life times, reuse/remanufacturing, data management, etc.).

BIBLIOGRAPHY

Agrawal, V.V. et al. (2012). Is leasing greener than selling? *Management Science* 58(3): 523–533. DOI: 10.1287/mnsc.1110.1428.

Baines, T.S. et al. (2009). The servitization of manufacturing: A review if literature and reflection on future challenges. *Journal of Manufacturing Technology Management* 20(5): 547–567. DOI: 10.1108/17410380910960984. Edited by R. Roy. Emerald Group Publishing Limited.

Dahmus, J.B. (2014). Can efficiency improvements reduce resource consumption? *Journal of Industrial Ecology* 18(6): 883–897. DOI: 10.1111/jiec.12110.

EEA. (2016). *Circular Economy in Europe: Developing the Knowledge Base.* Luxembourg: EEA.

Eichner, T. and Runkel, M. (2003). Efficient management of product durability and recyclability under utilitarian and chichilnisky preferences. *Journal of Economics* 80(1): 43–75. DOI: 10.1007/s00712-002-0607-0.

Ellen MacArthur Foundation. (2013). Towards the circular economy: Opportunities for the consumer goods sector. *Ellen MacArthur Foundation*, 1–112. DOI: 10.1162/108819806775545321.

Ellen MacArthur Foundation. (2015). Growth within: A circular economy vision for a competitive Europe. p. 100.

Finken, K.H. et al. (2013). *#4 PSS Tool Book – a workbook in the PROTEUS series.* Technical University of Denmark.

Goedkoop, M., van Halen, C., te Riele, H., and Rommens, P. (1999). *Product Service Systems, Ecological and Economic Basics.* The Netherlands: Pre consultants.

Madsen, M.B. (2015). *Deleøkonomiens klimapotentiale [The Climate Potential of the Share Economy].* Copenhagen, Denmark: CONCITO.

Matzen, D. (2009). A systematic approach to service oriented product development. Ph.D. Technical University of Denmark.

11 Key issues when designing solutions for a Circular Economy

Mattias Lindahl

INTRODUCTION

For almost a century, the consumption of products has been the dominant paradigm and mindset. It was promoted by John Maynard Keynes, who had a deep impact on modern macroeconomics and the economic policies of governments. In his 1936 classic *The General Theory of Employment, Interest and Money* (Keynes, 1936), he states 'I should support at the same time all sorts of policies for increasing the propensity to consume. For it is unlikely that full employment can be maintained, whatever we may do about investment, with the existing propensity to consume.' Other influential economists, such as Victor Lebow (1955), also supported this paradigm: 'Our enormously productive economy . . . demands that we make consumption our way of life, that we convert the buying and use of goods into rituals, that we seek our spiritual satisfaction, our ego satisfaction, in consumption . . . we need things consumed, burned up, replaced and discarded at an ever-accelerating rate.'

Today, however, the drawbacks following an ever-increasing consumption of materials and products (Sanne, 2002) are becoming more obvious, and a move towards more sustainable solutions[2] based on Circular Economy (CE) thinking is needed (Tukker and Tischner, 2006; Ellen MacArthur Foundation, 2013). Geissdoerfer et al. (2017) define the CE as a 'regenerative system in which resource input and waste, emission, and energy leakage are minimised by slowing, closing, and narrowing material and energy loops'. This can be achieved through long-lasting design, maintenance, repair, reuse, remanufacturing, refurbishing, and recycling. Therefore, the focus of CE solution (CES) design is to create solutions that are, from an economic, environmental, social and life cycle perspective, resource efficient, while maintaining the positive value within the overall system(s). Taking the example of an automobile, the aim would be to design-in a prolonged use phase in combination with a high level of reusability of the car and its components. This implies that, in comparison with concepts like Product Service System (PSS) and Integrated Product Service Offering (IPSO), the CES concept has a more explicit CE based focus, especially when it comes to maintaining the positive value within the overall system(s), e.g. by closing material and energy loops and taking an extended life cycle perspective.

Mont's (2004) PSS definition neglects the consideration of closing of resource loops in an 'extended life cycle perspective'[3] and the retention of value. Mont (2004) states that 'PSS is a system of products, services, networks of actors and supporting infrastructure that continuously strives to be competitive, satisfy customer needs and have a lower environmental impact than traditional business models'. In addition, Tukker and Tischner (2006) also neglect the closing of loops, extended life cycle perspective and retention of value issues and state that PSSs 'are a specific type of value proposition that a business (network) offers to (or co-produces with) its clients. PSS "consists of a mix of tangible products and intangible services designed and combined so that they jointly are capable of fulfilling final customer needs"'.

The manufacturing industry has a key role and opportunity to take the leadership in CES design. CES design provides a mechanism to turn environmental challenges into opportunities for change and innovation, and to transform existing businesses to use less, reuse, and preserve the value of resources, all while delivering more value to customers. This includes evolving from being a provider of products to one of solutions and focusing on an extended life cycle perspective, e.g. by life extension through repair and remanufacturing, adding on service and taking increased responsibility for the end-of-use phases.

This chapter presents four key issues that are important to consider when designing a CES.

MINDSET

CES implies the need for a design mindset with an extended life cycle perspective and with a focus on resource-efficient solutions: product/

service combinations that are durable with a long use phase, that require minimal service, spare parts and consumables, and which satisfy the customer as long as it is economically viable (for the CES provider). Furthermore, the design mindset stresses developing products that are easy to reuse as products or components with a view to maintaining positive value within the overall system(s).

Companies often start their move towards a CES by bundling their existing products with services (Sakao et al., 2008; Sundin et al., 2009). This is a problem, however, since the mindset needed for CES design differs significantly from traditional product design. In line with Lebow (1955), in general terms, the traditional product design mindset aims to identify customer needs, then to design the product, then encourage customers to buy and consume a product whilst producing it for as low a cost as possible, and finally selling it for as high a price as possible. This implies that the focus of the design process is on how to optimise and improve production – not on the design of an effective CES that maintains positive value within the overall system and takes an extended life cycle perspective. As a consequence, traditional design often does not consider future energy and consumables use, service, maintenance and end-of-life-treatment (Ulrich and Eppinger, 2000; Ullman, 2002), and what happens with used products after the use phase or contract is completed. Even if use phase, service and repair considerations are included in design thinking, e.g. as is in the case of some road and railway contracts in Sweden, infrastructure providers do not normally consider the infrastructure's value after the end of the contract in the design process. This implies a risk that the value of the infrastructure system during the contract degrades over time instead of remaining at a high level: i.e. the positive value within the system declines given the lack of extended life cycle perspective. Furthermore, at present, companies typically have a minor degree of integration between their physical product and service design, with the latter being done after product realisation or even after it has been put on the market.

However, a CES often also implies that the business models change from up-front payment to payment for the performance (value). This turns a lot of the traditional business logic, and therefore design logic, upside down. In other words, a CES implies a new design mindset, as further explained below.

- First, in contrast with the traditional sale of products, a CES provider normally does not want the customer to come back after a while and ask for a replacement or a new solution. Instead, the provider wants the customer to use the CES for as long as possible, as revenue is based on the provision of value and not on the use of products and services. Furthermore, if the use phase is prolonged, the ratio between the total initial environmental and economic cost for the production of the product(s) in relation to the use phase time decreases; this implies that the longer the use phase is, the more the provider can potentially earn and lower the total environmental impact in relation to the use phase.

- Second, traditionally, service, spare parts and consumables constitute an important income for manufacturers – often with high profit margins. However, since service, spare parts and sometimes consumables are normally included in a CES (see, e.g. Geissdoerfer et al., 2017), these become an unwanted cost – something that ought to be avoided or reduced (e.g., by more durable spare parts and a reduced need for consumables). Within a CES, the core issue is delivery of value: if the offer does not work, e.g. because of malfunctions, the provider loses money because the provider is not paid since the value is not provided.

- Third, in the case that the customer does not need the solution any longer, in line with Geissdoerfer et al. (2017) and BSI (2017), it is preferable that the used products are easy to repair, reuse, remanufacture, refurbish or upgrade so they can be used by other customers, e.g. to extend the use phase.

To conclude, as stated in the introduction, a CES implies *a design mindset change with a main focus on an extended life cycle perspective, and with a focus on resource-efficient and effective solutions.* This will be further elaborated on in next section.

EXTENDED LIFE CYCLE PERSPECTIVE

Designing a CES implies that an extended life cycle perspective is integrated into the design process and that there is a focus on lowering the total provider's and customer's life cycle cost, e.g. through a prolonged use phase or reuse, rather than a focus on achieving a low production cost for used products. The inclusion of the use phase implies that the solution space increases when designing a solution. This is positive, since it results in an increased possibility to optimise the total life cycle cost/environmental impact of the CES. Costs are often associated with the use of materials and energy, which in turn can create a negative environmental impact, implying that more cost-optimised solutions that take account of CE principles, see, e.g. BSI (2017), usually have lower environmental impact.

As highlighted earlier, in traditional design processes, services are often developed after the physical product is developed. As the work on the product progresses, knowledge is increased; at the same time, the degree of freedom of action decreases for every decision taken, since time and cost drive most projects. Related to economic costs are environmental impacts. Figure 11.1 illustrates, in general terms, the cumulative environmental impact over the product's life cycle and the influence of different life cycle phases on the environmental impact (BSI, 2017). Note that in reality, each use phase's duration differs substantially as different products have different profiles; in most cases, however, the use phase is the longest. Note also that the cumulative cost of a product is often closely linked with the cumulative environmental impact.

Even though different products will have different environmental impacts during their life cycle phases, the conclusion based on Figure 11.1 is that the design phase has a major influence on the total environmental impact. It is in the early phases of the design processes that the product specification is defined, including what parameters must/should be focused on, e.g. how the product will be used; how long it will work for; what type and amount of consumables will be used during the normal use phase; and what is the lifetime of the product (see, e.g. Ulrich and Eppinger, 2000). Furthermore, measures that can be taken to prolong the use, e.g. maintenance, repair, reuse, remanufacturing, refurbishing and recycling, are also generally preferable from a CE perspective since the total environmental impact in relation to the length of the use phase will decrease (see, e.g. Geissdoerfer et al., 2017; BSI, 2017).

To conclude, when designing a CES, the basic principle is to consider all life cycle phases (BSI, 2017) in order to optimise the solution from

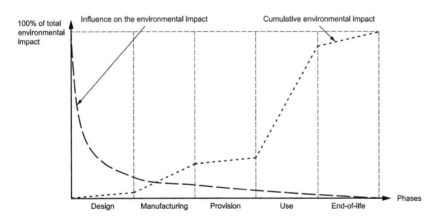

Figure 11.1 Illustration of the cumulative environmental impact over the product's lifecycle and the influence of different lifecycle phases on the environmental impact (BSI 2017)

a life cycle perspective (Lindahl, 2005), and to achieve the lowest total economic as well as environmental cost for the solution (Lindahl, Sundin et al., 2014).

IDENTIFICATION OF RELEVANT ACTORS AND THEIR REQUIREMENTS

In traditional product design, in order to avoid later changes, it is important to identify customers' requirements as early as possible (Ullman, 2002), as per the discussion relating to Figure 11.1. However, when designing a CES, the requirements usually differ from traditional sales of products. For example, since service is normally included, traditionally profitable work (e.g. maintenance and spare parts) becomes a cost, with no value for the provider. In addition, services are intangible and therefore more complex when it comes to measuring the quality of the outcome (performance and value), e.g. ensuring requirement fulfillment. This sets a higher demand on providers to deliver a CES which satisfies both expectations and demand (performance and value).

Furthermore, due to the inclusion of the extended life cycle perspective, a CES normally involves more actors with different requirements, and it is important to identify those that are relevant. An actor can be affected by and/or affect a CES, and it can be, e.g. an individual, a group, a function or a department, and can include designers, service staff, sales staff, users of the solution and consumables providers. An example of an actor within the CES provider could be a service technician who, in order to make the service less time consuming, requires a reduced number of sub-operations when changing tyres.

To conclude, in CES design, it is important to identify relevant actors and their requirements, and there are several methods that can support this, e.g. the Actors and System Map method (Lindahl, Sakao et al., 2014) and the Actor Maps (Tan, 2010). It is also essential not to neglect actors that traditionally would not be considered as being involved in a provided solution, e.g. NGOs and legislative functions (that might influence the solution) (Lindahl, Sakao et al., 2014).

CES DESIGN

Similar to traditional product design, CES design implies trade-offs among different requirements; however, the extended life cycle perspective can often make these easier to identify since the solution space is larger. Furthermore, as highlighted by Geissdoerfer et al. (2017), the CES concept is a driver for increased design for modular, robust and standardised products, and furthermore for reuse (of e.g. products and materials) and refurbishment of products, components and materials. A good CES design example is Polyplank, a company that is incorporating an extended life cycle perspective and resource efficiency into the design process, while aiming to maintain value within the overall system. More specifically, Polyplank has developed a process to transform plastic waste and wood fibres into a cheap, recyclable material used in a different CES (Lindahl, Sundin et al., 2014). In its design, the company has fully adopted the CES mindset, extended life cycle perspective and identification of relevant actors and their requirements.

Polyplank's most advanced CES (resulting from CES design) is core plugs used by paper mills that paper is rolled up on that is then shipped to customers, as seen in Figure 11.2 (Lindahl, Sundin et al., 2014). Its CES (re)utilises the used core plugs that are sent back to the paper mill by customers, as the paper mill then reuses them after Polyplank has washed and checked them. Furthermore, and also in line with the principles behind CE (see, e.g. BSI, 2017), Polyplank reuses broken core plugs for new core plugs or other types of products.

Polyplank has focused on designing a CES that incorporates modifications of the original core plug design in line with CE thinking (see, e.g. BSI, 2017). The first version of the core plug was designed based on the paper mill's initial requirements for single-use core plugs and was only intended for one use before being scrapped. However, Polyplank managed to convince the customer that a new, in effect, CES design would be more suitable from a resource perspective. The result was a design that improved the core plugs' durability while also making the core plug easier to produce, wash, reuse and transport (see Figure 11.3). The new core plug was 35 percent more durable and 30 percent lighter, with a significantly lowered environmental impact and at the same time improved economic benefit (Lindahl, Sundin et al., 2014).

Polyplank AB ⇄ Paper mill ⇄ Paper mill's customers

Figure 11.2 Core plugs for the paper mill industry

Figure 11.3 First version of the core plug (left); Final version of the core plug (right)

The higher durability meant the creation of more loops between the paper mill and its customers, and the reduced weight meant less transportation and production costs since less material was needed for the production process, e.g. in the injection moulding used for producing the core plug. The result was an environmental load and economic cost approximately one tenth of traditional product (Lindahl, Sundin et al., 2014). The largest gain from the design change is from the system for reuse – that means the more times core plugs are reused, the larger the gain. The second biggest gain relates to the recyclability of the Polyplank material which aligns with the core message of Figure 11.1, which is that an extended use phase via design for reuse and refurbishment is key for CES design.

To conclude, even though Polyplank creates its CES based on recycled materials in line with CE principles, the company prefers to design and use as little material as possible within its products, and with the highest level of recyclability possible. The longer the CES's products, components and materials are used, the lower the initial investment cost for those in relation to the cost for the use phase.

The Polyplank example illustrates that in order to facilitate the take back of products, it is also important to integrate reverse logistics into CES design to enable the retrieval of products, components and materials (Lindahl and Sakao, 2013; Lindahl, Sundin et al., 2014).

CONCLUDING REMARKS

This chapter highlights four key issues that are important parts of CES design thinking: mindset, extended life cycle perspective, identification of relevant actors and their requirements, and CES design. Related to these, it highlights what differs from traditional product design and why.

Finally, if a design process already exists within the company, it is worthwhile to review that process with the above issues in mind. One should consider how a CES design mindset might impact the design of both existing and new solutions, and how existing methods might need to be modified, or if new methods are needed.

NOTES

1 BS 8001 includes six guiding principles: Innovation, Stewardship, Collaboration, Value Optimization, Transparency and Systems Thinking (BSI, 2017)
2 A solution in this chapter is defined as a combination of product(s) and service(s).
3 A focus on more than just one use phase.

BIBLIOGRAPHY

BSI. (2017). *BS8001: 2017: 'Framework for Implementing the Principles of Circular Economy in Organisations: Guide'* [Online]. Available at: www.bsigroup.com/en-GB/standards/benefits-of-using-standards/becoming-more-sustainable-with-standards/Circular-Economy/

Ellen MacArthur Foundation. (2013). Towards the circular economy: Opportunities for the consumer goods sector. *Ellen MacArthur Foundation*, 1–112. DOI: 10.1162/108819806775545321

Geissdoerfer, M., Savaget, P., Bocken, N.M.P., and Hultink, E.J. (2017). The circular economy: A new sustainability paradigm? *Journal of Cleaner Production* 143(Supplement C): 757–768.

Keynes, J.M. (1936). *The General Theory of Employment, Interest and Money*. Harcourt: Brace.

Lebow, V. (1955). Price competition in 1955. *Journal of Retailing*, 31(1), 5–10.

Lindahl, M. (2005). Engineering designers' requirements on design for environment methods and tools. Doctoral Thesis, KTH.

Lindahl, M. and Sakao, T. (2013). Environmental and Economic Contribution of Design Changes in Integrated Product Service Offerings. Product-Service Integration for Sustainable Solutions. H. Meier. Bochum, Germany, Springer.

Lindahl, M., Sakao, T., and Carlsson, E. (2014). Actor's and system maps for integrated product service offerings: Practical experience from two companies. *Procedia CIRP* 16(0): 320–325.

Lindahl, M., Sundin, E., and Sakao, T. (1 February 2014). Environmental and economic benefits of integrated product service offerings quantified with real business cases. *Journal of Cleaner Production* 64: 288–296.

Mont, O. (2004). Product-service systems: Panacea or myth? Doctoral Thesis, Lund University.

Sakao, T., Napolitano, N., Tronci, M., Sundin, E., and Lindahl, M. (2008). How are product-service combined offers provided in Germany and Italy? Analysis with company sizes and countries. *Journal of Systems Science and Systems Engineering* 17(3): 367–381.

Sanne, C. (2002). Willing consumers: or locked-in? Policies for a sustainable consumption. *Ecological Economics* 42(1–2): 273–287.

Sundin, E., Lindahl, M., and Ijomah, W. (2009). Product design for product/service systems: Design experiences from Swedish industry. *Journal of Manufacturing Technology Management* 20(5): 723–753.

Tan, A.R. (2010). Service-oriented product development strategies. Ph.D. Thesis, DTU Management Engineering.

Tukker, A. and Tischner, U. (2006a). *New Business for Old Europe.* Sheffield: Greenleaf Publishing.

Tukker, A. and Tischner, U. (2006b). Product-services as a research field: Past, present and future. Reflections from a decade of research. *Journal of Cleaner Production* 14(17): 1552–1556.

Ullman, D.G. (2002). *The Mechanical Design Process.* New York: McGraw-Hill Higher Education.

Ulrich, K.T. and Eppinger, S.D. (2000). *Product Design and Development.* New York: McGraw-Hill Higher Education.

Laser printing and the Circular Economy

12 Kyocera challenges the status quo

David Parker

OVERVIEW

This case study doesn't simply consider an existing case of remanufacturing as an example of the Circular Economy (CE); it takes a well-known example of 'remanufacturing' in a product/service application – printing technology – and illustrates the approaches to prevailing circular models, how they emerged and how the associated technical solutions and business models can be continually evolved to challenge the status quo.

The laser printer is a common and virtually indispensable feature of offices worldwide and in many homes. Its speed and convenience at producing quality printed materials is taken for granted, as is the easy access to both printers themselves and the consumables – cartridges – which fuel them.

Although conceived in an age well before the invention of terms related to CE, the laser printer nonetheless serves as a fine example of a well-recognised and well-developed product/service showing numerous features of CE design. It illustrates how multiple business models can exist in parallel for both new and used products; how service may be delivered in different ways; how products can be designed for maintenance, life extension and – according to business drivers – engage with the consumables market by employing diverse material or product recovery and reuse tactics. In short, it highlights the complexity of any decisions made in the name of CE, particularly when the status quo is challenged by new entrants – with new technology, or low-cost structures – and the need to be clear about the underlying rationale for it.

REMANUFACTURING IN THE CIRCULAR ECONOMY

Remanufacturing is, according to *British Standard 8887–2:2009*:

> the return of a used product to at least its original performance with a warranty that is equivalent or better than that of the newly manufactured product.

It is a long-established industrial practice, although never as professionalised, systematised or extensive as it is today. With roots in the first world war, remanufacturing kept critical and hard-won weaponry in service; this continued through the twentieth century, most particularly in the aerospace and automotive sectors as a matter of necessity to offset reliability issues. It is apt, therefore, that it is now recognised as an exemplification of the highest CE principles in action, with demonstrable material, energy, financial and skill benefits.

Remanufacturing touches on all elements of the transformation from linear to circular operation, from the business model, product, service and process design, manufacturing, delivery, recovery, rejuvenation and upgrade. The next sections reflect on how remanufacturing in the printer market touches us at a somewhat more prosaic, everyday level.

LASER PRINTING – TECHNOLOGY EVOLUTION

Laser printing has evolved from an essentially business application to one with relevance to and accessibility by the whole range of consumers. The earliest evolution of the laser printer concept of Xerox and IBM in the early 1970s serviced the needs of a limited corporate market. Canon broke the mould in the late 1970s, creating the first desktop unit affordable by smaller businesses for routine office use. Their design set the template for the printers we see today as consumers: the printer shell coupled with a replaceable 'print engine', a convenient combined transfer drum and toner powder reservoir which persists to this day.

In those early days, it could not be claimed that these units were cheap, either the shell or the cartridges. To stimulate the market, Canon's cartridges were easily disassembled, repaired and reassembled – prime features of a remanufacturing service. There was open access to a spares industry that was not restricted to use by original equipment manufacturers (OEMs) only, which stimulated the growth of an independent cartridge refilling sector. This remanufacturing activity by both independents and OEMs has persisted, exploiting sound design for reuse principles, to the current day but in an increasingly competitive fashion and this is described further in the next section.

BUSINESS MODELS

Although based around the same core technology, there are two distinct printing markets: the high-volume printing market and the business/consumer market. The volume market is characterised by the large so-called print stations found in copy shops and corporations, multifunction machines which can collate and bind at high speed. The typical small office environment and consumer markets have converged on the smaller print units, cheaper and highly distributed in homes and office departments.

PRINT STATIONS

The way that manufacturers have responded to the needs of these two different markets illustrates how competitive pressures – even in the absence of overt CE imperatives – drives commercial responses. Print

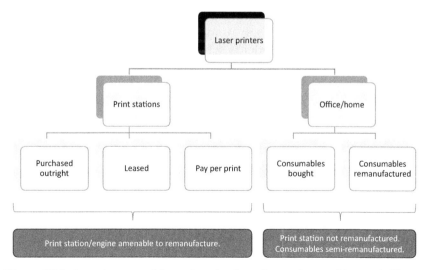

Figure 12.1 Asset/consumable options in the print station and home/office markets

stations, with their diverse capabilities and high-speed throughputs are expensive pieces of equipment. They are often purchased bundled with a service contract element which can include both the consumables and the print item itself. Even within this aspect there are numerous approaches which embrace a variety of delivery elements. As is seen in other sectors, such contracts cover on-demand purchase of consumables or pay-per-print, for example. Print stations may be purchased outright, or as part of a lease, with or without the consumables element. The high cost of the print stations has motivated a remanufacturing industry around the station itself.

One of the most notable examples of this is Xerox, well known for its regional centres for recovery, disassembly, remanufacture and reassembly of entire units. Either through take-back or end-of-lease, print stations are recovered and rejuvenated from the bottom up. The core print engine (laser drum, etc.) is part of the station, not a consumable, and will be replaced at this stage. In service, therefore, only the toners will be replenished, for example by use of a powder refill bottle. Because of the possibility (historically) of toner spillage, this system has not been widely adopted in the home/office market. It does, however, represent the most resource-efficient and cost-effective means of delivering the print service.

The example of print stations represents a well-functioning and financially sustainable example of a CE solution based on remanufacturing of the major capital component. It demonstrates many principles of the topic of closing product loops including the design of the business model, modular design of the product, servitisation of the product for user convenience, integration of new manufacture with remanufacture and improved design through product failure knowledge. This does not guarantee that the model is sustainable in perpetuity: continued enhancements to the home/office models increasingly encroach on the print station design space, reducing the size of the market. It is therefore timely to examine the evolution of the home/office market itself.

HOME/OFFICE

The home and office sector has adopted for the most part a '2-part' business model of a relatively modestly priced printer asset coupled with a relatively high cost 'consumables' element. Why is this so? It was already described that printers started as a relatively expensive capital purchase, but the market has expanded rapidly and is now saturated with over-supply of new product. Under these circumstances, revenue generation is driven by the sales of consumables, which can only happen if the corresponding brand of printer has been bought. This model therefore drives to a low cost – even loss-making – capital purchase, with an enhanced price on the consumables.

Such relatively high prices for OEM consumables have been the driver for sustained remanufacturing of consumables (as opposed to the printer, which is the case in the print station market) by a – to date – vibrant independent sector. As illustration, there are over 1,000 refillers or remanufacturers active in Europe. These agents recover cartridges either by directly engaging with corporations or by the use of core brokers who aggregate and sort for particular brands and types. Typically, remanufacturers can achieve a sales price which is around 50 percent of the OEM price.

There is an uneasy dynamic between OEMs and these independent agents. OEMs, with the notable exception of Lexmark and one or two others, do not remanufacture their own cartridges. In Europe, they are obliged under Article 4 of the European Commission's WEEE Directive (Council Directive 2012/19/EU), however, to arrange for the recovery of their own cartridges for either reuse or recycling. Except for the abovementioned OEMs, most cartridges are recycled. The reasons given for this practice centre on claims of quality of print achieved by the refilled units. When refilled units cannot meet OEM quality, it is claimed that users will reprint, and that this reprinting substantially outweighs the material and energy savings attributed to recovery and reuse of the cartridge itself. Be that as it may, it is the WEEE Directive which holds this dynamic in place. It mandates in addition that cartridges cannot entertain features that inhibit remanufacture and reuse.

Considering the competitive pressures apparent on market development of Figure 12 2., of late a further cost competition pressure is apparent. This relates to the import of low cost, lower quality or IP-infringing cartridge clones from the Far East. They cannot be remanufactured and act as a burden on genuine compliance efforts to achieve loop closure.

CIRCULARISATION AND THE GLOBAL ECONOMY

At heart, the concept of the CE is nothing more than a formalisation of a suite of existing approaches to manage manifest risks: materials supply, financial and skills risks identified by organisations themselves; and externality risks more often identified and formalised by regional, national and global agencies as requiring concerted action at a level above the company or sector.

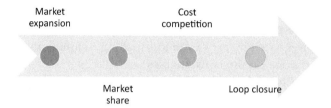

Figure 12.2 Market evolution

Has the laser printer sector been responding to global pressures to adopt CE principles? Only insofar as competition is international, and corporate commercial responses are correspondingly so. Has the sector responded to regional CE policy drivers? Most certainly so, and especially within Europe. The WEEE Directive (Council Directive 2012/19/EU) and the Ecodesign Directive (Council Directive 2009/12//EC) have explicitly motivated energy performance enhancements in printer energy usage and in stipulating that consumables (cartridges) must be recovered by the person placing them on the market. Even better, design measures that frustrate reuse are not permitted. Hence, even if OEMs themselves do not wish to remanufacture cartridges, the field is open for any third party to do so, provided they can access compatible spares. Since the primary purpose of a business is to make money, the apparently well-functioning consumables remanufacturing market appears to be good evidence that CE solutions which are material-efficient and profitable based on remanufacturing are feasible.

The above considerations apply only to the home/office market. The print station market, where the printer shell itself is the target for remanufacture, is different and sustains itself on a commercial basis without any need for regulatory incentives. Here, the printer asset price reflects its true value, it is inherently valuable, and financial forces which motivate recovery and remanufacture freely operate.

In the home/office market, the price of the print asset is kept purposefully low with the main functionality embedded within the cartridge consumable. The consumable has therefore become the commercial battleground with OEMs and third parties competing for the revenue share. European Commission efforts to impose material and environmental impact constraints in pursuit of CE objectives create some incentive for remanufacture, but they also highlight the peculiar incentives in Extended Producer Responsibility schemes which do not promote reuse-based options over simple materials recovery.

THE STATUS QUO IN SUMMARY

This long-existing dichotomy in practice between OEMs underlines the complexity of rational decision making in CE thinking. Considering environmental impacts of the choice of new over remanufactured cartridges is not as simple as might appear: whilst reuse or remanufacturing of the cartridge itself offer net benefits, a significant portion of the overall impact of a cartridge is in the other consumable – printing paper. A small deviation in cartridge print quality – if it translates into users having to reprint – results in a substantial and over-riding swing in the footprint towards dis-benefit. This is contentious, dependent on the quality demands of the user and hence open to exploitation by new cartridge sellers as a reason for sticking with premium OEM products. Without some clear mechanisms for users to differentiate the performance of various cartridges, or a blanket imposition of policy by the European Commission, it is unlikely that this debate will be settled soon.

There are clear business drivers which favour the high-cost OEM consumables model, but there is an uneasy tension with the new and remanufactured alternatives. The market is locked into a model which disfavours further reuse above the current 25-percent level instead promoting material recovery.

BREAKING OUT

The question arises of whether there is an alternative life-extension design challenge that can by-pass the current impasses in home/office printers.

Kyocera has placed on the market a printer family which spans the range from print stations through to office printing. This design avoids the debate about the print quality and focuses instead back to the longevity of the print device itself.

Kyocera is a diverse global corporation with expertise in ceramics. They have applied their ceramic technology to the core of the printer

Table 12.1 Summary of business CE responses by printer application

Application	Print Stations	Home/Office Now
CE response	Remanufacture printer body Replenish consumables/ drums	Bare bones printer body Recycle or remanufacture cartridge

engine, the photo-conductive drum. Their new design of drum has a silicon-based coating that is far more durable (typically five times as long-lasting) than those made from other materials, i.e. the conventional cartridges. The central elements of the print cartridge have been moved back into the body of the printer itself, thus segregating the low-cost toner reservoir, which is of a simple five-part cassette of two polymer design. This is easily and cheaply replaced and recycled, thereby saving the raw materials, manufacturing, transport and waste emissions associated with conventional complex parts.

In fact, Kyocera has fully embraced eco-design principles to make this product fit for the CE with design features such as:

- At the top end, a durable, robust metal sub-frame provides structural integrity in a product that is designed for using long-life components
- A modular design suitable for upgrades and novel features
- Arrangement of and access to parts to ease maintenance
- Design for disassembly by minimising fastener use; all screws used have the same head, so a single screwdriver can be used to remove them all
- Plastic parts clip apart and a symbol is embossed on them to indicate where to apply pressure
- The polymer ID symbol is used to identify recyclable parts

These principles apply throughout the printer range supporting remanufacturing at the top end of the range, and maintenance at the lower end, as well as designing out waste through the development of a consumables system that avoids repeated replacement of key components throughout the product's lifetime. Arguably, this is one of the most complete applications of what might be called CE design principles to a product range.

BUSINESS MODEL ADAPTATION

With lifetime support in mind, the delivery of this service is a critical consideration. For business-oriented products, Kyocera's current model is by leasing, with products sold through so-called 'servicing dealers' which provide service support using their own engineering teams, trained by Kyocera. The dealers access Kyocera spares to maintain a fleet of printers in operation. Customers may lease wholly remanufactured units or may accept remanufactured units as a means to deliver a specified service level in place of new units. Dealers also routinely harvest viable spare parts from failed products to maintain machines in the field.

Taking this one stage further, Kyocera has embraced the concept of Managed Document Services, a holistic approach which is centred around supporting the customer's document processes with an appropriate mix of hardware and software, rather than simply supplying hardware under a service contract. This has required new strategic alliances with software providers and restructuring the business to establish teams for professional services teams. The aim of a managed document solution is to understand the information flows into, around and out of an organisation and to design a system that enables information to be exchanged and stored with maximum efficiency and minimum use of resources. Paper is designed out of business processes, thereby reducing both the number of devices needed and the amount of energy consumed, with targets embedded in the project. This plays to the CE concept of servitization, and is transforming Kyocera from a hardware business to a professional services provider.

CHALLENGES FOR KYOCERA

Kyocera has outsourced the supply and maintenance of its devices to a third party. A limitation of this approach is that it is not part of the remanufacturing system and therefore cannot collect data on remanufacturing for product and process improvement. Currently, this is seen as too costly and complex (and perhaps not a core competence compared to the manufacturing).

The life extension process works best when Kyocera's channel partner leases the equipment. If instead a customer simply buys a product outright, there is less opportunity to recover it and it could end up in the waste stream where, even if it is working, it will be treated as waste and opportunities for remanufacturing, re-use or disassembly for retrieval of individual high value materials, will be missed. Building a means of retaining such customers in the re-use loop is therefore highly desirable and an area of opportunity.

CONCLUSIONS

The laser printer market offers some valuable lessons in circular design: it shows that there are multiple design and business model solutions to any market opportunity; that good design principles truly can support product reuse; but that in CE effectiveness terms, having the correct business and legal framework and associated outcome measures are vital to achieve material and environmental benefits.

BIBLIOGRAPHY

Directive 2012/19/EU of the European Parliament and of the Council of 4 July 2012 on waste electrical and electronic equipment (WEEE) (replacing Directive 2002/96/EC).

Directive 2009/125/EC of the European Parliament and of the Council of 21 October 2009 establishing a framework for the setting of ecodesign requirements for energy-related products.

Circularity Thinking

Systems thinking for circular product and business model (re)design: identifying waste flows and redirecting them for value creation and capture

13

Fenna Blomsma and Geraldine Brennan

INTRODUCTION

Circular Economy (CE) encompasses a wide range of strategies and tactics that aim to extend the productive life of resources, such as reuse, repair, recycling, remanufacturing, industrial symbiosis, Product Service Systems, buy-back systems, co-use and redistribution, refurbishment and upgrading, as well as material, product and energy cascading. How does one determine which of these strategies and tactics are appropriate to pursue? And where does one start with aligning both the product design and the business model with the chosen 'loops'?

In this chapter, we present the initial steps of a method for addressing these questions, titled Circularity Thinking. This method applies systems thinking in the context of CE-driven innovation: innovation with the goal to solve systemic resource availability issues or improve resource productivity. Circularity Thinking is the culmination of the authors' previous work into business approaches to CE (Brennan, 2015; Blomsma, 2016) that included a series of workshops and teaching sessions. Although other tools for systems thinking and CE-driven innovation exist, the strength of this approach lies in combining a systemic outlook with a focus on circular resource flows.

As part of Circularity Thinking, both the current industrial system and possible circular systems are explored, so that boundary conditions for product and business model (re)design can be established. Circularity Thinking is a tool that can support the early stage of innovation processes: where it is not self-evident how circular strategies can aid the achievement of the innovation goal. The method can also be used to take stock of circular strategies already in place by reviewing to what degree existing strategies contribute to resource productivity. The method can be used to gather insights into how business activities such as strategy formulation, design, sourcing, finance and customer relations can enable improved resource productivity as well as generate business value.

As a starting point, we define CE as an umbrella concept centred around assessing the wide variety of resource life-extending strategies with regards to their potential to generate value and reduce value loss and destruction (Blomsma and Brennan, 2017). That is: the authors regard all resource life-extension activities as having circularity potential.

The basis for Circularity Thinking is provided by systems thinking (e.g. Von Bertalanffy, 1969; Meadows, 2008). Systems thinking is a way of analysing interactions at different scales that is based on two central ideas. The first is the assignment of a boundary to the system under investigation. This defines the relationship of this system to the sub-systems it consists of as well as the larger system(s) it is nested in. This provides a system with internal throughputs as well as external inputs and outputs. The second idea is that relationships within and between systems are governed by feedback mechanisms, meaning that different outcomes are created by how different (parts of) systems interact or relate to each other.

In industrial systems both material, technical and infrastructural possibilities – i.e. 'hard' system components – and management practices or human related factors – i.e. 'soft' system components – are relevant (Hoffman, 2003; Baumann, 2004; Boons and Howard-Grenville, 2009). Although the influence of management practices is not always acknowledged in studies on how resources can be used productively, such practices are significant: using Life Cycle Assessment (LCA), Scott Paper compared 40 pulp-suppliers and found that despite fairly uniform technology for pulp-production used in tissue manufacture, CO_2 emissions (per tonne) varied by more than a factor 100 (ENDS, 1992). This discrepancy was largely explained by differences in the manner of operation and distribution, including operational procedures, maintenance policies and management systems.

Circularity Thinking builds on one additional pillar: Life Cycle Thinking (LCT), which is the consideration of various impacts from a product's inception, through its sourcing, manufacture, use and eventual disposal and end-of-use/life stages.[1] By including 'hard' as well as 'soft' components and combining it with LCT, Circularity Thinking creates a CE-specific 'populated flow' perspective, where one looks at 'what' substances flow as well as 'who' orchestrates their movement. This perspective, which originated in human geography as 'commodity chain analysis', has demonstrated the ability to generate new insights into chain-specific issues such as resource security, environmental impacts and sustainable sourcing (Baumann, 2012).

Circularity Thinking is not a detailed technical analysis method such as LCA, Material Flow Analysis and newer and emerging circularity metrics. Although such assessments are useful, Circularity Thinking focuses on structuring the analysis of value chain complexities by 'following the flows' and by making sure that one is 'asking the right questions' regarding scale, actors and technology. In other words: Circularity Thinking supports identifying available solution spaces: namely, what are feasible solutions given the constraints imposed by the system and an organisation's ability to affect change within that system.

Next, the two main Circularity Thinking tools developed by the authors – the Circularity Compass and the Circularity Grid – are briefly explained.

CIRCULARITY COMPASS

The Circularity Compass can be used to understand where waste in a system is being generated and how circular strategies might contribute to resource productivity (Blomsma, 2016). It uses thermodynamic principles to distinguish between 'high' and 'low' entropic resource states, which indicate where a resource is on its journey to becoming a finished product: see the state indicator on the left of Figure 13.1 Specifically, the Circularity Compass identifies three states: particles, parts and products. The *particles state* indicates a phase where one would speak of resources in terms of materials, molecules and substances. The operations in this state are primarily aimed at concentrating particles: purifying them and making them suitable for subsequent use. Think of, for example, the mining, smelting and manufacture of aluminium ingots and sheets. Next, particles are given an intermediary form in the *parts state*. This is where parts or components and (sub)assemblies are created.[2] In the example of aluminium, this would be when it is used to create the various parts of a car, such as the chassis and the doors and other parts are added to it to create sub-assemblies. Lastly, parts are assembled to form finished goods that end users can extract value and utility from in the *products state*. This is when the complete car is assembled from the parts and sub-assemblies.

Within each resource state the Circularity Compass identifies specific resource life-extending strategies, see Figure 13.1. The strategies are organised according to their technical renewal potential: the degree to which a product can be renewed compared to its initial specifications. For example: as-is reuse does not involve any renewal operations that negate wear-and-tear and does not restore function loss, such as repair or remanufacturing would accomplish. Recycling[3] can be placed at the other end of the spectrum in terms of renewal potential, as it allows for recreating the product on a molecular level. Rather than indicating a hierarchy, think of these strategies as representing different theoretical possibilities that may or may not be available or desirable depending on the context. See Figure 13.1 for a short description of the included strategies as used in Blomsma (2016).

By identifying these three resource states, specific issues can be identified more clearly, see right side of Figure 13.1. For example, analysis at a particle state level generally deals with issues of stock level depletion, renewal and preservation; the impact of material use on environmental and human health; and other macro-economic functions a substance enables or competes with. Think of, for instance, nexus interactions where the generation of biofuels may compete with food security. The parts state, on the other hand, deals with 'design for X' issues, or how products can be made suitable for repair, remanufacturing and upgrading. Knowing when parts become available and being able to extract information with regards to wear and tear to determine what circular operations are feasible are also important issues here. For example, when reusing construction beams, it is crucial to know whether they are still strong enough for use in new constructions. Instead, the *products state* deals with product energy-in-use, product life-time and user acceptance and behaviour. The latter is particularly important when transforming business models and designing interventions that involve users.

CIRCULARITY GRID

The Circularity Grid aims to generate an in-depth understanding of the relationships of the system parts in terms of cost, risk, dependency and infrastructure and knowledge requirements. This framework identifies

Circularity Compass

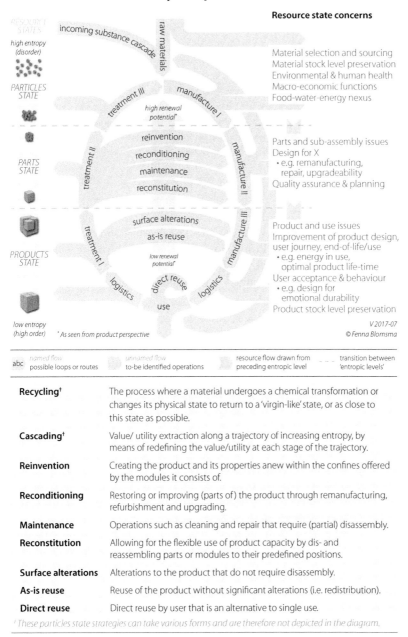

Resource state concerns

Material selection and sourcing
Material stock level preservation
Environmental & human health
Macro-economic functions
Food-water-energy nexus

Parts and sub-assembly issues
Design for X
• e.g. remanufacturing,
  repair, upgradeability
Quality assurance & planning

Product and use issues
Improvement of product design,
user journey, end-of-life/use
• e.g. energy in use,
  optimal product life-time
User acceptance & behaviour
• e.g. design for
  emotional durability
Product stock level preservation

V 2017-07
© Fenna Blomsma

abc	*named flow* possible loops or routes	*unnamed flow* to-be identified operations	resource flow drawn from preceding entropic level	transition between 'entropic levels'

Recycling†	The process where a material undergoes a chemical transformation or changes its physical state to return to a 'virgin-like' state, or as close to this state as possible.
Cascading†	Value/ utility extraction along a trajectory of increasing entropy, by means of redefining the value/utility at each stage of the trajectory.
Reinvention	Creating the product and its properties anew within the confines offered by the modules it consists of.
Reconditioning	Restoring or improving (parts of) the product through remanufacturing, refurbishment and upgrading.
Maintenance	Operations such as cleaning and repair that require (partial) disassembly.
Reconstitution	Allowing for the flexible use of product capacity by dis- and reassembling parts or modules to their predefined positions.
Surface alterations	Alterations to the product that do not require disassembly.
As-is reuse	Reuse of the product without significant alterations (i.e. redistribution).
Direct reuse	Direct reuse by user that is an alternative to single use.

† These particles state strategies can take various forms and are therefore not depicted in the diagram.

Figure 13.1 The Circularity Compass organises various circular strategies according to which resource state they occur in and their renewal potential as seen from a product perspective.

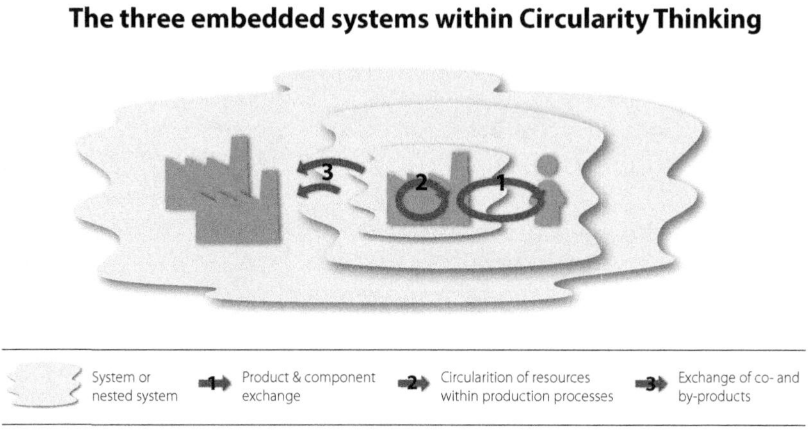

The three embedded systems within Circularity Thinking

Figure 13.2 Within the overall industrial system one can distinguish between systems-within-systems, or 'nested' systems. The product and component flows represent the middle 'layer'. Production processes are a separate subsystem, because of the amount of waste that they can create (e.g. O'Brien 2008). In turn, these systems are embedded in the wider economy with which it exchanges co- and by products.

three nested systems, see Figure 13.2, with the product and component flows representing the middle 'layer'. Production processes are designated as a subsystem because of the amount of waste they can create (e.g. O'Brien, 2008). In turn, these systems are embedded in the wider economy within which co- and byproduct exchanges take place. On each system level, flows can be governed by tight, semi- or open coupling. Think of these coupling types as a spectrum where tight coupling means a direct and highly controllable exchange managed by integration, whereas open coupling relies on much more loosely defined relationships (Weick, 1982; Boons, 1998).

Importantly, each coupling type has different implications. To illustrate, consider the types of coupling that can apply to fibre-based products, see Figure 13.3 (third column). Tight coupling involves closely controlling process parameters or direct contact among the actors involved. An example of this is the carpet manufacturer Interface, that operates a take-back scheme called 'Re-Entry' where it buys back its carpets from its customers at the end-of-life (Interface, 2017). In this example, there is a direct relationship between the resource-exchanging parts of the system.

Circularity Grid

Type of 'Coupling' (vertical axis: open, semi, tight)

Type of 'Flow' or 'Substance' (horizontal axis)

open

Waste supports process

Residual process heat is used to heat the space in which the process takes place.

A waste from a process is used to support the process without the existence of a (strong) feedback relation.

+ *Potential to save on energy and/or material costs;*
- *Can necessitate quality checks before waste can be used;*
! *Waste stream might be contaminated.*

Terracycle's bottle-cap scheme

Collection of bottle caps for specialised recycling to make optimal use of residual value.

Would-be-waste turns resource through ('open loop') recycling/ cascading.

+ *Wields the power of distributed networks;*
- *Exchange is not governed by strict rules on resource quantity, constituiton a/o delivery time;*
! *Contaminants may disrupt treatment.*

Patagonia & e-Bay

Online platform creates peer-to-peer market enabling redistribution of products.

Highly networked exchange links supply and demand for ('closed loop') resource cycling.

+ *Wields the power of distributed networks;*
- *Broad set of rules govern exchange and OEM not in control of resource quality;*
! *Flows dependent on incentives that can be changeable.*

semi

Coupling of processes

A process that generates heat is coupled to a different process that requires heat.

A would-be-waste from one process is used as an input in another process within the same facility.

+ *Potential to save on energy and/or material costs;*
- *Likely to require further or additional transport within a production facility;*
! *Creates dependency on (an) other process(es).*

Kalundborg Symbiosis

Factories exchange each other's waste streams in a system of industrial symbiosis.

Exchanges are governed by (contractual) relationships between partners.

+ *Access to extended facilities for processing would-be-waste;*
- *Range of exchanges determined by waste of co-located partners;*
! *Dependency: requires stable alignment of partner interests.*

Teijin's Eco-Circle

Chemical company works with apparel brands to recapture end-of-life fibre.

Exchanges facilitated by one or more intermediaries create tiered relationships.

+ *Extension of own capabilities and relations with that of partners;*
- *Likely to require additional material, energy, capital or labour inputs;*
! *Dependency: requires stable alignment of partner interests.*

tight

Adnams (brewery)

Using waste heat from kettles to preheat water used for the next batch of product.

Wasted resource from one process is used as an input to the same process.

+ *Potential to save on energy and/or material costs;*
- *Likely to require additional equipment;*
! *Can create reinforcing feedback loops when deviations occur.*

British Sugar

Transforming sugar production by-products into various sellable co-products.

Substance cascading, or industrial symbiosis, within the confines of focal organisation.

+ *Direct control over all exchanges and scheduling;*
- *Likely to require additional infrastructure & expertise;*
! *Deviations can create knock-on effects for interdependent products.*

Interface's 'Re-Entry 2.0'

End-of-life carpet is recaptured through a customer take-back scheme.

OEM engages directly with end-users to recover product.

+ *Continued contact with customer and possibility to set terms of exchange;*
- *Likely to require additional management & (legal) expertise;*
! *Variance in usage may make timing and quality of return flow unpredictable.*

production process (single facility level)

by-product & co-product

product & component

Figure 13.3 Overview of important positive (+) and negative (-) points as well as key aspects of risk (!) to consider when 'circularising' particular flows, illustrated with case and company examples (top of quadrants).

Semi-coupling, on the other hand, usually involves an extra pro-cess step, such as further or additional transport within or between production facilities, or the use of an intermediary. Whilst this might bring benefits, it has associated cost, risk, dependency as well as infrastructure and knowledge requirements. Additional investment, process buffers and management procedures might be necessary to minimise potential adverse effects. An example of this type of cou-pling is chemical producer Teijin's Eco-Circle fibre system. Here, Teijin partners with apparel producers to organise reverse-retail whereby used clothing made from this material is recovered from consumers who return used product back to the stores (Teijin, 2017). This means continued access to raw materials for Teijin but also a new relationship with its customers whereby the customers also become suppliers.

An example of open coupling is apparel company Patagonia's collaboration with the online platform e-Bay (e-Bay, 2017). Open-coupling usually involves only broad specifications regarding the resource quality and/or exchange frequency, and tends to rely on aggregates and can be highly-networked. Special attention needs to be given to how loop closing is incentivised and who benefits from it. By using e-Bay's capacity to aggregate supply and demand specif-ically for Patagonia products, redistribution of Patagonia products is encouraged and Patagonia benefits from an improved reputation for long-lived products. Also, Patagonia customers get a monetary return from reselling their apparel. However, no central infrastructure exists for this redistribution mechanism and standardised quality control procedures are absent.

PREPARING FOR CIRCULAR PRODUCT AND BUSINESS MODEL (RE)DESIGN

Next, the use of the Circularity Compass and the Circularity Grid is illus-trated by giving an overview of how the tools are used in the first four steps of Circularity Thinking, see also Figure 13.4. These four steps gen-erate an in-depth understanding of the problem, clarify the goal of the effort and identify potentially interesting directions for further explora-tion. More detailed steps, accompanying worksheets or facilitated work-shops are available upon request from the authors. In the following, particles (materials), parts (components) or products (finished goods) are, for simplicity, referred to as 'the product'.

Before you start: make explicit and share with the innovation team why the analysis is necessary: what problem are you aiming to solve? Also determine whether your analysis concerns (groups of) particles, parts or products and list the materials contained within them. The more specific you can be the better: use 'PET' instead of 'plastic' or 'aluminium alloy 6061' instead of 'metal' wherever possible. The method is suitable for both bio-based and technological materials. However, consider grouping flows and using more generic labels if this helps to keep things manageable or if detailed information is not at hand. Just ensure you understand what is required for the manufacturing of your product: conduct a material inventory if necessary. If applicable, include materials that are necessary in manufacturing processes or significant by- and co-products that are generated.

The first step in Circularity Thinking, see for an example Figure 13.5 (top), aids in identifying where and why waste is generated in the current system, where the most important problems or opportunities lie, what actors are present and what barriers to change exist. The second step, see for an example Figure 13.5 (bottom), explores what circular strategies could aid in achieving the desired goals by systematically reviewing the available options to address 'wastes' and identifying the possibilities for value creation and capture based on an initial screening of possible enablers. In the subsequent step, the relevant actors and their relationships are analysed in terms of cost, risk, dependency as well as infrastructure and knowledge requirements. This serves to review the relationships that are required for the operation of the pre-selected strategies and further clarify the implications of choosing a particular value chain configuration. Last, the position of the focal organisation is examined by looking at its sphere of influence and selecting what circular strategies are suitable from this perspective. The benefit of starting from a broad perspective and then zooming in on the organisation is that insights can be generated on a broad range of different actors' interests and one can identify other actors whose interests are or can be aligned with those of the focal organisation.

The Circularity Thinking process can be undertaken through a (series of) workshop(s) with relevant actors or simply be used as a guide by a team tasked with gathering insights. If workshops are conducted, ensure that some basic information is at hand, or better yet, (partially) pre-populate the Circularity Compass and use it as a discussion piece to make sure that all relevant material flows and actors are represented. Similarly, one might want to gather product or sector-specific examples

STEP 01 - Map the current system

Generate an overview of the current system. Use your own flow map or use the Circularity Compass worksheet (use of the worksheet is depicted in Figure 13.5).

1.1.   Sketch the flows under investigation
Sketch on the worksheet how the flows transition through the different resource states. Add flow quantities if available, but if not specify orders of magnitude by indicating the (estimated) proportional size of flows.

1.2.   Identify problem(s)/opportunities
Next, consider where waste is generated. Think of instances where particles are not returned to a virgin-like state, where more use could be obtained from particles through cascading, where product capacity is un- or underused or premature end-of-use/life of products occurs. Also gauge the extent of any additional problems in the value chain that merit addressing.

1.3.   Identify the actors
Name the actors involved in the various parts of the system. Consider both actors with a direct involvement such as suppliers, customers and companies that offer end-of-life services, but also other stakeholders such as governments, standards agencies or financing bodies.

1.4.   Identify barriers
What or who prevents change? Consider if and how the resource state specific issues regarding particles, parts or products apply. Identify where barriers originate.

STEP 02 – Explore the solution space

Explore the possibilities for extending the productive life of the resources in your system and pre-select feasible solutions.

2.1.   Available options to address 'wastes'
Think about what strategies – or 'loops' or 'cycles' are available, using Figure 13.1 as a guide. Not all strategies will apply or be feasible for all products. Sketch the options on the worksheet and indicate why other options are not desirable or feasible.

2.2.   Consider out-of-system options
Solutions do not necessarily lie within the boundaries of the industrial system the product is currently part of. Consider what it might mean when resources leave the system: think of cascades (e.g. forms of industrial symbiosis) and alternate use (use of products for other than their original purpose).

2.3.   Value potential: possibilities for value creation and capture
Can addressing the identified 'wastes' in the manner described above generate value? And for whom? Consider financial value but also social and environmental gains. If desired, conduct a more detailed value mapping exercise (e.g. Bocken et al 2013, Yang et al 2017).

2.4.   Implications and enablers
What is required for implementing the identified strategies? For example, does the product concept or the business model need to be rethought? And what enablers are necessary to overcome the earlier identified barriers? Also think of changes in information flows, infrastructure and energy requirements.

2.5.   Short list viable solution(s)
The previous steps have provided insight into which circular strategy or strategies can be considered feasible and have potential to generate value. Inventorise and short-list them.

Figure 13.4 An overview and summary of the first four steps of Circularity Thinking

More detailed steps, accompanying worksheets or facilitated workshops are available on request. Particles (materials), parts (components) or products (finished goods) are, for simplicity, referred to as 'the product'.

four steps of Circularity Thinking

STEP 03 – Understand system relationships
Turn to the Circularity Grid worksheet and make an inventory of the system relationships that are required for the operation of the selected strategies.

3.1.   Transfer from Circularity Compass to Circularity Grid worksheet
Consider where your selected solutions fit in the three levels of the Circularity Grid: are they flows that can be fed back into manufacturing processes, do they propose continued use of co- and by-products or do they represent product and component life-extension?

3.2.   Inventorise relationship options
Consider the relationships that are possible for each of your proposed solutions by putting your solutions in one of the boxes of the Circularity Grid. What are the implications of organising that particular flow that way in terms of cost, risk and dependency? Who would have access to what infrastructure and knowledge? Who captures what value and why? Can shared value be created with partners whose interested are aligned? How can resource quality be ensured? It is possible that the proposed solution can be implemented in different ways, as different configurations. That is: different types of coupling may be possible.

3.3.   Supplement your analysis
Consider including inspirational examples from your industry or from other industries on the Circularity Grid to sense-check your analysis. Think also of new and possibly disruptive technologies and consider how they might change the relationships for organising flows.

STEP 04 – Review your organisation's position in the system
Review your organisation's position in the system, select what circular strategies are suitable from this perspective and decide on an action plan.

4.1.   Consider your organisation's sphere of influence
Who has control over which parts of the system? Where can your organisation exert direct influence, where moderate influence and where none at all? On the worksheet, circle the parts that are within the focal organisation's 'sphere of influence'.

4.2.   Consider value, enablers and coupling
Where are the major opportunities for value creation in relation to your sphere of influence? This is a combination of the value potential uncovered, how difficult barriers are to address, where enablers are placed in relation to your sphere of influence, what relationships are required with which other partners and whether the interests of actors/ stakeholders are aligned or opposed.

4.3.   Select (a) promising option(s)
Do any of the options, separately or in (a) set(s) appear more attractive than others as a result of these considerations? Why?

4.4.   Is a change in product design required?
Does the selected (set of) options(s) require a change in material selection and/or product design? If so, what other parts of your value chain are involved in implementing them?

4.5.   Is business model change required?
Does the selected (set of) option(s) require a change in your business model? Or will additions/amendments suffice? Are other parts of your value chain involved in implementing them? Distinguish between short-, medium- and long-term options.

Workshops are available on request. Particles (materials), parts (components) or products (finished goods) are, for simplicity, referred to as 'the product'.

Figure 13.4 (Continued)

Worksheet Circularity Compass with Example

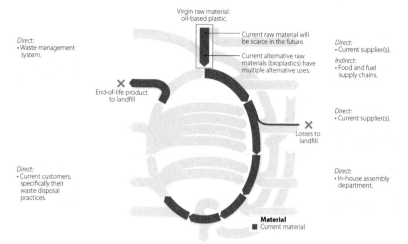

Business-as-usual - The situation to move away from.

*In example: significant losses appear in the second stage of manufacturing, which are landfilled.
Also: at the end-of-life the product is landfilled, due to the failure of specific parts. Additional drivers for innovation: the current material (oil) is predicted to be scare in the future, and current alternatives (bioplastics) have other uses as food and/ or fuel.*

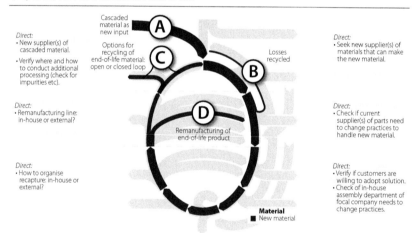

Proposed solution - The desirable situation to be created.

In example: material is changed to a geopolymer, made from waste from the mining industry. This allows for closed-loop recycling of the losses, as well as closed-loop recycling of the recaptured end-of-life product due to the chemical properties of material. Furthermore, through modularisation, part of the product can be remanufactured and reused.

Figure 13.5 Worksheet Circularity Compass with example

Simplified hypothetical case to illustrate the use of the Circularity Compass as a mapping tool. Depicted is a mapping after having conducted Steps 01 and 02. NB: One loop depicted only.

of coupling and put them on the Circularity Grid to kick off the conversation about system relationships.

CONCLUSION

Applying Circularity Thinking will provide you with a better understanding of what circular strategies to pursue and why. You will have collected the necessary information to inform decision-making as well as clarified the remaining questions regarding what changes to your product design, business model and value chain may be required. For the remaining questions, consider using one of the available tools which enable addressing specific areas in-depth, such as the Ecodesign Guide (McAloone and Bey, 2014) for product design; the Business Model Canvas (Osterwalder and Pigneur, 2010) for business model (re)design; and the Relational Capital Tool (Brennan, 2016) for leveraging your organisation's value chain position.

While CE is an intuitive concept, complexity quickly emerges when seeking to assess the different solution spaces it encompasses. Circularity Thinking offers a structured way to navigate this complexity and focus your circularity efforts. Ready, set . . . circularize!

NOTES

1 The combination of end-of-use/life is used here to indicate both strategies that relate to material revalorisation such as recycling and energy recapture traditionally designated as 'end-of-life' strategies, as well as the emergence concept of 'end-of-use' which encompasses product-oriented strategies such as reuse, redistribution, reconditioning, etc.
2 Note that this state can be present or absent both in the manufacturing and end-of-life treatment stage, depending on product design.
3 Here, we use recycling in the sense of 'upcycling' (Braungart & McDonough 2002, McDonough and Braungart 2013) or 'level-cycling' (Correia et al., 2015), or as close as this can be approached in reality. This deliberately does not include 'downcycling', which – in our view – represents a cascade, which is resource life-extension, but not 'true' recycling.

BIBLIOGRAPHY

Baumann, H. (2004). Environmental assessment of organising: Towards a framework for the study of organisational influence on environmental performance. *Progress in Industrial Ecology: An International Journal* 1(1/2/3): 292.

Baumann, H. (2012). Using the life cycle approach for structuring organizational studies of product chains. *18th Greening of Industry Network Conference*, Linköping.

Blomsma, F. (2016). *Making Sense of Circular Economy: How Practitioners Interpret and Use the Idea of Resource Life-Extension*. London: Imperial College.

Blomsma, F. and Brennan, G. (2017). The emergence of circular economy: A new framing around prolonging resource productivity. *Journal of Industrial Ecology* 21(3): 603–614.

Boons, F. (1998). Caught in the web: the dual nature of networks and its consequences. *Business Stratetgy & Environment* 7(4): 2014–2012.

Boons, F. and Howard-Grenville, J. (2009). *The Social Embeddedness of Industrial Ecology*. Cheltenham: Edward Elgar Publishing Ltd.

Braungart, M. and McDonough, W. (2002). *Cradle to Cradle: Remaking the Way We Make Things* 1st ed. New York: North Point Press.

Brennan, G. (2015). *Exploring the Impact of Power Dynamics on Sustainable Value Creation in a Business Ecosystem*. London, UK: Imperial College.

Brennan, G. (2016). *Workshop exploring Resources, Power and Value Creation in the Context of the Circular Economy*.

Correia, A.G. et al. (2015). A review of sustainable approaches in transport infrastructure geotechnics. *Transportation Geotechnics* (7): 21–28.

e-Bay. (2017). *Patagonia: Clothing, Shoes & Accessories* [Online]. Available at: http://www.ebay.com/bhp/patagonia [Accessed 11 August 2017].

ENDS – Environmental Data Services. (1992). *Report 214: Scott Ltd Cleans up Paper Chain*. London, UK.

Hoffman, A.J. (2003). Linking social systems analysis to the industrial ecology framework. *Organization & Environment* 16(1): 66–86.

Interface (2017). *The ReEntry^{TM} Carpet Recycling Program* [Online]. Available at: www.interface.com/APAC/en-AU/about/mission/ReEntry-en_ AU [Accessed 11 August 2017].

McAloone, T. and Bey, N. (2014). *Environmental Improvement Through Product Development: A Guide*. Lyngby: Technical University of Denmark.

McDonough, W. and Braungart, M. (2013). *The Upcycle: Beyond Sustainability - Designing for Abundance*. New York, NY: Charles Melcher.

Meadows, D.H. (2008). *Thinking in Systems: A Primer* (D. Wright, ed.). White River Junction, VT: Chelsea Green Publishing.

O'Brien, M. (2008). *A Crisis of Waste? Understanding the Rubbish Society*. New York, OX: Routledge – Taylor & Francis Group.

Osterwalder, A. and Pigneur, Y. (2010). *Business Model Generation: A Handbook for Visionaries, Game Changers, and Challengers*. Hoboken, NJ: John Wiley & Sons Inc.

Teijin. (2017). *Eco Circle^{TM}* [Online]. Available at: http://www2.teijin-frontier.com/english/sozai/specifics/eco-circle.html [Accessed 11 August 2017].

Von Bertalanffy, L. (1969). *General System Theory: Foundations, Development, Applications* (Revised). New York: George Braziller, Inc.

Weick, K. (1982). Management of organisational change among loosely coupled elements. In: *Change in Organisations: New Perspectives on Theory, Research and Practice* (P.S. Goodman, ed.). San Francisco: Jossey-Bass Publishers, pp. 375–408.

14 Design for product integrity in a Circular Economy

*Conny Bakker, Ruud Balkenende
and Flora Poppelaars*

INTRODUCTION

In the past century, global materials use per capita doubled from 4.6 to 10.3 tonne per annum, and currently seems to continue growing (Krausmann et al., 2009). This puts substantial pressure on global ecosystems, and has been one of the factors contributing to the popularisation of the concept of the Circular Economy (CE): a production-consumption system that uses cyclical material flows and renewable energy to limit resource throughput to a level that nature tolerates (Korhonen et al., 2018). The CE concept recognizes the importance of the raw material value that is lost and the environmental damage that is imposed when products are manufactured from extracted materials, used and then disposed of in a single cycle. The Circular Economy's goal is thus to preserve as much of the economic and environmental value of products and materials as possible by 'looping' them back in the economy and prolonging their useful lives.

This specific focus on high-value and high-quality product and material cycles sets the CE apart from other contributions to sustainability science (Korhonen et al., 2018). Exploiting the 'inner loops' of the CE creates an economic and environmental opportunity because the tighter the circle, i.e. the less a product has to be changed in reuse, refurbishment and remanufacturing, the higher the potential savings on the shares of material, labour, energy and capital embedded in the product. In other words, in a CE, a product should remain as much as possible identical to its original state, over time (Den Hollander et al., 2017). The extent to which a product remains identical is called 'product integrity'. The idea of product integrity originates from Stahel (2010), who postulated the Inertia Principle: 'Do not repair what is not broken, do not remanufacture something that can be repaired, do not recycle a product that can be remanufactured. Replace or treat only the smallest possible part in order to maintain the existing economic value of the technical system' (Stahel, 2010, p. 195).

Exploiting the 'inner loops' is however also a complex challenge. While in theory the benefits of the Inertia Principle and product integrity may seem logical and rather straightforward, in practice there are very different ideas of how product integrity in a Circular Economy can or should be realised. The goal of this chapter is to explore how the different conceptualisations of product integrity in a CE influence the design of products. Our approach is to take stock of how representatives from academia, industry and the policy arena are, often implicitly, promoting very different concepts of product integrity in a CE. An inventory of the principle stands in these debates through an analysis of the literature shows that there are currently two dominant and almost opposing concepts, which we have named the 'open-loop, open-source' concept and the 'closed-loop, closed-source' concept. Comparing the underlying philosophies, it becomes clear that these concepts vary widely in the extent of product transparency they propose, the responsibility for creating cyclical product and material flows, and the view of what constitutes a 'good' or a 'bad' circular product. These issues are however very relevant regarding the realisation of a CE and the provision of guidelines for circular product design.

The design strategies for product integrity are described first. The aim is to provide context for the next section where we explore the 'open' and 'closed' concepts.

DESIGN FOR PRODUCT INTEGRITY

Following the Inertia Principle, in an ideal circular world, products would stay 'whole' for as long as possible, after which they would loop through a number of consecutive use cycles. Design approaches for product integrity can be ordered according to the hierarchy imposed by the Inertia Principle. Table 14.1 gives an overview, with product integrity decreasing from left to right.

Products with a high physical and emotional durability that are intended to be used for a long time operate at a high level of product

Table 14.1 Design approaches for product integrity.

Design for Product Integrity		
Design Approaches for Long Use	*Design Approaches for Extended Use*	*Design Approaches for Recovery*
Design for Physical Durability	Design for Maintenance and Repair	Design for Recontextualising
Design for Emotional Durability	Design for Upgrading	Design for Refurbishment
		Design for Remanufacture
		Design for Recycling

Source: Adapted from Den Hollander et al. (2017).

integrity. In order to extend product use, designers can create products that are easy to maintain and/or upgrade. While maintenance is done to *retain* a product's functional capabilities and/or cosmetic condition, repair is done to *restore*, and 'upgrading' to *enhance* a product's functional capabilities and/or cosmetic condition. Product recovery takes place after a use cycle and is done to restore product integrity and ready the product for the next use cycle. To enhance the product's recovery potential, designers can create products that are easy to re-use in a different context ('recontextualise') (Den Hollander et al., 2017). Refurbishment and remanufacture are differentiated according to the quality of the recovered product relative to the original. In the case of remanufacturing, the product gets an extensive overhaul and is brought back to at least original equipment manufacturer (OEM) specification. In the case of refurbishing, the process is less comprehensive and the condition of the refurbished product may be inferior to the original specification (Gray and Charter, 2007). Design for recycling, finally, destroys product integrity and is aimed at recovering of a product's materials and their value.

Developing durable products with high levels of product integrity is not enough to achieve a CE. In conjunction, systems need to be in place that allow products to be returned (so that they can be repaired, refurbished, etc.). Current return systems have varying levels of sophistication. They can range from curb-side collection of (sorted) household waste to voluntary returns, and from incentive schemes for product return (like deposit systems, discounts on new purchases, buy-back programmes, etc.) to sophisticated rental, lease, and pay-per-use models.

PRODUCT INTEGRITY IN A CIRCULAR ECONOMY: TWO DOMINANT CONCEPTS

The following sections explore the concepts in more detail. The review is organized around four aspects, related to Table 14.1:

- Ways to prolong and extend the use of a product
- Ways to recover products
- Associated opportunities and threats
- Implications for design

Concept 1. Open-loop, open-source

The open-loop/open-source scenario is based on the premise that consumers want or need to be active participants in the creation of a CE. This concept has gained popularity since the rise of repair cafés, maker-spaces, sharing platforms and digital manufacturing, promoting alternative forms of consumption empowered by new technology.

Extending product use in the open-loop, open-source scenario

Following from the premise that consumers are active participants, the responsibility for care, maintenance, upgrade and repair rests with consumers and a wide network of, often informal, third parties. It is argued that for consumers to exercise this responsibility, they need to be empowered, for instance by enabling them to repair products themselves. The process of empowerment takes place through various stakeholders and mechanisms, including new businesses (i.e. repair platforms), grassroots initiatives (i.e. makerspaces, repair cafés), and regulation (i.e. product lifetime labelling, 'right to repair' legislation, laws against planned obsolescence). All seem to come together to create a powerful discourse: the best way to stimulate product integrity in a CE is to create an open, transparent production system with full product disclosure and with savvy consumers that are empowered to optimally exploit the value of the products they own.

Product recovery

The focus in this concept is on creating opportunities for products to last longer, and to have multiple use cycles, without pre-determining *how* this can or should be done. The philosophy behind open access to product information is that the market will take the opportunity to exploit products' residual values, which will stimulate innovation. There is, however, very little attention to what happens at a product's end of life. In the open-loop, open-source concept, the responsibility for a product's end of life lies with society, through collective systems for recovery. It is an open-ended concept: recovered products and recycled materials become available for the general market.

Opportunities and threats

The literature review reveals a number of positives and negatives of the 'open-loop, open-source' concept. The opportunities include:

- Consumer empowerment can bring back an appreciation of the 'materiality of consumption'. As consumers become more engaged with their products through conscious upgrading and repair, the likelihood increases that they become more attached to their products (Mugge et al., 2005).
- The problem of information asymmetry can be addressed; this is a situation in which the manufacturer knows far more about the product than the consumer. If consumers have better information, for instance regarding expected product lifetimes, availability of spare parts, repair information, etc., it is believed they can make better buying decisions.
- The 'open-loop, open-source' concept stimulates entrepreneurship. Companies can create revenue from exploiting product lifetime value gaps. Examples are repair businesses, vintage stores, businesses that service sharing platforms and businesses that refurbish used products. Also, consumers-as-entrepreneurs are enabled and stimulated to exploit their own(ed) assets.

There are also negative points that potentially undermine the concept:

- By offering consumers high levels of control over product lives, and therefore shifting the responsibility for product life extension, repairs, etc. to consumers and other third parties, original equipment manufacturers (OEMS) and product developers may be side-stepping responsibilities for providing high-quality, reliable and sustainable products. In the literature, this is described as 'transferring risks to consumers' (Martin, 2016).
- The 'open' concept may put too much expectation on consumers to shift the production-consumption system towards a more CE. As Akenji (2014) argues, there are limits to 'green consumerism as a driver of sustainability' (p 22), and not recognizing these limits is at best naïve and at worst 'consumer scapegoatism': a situation where the most visible actor (the consumer) is targeted, instead of the most influential one.

- Although there are many ways in which the 'open' concept can contribute to sustainability and a CE, this is not a given. Companies can exploit 'open' products for commercial gain without concerning themselves with environmental issues. For instance, upgradability of modular products may lower the threshold for excessive new module production and acquisition.

Implications for design

The role of design is to enable consumers, through the product's design, to be active agents in product life extension; for instance through designing for ease of maintenance and (self)repair, upgrading, etc. Modular design is considered one of the main characteristics of 'open' products, although modularity becomes increasingly more challenging as the complexity of the product increases. Given the open-endedness of the concept, in addition to design for repair and refurbishment, design for recycling will be crucial to prevent unnecessary losses at a product's end of life.

Concept 2. Closed-loop, closed-source

The closed-loop/closed-source concept is based on the premise that OEMs, and not consumers, are the most salient agents in a circular pro-duction-consumption system. It is therefore the responsibility of OEMs to shape a CE and to provide consumers with a comfortable, seamless (and circular) product experience.

Extending product use in the closed-loop, closed-source scenario

In the 'closed' concept, the responsibility for maintenance, upgrade and repair rests predominantly with the OEMs in both B2B and B2C markets. This can be achieved through the introduction of innovative consumption models such as lease and pay-per-use, where consumers no longer are the legal *owners*, but instead are given *access* to products for a predefined period in exchange for a periodical fee. This means that products, throughout their lives, are legally owned by the OEMs or by associated service providers, who then have an interest in making sure products are robust and easy to service. Maintenance and repair is organised through OEM-owned or OEM-authorized services. Expecta-tions of normal care for products given in access need to be managed, for instance through contracts that demand that customers exercise proper care. It follows that OEMs have no incentive to give consumers the possibility for self-repair or to allow non-authorized repair or refur-bishment. On the contrary, their business success relies on the ability to give consumers access to products of a consistent quality, reliability and durability. Allowing any kind of 'tinkering' with their products would make it harder for OEMs to guarantee quality. This is why this scenario is called 'closed-source'.

Product recovery

The philosophy behind the 'closed' concept is that OEMs, being the legal owners of their products, will take the opportunity to exploit the residual values of a product and ensure multiple product use cycles and eventually material recovery. They can do this through refurbishment or remanufacturing, but in order for this to be successful, OEMs need to be able to control the timing, quality and quantity of the product return flows, which will require extensive reverse supply chain coordination. The 'closed' scenario ensures that products are accounted for at all times, and that at the end of a product's life, the materials can be recycled in a closed-loop system.

Opportunities and threats

Opportunities of the closed-loop, closed-source concept include:

- The responsibility for closing loops is in the hands of the actor most capable of delivering: the OEM. From an environmental perspective, this opens up the possibility for optimized closed-loop systems using advanced technology. It doesn't put the onus on the consumer to take charge of the problem (Akenji, 2014).
- The 'closed' concept will create new jobs in the service industry to educate, assist and encourage consumers to accept 'access' models. In spite of OEMs taking the lead, the concept still relies heavily on the cooperation of consumers, which means that transparency and excellent service are needed to allay consumer mistrust (Poppelaars et al., 2016).

Several critiques of the 'closed' concept:

- In a B2C context, the concept denies consumers the possibility to own products, or to 'tinker' with their products, or generally to compromise product integrity. This will result in a different relationship with products. The question is whether this changing relationship will affect the level of product attachment and people's willingness to care for and maintain the products.
- Equity and exclusivity are points of critique as well. The owner of an asset (in this case the OEM) could potentially limit or deny access, for instance to specific groups of consumers.

Implications for design

For product designers, the 'closed' concept implies that processes that used to be far removed from the designer's table, such as remanufacturing and its associated business models, now need to become an integral part of the design process, starting at the product strategy level. It also implies that designers need to take a product's entire lifetime into account, and they need to design for the many potential use cycles the product will go through in its life. This creates a huge challenge for product design because it requires that designers anticipate future use cycles and create flexible, adaptable and compatible products, with a carefully managed level of 'openness'.

DISCUSSION AND CONCLUSION

Our review shows that there are different ways of conceptualising product integrity in a CE, and the roles of consumers and producers therein. These lead to different approaches to product design. Considering the 'closed-loop, closed-source' concept, this requires product designers to plan and design for a product's entire lifetime, with the product repeatedly cycling through the CE in different states of integrity. The challenge for designers is to create robust products with extensive adaptive possibilities that also can be refurbished or remanufactured, whilst at the same time limiting 'tinkering' through self-repair or unauthorized repair. Considering the open-loop, open-source concept, where product integrity is seen as a collective responsibility involving consumers as main agents, product designers have to prioritize repairability and upgradeability, which is often done through modular designs. Designers should, in principle, ensure that full access to products' insides is possible, without compromising their reliability and durability.

Although at casual glance, the design strategies used may seem alike (both concepts, for instance, value product durability, adaptability and upgradeability), these strategies are used in distinctly different ways, and with very different aims. Designers therefore need to be keenly aware of the Circular Economy context for which they are designing.

The two concepts were deliberately described as opposite ends of a continuum in which product integrity can take shape. There will of course be all kinds of variations, leading to a nuanced spectrum of product integrity highly dependent on the kind of product and business under consideration. The authors hope that this short review provides a basis for further empirical research which critically analyses the nature and impacts of product integrity in a CE in its many and varied forms.

BIBLIOGRAPHY

Akenji, L. (2014). Consumer scapegoatism and limits to green consumerism. *Journal of Cleaner Production* 63: 13–23.

Den Hollander, M.C., Bakker, C.A., and Hultink, H.J. (2017). Product design in a circular economy: Development of a typology of key concepts and terms. *Journal of Industrial Ecology* 21(3): 517–525.

Gray, C. and Charter, M. (2007). *Remanufacturing and Product Design: Design for the 7th Generation.* A report by The Centre for Sustainable Design ®, Farnham, UK.

Korhonen, J., Honkasalo, A., and Seppälä, J. (2018). Circular economy: The concept and its limitations. *Ecological Economics* 143: 37–46.

Krausmann, F., Gingrich, S., Eisenmenger, N., Erb, K.-H., Haberl, H., and Fischer-Kowalski, M. (2009). Growth in global materials use, GDP and population during the 20th century. *Ecological Economics* 68(10): 2696–2705.

Martin, C.J. (2016). The sharing economy: A pathway to sustainability or a nightmarish form of neoliberal capitalism? *Ecological Economics* 121(C): 149–159.

Mugge, R., Schoormans, J.P.L., and Schifferstein, H.N.J. (2005). Design strategies to postpone consumers' product replacement: The value of a strong person-product relationship. *The Design Journal* 8(2): 38–48.

Poppelaars, F.A., Bakker, C.A., and van Engelen, M.L. (2016). The (il)logic of ownership: Exploring alternative commercial offers for mobile devices. *Proceedings of Electronics Goes Green 2016*, 7–9 September, Berlin, Germany. Published by Fraunhofer IZM and Technische Universität Berlin.

Stahel, W.R. (2010). *The Performance Economy* (2nd edition). London, UK: Palgrave Macmillan.

15 Thinking life cycle in a Circular Economy

Louis Brimacombe

INTRODUCTION: UNDERSTANDING THE DRIVERS FOR A CIRCULAR ECONOMY

On the face of it, the CE is a noble concept. The aim is to consume fewer raw materials and to generate less waste than we do currently, set against a background that society will increasingly demand more materials and more products, particularly as the developing world aspires to make quality-of-life improvements. In this context, the notions of reusing, repairing, refurbishment, recycling or, even better, the development of a sharing society, seem attractive.

The implication is by designing products that are reusable, repairable, refurbishable and recyclable that we will avoid or reduce the need for virgin raw materials. However, in the development of new strategies it will become increasingly important to fully understand the wider implications of implementation. For example, when specifying a new material or product redesign, or the development of a new business model which might aim to improve one aspect of environmental or energy performance, it is important that the designer takes a life-cycle approach to assess other potential consequences and trade-offs.

LINKS TO PRODUCT DESIGN AND DEVELOPMENT

As we aspire to develop the CE, there is a need to realise how a new product design or a new business model can contribute towards 'circularity'. At the simplest level, the aim is to reduce (or avoid) raw material inputs and generate less waste – but without a clear understanding of a product's life cycle, and a comprehension of the environmental impacts in each life cycle stage, this aspiration could lead the designer to make ill-informed choices and perhaps over simplify potential solutions.

For example, the term 'less waste' could be rather complex to determine and will depend upon what is defined, or included, as waste. Noteably, CO_2 (carbon dioxide) is a waste gas from combustion of fossil fuels: should this be included as a waste ? We know that CO_2 in the atmosphere is contributing to global warming and also to ocean acidification, so should the amount of saved CO_2 by a new, more energy-efficient, product redesign be regarded as contributing to CE? This is important because there may be a dilemma faced by designers between products that are more energy-efficient and those that can be re-used, repaired or recycled.

This is illustrated in aircraft design which has moved towards the use of composite plastics to enable light-weighting of the fuselage over the last 50 years. This has helped to improve the fuel efficiency of air travel and so has reduced CO_2 emissions over the lifetime of an aircraft, but compared with the previous generation of fuselage materials (typically aluminium, which is recycleable) composite materials are much more difficult to recycle. Hence, there is a potential end-of-life recycleability and/or waste problem.

So in terms of the CE, was the selection of composites the right choice? In terms of avoided CO_2 emissions over the lifetime of the aircraft, the answer is (almost certainly) yes. Even with the end-of-life of 'solid waste' issue, the designer should acknowledge that the production of aerospace grade fossil fuels will produce some solid waste. So over the lifetime of the aircraft and with the improved fuel efficiency, this may result in higher levels of avoided waste than the mass of waste associated with the end-of-life composite aircraft fuselage. Similarly, there will be the avoided wastes of aluminium production compared to that from producing composite plastic.

This type of analysis is termed Life Cycle Thinking (LCT) and the numerical analysis and evaluation of the systems is termed Life Cycle Assessment (LCA) (ISO 14044:2006). Hitherto, CE ambassadors have tended to distance themselves from advocating LCA because of its potential complexity, both from a data and methodological perspective, but without it's use unintended consequences, which may be contrary to the initial aims of the design, may result. Using LCT, or taking 'a life cycle approach' to design however, although less exacting than LCA, will be a necessary requirement in the skill sets of CE designers. It will become more critical for the designer to set out to clarify and understand the actual aims and potential consequences, both direct and indirect, of the new design or a new business model and take this into account in the assessment of the overall benefits.

FUNCTIONALITY AND SOCIAL VALUE

Of course, the first aim of any product design is to deliver the expected functionality or to meet a product specification, i.e. making sure that it works as intended. This is where the concept of 'social value' (SV) of a product needs to be embraced, since this adds a further dimension to the term 'functionality'. In other words, a starting question is how well does the product deliver this functionality? SV is a collective term to evaluate or asses the relative experience of individuals or societal groups with respect to a range of parameters which can affect quality of life, both positive and negative, associated with circumstantial, systematic or existential change. This might include, for example, comparing one product with another in terms of visual appearance, tactility, safety, convenience, ease of use, noise levels and so on. But a critical consideration – from a CE perspective – is the durability and resilience of the product to continue to deliver a high level of SV for the longest duration. In the case of fast emerging product technology, the SV of the next generation of products tends to be higher so the current models become less desirable or obsolete. At this stage, users then tend to discard, recycle or of throw away the product with lower (outdated) SV. Technology companies have been criticised for designing-in built-in obsolescence and/or deliberately making updates and/or repairs difficult. In the CE, this approach will need to change and new business models will need to develop that can achieve viabilty but with extended product life spans and retained SV, thereby respecting that Earth's resources have been invested in the materials and products that they sell.

So in the CE, products will have to be more robust and have longer-lasting SV and therefore these considerations will need to be embedded in the design. Products should not only last longer but also be efficient in the delivery of SV (i.e., be energy-efficient, lightweight and reliable). Further, the designer should consider how at the end-of-life of the product, the SV can be carried forward in some way, through reuse, repair, refurbishment or recycling, thereby utilising the investment made in generating the materials embedded in the original product. Business models which provide services rather than selling products may be more capable of delivering this kind of long lasting SV. This is in part because the product life cycle can be integrated into the scope of the business and so incentivise greater attention to the efficiency of product/service performance across the life cycle, including, for example, the design of more durable and remanufacturable products.

REUSE, REPAIR, REFURBISHMENT, RECYCLING VERSUS MATERIALS AND ENERGY EFFICIENCY

There are good examples of where design can help to enable retained future value of materials; for example, by enabling components and/or materials to be easily separated for future reuse or recycling. Take, for example, a steel frame of a building, mainly composed of steel section beams (usually with the cross sectional shape of an H or an I) with the function of providing structural support for floors, external cladding or roof structures. Early designs may have included welded joints or rivets in the assembly of the total structure. This would mean that reusability of the beams was limited, since at the end-of- (building) life, although the steel could be recovered and recycled by melting the scrap to make new steel, the option of reusing the structural beams would have meant cutting and separating the structural components, with some material losses. Today's design would include the bolting of joints which would ease the separation and retaining the original integrity (and shape) of the whole beam, potentially for future reuse in another building. In this case, bolted joints rather than welds have improved the potential to retain the SV of the product.

Whilst the above is a simple example where the benefits may be obvious, in many cases the designers can be faced with decisions which on the face of it appear to be sound but which in fact can lead to unintended consequences. For example, to make products more robust with an extended service life or to improve the potential for future reuse, this may require more energy or more intensive processing of the original product. In some cases, the light weighting of products may result in the use of higher embodied energy materials, so there is a need to understand whether selecting this material is worthwhile across the whole life cycle of the product, including the end-of-life potential for reuse, recovery, refurbishment and recycling.

Another dilemma is that designing and building for product longevity may compromise on potential future recyclability. An example is the galvanising of steel products (zinc coatings) which will improve the corrosion resistance of the steel product and help to maintain the SV of the products (surface finish appearance, structural integrity) for extended periods without the need for repainting and repairs. Yet galvanising will add embodied energy to the original product and will make the end-of-life recycling more complex (the zinc, as well as the steel, will need to be recovered in the recycling process).

LIFE CYCLE THINKING (LCT) AND LIFE CYCLE ASSESSMENT (LCA)

As described in the section above, it is recommended that all new developments and endeavours towards the CE should be assessed upon a life cycle basis. The main reason for this is that with all good intentions there are occasions when new developments in design, manufacturing or product development can lead to unintended consequences. There is a need to consider how material selection and product design should embrace not only the end-of-life scenarios, where higher levels of recycling may be desirable, but all aspects of environmental, social and economic impacts across the life cycle. These should be assessed collectively to help make informed and soundly-based decisions on the preferred options.

The two challenges in this approach are data availability and deciding on the most appropriate and fair methodology which reflects the most likely consequences of a decision. Several methods have been proposed, and standards and guidance exist, but the range of options can be confusing and sometimes these have been driven by political or market preferences.

Clearly the concept of the CE needs to embrace LCT for it to be effective in delivering real improvements. Ultimately, we are trying to make things better not worse, so we should at least use a life cycle approach to understand the wider consequences of our decision making (BS8905 Framework for the Assessment of the Sustainable Use of Materials).

One of the key aspects which is fairly new in the field of LCT and which needs to be better understood is the concept of SV (of a product), as described above. A poorly designed product, which does not deliver the necessary positive SV will most likely fail and be replaced or disposed of before the value of the investment of raw materials is fully utilised. This is discussed further in the section below.

BALANCING THE QUALITATIVE AND QUANTITATIVE IN DELIVERING PRODUCT SOCIAL VALUE (SV) FOR A CE

As described earlier, products and services are designed to, or set out to, deliver a societal benefit or to add SV in some form. Whilst this may be patently obvious to designers, engineers, as well as consumers (this is the reason why consumers buy things), the understanding of SV assessments in sustainability and LCT has become something of a stumbling block. This is because the life cycle practitioner, in doing LCA, strives for quantitative results which can be interrogated to support decision making. Whereas at the core of SV assessment, there is a need to understand the influence of inevitably qualitative parameters which can affect preferences and choices, although some elements can be quantified. Whilst scientists will always be strong advocates of the numeracy of LCA we should not underestimate the value of the qualitative elements of circularity. Instead, these should be rationalised, explained and embraced as a necessary component of circularity and should be presented in combination with the quantitative aspects as a part of sustainable design.

An example of where SV considerations become important in product selection is in the development of energy-efficient lighting. The early designs of low-energy light bulbs struggled to provide sufficient light to be fit for purpose or perhaps took a long time to deliver adequate levels of light. Either way, the SV (to provide sufficient light to, say, read a book) was compromised and the consequence of that was that the bulbs were either replaced with less efficient ones that worked and then were discarded as waste. In CE terms, the early low-energy light bulbs did not save energy and potentially created more waste. In other words, the failure to deliver SV probably resulted in greater overall environmental impacts because the manufacturing impacts of the low-energy bulbs was not offset by the potential energy saving benefits of the use phase.

Of course, the last two decades has seen the emergence of fantastic innovations like LED lighting technology, which has enabled low-energy lighting with adequate light levels to become a reality; also Philips have started to sell the product-service function of 'light' rather than lighting products. There is additional SV from the long life of LEDs which require fewer bulb replacements within the lifetime of an installation and so are more convenient. In CE terms, these are low-energy, long-life, provide adequate light and require less maintenance than conventional bulbs.

SV IN A LIFE CYCLE CONTEXT

It is also important to consider SV in a broader life cycle context, so as with the example described above which concentrated on the SV aspects of the use phase (i.e. providing sufficient light) it is also necessary to consider the SV of the supply chain (for example through the responsible sourcing of materials) and the SV associated with end-of-life. Figure 15.1 (Brimacombe, 'Thinking Life Cycle in a Circular Economy', EMECR2017) is an illustration of how SV and LCT can be represented. The first column is about the provenance or sourcing of a product (or material) where the integrity of the supply chain can be verified, perhaps by attaining recognised responsible sourcing certifications such as the BES 6001 for construction products (BES 6001). The second column represents the use phase aspects of the SV attributes, many of which may be qualitative or may be prioritised by the user to assist with quantification. (For example, how important is it for the product to be visually appealing to users or to society?) The third column represents the time that the SV can be retained; this is not just a consideration of the end-of-life recycling. The designer should be considering how the SV can be retained by durability and/or technology future proofing, etc., as well as through repair, reuse, refurbishment and recycling.

Inevitably, the most sustainable designs (that incorporate circularity) are those which provide highest levels of SV for the longest duration across the whole product life cycle.

To summarise, the delivery of SV, although difficult to quantify, is perhaps the most important aspect of truly sustainable design – and within that CE design – and should be the pre-requisite of all sustainable decision making.

THE CHALLENGE TO BALANCE DURABILITY WITH AFFORDABILITY AND RECYCLEABILITY

Having set out that delivering (and maximising) SV is a prerequisite to CE design, the challenge for achieving circularity is to maintain this SV for the longest period possible with the least resource-intensive means. So a first obvious step is to design and build robust and resilient products that will enable SV to be available to users for the maximum period of time. So let's consider an example of the engineering and construction of buildings and infrastructure in the context of circular design. A bridge structure delivers SV by enabling the connection of communities across some physical boundary thereby improving the economic viability of trade and labour, making tourism more convenient, improved access to hospitals, schools, etc. To achieve this, the designer and/or engineer sets out to build something that delivers this functionality safely and with improved SV. For example, he/she may strive to make the bridge as aesthetically pleasing as possible, even beautiful, although this

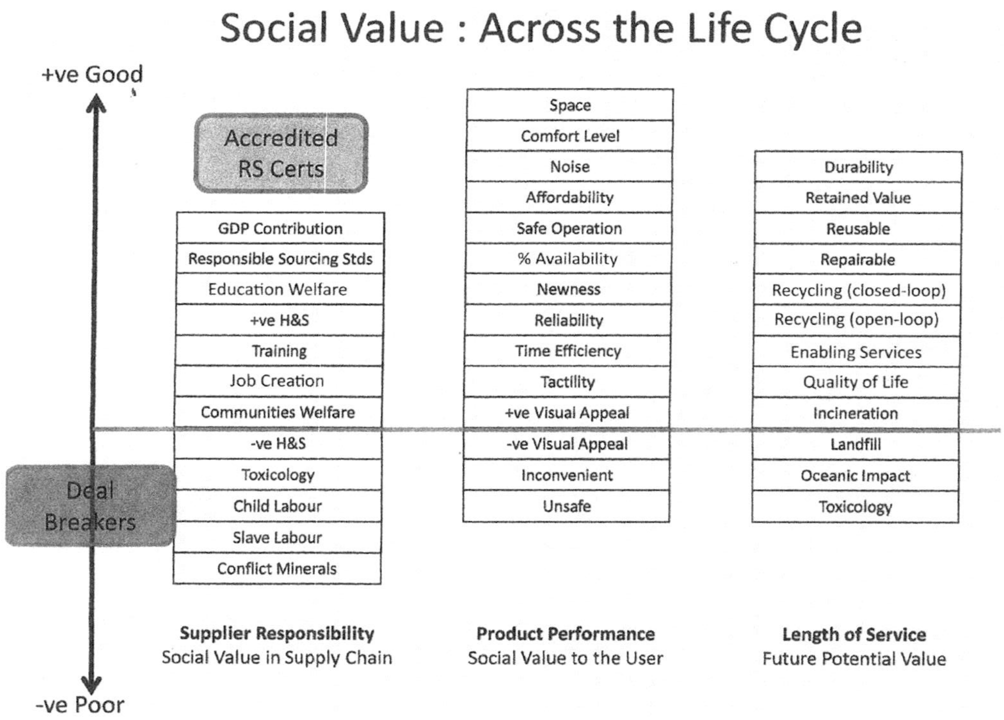

Social Value : Across the Life Cycle

Accredited RS Certs		Space		Durability
GDP Contribution		Comfort Level		Retained Value
Responsible Sourcing Stds		Noise		Reusable
Education Welfare		Affordability		Repairable
+ve H&S		Safe Operation		Recycling (closed-loop)
Training		% Availability		Recycling (open-loop)
Job Creation		Newness		Enabling Services
Communities Welfare		Reliability		Quality of Life
		Time Efficiency		Incineration
-ve H&S		Tactility		
Toxicology		+ve Visual Appeal		Landfill
Child Labour		-ve Visual Appeal		Oceanic Impact
Slave Labour		Inconvenient		Toxicology
Conflict Minerals		Unsafe		

Deal Breakers

+ve Good

-ve Poor

Supplier Responsibility
Social Value in Supply Chain

Product Performance
Social Value to the User

Length of Service
Future Potential Value

Figure 15.1 An illustration of product Social Value in a life cycle context

will be subjective. It may be possible to build something that meets the specification within the constraints of a budget but the next step (or the extra mile) to achieve circularity would be in identifying sustained performance for (perhaps) decades and by ensuring that the engineering is sound, long-lasting and that the bridge is future-proofed in terms of foreseeable technology development. The challenge then becomes one of increased initial costs. Will the increased upfront costs associated with in-built durability be recoverable or be made worthwhile by the extended economic service life or the reduced future maintenance costs? In these cases, short-term 'affordability' can become *the* barrier to CE (within the context of sustainability) even when the life cycle costs make it overall worthwhile.

THE NEED FOR NEW BUSINESS APPROACHES

The CE will require new approaches and a radical re-think of business and investment models. Traditional models aiming for 'increased revenues by selling more' will need to be replaced with a new mindset of 'added value, less consumption'. The learning point here is that 'added value' will need to be 'felt' by the consumer as well as by the businesses. Social Value (SV) of products and services will be a critical element of what is 'felt' and will be central to the success of CE approaches. This leads onto the challenge that as new business models might strive to make products more robust, more efficient and more repairable, it is more likely that there could be increased (and perhaps unaffordable) upfront costs to the user and/or consumer. One of the greatest barriers to establishing the CE is short-term affordability, or the initial cost investment; yet one of the greatest incentives is that the through-life-costs (or life cycle costs) may be much reduced by longer-lasting, more efficient and more available products. So new service business models which invest in the initial capital costs and/or recover these by spreading (and perhaps sharing) the costs to the customer by ongoing rental and revenue charges may be one solution. The challenge then becomes the set up of the right cost structures for the service and the inevitable increase in business risk as the return on the (higher initial) investment may be longer-term and less predictable. There is a role for policy makers and governments in incentivising these business models and supporting the demonstration of innovations in this field.

BIBLIOGRAPHY

BES 6001: The Framework Standard for the Responsible Sourcing of Construction Products

Brimacombe. 'Thinking Life Cycle in a Circular Economy' EMECR2017; 1st International Conference on Energy, Materials Efficiency and CO_2 Reduction in the Steel Industry, Kobe, 2017.

BS8905. Framework for the Assessment of the Sustainable Use of Materials. Guidance.

ISO 14044:2006. Environmental Management – Life Cycle Assessment – Requirements and Guidelines.

16 Design for Resource Value

Ab Stevels

INTRODUCTION

The current dominance of energy consumption in the use phase

EcoDesign of products started in the last decade of 1990s. Its aim was to minimise the environmental impact of products over the life cycle. For operational purposes, the activities under the EcoDesign umbrella were split into six focal areas: energy, materials application, packaging and transport, chemical content, reuse/recycling and life time extension. The first focal areas addressed were recycling and chemical content. Important drivers for doing so were scandals associated with waste and waste handling (landfill, incineration). Soon after, reduction of materials use in the design and production of artefacts came into the picture as well. For electronic products, energy consumed in the *use* phase took over as the number one priority by the turn of the century. This was due to – amongst other things – the breakthrough of new methods for environmental evaluation like Life Cycle Analysis (LCA). These were 'emission-based', so the design focal area of energy in *use* turned out to be dominating the life cycle phase. Moreover, LCA is based on science, which means that governmental policies (which are not necessarily science-based) and consumer preferences (which can be very subjective) are not well reflected. For EcoDesign in companies, this meant a balancing act: minimise the (science-based) environmental load, comply with the environmental legislation and make sure consumer emotions are turned to the positive as much as possible. For these reasons, EcoDesign in the first decade of this century became strongly oriented towards energy in the *use* phase.

The revival of attention on materials and resources

The price peak for raw materials was in 2007–2008, and supply restrictions for some critical materials and the notion of supply risks subsequently resulted in a revival of attention on resources and material application. As a result of this, the concept of 'Circular Economy' (CE) emerged covering a range of issues including longer life of products, reuse and recycling. This development means that EcoDesign now has to serve three goals: (1) Emission control: the chief focal area of EcoDesign here is energy consumption; (2) CE: the chief focal areas of EcoDesign here are materials application, reuse, life-time extension and recycling. (3) Control of (potential) toxics: the chief focal area of EcoDesign here is chemical content. This comparison makes clear that the priorities for design for the CE are different from design for emission control (DEC). Including design for the CE into the EcoDesign activities means that the design priorities will have to change. In order to establish this, new metrics have to be developed and applied. However, essentially the EcoDesign methodology as such does not have to be changed. In order to assess the impact of EcoDesign on society, one has to think more broadly than a focus on individual products. In order to determine the impact of design for CE, the impact per (CE-designed) product has to be multiplied by the total number of products produced and sold. As a result, the users/buyers (the 'demand side') come explicitly into the equation. This needs to be considered because in the end consumers ('the demand side') will determine – through their buying behaviour – the total resource consumption. Unfortunately, 'green', irrespective of whether it concerns resources or emissions, does not rank high in the considerations of many consumer segments. The idea that if such groups are 'educated' that this will move up the consumer's priorities has not happened in the last 25 years. A much better link to the demand side is 'value' for their money which consumers are keenly interested in. In section 2, consumer behaviour will be explored in more detail. In particular, how 'green' can contribute to enhancing functionality value will be highlighted. This also has links to economic value: higher perceived value means that, in general, higher prices will be paid. If so, the ratio between the price paid and environmental load increases and is best demonstrated in the category of premium products. Modern EcoDesign is therefore creating 'EcoValue' (EV) (see Stevels, 2007a) instead of just lowering environmental load over the life cycle. The EV concept is explained further in section 3. This concept is also is relevant for specific strategy of Design for Resource Value (DfRV). DfRV is a specific form of EcoDesign that focuses on the optimisation of resource use. In section 4, there will be a particular focus on the link between this resource productivity and value creation. The methodology to address this is identical to all other forms of EcoDesign that have a different focus (for instance, EcoDesign for legal compliance or EcoDesign for cost reduction). However, the metrics applied will be different as the priorities will be different. Companies have to make a choice as to the focus areas of their EcoDesign activities. This should tackle fundamental environmental considerations (such as emissions, resources and toxicity that may include difficult trade-offs) and external drivers (legislation and consumer demands). Finding the' best' compromise is even more complicated because there are technological and economic constraints to be considered as well.

CONSUMER BEHAVIOUR: THE DEMAND SIDE FOR DFRV OF CONSUMER PRODUCTS

Having a positive environmental image is a necessary but not a sufficient condition for selling products to individual customers (as their interest usually relates to personal benefits rather than to those of society in general). Although 70 to 80 percent of consumers in Western Europe say that they will buy 'green products' (even if these cost a little more), actual behaviour is different: only 25 to 30 percent show real interest (see Stevels, 2007b). Therefore, only a minority of potential consumers are exclusively interested in buying products that are presented as green. Other benefits have to be present in the value proposition to create interest for a broader group of consumers.

Having recognised this, a successful 'linked benefit' marketing and communication approach was developed at Philips Consumer Electronics (Stevels, 2007b). In this approach, environmental benefits for consumers themselves and for society were linked to other product benefits. Examples of such benefits for electronic products are: lower energy costs/lower watts, simple/easy to operate, quality feel/nice design but also fewer environmentally-relevant substances and higher recyclability. Through this, environmental performance became a supportive or an extra positive product attribute rather than a new item competing with the usual three chief consumer concerns: performance, price and quality. Further research indicated that consumers of electronic products were split broadly into three segments:

- Price buyers (approx. 1/3 of the total in Western Europe)
- Tech buyers (approx. 1/3 of the total in Western Europe)
- Quality buyers (approx. 1/3 of the total in Western Europe)

For products catering chiefly to the price buyers, the prime environmental primary concern was 'reduction' (of energy and/or material).
Resource reduction also appealed to this group, since it is perceived
that such a reduction will lead to lower prices. In line with this, repairability is likely to appeal to this segment. When the (mostly) cheap products in this category are discarded, design for material recycling is the
best DfRV strategy. For products catering to tech buyers, the emphasis should be 'green through technology' (latest components, miniaturisation, smart materials). In practice, the latest 'tech' in almost all
cases, uses fewer resources, although more sophisticated materials often
includes more use of scarce resources as well. Tech buyers will have a
tendency to discard products before they reach the end of their functional life. This is chiefly because before that moment, new products
often become available with new features and/or increased functionality ('sexier products') that can result in premature discarding of products. Design for reuse of such products (sold to price buyers) seems to
be the best strategy – in this category – to optimize resource value. For
the quality segment, the environmental element adds 'positive emotion'
(recyclability, less chemicals, less (packaging) waste). In this category,
there are generally plenty of opportunities to include resource reduction aspects in the value proposition. These generally have higher initial prices but in the end could have lower cost of ownership over the
life cycle. These include selling upgrades, remanufacturing and design
for longer life. In general, the business conclusion of this section is
that knowing the environmental attitudes of potential customers will
be helpful to define the best product offering; in the end, consumers
decide through their spending behavior what the total environmental
effect for society will be. Optimal results are obtained if the 'green perceptions' of the potential customers' can be matched with the 'green
ambitions of the company'. Just having the 'greenest' of products is not
a good strategy for a company wanting to cater to a broad public – it can
be a niche strategy only.

THE ECOVALUE CONCEPT

In section 2, EcoDesign has been positioned as a contributor to value
creation. Value relates specifically to the buying process and is therefore
oriented towards the demand side (the external value chain, in particular to the customer). In order to achieve this, it is also necessary to link
the supply side (the internal value chain) and the demand side. This is
particularly relevant for balancing the product portfolio offered to the

market with respect to the customer base. For this purpose the concept of EcoValue (EV) was developed at Philips Consumer Electronics. EV links environmental issues and money. It is the ratio between the price paid by the customer (or the life cycle costs of a product) and the environmental load of the product (for production or over the complete life cycle). High-scoring EVs compared to the competition means that relatively attractive prices can be obtained through high perceived functionality or through environmental loads being reduced (through good EcoDesign) A good design approach is therefore to increase the attractiveness of products, so that higher prices can be obtained whilst the environmental load is kept constant. A more extreme strategy could be to increase the attractiveness enormously so that a much higher price can be obtained allowing the environmental load to increase a little – in both cases, the environmental load per currency unit decreases, which is positive for the environment. This is not a theoretical construct; a company like Apple follows such a design strategy.

For an organisation wanting to cater to a broad public, this would imply that its product portfolio would have to be further tailored to target groups like quality buyers, see section 2. Apart from this perspective, EV creation strategies deserve attention for another environmental reason: the so-called rebound effect. Traditional EcoDesign generally results in cost reductions as well a reduction of environmental impact, e.g. less energy and less materials. This means that consumers with a constant income can basically buy more goods. Through this mechanism, part of the environmental gains for individual products are often lost through this negative rebound effect. However, products with a high functionality can command a higher price and have therefore a positive rebound effect.

DESIGN FOR RESOURCE VALUE (DFRV)

As discussed in section 3, the design procedure for DfRV is essentially identical to traditional EcoDesign. Although, 'design' is still at the core, DfRV pays a lot more attention to the upfront functionality analysis, because it is in this stage that a close link should be made to the requirements of the customer segment which is targeted (see section 3 above). The design procedure for DfRV is highlighted in the Figure 16.1.

Central to DfRV are the three steps in the middle: functionality analysis, design and design result. As will be discussed in section 5 below, the metrics to evaluate the design result are different. The upper and lower blocks are the 'supporting activities' for the design itself. For

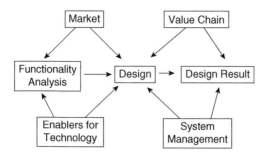

Figure 16.1 Procedure for Design for Resource Value

DfRV, these are very specific since they are focused on identifying and fulfilling the needs of specific consumer segments for which the DfRV activity is targeted. Among the activities at the bottom of Figure 16.1 are the identification of technologies (manufacturing, electronics, IT) which can effectively support specific DfRV strategies. In addition, the quality of sales and services strategy ('trade in', 'trade up', after sales services, refurbishment, remanufacturing, take-back and treatment) will determine the effectiveness of design for upgrading, reuse and/or recycling. Having insights into market trends (top of Figure 16.1) like, for instance, the size of the target consumer groups for products designed for Resource Value (RV) is a necessary condition for success. Also there is a need for the value chain – in a particular trade, e.g. retailers – to 'buy in' to the approach. The three general types of buyers (price, tech, quality) identified in section 2 should each be linked with specific retail sales channel. The appropriate choice of retail sales channels, e.g. discount stores, department stores, specialty stores, etc., will determine to a large extent whether products designed for RV achieve an optimal market reach.

METRICS FOR DESIGN FOR RESOURCE VALUE (DFRV)

Proper RV creation mean taking account of environmental issues (such as the environmental load associated with production), 'supply risk' and societal aspects (see Graedel et al., 2012). At the design (front end), supply risk include: a geological risk (risk of depletion) and a geopolitical risk (stability of supply countries) associated with access to materials. The potential 'supply risks' also include monopolisation by a few key suppliers. At the back end (discarded products), there are technological and regulatory risks. Moreover there is a 'treatment risk', e.g. products after use do not get collected in sufficient volumes and/or are treated inadequately to keep materials in the loop. Such 'risk' is associated with materials which occur in products in low amounts or in low concentrations. In this risk category there are also a lot of materials with high environmental and supply risks.

In order to allow the designer to take into account such resource aspects, it is proposed to develop a one-point score taking into account the aspects described above. This is a factor method approach which was popular in EcoDesign in the period before LCA was practiced more extensively [[Griese H-J et al, Kreislaufwirtschaft in der Elektronik Industrie, VDE-Verlag, 1997, ISBN 3-8007-2196-1]] Stevels, A. (2007c). The method was very effective because it gave clear design directions in complex situations. This is because in a factor approach, comparisons are made with a previous situation ('comparative analysis'). The ratio between the factor score for the old situation and the new situation indicated whether an 'action', e.g. if a design change, works out positively or negatively. An additional advantage of factor scores is that apart from environmental scores (based on LCA for instance), other factors are taken in account, e.g. stakeholder perceptions and legislative requirements. It is also beneficial as designers do not need to be environmental specialists to be able to use the system effectively. Once designers have got the 'factor list'– preferably prepared by the environmental manager – experience at Philips Electronics showed that designers were better able to implement solutions. Despite the subjectivity of the factors – e.g. they were 'educated guesses' – they reflected the business reality very well and could be easily explained to the internal value chain. This simplified approach worked well because many organisations are conservative and have difficulty in accepting new issues, particularly when they are perceived to be complex, scientific and sustainability oriented. Unfortunately, newness and complexity are often perceived as a threat rather than an opportunity which can provoke opposition. Complexity in such a situation can be used as scapegoat by some managers, e.g. 'this is complicated and won't work in practice the company'. In contrast to LCA, factor methods are simple to apply. Moreover, no big databases have to be developed to operate such systems. The author is still in the process of development of a full set of factors to develop the DfRV concept further. When these are applied to design, it will be interesting to find out which DfRV design decisions will be different from the ones based on traditional EcoDesign.

CONCLUSIONS

Design for Resource Value (DfRV) considers the front end of the product life cycle and is therefore an indispensable part of a holistic approach of design for the CE. As such, it is an EcoDesign approach that has a specific emphasis on material or resource issues. It requires that new paradigms are to be added to current EcoDesign. The first is the consideration of the demand side because the end consumers – through their spending and their discarding behavior – determine the success and/or failure of the CE concept.

The second is the consideration of ratios between environmental load and money-related items such as price and value. DfRV calls for extracting more economic value from resources used to realise a certain physical functionality. This is a new challenge for the (Eco)designer as it includes this economic dimension. It is not meant to replace the aim of reducing the environmental load over the life cycle, rather it is meant to open a new avenue for creativity. DfRV should therefore not be operated in isolation but rather identify those design aspects which are different either in terms of content or in terms of priority. After this, a balanced action agenda can bet set. The methodology for DfRV is essentially the same as EcoDesign. However, DfRV metrics include an environmental dimension, a supply risk dimension and a factor that takes into account the effectiveness of end-of-life treatment.

BIBLIOGRAPHY

Ecoindicator. (1999). [Online]. Available at: https://www.pre-sustainability. com/download/EI99_Manual.pdf

Graedel, T.E. et al. (2012). Methodology of criticality determination. *Environmental Science and Technology* 46: 1063–1070.

Griese, H.-J. et al. (1996). *Kreislaufwirtschaft in der Elektronik Industrie.* VDE-Verlag, ISBN 3-8007-2196-1

Stevels, A. (2007a). *Adventures in EcoDesign in the Electronic Industry, 1993–2007* [Online], Chapters 2.4. Available at: www.aeki.se

Stevels, A. (2007b). *Adventures in EcoDesign in the Electronic Industry, 1993–2007* [Online], Chapters 5.4. Available at: www.aeki.se.

Stevels, A. (2007c). *Adventures in EcoDesign in the Electronic Industry, 1993–2007* [Online], Chapters 6.2. Available at: www.aeki.se.

17 Circular textile design
Old myths and new models

Rebecca Earley and Kate Goldsworthy

INTRODUCTION

The Mistra Future Fashion programme[1] brings together design and scientific researchers with industry experts to create new insights based on collective endeavour, focusing on the need to use design to create a circular future through evolving new economic, environmental and social values. Design can work at both micro and macro levels (from materials to products to systems) to avoid the, often unintended, consequences which can come from looking only at parts of the life cycle and value chain, rather than the whole.

Designers need to work with circularity principles within a sustainability framework and need to fully understand the technical and biological cycles. Yet innovation in the field has shown us that for textile designers, circular design also needs to consider how these cycles can interconnect; and how understanding the speed of cycles is important too. Inter-disciplinary practice-based textile design research can generate new insights for this emerging design field.

This chapter presents four projects which challenge and provide a basis for different approaches to circularity. In defining circular design in part one, we consider how a polarization of thinking has occurred before we consider how boundaries are blurring between the biological and technical cycles. The practice work in this section addresses designing for future material cyclability[2]: the 'Laserline' project shows how a single-fibre property approach combined with laser technology can keep polyester materials pure for future reprocessing.

As our desire for functionality from materials grows – think non-iron shirts, waterproof Teflon or anti-bacterial coatings – keeping these technical and biological cycles separate becomes increasingly complex and new approaches are needed. Part two looks at innovations that are leading the way.

In part three, we question the idea of speeds for circular textile design and we present research that extends these ideas to 'super-slow' and 'ultra-fast'. 'Fast ReFashion' and 'Twice Upcycled' keeps polyester shirts in use for extended periods of time through new business practices and user engagement approaches. A.S.A.P. (paper cloth) experiments with new materials for clothes we don't intend to keep for long, for whatever reasons.

The chapter concludes by applying these insights from original practice-based research to other disciplines to show that textile design has an important role to play in understanding the potential for material flows.

CIRCULAR DESIGN AND MATERIALS

Circular design first became relevant to textile materials through McDonnough & Braungart's *The Hannover Principles* (1992) followed by the more widely cited *Cradle to Cradle* in 2002, where the sixth principle 'eliminate the concept of waste' pointed towards a far more holistic notion of materials recovery as compared to the 'reduce, reuse, recycle' mantra. They called for the optimisation of the 'full life cycle of products and processes to emulate the state of natural systems, in which there is no waste', and suggested that current methods perpetuated a cradle-to-grave strategy, which was ultimately linear in nature.

Circular design should not be confused with 'sustainable design', although they undoubtedly overlap in ethos and approach. Circularity aims to be sustainable by default but sustainable intentions are not always circular. It is also not just about recycling materials, which can often be a linear process in real terms, ultimately ending up in landfill, albeit a little later in time. In fact, it is not always about closed loops, with materials being directed neatly back to the beginning of the same product life cycle. For design, the key concept is one of systems thinking.

Connected solutions

All too often, approaches to sustainability and even circularity are at odds, with competing strategies almost battling it out for top billing. Yet the potential for circular design is that it 'connects' through holistic relationships, participation and collaboration. Circular systems thinking is built upon the oldest system of all – our ecological system. The model we aspire to is based on a synergistic network of cycles and open loops, which feed each other at multiple scales and speeds. These are complex and sophisticated transformations of materials and living matter. Within this network we will undoubtedly see both old and new technologies and processes contribute to the whole, with hi- and low-technology working together. The same system could include slow garments, upcycled from pre-loved ones or fibres chemically recycled back to virgin quality in a closed-loop system where nothing is lost.

MYTH 1: NATURAL MATERIALS ARE GOOD, SYNTHETIC MATERIALS ARE BAD

In existing versions of circular design – for example models by *Cradle to Cradle* 2002; Ellen MacArthur Foundation 2014; *RSA The Great Recovery* 2014 – there is a polarised view of the material world as either relating to biological or technical nutrients with a suggestion that these two worlds should be kept firmly apart. All technical resources should be recovered through industrial processes and kept in closed loops away from biological systems, where 'natural' materials should be retained. However, this approach can be problematic in an increasingly complex material landscape and it's not always easy to define boundaries so simply. The following examples show work which follows this material division in order to build-in recovery at end-of-life but also examples where boundaries are more blurred.

Designing for the technical cycle

In the fashion and textiles industry, one of the most prominent technical fibres – polyester – represents over 48 percent of total global fibre production (The Fiber Year, 2013, p. 101). As fibre-to-fibre polyester recovery comes closer to commercialisation (first industrialised by Teijin with Eco-Circle[3] in 2006) then designing production processes to fit with this recovery system becomes vital. One approach is to design materials which fit within the constraints of this system, i.e. are monomaterial in content to enable efficient recovery with minimum waste.

LaserLine (2011) (Figure 17.1), developed by Goldsworthy as part of a doctoral project (2012), was focused on this challenge. Research identified monomateriality (sometimes also called 'unimateriality') as the key to designing polyester fabrics for chemical recyclability and a new laser-based technology was developed as an alternative to existing finishing

Figure 17.1 'Seamsdress' (Goldsworthy & Telfer 2014), evolved from the 2011 'LaserLine' work

techniques which often rendered materials unrecyclable. Rapid advances in chemical fibre-to-fibre recovery are being made which save not only resources but also chemical and energy use when compared to virgin materials; companies such as Worn Again,[4] Renewcell[5] and Evrnu[6] and researchers at VTT[7] Aalto Chem,[8] RiSE[9] and Swerea IVF[10] lead the way in this area. Projects like Trash-2-Cash[11] – an EU-funded Horizon 2020 venture – is bringing some these researchers together to join up the approaches by striving for Design-Driven Material Innovation (DDMI).

Designing for the biological cycle

Perhaps with more obvious links to sustainability principles, new materials from the biological cycle represent a fast-growing area of innovation. Materials such as organic cotton or hemp are well established alternatives to traditional fibres, but a new material world is opening up by utilising the waste streams found in agriculture and the food industry.

Materials made from food waste streams are an exciting way to link up industries which can benefit from each other's waste. Pinatex[12] is a vegetable leather produced from agricultural waste from the pineapple industry; Grape Leather[13] is made from the waste materials in wine production; Manure Couture[14] even uses the cellulose in cow dung to create a bio-fabric like viscose. The important factor here is that *all* aspects of the materials and processing must be biocompatible to ensure safe return to the environment.

Blurring material boundaries

Keeping these material 'opposites' apart is sometimes problematic. Often we need properties from both natural and synthetic materials in order to produce the most functional fabrics (polycotton is a common blend often used for its easy-care properties and durability). It is also often difficult to firmly place materials into either the biological or synthetic cycle. Raw materials of natural origin can be processed to produce at least semi-synthetic materials (for example bamboo becomes viscose, corn becomes polyester, etc.); whilst experimental material innovations often prove that even synthetic materials can be transformed back across the divide into bio-nutrients. Fungi Cutlery[15] uses mycelium fungi to create plastic cutlery; at Exeter University, the e-coli bacteria has been engineered to produce a renewable propane biofuel (Howard et al., 2013). CiClO[16] technology allows plastic-based fibres like polyester to degrade more like natural fibres in landfill conditions. If we are to create a truly 'networked' ecology of future materials, designers need to understand these continually blurring boundaries and material stories and adapt the design of products accordingly.

MYTH 2: SLOW FASHION IS GOOD, FAST IS BAD

Design and production has changed to meet the need for speed, growing populations and the cultivated fast fashion appetite. Conversely, the idea of designing durable and long-lasting fashion textiles has been a part of the fashion industry from the outset – long before product obsolescence had been dreamt up in the 1950's, yet the idea of slow fashion has been promoted in recent years as a new counter approach to *fast fashion.*

The concepts of fast and slow fashion (Tham, 2012) have gained increased attention during recent years since Fletcher & Tham first published around clothing *rhythms* (*Lifetimes,* 2004). This may in part be due to a renewed and intensified media coverage of the unwanted implications of the fast fashion industry, which can be seen on a local, regional and worldwide scale (including water, air and soil pollution, climate impact, shortage of arable land, harmful and unsafe working conditions and poor worker's rights', etc.). In addition, slow fashion, coined by Fletcher (2010), has been promoted by NGOs and other devoted individuals for the last decade, and is growing stronger. Slow living, spanning from food to fashion to other daily practices, is now an established phenomenon of the Western world – as an antidote to the fast-paced living that dominates our societies.

However, if we are to look to nature's systems as a blueprint for circularity, there are examples of all speeds in the natural world which point towards positive appropriation of both fast and slow systems. We see the same positive examples of fast in food, fashion and architecture. Perhaps slowing down is not the only solution to the environmental challenges we face. Rather than pursue a polarised approach to viewing 'speed of use' (which often limits attention to a small part of the whole life cycle), we would argue that a more nuanced method of analysing speed is needed which acknowledges the entire life cycle of a product. We should in fact be considering the right speed for each garment within specific life cycle stages.

Our research intends to move the discourse on from simply fast and slow, to a level where multiple and proportionate speeds can be both understood, tested via life cycle analysis (LCA) and ultimately engineered, to improve the circular efficiency of a product. The idea presented here is that both long-life (slow) *and* short-life (fast) can both be models for clothing to suit a broad range of user contexts – different needs, tastes, incomes and styles.

Designing super-slow

Examples of slow (and circular) design can be seen in the *Textile Toolbox* (Earley & Goldsworthy 2014) exhibition, in the project *Fast ReFashion* (Figure 17.2) and the Top 100[17] project work, *Twice Upcycled* (Figure 17.3) where the retention of products in 'super-slow' use results in product longevity. The approach is to transform the industry through designing fashion services which extend a product's useful lifespan, rather than solely the creation and sale of new products. This is about design interventions or facilitated consumer instructions that can inspire designers and consumers to engage with materials and products towards closed-loop thinking and action.

In *Fast Refashion* (Earley, 2013), users are encouraged to create a monomaterial refashioned garment for themselves, using readily available tools and resources like irons, paper and dry foods. This project references the speed of high street trends, but draws consumers back to their wardrobes or a second-hand shop for the garment that will begin the fashion process – the material and the personal transformation.

In *Twice Upcycled*, (Earley and Goldsworthy, 2008) the original shirt has been bought and worn by a consumer, and then handed on to a second-hand or charity shop, with the first upcycling occurring through reshaping and overprinting by the upcycling SME. On resale of the garment, the consumer agrees to return the shirt at a later date. Following a period of wear by the same or next consumer, the shirt can be returned to the SME and its third life can be created. In this case, the shirt becomes a quilted waistcoat, where it has been recut and lined in recycled polyester fleece, using an innovative laser-welding process.

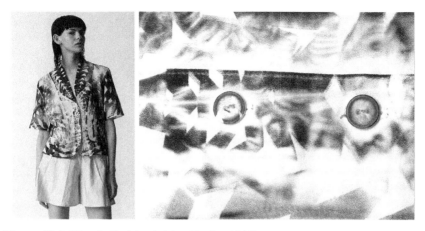

Figure 17.2 'Fast ReFashion' shirt (Earley 2013)

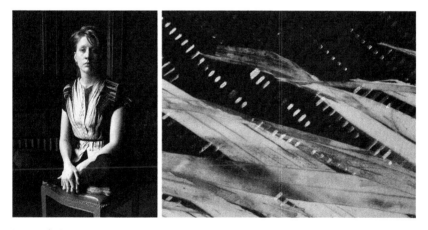

Figure 17.3 'Twice Upcycled' (Earley & Goldsworthy 2008)

Upcycling is achieved without any material resources and the resulting product retains its inherent recyclability for another lifetime.

Designing ultra-fast-forward

ASAP (paper cloth) (Figure 17.4) is designed to be 'ultra-fast' but also to enable material longevity through efficient recovery at its end-of-life. The collection made from a wearable, non-woven material developed for the Mistra Future Fashion work in a collaborative project between CCD and Innventia[18] (part of RiSE,[19] a world-leading Swedish research institute). The premise for the project acknowledges the consumer's many reasons for buying clothes and addresses the damage caused by fast fashion by creating materials appropriate for this market. It enables

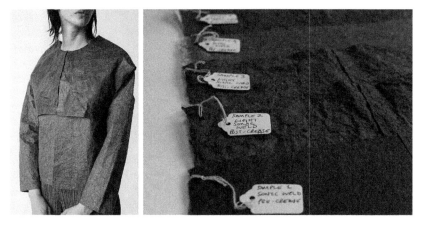

Figure 17.4 'ASAP' (Politowicz, Goldsworthy, Granberg, MacLennan & Telfer, 2014)

the prevailing 'disposable' culture in fashion to be transformed by the development of inexpensive, bio-based 'recoverable' garments with sustainable credentials. It also aims to eliminate the 'consumer washing' phase and therefore remove its large carbon footprint. Through the collaboration of designers and scientists, this collection relies on the mass production of various blends of wood fibres and polylactose acetate (PLA) fibres, which can be recovered to break new ground in cyclability. Raw materials are developed to offer alternative, renewable qualities as a complement to the resilience and durability of an existing, classic wardrobe.

More agile and adaptable business and production models are key to this area. Automated and hi-tech production can be used to enable more responsive (redistributed) manufacturing tailored to the individual whilst reducing associated impacts. Unmade[20] (UK) enable bespoke knitwear products to be manufactured at an industrial scale whilst responding to individual needs; Dyecoo[21] have led the way in water-free and process chemical-free dyeing; the Post Couture Collective[22] designs clothing based on open-source principles to provide a blueprint service for the maker movement generation.

CONCLUSION

In conclusion, we can draw some insights around the principles for circularity from this review of practice and find strategies for impacting our future design decisions; the beginnings of a manifesto for circular design.

- *Circular resources* can be designed with recovery in mind at the outset or upcycled from existing waste streams to retain their value in use.
- *Circular material flows* are not only based upon industrial systems (even when they relate to the 'technical cycle') but need to be part of the ecosystem as a whole. Anything which escapes an industrial cycle should aim not only to do no harm but to be an active nutrient in the biosphere.
- In a *connected system* it is possible to see seemingly polarised approaches exist in balance; old and new, fast and slow, natural and synthetic, large and small working together.
- Whilst there is often an argument for designing for purely biological or technical cycles, in order to enable forward recyclability, there are also materials and processes which *blur the boundaries* and in doing so also enable circularity through new material networks.
- *Circular system opportunities* can often be found outside of industry boundaries. Food waste streams into textile fibres point to open not closed loops.
- *Speed of cycle* is an important and under-explored consideration for circularity. The speed of raw material creation, fibre through to garment production and use-phase need to be considered along with ease of recovery in order to make appropriate design choices.

There are many challenges ahead in the move towards a circular industry; improving technology, economic and political pressures, finding and moving towards new untested models, overcoming misunderstandings and myths, accurately understanding the impacts we are having (across the whole system). These are complex and wicked problems but many brands and researchers are putting enormous efforts into resolving these challenges.

NOTES

1 http://www.mistrafuturefashion.com/
2 'Cyclability' is a term which describes something that can be recycled (the term originates from the development of recycled batteries) and which Goldsworthy used as a conceptual framework in her PhD thesis (Goldsworthy 2012).
3 Teijin, *Eco-Circle*, http://www2.teijin-frontier.com/english/sozai/specifics/ecopet-plus.html

 4 Worn Again, http://wornagain.info/
 5 Renewcell, http://renewcell.se/
 6 Evrnu, www.evrnu.com/
 7 VTT, www.vttresearch.com
 8 Aalto Chem, http://chem.aalto.fi/en/
 9 RiSE, www.ri.se/en
10 Swerea IVF, www.swerea.se/en/ivf
11 Trash-2-Cash, www.trash2cashproject.eu/
12 Pinatex, www.ananas-anam.com/pinatex/
13 Grape Leather, www.youtube.com/watch?v=mGCLlJxdYXc
14 Manure Couture, Jalila Essaïdi, www.youtube.com/watch?v=OuhMIMs1gJs
15 Fungi Cutlery, by Livin Studio and Utrecht University, www.livinstudio.com/fungi-cutlery
16 www.ciclotextiles.com
17 Top 100, www.upcyclingtextiles.net/
18 Innventia, www.innventia.com/en/
19 RiSE, www.ri.se/en
20 Unmade, www.unmade.com/
21 Dyecoo, www.dyecoo.com/
22 Post Couture Collective, www.postcouture.cc/

BIBLIOGRAPHY

Braungart, M. and McDonough, W. (1992). *The Hannover Principles: Design for Sustainability*, Commissioned by City of Hannover, EXPO 2000, The World's Fair Hannover: Germany.

Braungart, M. and McDonough, W. (2002). *Cradle to Cradle: Remaking the Way We Make Things*. New York: North Point Press.

Earley, R. (2013). *Fast Refashion* [Online]. Available at: www.upcyclingtextiles.net/#/black-hack-chat-2013/ [Accessed 25 August 2017].

Earley, R. and Goldsworthy, K. (2008). *Twice Upcycled* [Online]. Available at: www.upcyclingtextiles.net/#/concert/ [Accessed 25 August 2017]

Earley, R. and Goldsworthy, K. (2014). *The Textile Toolbox* exhibition, London, touring and online. Available at: www.textiletoolbox.com [Accessed 24 March 2016]

Ellen MacArthur Foundation. (2014). *Towards the Circular Economy Vol.3: Accelerating the Scale-Up Across Global Supply Chains* [Online]. UK: Ellen MacArthur Foundation. Available at: www.ellenmacarthurfoundation.org/business/reports/ce2014 [Accessed 24 March 2016].

Fletcher, K. (2010). *Slow Fashion: An Invitation for Systems Change, Chapter in Fashion Practice, Vol.2, Issue 2, 2010*. Sheffield: Centre for Sustainable Consumption, Sheffield Hallam University.

Fletcher, K. and Tham, M. (2004). *Clothing Rhythms*, in *Eternally Yours: Time in Design: Product, Value, Sustenance*. Rotterdam: 010 Uitgeverij, pp. 254–274.

Goldsworthy, K. (2012). Laser Finishing; a new process for designing recyclability in synthetic textiles. Ph.D. Thesis, University of the Arts, London.

Howard, P. et al. (2013). Synthesis of customized petroleum-replica fuel molecules by targeted modification of free fatty acid pools in Escherichia coli. *Proceedings of National Academy of Sciences* 110(19): 7636–7641. Available at: www.pnas.org/content/110/19/7636 [Accessed 25 August 2017].

Politowicz, K. and Goldsworthy, K. (2014). *A.S.A.P.* [Online], Available at: www.textiletoolbox.com/exhibits/detail/sp-paper-cloth/ [Accessed 25 August 2017].

RSA. (2014). *The Great Recovery Project* [Online]. Available at: www.greatrecovery.org.uk/ [Accessed 24 March 2016].

Tham, M. (2012). *Slow and Fast Fashion. The Sustainable Fashion Handbook.* London: Thames & Hudson, pp. 216–218.

The Fiber Year Consulting. (2013). *The Fiber Year 2013: World Survey of Textiles and Nonwovens.* Available at: www.thefiberyear.com/home/ [Accessed 20 August 2017].

Circular Economy
18 and design for remanufacturing

Erik Sundin

INTRODUCTION

This chapter focuses on Circular Economy (CE) and how to design products for remanufacturing. CE is a concept that has gained popularity in recent years, and especially within Europe. For many original equipment manufacturers (OEMs), e.g. within aerospace and automotive industries, remanufacturing is a natural and essential part of their business. Remanufacturing is one of many ways to stay competitive, since it brings business benefits such as reduced costs, meeting new customer needs, brand protection and increased market shares as well as improving environmental performance.

An important starting point with CE is the design of products and manufacturing processes. Products can be designed and redesigned to be used longer, repaired, upgraded, remanufactured or eventually recycled, instead of being thrown away after its first use. Manufacturing processes can be based more on the reusability of products, components and materials and the restorative capacity of natural resources, while innovative business models can create a new relationship between companies and consumers, e.g. through product service systems (PSS). In a PSS, a company provides the function of a product instead of the actual product. This is done, for instance, when a customer is paying for a number of copies rather than purchasing a photocopy machine (see, e.g. Sundin and Bras, 2005).

This chapter also reviews the industrial sector of photocopiers since it is one of the sectors that have had long experience within circular thinking and remanufacturing already in the product design process. This means that the companies within this industry sector have achieved a deeper understanding of the drivers and barriers when conducting remanufacturing. The chapter is based on research conducted at several remanufacturing companies and especially at four OEMs that both manufacture and remanufacture photocopiers: FUJI Xerox, Canon, Ricoh and Kyocera.

CIRCULAR ECONOMY (CE)

The concept of CE is described in many ways. The Ellen MacArthur Foundation (EMF) defines it as 'Restorative and regenerative by design, and which aims to keep products, components and materials at their highest utility and value at all times, distinguishing between technical and biological cycles[1]'.

CE is often visualized in diagrams with focus on circularity of materials. One of the most popular illustrations of the Circular Economy is from the EMF, known as 'the butterfly'[2] (Figure 18.1). In this diagram, CE consists of two major flows of materials: *biological* and *technical*. EMF's view of CE is that materials should be kept within circular loops from extraction and throughout their life cycles, while minimizing the material flows going to incineration (energy recovery) and landfills. Remanufacturing is in EMF's description of CE mentioned as one of the options for getting the product, components and materials back in use.

Furthermore, the European Union has illustrated CE in a circular diagram[3] with seven main phases connected to each other in a circle: *raw material, design, manufacturing/remanufacturing, distribution, consumption/use/reuse/repair, collection,* and *recycling.* These seven phases are interlinked, as materials can be used in a cascading way; for instance, industry exchanges by-products, products are refurbished or remanufactured, or consumers choose to buy the function rather than the product itself (Product Service System (PSS)). The aim with these circular flows is to minimise the resources leaving the circle so that the system functions in an optimal way. This means that CE occurs in the seven phases with the products, components and material to keep product value in a resource-efficient manner while avoiding residual waste. Resources within the CE should be kept when

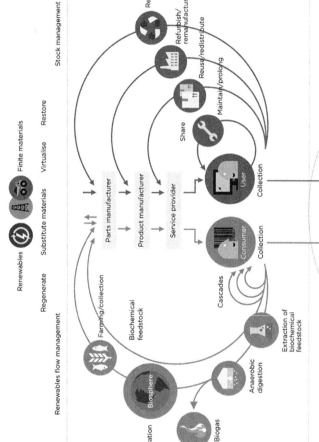

Figure 18.1 The butterfly diagram of Circle Economy by Ellen MacArthur Foundation (used with permission)

Source: Ellen MacArthur Foundation, SUN, and McKinsey Center for Business and Environment: drawing from Braungart & McDonough, Cradle to Cradle (C2C).

a product reaches its End-of-Use so they can be reused several times to create further value for the product's next customers. This means that CE systems keep the added value in products for as long as possible and eliminate waste.

However, a transition to a more CE requires changes throughout the entire product value chain, from new business models to product and process designs. Thus, there is a need for solutions all the way from finding new ways of turning waste into resources to changes in the behavior of product users and consumers. This implies systemic changes on a large scale, and innovation not only in technologies but also in organizations, society, and finance methods.[4]

When studying different diagrams and descriptions of CE and life cycles of products, one understands that the authors of these mean similar things. As illustrated in Figure 18.2, the physical life cycle of a product can be divided into the three major phases: *Beginning-of-Life* (BoL), *Middle-of-Life* (MoL) and *End-of-Life* (EoL), where these phases include:

Beginning-of-Life: material extraction, design and manufacture of part and components which are assembly into products, product delivery and installation.

Middle-of-Life: use, repair, maintenance, upgrade, refurbishment, remanufacturing, second use, nth use and final use.

End-of-Life: material recycling, downcycling, energy recovery and landfilling.

Figure 18.2 is similar to the right wing of the EMF's butterfly (Figure 18.1). Note here that *remanufacturing* takes place in the *Middle-of-Life* and not in the *End-of-Life*, as the remanufacturing of products and parts/components contribute to the *use* time extension of that specific part before it reaches its *End-of-Life*. Most often within *remanufacturing*, the owner/user of the product has been changed between the nth and n+1th user, whereas in *repairs* the owner/user stays the same. At the *End-of-Life* it is, however, still possible to recover some value through material recycling and/or energy recovery through incineration. During incineration, the heat can be used for electricity generation and districted heating of buildings, where possible.

According to the EU report[5] previously mentioned, the existing infrastructure, business models and technology, together with established behaviour, keep economies 'locked-in' to the linear economy. Traditionally, companies may lack the information, confidence and capacity to move to CE solutions. In addition, the financial system often fails to provide for investment in efficiency improvements or innovative business

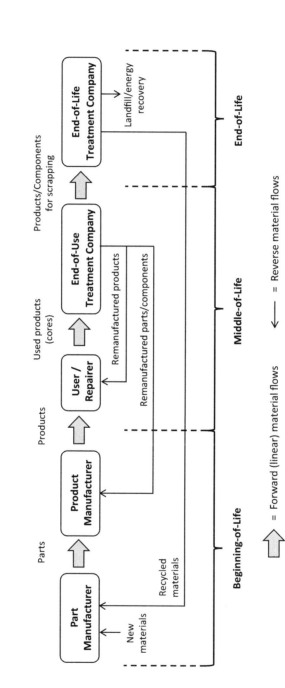

Figure 18.2 A diagram visualizing the major life cycle phases of a product (Beginning-of-Life, Middle-of-Life and End-of-Life) including the forward and reverse flows of products, parts/components and materials

models, which are perceived as more risky and complex, deterring many traditional investors. Conventional consumer habits can also hinder new product and service development. Such barriers tend to persist in a context where prices do not reflect the real costs of resource use to society, and where policy fails to provide strong and consistent signals for the transition to a CE.[6]

REMANUFACTURING

As seen in the diagrams and descriptions of CE in the previous section, remanufacturing is an essential part of CE. The concept of remanufacturing has been defined by researchers, but most are variations of the same basic idea of product restoration. The author's definition of remanufacturing is:

> 'Remanufacturing' is an industrial process whereby used products (a.k.a. cores) are restored to useful life. During this process, the core passes through a number of remanufacturing operations, e.g. inspection, cleaning, disassembly, reprocessing, reassembly, and final testing, to ensure it meets the desired product standards.
>
> (modified from Sundin, 2004)

A 'core' is here defined as the discarded/worn-out/used product that is used for remanufacturing. In some cases, for example a laptop computer, the used laptop is remanufactured to a remanufactured laptop. In other cases, components of a product are remanufactured, e.g. brake calipers for cars or toner cartridges for printers. In addition, remanufactured parts could be used in new manufacturing.

'Repair' is 'to put something that is damaged, broken, or not working correctly, back into good condition or make it work again'.[7] This means that repair can be conducted at the user and without having an industrial restoration process as in the case of remanufacturing.

'Material recycling' is 'when a product is reduced to its basic elements, which are reused' (Rogers and Tibben-Lembke, 1999).

The order and purpose of the different process steps are not standardised, but rather case dependent. This means that a remanufacturing process can be organised in many different ways. From the author's experience, remanufacturing companies use different sequences to execute the remanufacturing steps depending on, e.g. type of product and

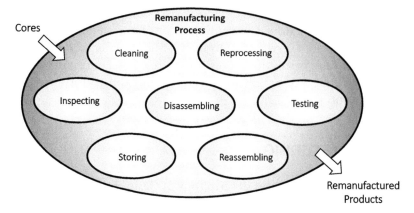

Figure 18.3 A generic remanufacturing process containing seven general process steps

Source: modified from Sundin, 2004.

remanufacturing volume. However, a generic remanufacturing process can be illustrated as seen in Figure 18.3, with seven generic steps that the cores pass through in order to become remanufactured products (modified from Sundin, 2004).

Remanufacturing is generally very different in comparison with traditional manufacturing. For example, the remanufacturing batch sizes are normally smaller, the degree of automation is lower and the amount of manual labour is higher in comparison to manufacturing (Steinhilper, 1998). However, as robot technologies are improving there are now better opportunities to include more automation in remanufacturing to deal with, e.g. operations that sometimes have a bad work environment. This could, for example, be cleaning and disassembly of dirty cores from the automotive industry.

REMANUFACTURING IS AN ESSENTIAL PART OF THE CE

In the diagrams and descriptions of CE (in first sections), the authors stress that the circular loops of products should be kept as tight as possible around the users in order to achieve good economic and environmental benefits, and leave fewer products, components and material for the outer loops e.g. material recycling, incineration and landfill. Hence, remanufacturing is essential for CE since it keeps the added value in products for the users in several circular loops.

Many OEMs in different industry sectors manage to create economic and environmentally sustainable businesses from their remanufacturing operations. However, there are barriers to overcome for CE and remanufacturing to become more common in today's society. These deal with, e.g. customer acceptance, legislative issues, company policies and an understanding of what the real benefits of remanufacturing are. If the general mindset of both company management and product users can be changed to a more circular mindset and towards increasing awareness of the benefits of remanufacturing, adoption of the CE and remanufacturing will accelerate.

ENVIRONMENTAL IMPACTS OF REMANUFACTURED PRODUCTS

Studies have indicated that remanufacturing is an environmentally beneficial way of closing the flows of products, components and materials (Sundin and Lee, 2011). The reasons why remanufacturing is beneficial from an environmental perspective, is that all efforts used in material extraction, part/component shaping and product assembly, are fully or partly salvaged through remanufacturing. With product remanufacturing, the geometrical form of the product is retained and its associated economic value is preserved.

Figure 18.4 shows how a product's environmental impact accumulates during its product life cycle. Typically, for energy-using products, most of the environmental impact occurs during use. For products not using energy, most environmental impact usually occurs during *Beginning-of-Life* and at *End-of-Life*. However, when a product is being remanufactured its *use* time will be extended, and therefore the environmental impacts from, e.g. *Beginning-of-Life* and *End-of-Life* become less severe in comparison with a product with a more traditional linear flow without remanufacturing. By this, the environmental impact is reduced in comparison to a traditional linear economy that requires that new products are manufactured to meet new customer needs.

According to Figure 18.4 it is in the early design phase that one has the largest possibility to influence the product's environmental performance during its life cycle phases. This means that increased effort in design can improve the product's environmental performance during its life cycles. In addition, there are indications that if a product is designed for remanufacturing (see next section), even more environmental benefits are gained (Kerr and Ryan, 2001). Having products designed for several use periods with remanufacturing

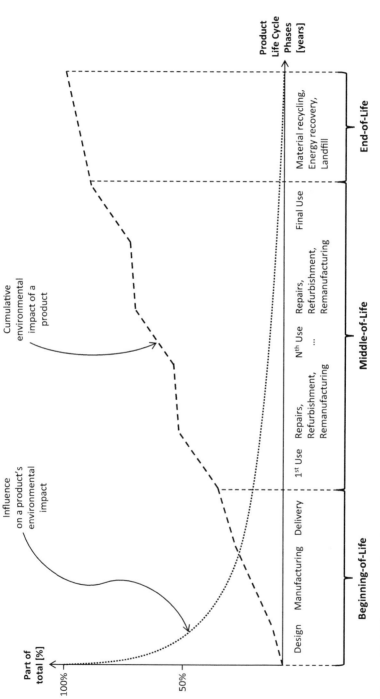

Figure 18.4 The accumulated environmental impact during a product's life (dashed line). In addition, the dotted line shows where the most influence on the environmental impact occurs

Source: modified from Lindahl and Sundin, 2013.

occurring in between therefore extends the use-time of products (Sundin and Bras, 2005).

DESIGN FOR REMANUFACTURING

To facilitate remanufacturing, the individual steps of the remanufacturing process, described in previous 'remanufacturing' section, should be facilitated (Sundin and Bras, 2005). It has been found by Sundin and Bras (2005) that there are specific product properties that are preferable for a product to have to facilitate the remanufacturing steps as illustrated in the RemPro-matrix in Figure 18.5.

Although the application of design for remanufacturing is known, few companies apply such methods (see, e.g. Hatcher et al., 2011). One reason why design for remanufacturing is not happening to a larger extent is that few companies have been able to establish information channels for retrieving feedback from remanufacturing operators to product designers. In order to overcome this lack of feedback channels one can use the '*Genshen Gemba*' principle which means 'go and see' where the product designers go to the remanufacturing facility and disassemble their products with the purpose of understanding what improvements

*Remanufacturing **Product** Property **Matrix***

Preferable Product Property \ Remanufacturing Process Step	Inspecting	Cleaning	Disassembling	Storing	Reprocessing	Reassembling	Testing
Ease of Identification	X		X	X			X
Ease of Verification	X						
Ease of Access	X	X	X		X		X
Ease of Handling			X	X	X	X	
Ease of Separation			X		X		
Ease of Securing						X	
Ease of Alignment						X	
Ease of Stacking				X			
Wear Resistant		X	X		X	X	

Figure 18.5 The RemPro-matrix showing which product properties those are preferable for the generic remanufacturing process steps

Source: Sundin and Bras, 2005.

that can be done to the product design. Manufacturing companies with longer experience of remanufacturing are, in general, good at establishing feedback channels and performing design for remanufacturing, e.g. within the industry of photocopiers.

REMANUFACTURING OF PHOTOCOPIERS

Within the photocopy industry, manufacturing companies have had a long experience of both manufacturing and remanufacturing their machines as well as their parts and components. For environmental and economic reasons FUJI Xerox, Kyocera, Ricoh and Canon started to use reused parts and remanufacture their photocopiers around the mid-1990s. Another reason why these companies started to remanufacture was that the users were more willing to *pay-per-copy* rather than buying the photocopier (PSS). This was because a photocopier is not fashion or status-related, it should just work when needed. Therefore, it is suitable to sell the photocopy function where one *pay-per-copy* (see e.g. Sundin and Bras, 2005). Currently the reuse rates of reused parts are between 30 to 80 percent (in weight) for the remanufactured photocopiers. An example of part replacement of a photocopier is shown in Figure 18.6.

FUJI Xerox uses many quality checks to ensure their remanufactured products are of high quality, e.g., image quality and occurrence of paper jams. In addition, FUJI Xerox let their designers 'go and see' how their products are performing in the remanufacturing process. This close connection between remanufacturing and design department have led to photocopy machine design that facilitates their remanufacturing process, e.g. through modularisation. In addition, a *Design for Remanufacturing* manual has been developed to be used when designing all their photocopiers.

Kyocera is practicing remanufacturing because resource efficiency is a strategic focus within the company. Their photocopiers are being sold and remanufactured by their servicing dealers. The dealers are selling many products on leasing contracts and recover spare parts from broken products to be re-used in remanufacturing. In the early 1990s, Ricoh started to design their photocopiers for reuse and now remanufactures to lower the risk of increased resource cost in the future. Table 18.1 shows examples of how OEMs implemented *Design for Remanufacturing* of their photocopiers.

From a marketing perspective, Canon has introduced their own EcoDesign label, EQ80, for their photocopiers that has 80 percent or more reused parts. An example of this is illustrated in Figure 18.7.

Figure 18.6 Replacement of parts in a photocopy remanufacturing process

Table 18.1 Design for Remanufacturing attributes at photocopy manufacturers/remanufacturers

FUJI Xerox	Kyocera	Ricoh
• Using standard parts as much as possible • Family parts are reused within the product family • Modules are reused within the same product family • Standard parts are reused in several families	• Use of long-lasting sub-frame in metal • Upgradeable and modular design • Easy replacement of parts • Minimizing the use of fasteners • Standardized head of screws • Plastic clips with indication about where to push them for disassembly	• Reuse of high-value components • Easy dismantling/ segregation • Adaptable outer plastic housing for easy serviceability • Avoidance of stickers and labels over multiple components that are easy to disassemble

Figure 18.7 The Canon Image Runner Advance C5000 which has the EQ80 label meaning that 80 percent or more of its parts are reused

Source: https://www.canon.se/for_work/products/office_print_copy_solutions/office_colour_printers/imagerunner_advance_c5000_series/

CONCLUSIONS AND FUTURE PROSPECTS

There are some products, for example car parts, where remanufacturing is almost second nature, while for other products, such as smartphones, remanufacturing is still rather young. In either case, the remanufacturing industry is growing and makes a significant contribution in the transition from current linear economy towards CE. Below is a statement about the future made by APRA[8]:

> As people grow more and more concerned about the environment, we must seek public policies that will encourage even more remanufacturing. There are enough social and environmental benefits to justify remanufacturing. Imagine the added benefits to society if EVERYTHING we buy could be remanufactured, from small appliances to lawn mowers. Also imagine if products were originally manufactured with the sole purpose of being rebuilt and not thrown away.

In the future, business models for CE will lead to more remanufacturing and more understanding of how to make remanufacturing more efficient through *design-for-remanufacturing* thinking, as in the case mentioned from the photocopy industry.

NOTES

1 www.ellenmacarthurfoundation.org/circular-economy/
2 www.ellenmacarthurfoundation.org/circular-economy/interactive-diagram
3 EU. (2014). The EU report "Towards a circular economy: A zero waste programme for Europe" found at: http://eur-lex.europa.eu/legal-content/EN/TXT/?uri=CELEX:52014DC0398
4 Ibid.
5 Ibid.
6 Ibid.
7 Cambridge Dictionary. (2017). Definition of 'repair' found at: http://dictionary.cambridge.org/dictionary/english/repair
8 APRA (2015). www.apra-europe.org/dateien/News/News2015/APRA_Position_Paper.pdf

BIBLIOGRAPHY

Hatcher, G.D., Ijomah, W.L., and Windmill, J.F.C. (2011). Design for remanufacture: A literature review and future research needs. *Journal of Cleaner Production* 19(17–18): 2004–2014.

Kerr, W. and Ryan, C. (2001). Eco-efficiency gains from remanufacturing: A case study of photocopier remanufacturing at Fuji Xerox Australia. *Journal of Cleaner Production*(9): 75–81.

Lindahl, M. and Sundin, E. (2013). Product design considerations for improved integrated product/service offerings. In: *Handbook of Sustainable Engineering*, J. Kauffman and K. Mo Lee (eds.) Springer, pp. 669–689. ISBN 978-1-4020-8938-1.

Rogers, D.S. and Tibben-Lembke, R.S. (1999). *Going Backwards: Reverse Logistics Trends and Practices* [Online]. Reverse Logistics Executive Council. Available at: www.abrelpe.org.br/imagens_intranet/files/logistica_reversa.pdf

Steinhilper, R. (1998). *Remanufacturing: The Ultimate Form of Recycling*. Fraunhofer IRB Verlag, Stuttgart. ISBN 3-8167-5216-0.

Sundin, E. (2004). Product and process design for successful remanufacturing, Linköping studies in science and technology. Dissertation No. 906, Department of Mechanical Engineering, Linköping University, SE-581 83 Linköping, Sweden. (Open access) [Online]. Available at: http://liu.diva-portal.org/smash/get/diva2:20932/FULLTEXT01.pdf

Sundin, E. and Bras, B. (2005). Making functional sales environmentally and economically beneficial through product remanufacturing. *Journal of Cleaner Production* 13(9): 913–925.

Sundin, E. and Lee, H.M. (2011). In what way is remanufacturing good for the environment? *Proceedings of the 7th International Symposium on Environmentally Conscious Design and Inverse Manufacturing (EcoDesign-11)*, November 30 – December 2, Kyoto, Japan, pp. 551–556, ISBN: 978-94-007-3010-6.

Repair cafés

Potential implications for product design and development

19

Scott Keiller and Martin Charter

INTRODUCTION

Repair cafés are part of a rapidly growing movement in civil society that advocates repair as a means of extending the useful life of consumer goods. Product longevity is a key element of Circular Economy (CE) thinking (Cooper, 2010), which can delay the generation of waste from disposal and slow down the consumption of resources in the production of replacement products. Since the first repair café opened in the Netherlands in 2009, their number has roughly doubled every two years and by 13th April 2018, there were 1,538 from 34 countries registered with the Repair Café Foundation.[1]

At each repair café, members of the local community bring a wide range of faulty or broken items — most commonly electrical equipment and clothing – for repair and repair advice. Volunteer 'fixers' guide and assist visitors with the repair. Visitors are therefore exposed in a very 'hands on' way to the notion that they can personally intervene in the product life cycle and through repair, preserve the value of their possessions.

In a survey of visitors to Farnham Repair Café, UK (Charter and Keiller, 2016), 60 percent said that attending the repair café had made them more likely to attempt to repair their own products in the future. So as well as providing a valuable service to local communities, it is probable that repair cafés are changing the attitudes of attendees and increasing their motivation to attempt to repair, rather than dispose of and replace, faulty products. In this way, repair cafés advocate longevity through repair on a one-to-one basis with consumers. On average, each of the world's 1,538 repair cafés attracts 29 visitors that bring 19 items for repair each a month (Chapter Charter & Keiller). Annually, this equates to 350,664 products being examined for repair and 535,224 visitors exposed to some degree to the possibility of attempting to repair their own products. Sabbaghi et al. (2016), found that consumers with personal experience of undertaking the repair of electronic products using the guidance on iFixit[2], a Wiki-based website for repair manuals, found that factors related to reparability, including complexity of repair and usefulness of repair information, have a significant effect on brand loyalty and future purchase recommendations. If greater numbers of consumers see reparability as an important factor in buying decisions, then manufacturers of consumer products might be expected to give it greater consideration in the design and development stage.

This chapter explores the role of repair cafés and other repair organisations in influencing policy-makers to design more reparable products and examines the lessons learnt from the first two years of repair data collected at Farnham Repair Café and their implications for product design.

ADVOCACY ON REPARABILITY AND LONGEVITY

The willingness of consumers to repair some electronic devices is increasing rapidly (Scott and Weaver, 2014). However, design for reparability is not a priority for most designers of consumer products. For the Repair Café Foundation and notably, iFixit and the Restart Project, improving product reparability is a key focus of their communications and advocacy activity. Seventy percent of respondents to the first global survey of repair café volunteers in 2014 (Keiller and Charter, 2014) expected repair cafés to have greater involvement in campaigning to improve the reparability and longevity of products. This expectation came to fruition in 2015 with the publication of a joint mission statement; *Sustainable Consumption and Production: Improving Product Durability and Reparability* by the Repair Café Foundation, iFixit, Rreuse and other European environmental advocacy organisations (Repair Café, International, 2015). The joint mission statement called for:

- Obligations on manufacturers to provide independent re-use and repair organisations with free access to repair and service documentation, diagnostic tools, circuit diagrams and software
- Batteries and other consumables in electrical and electronic equipment be adhesive-free and easily replaceable

- Design requirements for products to guarantee a minimum lifetime and ensure non-destructive disassembly of the product and components
- Provide consumers with information on average expected product lifetimes
- Spare parts to be widely available and affordable for a minimum number of years following the last batch of manufacture. Reuse of remanufactured and used components must be allowed
- Standards to be developed to rate the durability and reparability of products on the European market
- Explore the effects of extended minimum legal product warranties
- Lower taxes on repair service activities and increased taxes on single-use, resource intensive products

The Joint Mission Statement was developed in *Routes to Repair – Improving Product Reparability – Policy options at EU level,* (Rreuse, 2015), supported by the Repair Café Foundation, iFixit and others, which sought to inform the European Commission's (EC) Circular Economy Action Plan (EC, 2015). The action plan places greater emphasis on product durability, reuse and materials efficiency and in 2017, the EC announced a work programme for the development of standards on *Energy-Related Products – Material Efficiency Aspects for Ecodesign.* The proposed standards cover methods for the assessment of product durability, upgradability, reparability and re-use (CEN-CENELEC, 2017) and are an essential step in the development of new regulation.

Five leading community repair organisations; *The Restart Project,*[3] *The Repair Café Foundation, iFixit,* the Germany-based *Anstiftung Foundation*[4] and the US-based *Fixit Clinic,*[5] announced their collaboration with the launch of the *Open Repair Alliance*[6] in October 2017. The alliance aims to present a stronger case to manufacturers, designers and consumers through sharing data on recurrent faults in order to promote and demand greater reparability. A key objective of the alliance is to develop an *Open Repair Data Standard* for its members to combine and share open data on electronics repair. Although, Charter & Keiller (Chapter 25) found that 56 percent of repair cafés collect data on the types of fault or repair undertaken, there is no shared methodology for data collection and therefore the introduction of a standard could open up a potentially valuable source of information for product designers. The remainder of this chapter examines the repair activity and data collected at Farnham Repair Café (FRC), which from its inception has recorded detailed information on product faults and repairs.

CASE STUDY: FARNHAM REPAIR CAFÉ

Farnham is a medium-sized town in Surrey, UK. Farnham Repair Café (FRC) was launched in February 2015 and sessions take place in a hall in central Farnham and are held for three hours on the second Saturday of every month, excluding August. Repair volunteers, fixers, are from the local community and at each session, they provide 'hands-on' repairs and repair advice. It is a key requirement of FRC that product owners are present and observe or participate in any repairs undertaken. Regular 'Repair Stations' include; electrical and electronic, mechanical, textiles and furniture; a bicycle 'Repair Station' operates less frequently. In addition, a 'Creative Station' operates where visitors are encouraged to create a variety of artefacts from upcycled materials and waste products.

Between February 2015 and January 2017, over 1,000 visitors attended FRC sessions and 382 items were brought for repair. All items were logged with details of item type, fault diagnosis, repair outcome, an estimate of the cost of the repair in terms of consumables and parts and notes on advice given to the product owner.

Volunteer fixers successfully repaired 243 items; a 64-percent repair rate and a further 18 percent were partially repaired. A partial repair is recorded when the diagnosis of a failure is made, and the repair is started, but not completed due to time constraint, economic viability or lack of available spare parts.

The remaining 18 percent of items were not repaired during sessions. This includes repairs that were too difficult, costly or time consuming to repair safely. Owners were advised to seek professional repair expertise or, if the product was beyond repair, advice was given on routes for disposal and recycling. The frequency of products by category presented at FRC and repair outcomes are presented in Figure 19.1.

Seventy-three percent of items were repaired for less than £1 (Figure 19.2). These include repairs that cost nothing, e.g. the removal of blockages in vacuum cleaners and those repairs that required consumables, including adhesives, lubricants, solder, cotton thread, wiring, offcuts of material used in patching and low-cost electronic components. A further 22 percent of products were repaired for between £1 and £5, reflecting the cost of electrical components and zips for clothing. Costs over a £1 were generally born by product owners who purchased parts on the advice of FRC fixers. Just 5 percent of items cost £6 or more to repair.

All of the 382 products brought to FRC were examined and assigned to one of 31 fault types. Figure 19.3 shows the 15 most frequent product

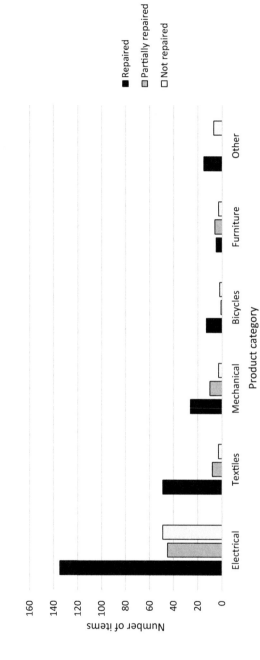

Figure 19.1 Number of items presented at FRC and repair outcome by product category

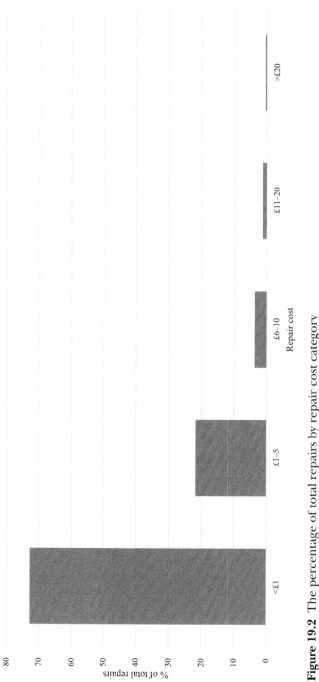

Figure 19.2 The percentage of total repairs by repair cost category

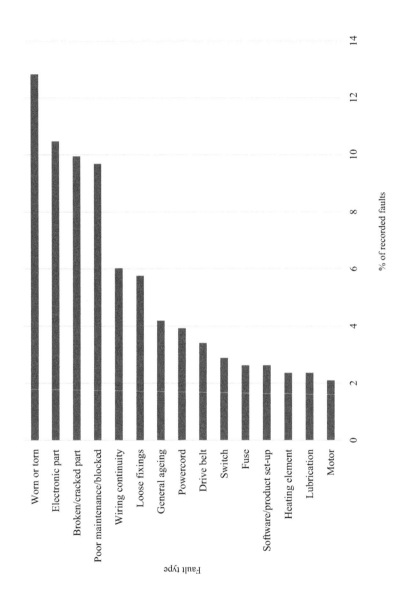

Figure 19.3 Fifteen most frequently observed faults as a percentage of all 382 items brought for repair

faults across all categories and includes 81 percent of the products brought for repair. A further 11 percent of products had faults that could not be diagnosed by FRC.

The most common single failure type was 'worn or torn', which related primarily to textiles and clothing. Ten percent of products were not faulty but were believed to be faulty because of poor maintenance or adjustment. These tended to be electro-mechanical products, and included blocked vacuum cleaners and incorrectly tensioned sewing machines (Table 19.1). The following two sections describe repairs to electrical and electromechanical equipment and clothing, which together made up over 90 percent of all items presented at FRC. Repair

Table 19.1 The 10 most frequent EEE items presented at FRC and their most frequently and second most frequently diagnosed fault types

Item type	Number of items examined	Most frequent fault (number of items)	Second most frequent fault (number of items)
Radio/CD/HIFI	47	Electronic component (15)	Wiring continuity (7)
Lighting	37	Loose fixings (7)	Electronic component (7)
Vacuum cleaners	19	Poor maintenance or adjustment (6)	Drive belt (4)
Gardening tools – electrical	19	Motor (5)	Drive belt (4)
Personal health & haircare	18	Poor maintenance or adjustment (2)	Heating element (2)
Sewing machines	17	Poor maintenance or adjustment (10)	Broken or cracked part (2)
Laptops	10	Electronic component & ageing (4)	Broken or cracked part (3)
Toasters	10	Heating element (4)	Electronic component (3)
Irons	7	Broken or cracked part (2)	Poor maintenance or adjustment (1)
Kettles	6	Heating element (2)	Broken or cracked part (2)

details for bicycles and furniture are not described further because of the small number of items presented.

REPAIRS TO ELECTRICAL AND ELECTROMECHANICAL EQUIPMENT

Almost all faults were diagnosed and repaired without access to repair manuals or user documentation, which product owners had not usually retained. Often diagnosis and repair can be completed in less than 15 minutes; for example, a number of vacuum cleaners have been repaired simply by removing dust and hair from tubes and rotating brushes and the owner advised about on-going product maintenance. Some fans presented as faulty simply needed to be rotated by hand for a minute or so to free up a sticking rotation mechanism.

However, the majority of appliances require disassembly to diagnose faults and this is often the most time consuming element of repair, together with reassembly. Different types of screw fittings and awkwardly positioned snap closures on appliances increase complexity and handling time. Some appliances, particularly small haircare products, had degraded and brittle plastic snap closures in the outer casing which were damaged during disassembly, effectively rendering them beyond repair. Plastic snap closures are considered by many experts as being indicative of good eco-design, because they reduce the need for different types of fixings and reduce handling time for dismantling at end-of-life, but they have often been a barrier to repair particularly in small electrical items. Faulty sealed external power supplies were also deemed to be beyond repair, although the faults were likely to be from blown fuses, capacitors and diodes that if accessible could have been replaced.

Almost 11 percent of faults were due to faulty electronic components, mainly transistors and capacitors. For most citizen repairers, these are challenging repairs to undertake. Fault diagnosis can be straightforward, in the case of spotting a blown capacitor, but might also require the use of multi-meter and other specialist equipment. Soldering replacement components is a skill that must be learned and product owners were guided through this process to give them an insight into the technique.

Broken or cracked plastic parts were common faults across all appliances and included broken on/off switch mechanisms or cracks in the outer casing of appliances, which were repaired with adhesives or replacement parts if available. Breaks in the continuity of internal wiring were repaired with new wiring and on some occasions wire connectors had simply become dislodged and were reconnected and crimped in place.

REPAIRS TO TEXTILES

Most of the textile repairs and advice provided by fixers has related to clothing. Common repairs included sewing outer fabric and linings, patching holes and repairing or replacing faulty zips.

Product owners are encouraged to learn how to hand-stitch and use sewing machines under supervision. The emphasis in textiles repair is to give people the confidence that they are able to complete many of the repairs themselves. Often repairs have required very basic skills, including how to correctly sew a button on a garment. Patagonia, the clothing manufacturer, actively encourages its customers to maintain and repair its products and has collaborated with iFixit to share online repair guides.[7]

Charter & Keiller (Chapter 25) found that volunteers at 34 percent of repair cafés around the world undertake modifications to clothing, taking in fabric to reduce size and letting it out to increase size, and this has also been a frequent activity at FRC. In addition, some of the modifications and repairs have been completed to accentuate the repair, including darning holes in knitted garments with different colour yarns and sewing obvious patches over holes to add character to the garment. This practice is similar to the Japanese art of *Kintsugi* in which broken pottery is repaired using gold and silver lacquers to draw attention to the repair, effectively treating breakage and repair as part of the character and history of an object, rather than something to disguise.

SUMMARY OF FINDINGS AND DESIGN CONSIDERATIONS EMERGING FROM THE EXPERIENCES OF FARNHAM REPAIR CAFÉ

The following summary of findings from two years of operation at FRC focuses on electrical and electronic equipment (EEE) and clothing, the two most common categories of goods brought for repair.

1. Most products can be repaired very cheaply – 73 percent for less than £1.
2. Products which are designed with built-in obsolescence, e.g. sealed power supplies and products with sealed batteries, electric toothbrushes, etc. are irreparable and unsustainable.
3. Most products are not designed for disassembly and repair. Some products are better designed for disassembly at end-of-life

than for repair and reassembly. Plastic snap closures are prone to degradation and breakage and so can therefore prevent non-destructive disassembly and reassembly following repair.

4. Manuals on product maintenance and trouble-shooting are frequently not retained by the owners but correct maintenance can prolong the product lifetime. The printing of QR codes directly on products could direct the user to online documentation. Simple schematic diagrams could be printed on the internal panels of products and the labelling of connectors and voltages on printed circuit boards would improve repair efficiency.

5. In EEE, there are often weakened solder joints and wire connectors, connected to or near to moving parts, i.e. on/off switches are a frequent cause of product failure. Where components fail in flat-screen TVs, these are most often standard components, e.g. capacitors, transistors, diodes and resistors in the device's power supply that can be replaced easily and cheaply.

6. Spare parts can be sourced online for many products, from companies like eBay and iFixit. Service documentation can also be sourced online for many EEE products, although it is usually unclear whether this is with the agreement of manufacturers.

7. Basic sewing and clothing repair skills have declined as new clothing has become cheaper. Simple repair skills are easy to teach and learn. Companies like Patagonia actively encourage their customers to repair their own clothing.

8. Clothing repairs, in which the repair is accentuated on purpose, e.g. through obvious patching or darning can bring character to a garment and makes a fashion statement about repair.

DISCUSSION

The first repair café opened in the Netherlands in 2009 as a way of reducing waste and actively engaging the public in sustainability at a local level. The Repair Café Foundation, which now represents 1,538 repair cafés in 34 countries, seeks to exert greater influence over man-ufacturers and policy-makers to improve the durability and reparability of consumer goods by channelling the expectations and observations of over 15,000 volunteers. As a grassroots organisation that started as a means to 'act locally but think globally', the growing popularity of repair cafés and collaborations with others, like iFixit and Restart, promises to give these citizen-powered local initiatives the opportunity to also 'act globally'. In a similar way to citizen science projects that have enabled the collection of large scientifically valuable datasets on biological populations (e.g. garden birds, butterflies etc.) by motivated individuals, the Open Repair Alliance offers the possibility of bringing together annual data from thousands of locations and hundreds of thousands of citizen repairs.

Although repair cafés enable the repair of a wide range of consumer goods, electrical and electronic equipment (EEE) are the most frequently repaired items. Waste from EEE is the fastest growing waste stream globally (Baldé et al., 2015) and many products with small faults are disposed of and replaced (Green Alliance, 2015). The finding that 73 percent of the products at FRC were repaired for less than £1 suggests that much of the waste disposed of each year could be repaired at negligible cost. Also, the fact that 10 percent of items brought to FRC for repair needed simple maintenance rather than repair could potentially be addressed by manufacturers, simplifying the maintenance process and providing maintenance information printed on the product, rather than solely in manuals that are commonly lost or discarded by product owners.

The design implications and themes emerging from two years' repair experience of FRC show the types of data and observations that can be collected at a repair café. Gathering and analysing data from thousands of community repair organisations as envisaged by the Open Repair Alliance could provide valuable data for manufacturers on repair in a real-world, non-specialist setting. There is an opportunity for some manufacturers to become actively involved in describing the types of data that could be collected about their products. In this way, manufacturers committed to improvements in durability and reparability could be part of this new progressive alliance and potentially make a significant contribution towards a more Circular Economy.

NOTES

1 https://repaircafe.org/en/
2 www.ifixit.com/
3 https://therestartproject.org/
4 https://anstiftung.de/english
5 http://fixitclinic.blogspot.co.uk/
6 https://openrepair.org/
7 www.ifixit.com/Patagonia

BIBLIOGRAPHY

Baldé, C.P., Wang, F., Kuehr, R., and Huisman, J. (2015). *The Global e-Waste Monitor: 2014*. Bonn: United Nations University, IAS – SCYCLE.

CEN-CENELEC. (2017). *Work Programme 2017: European Standardisation and Related Activities* [Online]. Available at: www.cencenelec.eu/News/Publications/Publications/cen-cenelec-wp2017_en.pdf [Accessed 20 November 2017].

Charter, M. and Keiller, S. (2016). *Farnham Repair Café: Survey of Visitors and Volunteers* [Online]. Available at: http://cfsd.org.uk/site-pdfs/Farnham%20Repair%20Cafe%20Survey%202016.pdf [Accessed 20 November 2017].

Cooper, T. (2010). Policies for longevity. In: T. Cooper (ed.) *Longer Lasting Products: Alternatives to the Throwaway Society*. Farnham: Gower, pp. 3–36.

European Commission. (2015). *Closing the Loop: An EU Action Plan for the Circular Economy* [Online]. Available at: http://eur-lex.europa.eu/legal-content/EN/TXT/?uri=CELEX:52015DC0614 [Accessed 20 November 2017].

Green Alliance. (2015). *A Circular Economy for Smart Devices: Opportunities in the US, UK and India*. London: Green Alliance.

Keiller, S. and Charter, M. (2014). A study of member motivations and activities in Hackerspaces and Repair Cafés. *Proceedings of 19th International Conference on Sustainable Innovation*, pp. 125–138. ISBN 978-0-9543950-7-0.

Repair Café International. (2015). *Joint Mission Statement* [Online]. Available at: http://repaircafe.org/wpcontent/uploads/2015/03/Mission_Statement_Reparability_and_Durability_of_Products.pdf [Accessed 21 October 2015].

Rreuse. (2015). *Routes to Repair* [Online]. Available at: www.rreuse.org/wp-content/uploads/Routes-to-Repair-RREUSE-final-report.pdf [Accessed 20 November 2017].

Sabbaghi, M., Esmaeillian, B., Cade, W., Wiens, K., and Behdad, S. (2016). Business outcomes of product repairability: A survey-based study of consumer repair experiences. *Resources, Conservation and Recycling* 109: 114–122.

Scott, K.A. and Weaver, S.T. (2014). To repair or not to repair: What is the motivation? *Journal of Res. Consum.* (26): 1.

Dislocated temporalities

20 Valuing difference and working together

Jonathan Chapman and Konstantinos Chalaris

AN ESTABLISHED, BUT OVERLOOKED, IDEA

Despite environmental and social framings of sustainability continuing to become an increasing object of design focus, sustainability concerns, until recently, have remained somewhat marginal. With the advent of design for the Circular Economy (CE), some larger institutions and industrial sectors are becoming aware of its value, and even though we are in an experimental stage, organisations outside of the mainstream are integrating these into their core business and strategies.

The roots of the CE run deep and wide, forming meaningful connections across a broad array of earlier works, spanning systems thinking, biomimicry, industrial ecology and the study of living systems (Pearce and Turner, 1989). Indeed, as many of the chapters in this book (*Designing for a Circular Economy*) show, the CE is not an especially new idea – it's been around for some time. Circular material and production practices have been embedded within industrial systems for some time, though not referred to as CE approaches. Today, CE has only become a more common focus of sustainable design discourse for those few specialised in teaching and researching this area.

In a 1976 research report to the European Commission in Brussels, entitled: 'The Potential for Substituting Manpower for Energy', Stahel first described his vision for an economy of loops, cycles and flows, explaining how economic actors in a loop economy can achieve a higher profitability than their competitors in the throughput economy (Stahel, 1976). Let's not forget, during the 30 years or more in which Stahel developed these radical new economic models, almost all waste was dumped in landfill sites, and there was no alternative energy infrastructure to speak of – such were the norms of the period.

There are several definitions developed in the recent years as CE has become a more mainstream topic (from WRAP in the UK, the Scottish and Welsh governments, to the European Union), but the one that most appropriately reflects our approach was developed by the Ellen MacArthur Foundation and states:

> A circular economy is restorative and regenerative by design, and aims to keep products, components, and materials at their highest utility and value at all times. A concept that distinguishes between technical and biological cycles, the circular economy is a continuous, positive development cycle. It preserves and enhances natural capital, optimises resource yields, and minimises system risks by managing finite stocks and renewable flows. A circular economy works effectively at every scale.

We are interested in this definition because it helpfully refers to technical and biological cycles that are reflected in the way we understand and work with CE (discussed later in this chapter).

MORE IS KNOWN THAN IS KNOWN IS KNOWN

Far more is happening in the CE space than one might realise and levels of engagement are on the rise. For example, the China Association of Circular Economy reported that – in relation to recycling and remanufacturing – China's CE grew 15 percent every year from 2006–2010 and a doubling in value from 1 trillion yuan in 2010 to 1.8 trillion yuan in 2015. Activities over the past several years have shown that, in China, CE is emerging as an economic strategy rather than a purely environmental strategy (Yuan et al., 2006). Internationally, levels of industrial and commercial engagement with CE are rising, overall, and many manufacturers are actively engaged in the search for more resource-efficient ways to design materials, products and services.

In addition to fuller engagement, radical reinterpretations of CE are also emerging from small-scale businesses like Nudie Jeans – a business-to-consumer (B2C) model – where customers can have their old jeans repaired for free, resell as second-hand or donate to the company's recycling programme. Others design in a way that draws clear distinction between 'biological nutrients' (designed to re-enter the biosphere safely and build natural capital) and 'technical nutrients' (which are designed to circulate at high quality without entering the biosphere) (Braungart and Mcdor, 2002) to ensure ease of disassembly and recycling downstream. Considering product flows and systems, Good to Go's cup-sharing programme allows customers to buy coffee from one coffee shop and return their mug to another once they are finished with their drink. Much of this is due to their smaller scale, which affords a degree of agility that allows them to 'pivot' their practice relatively quickly and realign their business model with the principles of the CE. These businesses take these understandings and weave them into the design process itself. Medium-scale business like Freitag, which works both on a business-to-business (B2B) and a B2C level, create customer value and experience by producing, for example, bags from used truck tarpaulins, and Timberland who collaborates with a vehicle tyre manufacturer and Omni United to create soles for their new line of shoes.

In this new creative landscape, there has never been a more exciting time to be a designer. Unfortunately, though, design schools are falling behind in engaging, not only with CE, but overall sustainability teaching in the curriculum. For a range of reasons, the majority of design educators believe that sustainability is not 'their subject' as they view the consideration of issues of sustainability as an area of expertise rather than a vital necessity. This comes from personal experience, but we can also find evidence in the Future Fit Framework (Ryan, 2011), which argues that to transform the curriculum and pedagogy at the core of their higher education experiences requires deeper innovation in staff development and across institutions (UNESCO, 2014). The past five years has seen an upsurge of participation in design for the CE projects in a number of the world's more forward-thinking design schools – from TU Delft in the Netherlands, to Parsons The New School for Design in the US – but participation amongst the majority of design schools is still limited.

ACTION TRUMPS MOTIVE

Many of the 'moves' made by global businesses toward the CE are not always motivated by ecological concerns. Often, they are driven by anxieties over material quality and establishing control over unstable resource markets and material flows. In many cases, the 'sustainability' or 'ethical' dimension of their transition to the CE is more of a secondary concern. This does not matter. What matters is that businesses are making the transition, and doing so in a way that is simultaneously good for business and the planet. Too often we get caught up in unhelpful and polarizing debates surrounding the deeper motivations behind a particular business and their effort toward making sustainable change. H&M was one of the first global fashion companies to launch a CE collection, taking in fibres not only from their own brand goods but that of other brands too. In 2012 they launched the 'Conscious Collection' in an attempt to embrace CE, where they used recycled yarns (made out of plastic bottles) for their garments, and avoided certain toxic fibres and unethical material sources. Many criticized these attempts as cynical marketing stunts. Yet, behind the scenes at H&M Design, things have changed as a result of this collection, which empowers staff – from fashion designers to pattern cutters – to more effectively adapt to a new creative and ethical operating environment; one where creative success is closely aligned with social and environmental concerns. Linked to this shift in the industry, we witness the worldwide emergence of new fashion and textile design programmes that re-invent themselves in the name of sustainability and in many cases, circularity.

When framed as a systemic approach to better management of resource flows, one could argue that we have been living with the ethos of CE for some time. For example, some readers of this text may even remember the glass soda bottles that you could bring back to shops in return for some small change? Some of you may have, as we did, hoarded these empty bottles, then one day, took them back to the store to claim your windfall. At the age of seven, we would stockpile these resources, then choose the optimal moment to trade-in our material economies . . . usually, until they were worth enough to buy an ice cream! Of course, these processes were not engaged with through any concern for resource depletion, environmental degradation or climate change. Instead, we engaged heartily within these systems because they had been designed in such a way that materials and resources had a tangible monetary value. As custodians of those materials, we had agency over that value, and therefore it was in our own interest to take care of them. Nowadays system like that usually exists with white goods, where companies offer to pick up your old fridge when you buy a new one. But in that case, we are missing the educational factor, as the user becomes passive and not engaged with the process.

Businesses like The Body Shop – founded by Dame Anita Roddick (1976) – successfully integrated product take-back into their business model, with stores being places to take-back empty containers and have them washed and refilled. Not only was this an excellent way to cut waste and increase resource efficiency, but it also provided a platform for awareness-raising and customer education. However, because of the rising social emphasis on convenience and speed at all costs, less than 1 percent of customers were using the refill service at the time the system was halted in 2002 and has yet to re-emerge.

THE BODY SHOP – A DESIGN RESEARCH PARTNERSHIP

In the CE, partnerships are essential, but difficult – a process of messy encounters characterised by ongoing negotiation and cultural appropriation. Collaborations between a university and a global retailer, for example, expose deep cultural and structural incompatibilities on both sides. When managed correctly, partnerships lead to the co-creation of mutually-beneficial intellectual and practical environments. It is in these neutral spaces that co-creation and innovation occurs.

In the case of a recent collaboration between the authors and The Body Shop, it was clear that the co-development process of the research was as valuable as the results of the research itself. Established in 2015 by Professor Jonathan Chapman, and developed in collaboration with Research Fellow Konstantinos Chalaris, this ongoing partnership supports The Body Shop in their transition to CE by increasing resource efficiency, enhancing product experience and cultivating brand value. One of the primary aims of this collaboration is to reinvigorate a culture of informed risk-taking and adventure within design and business thinking at The Body Shop; overcoming the restrictive cultures and norms that so often stifle innovation in large, established businesses. In addition to innovation in new sustainable materials, manufacturing processes and product innovation, this research partnership is underpinned by an ongoing body of field studies, interviews and empirical research, to better understand users in relation to their particular contexts and realities.

Through this partnership, we have developed practical and theoretical bodies of research that support The Body Shop in:

- **Enriching materials:** not only do we seek to enrich the ecological performance of materials and manufacturing processes at The Body Shop, but we also work to extend their social and experiential impacts.
- **Enriching products:** we optimize user experience and product performance with a focus on circular product design and integrated systems thinking.

- **Enriching people:** this strand relates to how The Body Shop can support, develop and nurture people; from the way users experience products and services to how workers are cared for at different points along the supply chain.

The research process features several clearly defined long-term 'programmes', each comprising several interlinked shorter-term 'projects'. This research structure has been designed to allow the research agenda to grow and flex (as business objectives continually grow and flex), without shattering the overarching theoretical frame.

Supporting a business in their transition to the CE requires a deeper shift in the culture and values of the organisation. This approach represents a more generative and reflexive way of establishing a partnership – that goes beyond the didactic format of many conventional 'consultancy' relationships – to cultivate more optimal conditions for innovation to take place. We mapped out technical and natural based circularities for projects that take a variety of forms: from gift box packaging that became a bird nesting box after use, through to an in-store system to encourage users to bring bottles back and the have them customised whilst refilling them.

Through our ongoing commercial engagements, we have found that many businesses already possess much of the skill and capability required to operate successfully within the CE context. What stands in their way, often, are the 'bad habits' and unhelpful 'norms and assumptions' which prevent them from seeing the opportunities that lie before them. We also found that design schools also exhibit such creative blind spots and latent prejudice against certain forms of idea; frequently dismissing things that we hastily deem unimportant or invalid. Hence, the Keynesian assertion: 'The difficulty lies not so much in developing new ideas as in escaping from old ones' (c. 1935).

TOWARD HYBRID TEMPORALITIES

Our research working in the design and CE space with The Body Shop has shown that a key limitation to the success of partnerships between design schools and businesses is that of 'dislocated temporalities'. That is to say, we work at a different pace and depth, with one partner often struggling to see the value in the temporal culture of the other. Our contention is that for partnerships to first establish, and then endure fruitfully, a far deeper appreciation of each other's temporal culture is needed. Much of this relates to the effective setting of expectations at the outset. Yet, many academics are afraid to do this, as they fear appearing 'slow' or 'unable to keep up' with fast-paced industrial cycles. For us, it is more about showing the value in slowing down, and the richness of results this shift in pace can lead to. In fast-paced business environments – and especially in the retail arena – companies are competing to create unique ideas, novel ways to increase profit and maintain currency with customer demand. Whilst also concerned with competition, design schools compete at a slower pace, spending longer on each iteration whilst also committing considerable time to the 'is this even the right thing to be doing?' types of questions. In the CE context, both forms of enquiry are essential. Clearly, a more reflexive process is required, that critically speculates upon underpinning questions, whilst practically developing strategies for effectively engaging those questions. Our research process aimed to draw these two dislocated temporalities closer together, and create a more reciprocal, empathetic research environment. In doing so, we created a new 'hybrid temporality' in which both partners could effectively collaborate and work together on solving complex problems – a process that benefits both partners; creating fertile ground for the growth of unexpected ideas, opportunities and research outputs.

CONCLUSIONS

Many businesses are beginning to experiment with design for CE, with varying degrees of success. Whether these engagements are motivated by economic or environmental concern is less relevant for us. Universities, and design schools in particular, are also beginning to take up the challenge to develop more circular ways of thinking and designing. In many market sectors (e.g. white goods, consumer electronics, automotive), too often, the parallel research efforts of industry and academia fail to connect and are carried out in isolated ignorance of one another. If we are to more effectively integrate academic and industrial discourses around CE design, for example, we must first develop a more collaborative 'mindset and posture' (Irwin, Kossoff and Tonkin, 2015). One which has academics working with, not for, industry – a more reflexive mode of research and partnership. Of course, embedding the tools and practices of the CE into design represents a major challenge. However, until these temporal roots are firmly grasped, design for the CE will always teeter around the edges of impact but never fully drive the transformational changes it so passionately advocates. Indeed, systemic challenges like climate change, loss of biodiversity and resource scarcity will persist until we fundamentally redesign their underpinning systems. This is far from simple, as Dan Lockton urges, 'understanding how to act to change the systems we're in is arguably the biggest meta-challenge of our age' (Lockton, 2015).

BIBLIOGRAPHY

Braungart, M. and Mcdonough, W. (2002). *Cradle to Cradle: Remaking the Way We Make Things.* New York: North Point Press.

Irwin, T., Kossoff, T., and Tonkinwise, C. (2015). Transition design: An educational framework for advancing the study and design of sustainable transitions. *Proceedings, International Sustainability Transitions Conference,* University of Sussex, UK, p. 8.

Lockton, D. (2015). *Let's See What We Can Do: Designing Agency,* cited from Medium. Available at: https://medium.com/@danlockton/let-s-see-what-we-can-do-designing-agency-7a26661181aa#.9d9vhbtu5 [Accessed 26 September 2017].

Pearce, D.W. and Turner, R.K. (1989). *Economics of Natural Resources and the Environment.* Johns Hopkins University Press.

Ryan, A. (2011). *Education for Sustainable Development and Holistic Curriculum Change* [Online]. Gloucester. Available at: http://efsandquality.glos.ac.uk/toolkit/AR_HEA.pdf.

Stahel, W. and Reday, G. (1976). *The Potential for Substituting Manpower for Energy.* New York, NY: Vantage Press.

UNESCO. (2014). *Shaping the Future We Want – UN Decade of Education for Sustainable Development.* Final Report, Paris: UNESCO.

Yuan, Z., Bi, J., and Moriguichi, Y. (2006). The circular economy: A new development strategy in China. *Journal of Industrial Economy, Yale.* Available at: http://onlinelibrary.wiley.com/doi/10.1162/108819806775545321/abstract.

21 Design for a Circular Economy in Industry 4.0

Rhiannon Hunt

INTRODUCTION

With each industrial revolution, the ability of manufacturers to convert raw materials into value-added products has increased in terms of efficiency, rate and capacity. Whilst this technological advancement has afforded industrialised nations continued development and economic growth, it has relied on a linear, 'take-make-dispose' economic model, which continues today. In a world of finite resources and limited carrying capacity, a prolongation of growth under a linear model is inherently unsustainable (Suavé et al., 2016). As a result, and with industry facing mounting pressure in the forms of price volatility, resource scarcity and increasingly stringent environmental legislation, an alternative model, the Circular Economy (CE), has been gaining interest worldwide.

The Ellen MacArthur Foundation, a prominent advocate for the concept, describes the CE as:

> ". . . one that is restorative and regenerative by design and aims to keep products, components, and materials at their highest utility and value at all times, distinguishing between technical and biological cycles."
>
> (Ellen MacArthur Foundation, 2015, p2).

The CE therefore represents an alternative approach to achieving sustainable production and consumption by encouraging a systems perspective and avoiding the limitations of incremental eco-efficiency efforts, such as the 'rebound effect'.[1] By redesigning the product value chain and employing practices, such as reuse, repair, remanufacture and recycling, the CE aims to decouple economic growth and development from the consumption of raw materials, eliminating waste and pollution and conserving natural resources. Transitioning to a CE will therefore involve significant changes to the ways in which value is generated and delivered to consumers, requiring business model innovation and the design of new products and services (Preston, 2012).

As such, design is a key facilitating factor in the implementation of a CE (Andrews, 2015). Further it has been recognised that the design stage benefits from its position early in the product development process, at which point there exists the most potential for radical innovation before considerable time and resources have been committed to any particular design or direction (Bocken et al., 2016). However, within the current industrial system, design for a CE faces a number of challenges, including those related to designer awareness and education (Andrews, 2015), the availability and provision of product and material data (Winans et al., 2017), consumer expectations (Tukker, 2015) and technical and economic feasibility (Preston, 2012). As such, the CE concept remains at the early stages of implementation and, generally, has not yet progressed from theory to practice (Ghisellini et al., 2016).

In parallel, industry is now entering what is widely believed to be a fourth industrial revolution, commonly referred to as 'Industry 4.0' (Kagermann, 2015). As with those that have preceded it, the next paradigm shift in manufacturing technology is expected to bring about significant changes, not only to production processes but also to products themselves, their design and consumption (Stock and Seliger, 2016). Industry 4.0 is therefore likely to result in a period of inevitable disruption and transition within the industrial landscape, in turn presenting new opportunities and challenges for a CE. Further, whilst previous industrial revolutions have been observed retrospectively, Industry 4.0 is a somewhat orchestrated phenomenon that has yet to fully unfold, suggesting that shaping it remains a possibility (Kagermann, 2015).

This chapter therefore provides an introduction to Industry 4.0 and a brief explanation of the key technologies and developments associated with its implementation. This is followed by an exploration of its potential relevance to design and the CE. Possible implications are discussed and examples of the early adoption of Industry 4.0 technologies are presented. Whilst certainly not definitive, the aim is to illustrate the intersection that exists between Industry 4.0, design and the CE, providing an early outline for further preparatory research, helping to direct this period of industrial transformation towards a more sustainable, circular future.

INDUSTRY 4.0

Industry 4.0 is a phenomenon driven by both an application pull and technology push. In terms of application pull, Industry 4.0 presents opportunities for differentiation and competitive advantage by enabling manufacturers to adopt more intelligent, automated, flexible and agile production processes (Lasi et al., 2014). In a globalised market dominated by mass manufacturing of standardised products and components in low-wage economies, manufacturers in countries with higher wages have faced increasing competition (Brettel et al., 2014). As a nation with a large domestic manufacturing sector, Germany was quick to recognise the potential of Industry 4.0, coining the term and incorporating the initiative into its national 'High-Tech Strategy 2020 Action Plan'. However, whilst Germany was certainly an early adopter, many other countries have since followed with their own version of Industry 4.0, including the UK, USA, China, South Korea and Japan (Liao et al., 2017).

In terms of technology push, Industry 4.0 is made possible due to a number of converging technological developments. The first is widespread Internet connectivity, including wireless digital communication channels, which support both human-to-machine and machine-to-machine communication. The second is the increasing miniaturisation, affordability and power of hardware, such as sensors, actuators and processors, making it technically and economically feasible to produce and deploy these components en masse (Kagermann, 2015).

Combining these two elements, it becomes possible to create 'cyber physical systems' (CPS), through which live data is automatically captured and exchanged in real-time between the physical world and the digital sphere (Jazdi, 2014). Building on CPS, numerous applications and complementary technologies have emerged and are included under the scope of Industry 4.0, including the Internet of Things (IoT), Big Data analytics, cloud computing, robotics, digital fabrication, artificial intelligence and virtual reality (Prisecaru, 2017).

IMPLICATIONS FOR DESIGN AND THE CE

Manufacturing in Industry 4.0

The integration of CPS within manufacturing will see production processes become increasingly automated, intelligent and flexible, giving rise to the smart factories of the future. As digital fabrication technologies, such as 3D printing, laser cutting, CNC (computer numerical control) milling and agile robotic assembly, enable the direct translation of data into objects, mass customisation and small batch production become economically and technically feasible (Brettel et al., 2014). In turn, the level of risk and initial investment associated with the production of new products, such as the expense of tooling, are reduced, which could see an increase in product innovation, including eco-innovation for a CE (Rudtsch et al., 2014).

Digital fabrication technologies also enable the division and geographical distribution of supply chains to create flexible, modularised and networked production processes. As a result, it becomes possible to replicate digital designs in any given location, on demand. Opendesk is an example of a furniture company embracing distributed manufacturing and digital fabrication technologies (Figure 21.1 & Figure 21.2). Consumers select a digital design from the Opendesk online platform and send this to a local manufacturer. The manufacturer then machines the design from sheet material to create the flat-pack furniture components, which are then delivered to the consumer ready for assembly. This type of manufacturing model allows the consumer greater control over the production process, whilst encouraging the selection of locally available materials.

With the point of consumption close to the point of production, new opportunities for closed-loop material recycling also emerge, as the time, expense and administration associated with transporting post-consumer materials back to distant manufacturing centres may be avoided (Pohlen and Farris, 1990). One example of this is Reflow, a company that seeks out local waste streams and endeavours to turn them into high-quality, recycled 3D printing filaments for local designers and makers. With access to both locally recycled materials and accessible and affordable digital fabrication methods, designers will likely be presented with new opportunities for creating circular products and business models.

Another Industry 4.0 development that may have relevance for design and the CE is the ability for products to guide themselves through automated manufacturing processes using near field communication (NFC) and radio frequency identification (RFID) technologies.[2] Should it be possible to run these processes in reverse, there exists significant potential to reduce the labour costs associated with product disassembly; a significant barrier to closing the loop (Makris et al., 2012). This would still depend on whether products are designed with disassemblable fixings, avoiding the use of adhesives, for example. However, automated, smart disassembly has the potential to make the difficult task of designing products for both durability during use and ease of disassembly at end of life a simpler process for designers.

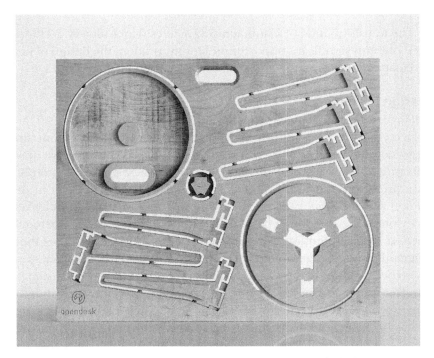

Figure 21.1 Edie stool by David and Joni Steiner for Opendesk, 2013

Source: Image by Rory Gardiner.

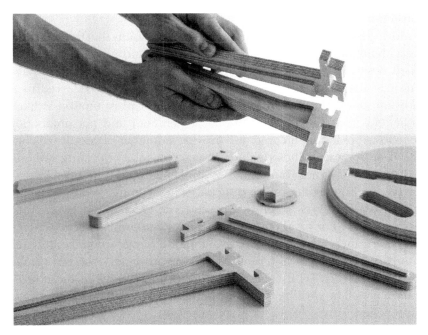

Figure 21.2 Edie stool by David and Joni Steiner for Opendesk, 2013

Source: Image by Rory Gardiner.

The transformation of manufacturing as a result of Industry 4.0 therefore presents significant opportunities for innovation, the design of new circular products and the adoption of closed-loop material cycles.

Design in Industry 4.0

Changes to manufacturing capabilities, as a result of Industry 4.0, are expected to not only impact on how products are fabricated but also how they are designed. The transition from the centralised, mass manufacture of standardised products to decentralised mass customisation presents opportunities for greater consumer participation in the design process (Kiel et al., 2016). One way that this can be achieved is through the development of co-design platforms, as demonstrated by Assa Ashuach Studio's 3D printed 'Helix Bracelet', which uses their Digital Forming® technology[3] (Figure 21.3). Whilst the designer specifies core product features and a set of design parameters, consumers are free to adapt the colour and shape of the bracelet, according to their own tastes and requirements, via the interactive design platform. It has been suggested that involving the consumer in the design process can help to ensure products meet individual consumer needs and strengthen the emotional attachment between consumer and product (Kohtala, 2015). This could help to keep functional products in use for longer, extending product life cycles and countering 'throw away' consumer culture.

Moving beyond co-design, there exists the possibility that the increased accessibility of digital fabrication technologies and intuitive computer aided design (CAD) software could drive more consumers to design and manufacture their own DIY products, in a process referred to as 'prosumption' (Smith and Light, 2017). Whilst prosumption is likely to benefit from the same emotional attachment and personalisation benefits as co-design, it could also present a number of additional complications for a CE. These include the challenge of educating not only professional designers but also every prosumer about the principles of the CE. It also becomes more difficult to regulate the quantity, quality, safety, toxicity and recyclability of products designed and manufactured by individuals. For example, within makerspaces, which serve as accessible fabrication workshops, the proliferation of discarded trinkets and prototypes referred to as 'crapjects' has already been observed (Smith and Light, 2017). Whilst the development of solutions to these problems may well be possible, it will require significant changes to existing approaches.

In terms of the process of design and who is making design decisions, it is evident that Industry 4.0 will present new opportunities and

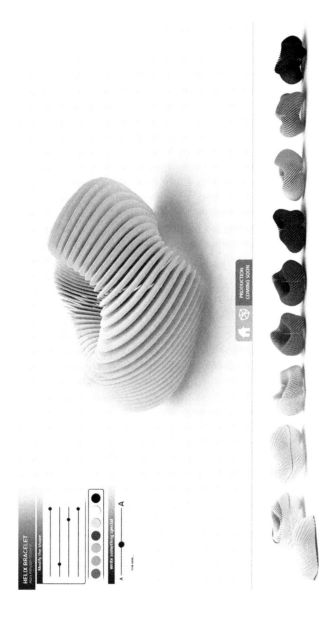

Figure 21.3 Helix bracelet.

Source: Objects, technology design and images by Assa Ashuach Studio.

challenges for a CE. Addressing the design of products will therefore be key to ensuring the necessary supporting systems are in place as new technologies are introduced.

Products in Industry 4.0

As Industry 4.0 brings about changes to manufacturing methods and design processes, new products are also likely to emerge, with implications for a CE. Where products become increasingly customised and individual, afforded by digital fabrication and smart manufacturing, it's possible that this will limit the potential for resale in second-hand markets, as consumers come to expect products to be tailored specifically to their needs. The lack of product standardisation may also complicate maintenance and repair efforts, as each product will require unique treatment, for which instructions and documentation may not be available. As a result, this could reduce the circularity of products in Industry 4.0, limiting end-of-first-life options to recycling.

The other major development is the networked connectivity of everyday products as part of the Internet of Things (IoT). This could provide designers with added visibility of products in use, past the point of sale, informing the design process and in turn helping to secure market success for radically new products designed for a Circular Economy. Connected products could also facilitate the transition towards alternative, use-based business models by enabling the remote monitoring, organisation and operation of physical assets. The move away from product ownership, towards service provision, generates a financial incentive for businesses to maintain, repair and reuse the products that they themselves own, encouraging the transition to a CE (Bocken et al., 2016). Whilst consumers can associate a loss of ownership with loss of control, preventing the uptake of product services (Tukker, 2015), the added visibility, reliability and convenience afforded by the real-time exchange of live data between connected products could present opportunities to overcome these preconceptions. Another opportunity provided by connected products is the potential to retain detailed information on their materials and construction, helping to facilitate repair, remanufacturing and recycling. This could overcome the issues associated with the individuality of customised products discussed earlier.

The connectivity of consumer products could also present designers with new aesthetic possibilities and consumers the ability to update their products. One example is ShiftWear™, footwear with integrated digital displays that allow the wearer to continually update the visual appearance of the product via their mobile phone (Figure 21.4.).

Figure 21.4 ShiftWear sneakers

Source: Objects, technology design and image by ShiftWear™.

Enabling consumers to customise and regularly update their products digitally could help to prolong their use, especially in the case of products that tend to be discarded due to changing fashion trends long before a loss of functionality. However, it should be noted that integrating electronic components into traditionally unconnected products, such as furniture and apparel, could also present challenges for a CE by adding an additional point of functional failure and complicating disassembly and recycling (Köhler, 2013). As such, it will be important for designers to consider both the opportunities and barriers to CE implementation as early as possible in the development of new products as a result of Industry 4.0.

SUMMARY

In conclusion, Industry 4.0 is expected to significantly transform not only the manufacturing sector but also the design process and those involved in making design decisions. This, combined with the diffusion of Industry 4.0 technologies into everyday life, is likely to give rise to new products and new methods of delivering value to consumers, such as product-services. These changes will present new possibilities and barriers for designing circular products and for transitioning to a CE. As such, further research is required to provide stakeholders and decision makers with the information necessary to navigate the transition to the fourth industrial revolution. Key topics of relevance for design and the CE include preserving product information in the case of mass customisation and distributed manufacturing, the regulation of prosumption and the EcoDesign education of prosumers, the opportunities presented for product innovation and servitisation and the potential implications for product and material circularity.

NOTES

1 'a behavioural or other systemic response to a measure taken to reduce environmental impacts that offsets the effect of the measure' (Hertwich, 2005, p. 86).
2 See Scholz-Reiter & Freitag (2007).
3 Digital Forming® is a software company founded by Assa Ashuach together with a team from the fields of engineering, business and online marketing in the 2000s.

BIBLIOGRAPHY

Andrews, D. (2015). The circular economy, design thinking and education for sustainability. *Local Economy* 30(3): 305–315.

Bocken, N.M.P., de Pauw, I., Bakker, C., and van der Grinten, B. (2016). Product design and business model strategies for a circular economy. *Journal of Industrial and Production Engineering* 33(5): 308–320.

Brettel, M., Friederichsen, N., Keller, M., and Rosenberg, M. (2014). How visualisation, decentralisation and network building change the manufacturing landscape: An industry 4.0 perspective. *International Journal of Mechanical, Aerospace, Industrial, Mechatronic and Manufacturing Engineering* 8(1): 37–44.

Ellen MacArthur Foundation. (2015). *Towards a Circular Economy: Business Rationale for an Accelerated Transition*. Cowes: Ellen MacArthur Foundation.

Ghisellini, P., Cialani, C., and Ulgiati, S. (2016). A review on circular economy: The expected transition to a balanced interplay of environmental and economic systems. *Journal of Cleaner Production* 114: 11–32.

Hertwich, E.G. (2005). Consumption and the rebound effect: An industrial ecology perspective. *Journal of Industrial Ecology* 9(1–2): 85–98.

Jazdi, N. (2014). Cyber physical systems in the context of industry 4.0. In: L. Miclea and I. Stoian (ed.) *Proceedings of the 2014 IEEE International Conference on Automation, Quality and Testing, Robotics*, 22–24 May, Cluj-Napoca. Los Alamitos: IEEE.

Kagermann, H. (2015). Change through digitization: Value creation in the age of industry 4.0. In: H. Albach, H. Meffert, A. Pinkwart, and R. Reichwald (eds.) *Management of Permanent Change*. Wiesbaden: Springer Gabler.

Kiel, D., Arnold, C., Collisi, M., and Voight, K. (2016). The impact of the industrial internet of things on established business models. *Proceedings of the 25th International Conference for Management of Technology,* 15–19 May, Orlando. Coral Gables: International Association for Management of Technology.

Köhler, A.R. (2013). Challenges for eco-design of emerging technologies: The case of electronic textiles. *Materials & Design* 51: 51–60.

Kohtala, C. (2015). Addressing sustainability in research on distributed production: An integrated literature review. *Journal of Cleaner Production* 106: 654–668.

Lasi, H., Fettke, P., Kemper, H., Feld, T., and Hoffmann, M. (2014). Industry 4.0. *Business & Information Systems Engineering* 6(4): 239–242.

Liao, Y., Deschamps, F., de F. R. Loures, E., and Ramos, L.F.P. (2017). Past, present and future of industry 4.0: A systematic literature review and research agenda proposal. *International Journal of Production Research* 55(12): 3609–3629.

Makris, S., Michalos, G., and Chryssolouris, G. (2012). RFID driven robotic assembly for random mix manufacturing. *Robotics and Computer-Integrated Manufacturing* 28(3): 359–365.

Pohlen, T.L. and Farris, M.T. (1990). Reverse logistics in plastics recycling. *International Journal of Physical Distribution & Logistics Management* 22(7): 35–47.

Preston, F. (2012). *A Global Redesign? Shaping the Circular Economy* (EERG BP 2012/2). London: The Royal Institute of International Affairs.

Prisecaru, P. (2017). The challenges of the industry 4.0. *Global Economic Observer* 5(1): 66–72.

Rudtsch, V., Gausemeier, J., Gesing, J., Mittag, T., and Peter, S. (2014). Pattern-based business model development for cyber-physical production systems. *Procedia CIRP* 25: 313–319.

Scholz-Reiter, B. and Freitag, M. (2007). Autonomous processes in assembly systems. *CIRP Annals* 56(2): 712–729.

Smith, A. and Light, A. (2017). Cultivating sustainable developments with makerspaces. *Liinc em revista* 13(1): 162–174.

Stock, T. and Seliger, G. (2016). Opportunities of sustainable manufacturing in industry 4.0. *Procedia CIRP* 40: 536–541.

Suavé, S., Bernard, S., and Sloan, P. (2016). Environmental sciences, sustainable development and CE: Alternative concepts for transdisciplinary research. *Environmental Development* 17: 48–56.

Tukker, A. (2015). Product services for a resource-efficient and circular economy: A review. *Journal of Cleaner Production* 97: 76–91.

Winans, K., Kendall, A., and Deng, H. (2017). The history and current applications of the circular economy concept. *Renewable and Sustainable Energy Reviews* 68: 825–833.

3D printing

22 Revolutionising the way we repair things

Nazli Terzioglu

INTRODUCTION

The Circular Economy (CE) is becoming a part of a new business agenda for companies worldwide. Rather than selling significant numbers of low-cost products, innovative business models are focusing on 'closing the loop', reusing and repairing products, selling services instead of items, and proving that it is possible to generate financial profit while respecting both the environment and society. We are transitioning towards a CE, but the world is now full of low-quality and short-lifespan products that are not designed for repair, disassembly and recycling. These products cannot just be discarded because they are not suitable for the circular system. The most environmentally friendly product is the one you already own because it does not require raw materials extracted from the earth and energy for manufacturing. The aim should be to make the most of existing products during the transition stage towards a CE. The throughput-based economic system has made it virtually impossible for citizens to get an economic repair service and to find spare parts for everyday household products. However, technological developments including 3D printing (3DP), computer technologies and online platforms have become widespread and provide various new opportunities to users, designers and manufacturers. More than 25,000 digital files of various products, ranging from a lens cap to a stove knob, are now available on Thingiverse[1] to download and make (MakerBot,

2012). It can be seen from online user platforms that there are people who want to fix their broken stuff. However, factors such as the design of products, unavailable spare parts and the high cost of repair prevent some of them from doing so (Terzioğlu et al., 2015).

3DP is an additive manufacturing process that builds up objects out of individual layers based on a digital file (Warnier et al., 2014). Since its invention 20 years ago, 3DP has drawn attention from a wide range of disciplines, used in diverse application areas including architecture, product design, fashion, food, medical industries, etc. (Manyika et al., 2013). It has affected the way we think about manufacturing. The interest in 3D printers has grown further after the maker-movement became widespread (Hagel et al., 2014). The technology has developed very fast and paves the way for businesses that provide 3DP services as well as low-cost desktop 3D printers. Although the main current application area of 3DP is prototyping in product design, today it is possible to produce many products; for example, bicycles, buildings, cars and even organs using living cells as a raw material.

The aim of this chapter is to explore the opportunities for and barriers to utilising 3DP technology for product repair. Twenty physically damaged products were fixed by using 3D-printed parts. The resulting artefacts are intended to help stimulate exchanges between the author, the audience and the wider world.

OPPORTUNITIES

3DP technology presents chances for businesses, designers and users to create, innovate and repair. This research has revealed six specific opportunities that have the potential to transform the way we produce and consume.

Producing spare parts

Unavailability of spare parts is one of the common barriers to product repair. It is very hard and sometimes impossible to find spare parts to repair or upgrade products, as the current linear economic system expects users to buy new products when they are damaged.

Consequently, it is a common user behaviour to throw away an umbrella with a broken handle. However, 3D printing the handle and fixing the umbrella and extending its lifespan is a more environmentally friendly option (Figure 22.1).

Although it is not widespread currently, it is possible to download CAD (computer-aided design) models and 3D print spare parts with

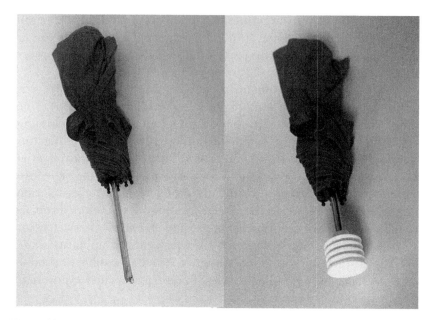

Figure 22.1 3D printed umbrella handle

desktop 3D printers or in 3DP facilities. Sometimes it could be easier and cheaper to repair a product with 3DP than buying a new one. Prescription glasses could be a good example. It could be easier to 3D print and replace temples as can be seen in Figure 22.2, instead of finding suitable frames for your face and buying the lenses.

Improving/altering product design – adding extra features

3DP is capable of creating complex shapes, unlike conventional manufacturing methods, which are restricted in the types of shapes that can be achieved (Warnier et al., 2014). 3DP offers the potential to create even eccentric designs. The spare parts do not have to be the same as the originals; instead, they could be designed in a different way to improve the products or personalise them. The toy sword in Figure 22.3 is an example of this category. The owner wanted it to be stronger and longer than before and wanted his name to be written on it.

A similar example is the Victorian glass candle holder in Figure 22.4. It was sitting on the shelf of an antique shop since the owner had accidentally dropped it on the floor. Unfortunately, all the broken parts were thrown away. However, this restriction resulted in a stimulating experimentation as 3DP provides the opportunity to try different designs to alter the shape of the object or add new functions. The missing parts were designed in a way that they would emphasize the difference of

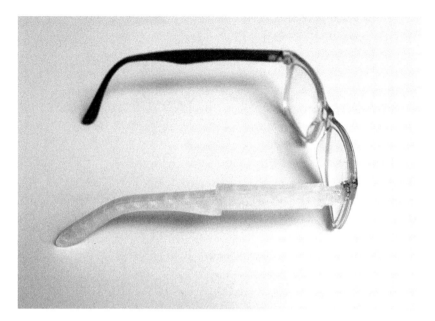

Figure 22.2 3D printed eyeglasses temple

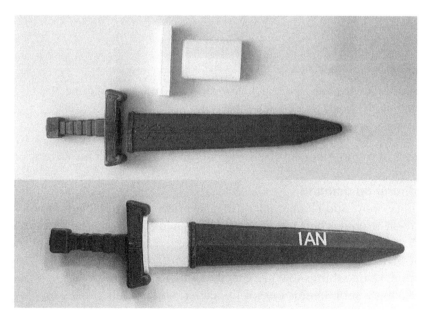

Figure 22.3 Toy sword repaired with a 3D printed part

Figure 22.4 Victorian candle holder repaired and augmented using 3D printing

materials and the production methods. The final piece became a synthesis of traditional manufacturing methods and new technologies.

Printing on demand

Unlike conventional manufacturing, 3D printers are suitable for making one-off products because previous investments such as unique moulds for each product or different manufacturing machines are not required for 3DP. One of the most significant potentials of 3DP is its ability to create unique things that are exactly suited to their purpose.

Fixing a shoe heel is one of the easiest shoe repair processes. However, if one wants to create a unique shoe heel due to aesthetic or health reasons, it could be very expensive or impossible with conventional methods depending on the design. The user owns his/her product and 3DP gives them the opportunity to customise it as much as they want to or are able to. The examples in Figure 22.5 and Figure 22.6 were

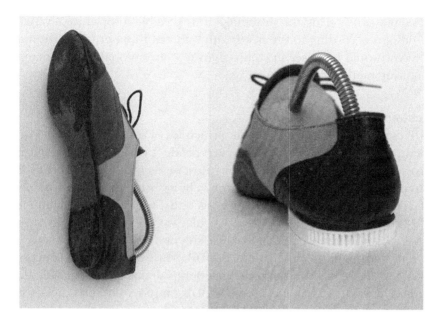

Figure 22.5 3D printed shoe heel

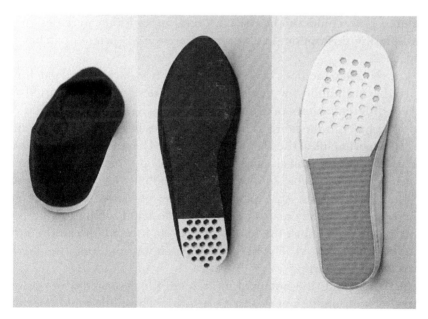

Figure 22.6 A 3D printed shoe heel and a shoe sole

designed considering this advantage. It is possible to produce a variety of designs according to the needs and wants of the user with 3DP, and the cost would be lower in comparison to conventional one-off manufacturing methods.

Sustainability implications

3DP contributes to the three main principles of sustainability (environment, economy and social). However, product design, manufacturing processes and post-use opportunities must be reconsidered and restructured fundamentally. Current literature about sustainability implications of 3DP mainly focuses on energy costs and CO_2 emissions (Baumers, 2012; Lindemann et al., 2012). Particularly, Gebler et al. (2014) provides a comprehensive and global assessment of this topic.

The sustainability implications of 3DP on the environment encompass the decrease of resource and energy demands along with the carbon dioxide (CO_2) emissions as 3DP employs additive means of production (Gebler et al., 2014). 3DP enables product life extension through repair and upgrade. In addition, end-of-life products can be recycled with a 'recyclebot' that uses household polymer waste and turns it into 3D printer filament (Kreiger et al., 2013). Thus combining the 3D printer with a 'recyclebot' would enable 'closing the loop' and positively affecting environmental dimension of sustainability. The 3D printed parts could also be reused several times if they were designed considering this option, like, for example, the 3D printed patches in Figure 22.7.

Conventional methods of textile repair such as darning and patching were the inspiration for this example. The design process started by trying different shapes of 3D-printed patches that could be pinned or sewn on holes in the fabric. The four examples in Figure 22.8 were the initial experiments of the 3D printed patches. These 3D printed patches were made out of semi-circular button-like 3D printed parts, strung on a fishing line to enable some degree of flexibility to make it suitable for mending textiles. An exploration of the movement of sewing and the form that thread created inspired this design. Each button has two holes. Users can adjust the length of the patch by adding and removing beads as required. The 3D-printed patch was sewn onto the fabric through the buttons.

3DP also holds the potential to increase the accessibility of objects together with online open-source platforms. Thus, this could improve the living conditions in rural areas affecting the socioeconomic conditions positively.

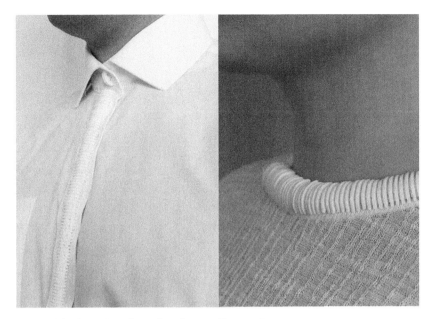

Figure 22.7 3D printed patches for textile repair

The interest in 3D printing

Damaged, frayed and repaired products are often associated with economic hardship and poverty. 3DP can be effective to encourage people to try repairing and to overcome the barriers and negative stigma attached to repair activity.

A 3DP pen was included in this study because it draws people's attention. As people are naturally interested in this technology, it becomes easier for them to focus on the positive and interesting aspects of the repair process. The working mechanism of a 3DP pen is similar to a glue gun. It heats up in one minute after it is plugged in. Then a polylactic acid (PLA) or acrylonitrile butadiene styrene (ABS) plastic string inside the pen melts with the heat and comes through the nozzle. The product is easy to operate, but it is very hard to create neat shapes with it.

A damaged lace doily was repaired with the 3DP pen as it can be seen in Figure 22.9. The repair process started with drawing the pattern on paper and following the lines with the 3DP pen. Although the pattern was two dimensional, it was hard to create the exact shapes. The final result was both aesthetically pleasing and interesting. The glass in Figure 22.10 was also repaired with 3DP pen. The broken part was filled with the filament by creating small dots. This process was easier compared to the doily example.

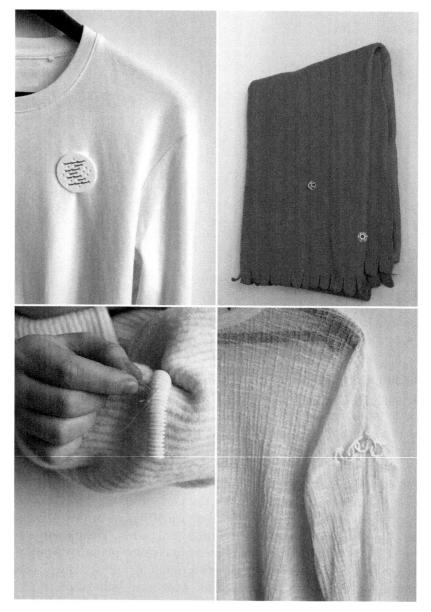

Figure 22.8 Initial experiments of the 3D printed patches

Possible future developments

A myriad of innovations in manufacturing technology is taking place at the moment. People will 3D print food, living tissue and fully assembled electronic products when these innovations are more fully diffused (Lipson and Kurman, 2013). It is conceivable for manufacturers

Figure 22.9 Lace doily repaired using 3D printing pen

to provide 'official' downloadable 3D models of spare parts of products which they produce in the near future. Moreover, it will be possible to print active systems like a working mobile phone instead of passive parts (Lipson and Kurman, 2013).

Figure 22.10 Glass repaired with 3D printing pen

The ripped USB cable and damaged earphone jack in Figure 22.11 could be given as examples to this category. These cannot be repaired if the wire is damaged. However, it is possible to design cables with detachable parts and these parts would be 3D-printed with the wire inside in the future.

BARRIERS

Despite the opportunities that 3DP technology offers, several factors are preventing its wider adoption. The barriers of employing 3DP in repair are discussed under three categories below.

Knowledge, skills, and time required

Developing 3D CAD models requires skills, knowledge and time. However, there are open-source websites such as Thingiverse where one can find CAD models of various product parts and instructions for repairing products with 3D printed parts; currently, the variety of these 3D CAD models is not sufficient enough to answer the need.

In some cases, it might be easier to find a replacement part or a similar one rather than 3D printing it because of the knowledge, skills and time required. The watch strap in Figure 22.12 and the little teapot in

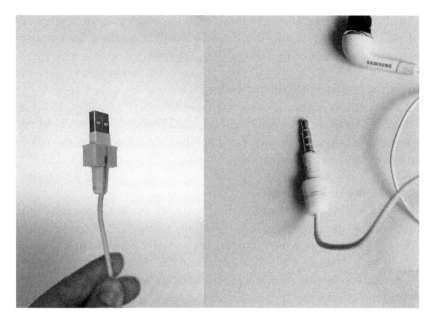

Figure 22.11 A USB cable and an earphone jack fixed with small 3D printed parts

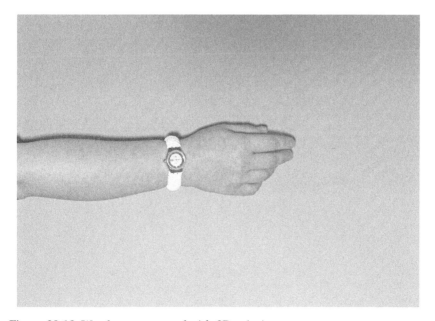

Figure 22.12 Watch strap created with 3D printing

Figure 22.13 can be given as examples of this case. Plenty of watch straps are available in stores and it is possible to find another lid from second-hand shops or antique shops.

Precision needed in CAD modelling

Digital precision is one of the advantages that 3DP provides. However, it could be difficult to create a precise CAD model, especially for the products with organic shapes. For example, it was not easy to create a spare part that fits the damaged spout of the teapot in Figure 22.14.

Accessibility of facilities

Creating the CAD model and finding a 3D printer are some difficulties that could be faced when fixing products using 3DP. However, these issues could be addressed when 3DP technology gets more widespread in the future. For example, 3D Hubs[2] is an online 3DP service platform that tries to solve this problem. It connects people who want to make 3D prints with 3D printer owners in the local area. It was founded in April 2013 in Amsterdam. Printer owners can provide information about their 3D printers on the platform to offer 3DP services. Users can upload their design and choose the available print locations on an

Figure 22.13 3D printed teapot lid

Figure 22.14 Teapot with a damaged spout

interactive map. If CAD models of various product parts and the 3DP service become more widespread in the future, it would become easier to download, and 3D print product parts according to our needs and wants with the desktop 3D printers or in local stores.

IMPLICATIONS OF FINDINGS IN RELATION TO CIRCULAR ECONOMY (CE)

3DP has a great potential for prolonging the useful life of products and helping transition towards a CE. Businesses and designers play a crucial role in achieving this. First of all, the design of products should enable circularity through 3DP for repair. That means designing products that are possible to repair, considering frequently broken product parts, and designing spare parts for 3DP. These parts could also be designed to personalize or upgrade the product. Additionally, this potential of 3DP and other technologies could be used by designers and manufacturers for encouraging people to repair their products and participate actively in the transition process towards a CE.

The categories and examples discussed here offer businesses new opportunities. Especially, 'producing spare parts' category stands out in this aspect. Some companies are still not fully aware of this potential.

Licensing the production of parts for repair, providing a 3DP service and renting design files for components at online platforms are some of the examples where they could generate profits.

The barriers discussed here would be useful for businesses that wish to integrate 3DP into their business models as a repair and upgrade strategy. The barriers should be considered with possible future developments. Additionally, some of them could be overcome by offering 3DP as a service.

CONCLUSION

This chapter discusses the current opportunities for and barriers to utilise 3DP technology for product repair. Twenty physically damaged products were fixed by using 3D printed parts, and the process helped define the opportunities and barriers of 3DP considering the repair of physically damaged products. The possible future developments that might affect the economic system and business strategies were also mentioned. Business leaders, designers and researchers should look ahead and identify how these technological developments could affect them if they want to be a part of the circular system. It would be exciting to see the transformation that 3DP technology brings to product design, repair process and to the production and consumption system in time.

NOTES

1 www.thingiverse.com/
2 www.3dhubs.com

BIBLIOGRAPHY

Baumers, M. (2012). Economic aspects of additive manufacturing: Benefits, costs and energy consumption. Doctoral dissertation, Loughborough University, Loughborough.

Gebler, M., Uiterkamp, A.J.S., and Visser, C. (2014). A global sustainability perspective on 3D printing technologies. *Energy Policy* 74: 158–167.

Hagel, J., Brown, J.S., and Kulasooriya, D. (2014). *A Movement in the Making*. Westlake, TX: Deloitte University Press. Retrieved from: https://dupress. deloitte.com/content/dam/dup-us-en/articles/a-movement-in-the-making/DUP_689_movement_in_the_making_FINAL2.pdf.

MakerBot. (7 November 2012). *Introducing MakerBot Thingiverse Dashboard and Follow Features.* Retrieved from: www.makerbot.com/blog/2012/11/07/introducing-makerbot-thingiverse-dashboard-and-follow-features/

Manyika, J., Chui, M., Bughin, J., Dobbs, R., Bisson, P., and Marrs, A. (2013). *Disruptive Technologies: Advances That Will Transform Life, Business, and the Global Economy,* Vol. 12. New York: McKinsey Global Institute. Retrieved from: www.mckinsey.com/business-functions/digital-mckinsey/our-insights/disruptive-technologies.

Kreiger, M., Anzalone, G.C., Mulder, M.L., Glover, A., and Pearce, J.M. (2013). Distributed recycling of post-consumer plastic waste in rural areas. *Proceedings of MRS,* Cambridge University Press, Vol. 1492, pp. 91–96.

Lindemann, C., Jahnke, U., Moi, M., and Koch, R. (2012). Analyzing product lifecycle costs for a better understanding of cost drivers in additive manufacturing. *Proceedings of Solid Freeform Fabrication Symposium,* Austin, TX, pp. 177–188. Retrieved from: https://sffsymposium.engr.utexas.edu/Manuscripts/2012/2012-12-Lindemann.pdf.

Lipson, H. and Kurman, M. (2013). *Fabricated: The New World of 3D Printing.* Indianapolis, IN: John Wiley & Sons.

Terzioğlu, N.G., Lockton, D., and Brass, C. (2015, November 9–10). Understanding user motivations and drawbacks related to product repair. *Proceedings of the Sustainable Innovation 2015 Conference,* pp. 230–240. Surrey, UK.

Warnier, C., Verbruggen, D., Ehmann, S., and Klanten, R. (eds.) (2014). *Printing Things: Visions and Essentials for 3D Printing.* Berlin, Germany: Gestalten.

Exploring circular design opportunities for wearable technology

23

Anne Prahl

WEARABLE TECHNOLOGY INNOVATION IN THE CONTEXT OF THE CIRCULAR ECONOMY

Over the last couple of years there has been an unprecedented rise in the sale of activity trackers and smartwatches, and in line with this trend, we are also seeing more fashion and sports clothing with integrated sensors and electronics coming to the market. While textile-based wearable technology is still considered a niche product, the US market for e-textiles or smart clothing is predicted to reach over US$3 billion by 2026.[1] Activity trackers and smart watches have a relatively short life span, and a third of users are believed to discard their trackers within six months.[2] Although there are no figures on textile-based wearable technology such as electronics and sensor-enabled bras, t-shirts and shorts yet, technology obsolescence, wash care issues and changing consumer preferences are likely to contribute to a relatively limited life span for these types of products too.

The challenge

From an environmental perspective, one could highlight an array of issues with the manufacture of wearable technology, including non-renewable resource depletion (for textiles and electronic and conductive components) and the use of potentially hazardous and toxic substances, which could have negative health impacts on workers as well as end-users. Within the context of the Circular Economy, end-of-life issues for textile-based wearable technology is a particular concern, as electronics and sensors are often deeply embedded within the yarn, textile or garment, thus creating hybrid products, which are extremely difficult to identify and recycle at end-of-life. In 2008, researcher Andreas Köhler highlighted these potential consequences and stated that by integrating electronics into textiles, the industry is creating a new waste stream (Köhler, 2008), which current textile or electronics recycling facilities and systems are not equipped to deal with yet.

Seamless integration appears to have become the Holy Grail for textile-based wearable technology design, as permanent and often invisible integration such as knitted, woven, printed, embroidered, laminated and bonded technologies seem to prevail on the innovation agenda (Prahl, 2015). These challenges are made even more difficult when we consider that many of the new generation materials are blended together on a nano-scale, which is imperceptible to the naked eye. Despite the growing momentum around circular design innovation in the textile and clothing industry, wearable technology stakeholders appear reluctant to acknowledge and address any environmental challenges associated with the manufacture, use and disposal of their products, seemingly pushing through long-awaited commercial success at any costs. This situation is not helped by the fact that these hybrid products fall into a grey area between electronic consumer goods and clothing, and are therefore not yet explicitly addressed by the WEEE Directive, which lists various electrical and electronic equipment categories, although none of these include electronic textile or sensor-enabled clothing. Furthermore, even hardware products, such as smartwatches or fitness trackers, are not clearly identified as part of the electrical and electronic equipment list.[3]

CIRCULAR DESIGN CONCEPTS FOR TEXTILE-BASED WEARABLE TECHNOLOGY

Design for circularity eliminates waste as part of the design process and replaces the idea of a product's 'end-of-life' with 'the end of its period of primary use' (Ellen McArthur Foundation, 2015). The circular system builds on the differentiation between the technical cycle, where durable technical components can be reused, remanufactured or recycled into new materials and products of the same or higher value in continuous cycles (i.e. Teijin ECO CIRCLE polyester recycling[4] for clothing), and the biological cycle, where biological components can be safely returned to the environment without causing any negative impact (i.e. C & A's first Cradle to Cradle Certified™ t-shirt, which can be recycled or composted[5]). In addition, products should be designed to be durable, repairable and reusable in the first instance, so that the product's active lifespan can be extended for as long as possible.

Practice-led PhD research (Prahl, 2015) investigated design opportunities for wearable sensors, which could detect biochemical and environmental stimuli and data, in order to monitor and improve the user's health and wellbeing. Inspired by the end-of-life challenges identified, the research project explored the creation of new types of wearable sensors, designed with closed-loop solutions in mind. In particular, the work sought to anticipate and eliminate the end-of-life issues caused by seamless technology integration, which includes approaches such as electronics and sensors permanently attached or embedded into textiles and clothing. As an alternative, Prahl proposed non-integrated form factors (*ibid.*); where instead of being merged with an item of clothing, the wearable becomes a stand-alone accessory that can be worn directly on the skin (such as the temporary tattoo sensor developed by UCSD[6]), a particular part of the body (such as the fingertip sensor developed at the University of Illinois at Urbana-Champaign[7]) or temporarily attached into clothing (such as the cancer-detecting bra developed by First Warning Systems[8]).

Furthermore, instead of being restricted to traditional knitted and woven textiles, the aim was to experiment with nonwoven 'wearable materials' (*ibid.*), inspired by ground-breaking new technologies such as 3D knitting, printing and spray printing, as well as materials 'grown' from bacteria or mycelium. Additional inspiration came from emerging material technologies from the field of medical science, such as flexible and stretchable electronics, epidermal and electronic tattoos and paper-based electronics and sensors. Many of these types of substrates could potentially be engineered to be reusable, and recyclable or biodegradable at the end of the product's life and therefore provide inspiration for future wearable technology design and development. Building on the design, review and dissemination of the research project's conceptual collections, three concepts – design for durability, reuse and repair; design for recycling; and design for biodegradability – were proposed to inspire more disruptive innovation in the field of commercial wearable technology design and manufacture in order to rise to the challenge of developing products and services fit for the Circular Economy.

Design for durability, reuse and repair

Design for durability, reuse and repair is a concept that responds to planned obsolescence of electronic consumer products, where products are deliberately designed to have a limited useful lifespan. In line with the Circular Economy philosophy, products should be designed to be durable, both physically and emotionally, so they can be utilised for a long time, by one or several users. In the case of wearable technology, physical durability would include the use of durable materials and components, which should also be easy to repair, while software should be updateable. In addition, emotional durability describes the consumer's desire to want to keep and use a product for a long time, as it continues to fulfil their needs and preferences. This can be achieved through involving the consumer in the design of the product, such as offering customisation and co-creation opportunities to provide a truly unique product and further taps into the trend of DIY manufacture by individuals.[9]

This concept therefore aims to appeal to a consumer who is keen on customising products to their personal specification and taste. Wearables could be created with 3D printing pens[10] or 3D printers at home or in makerspaces and enabled through electronic and conductive painting[11] or printing. A key feature of this concept is the use of patch and plaster-like accessories, which are worn directly on the skin (Figure 23.1), or attached to the wearer's clothes, footwear or accessories to fit into the existing routines and outfits of the user. Sources for inspiration include the heart-rate monitor band-aid, developed at Stanford University[12] and biosensor tattoos developed at UC San Diego.[13]

Another relevant strategy is to design modular and versatile products, which can adapt to the changing user needs. An interesting example is the BLOCKS smartwatch,[14] available to pre-order and due to be shipped in 2018, which encourages the consumer to select from a range of modules to build their perfect smartwatch. In terms of reusability, another example from the wearable technology sector is an initiative based at Tufts University, whose Recycle Health charity[15] collects unwanted wearable activity trackers and refurbishes them to provide wearable devices to people who aren't able to afford them. In the future, 3D printers could also be utilised to repair and upgrade wearables, or products could be designed with repairability in mind from the start. A good example is the Fairphone,[16] which is designed to last and to be repairable; this is achieved through a six-piece modular construction, where individual elements can be replaced or repaired easily.

Design for recyclability

Design for recyclability is an important principle to enable product disassembly and subsequent reuse and recycling of the product's inherent materials and components. In particular view to textile-based wearable technology, this concept aims to develop products that can act as a

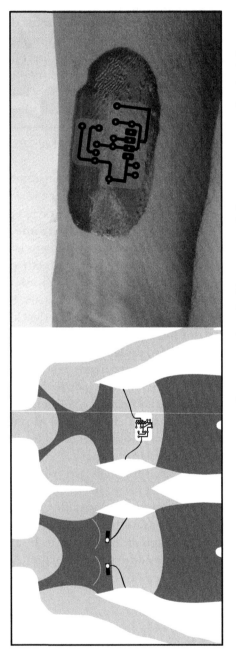

Figure 23.1 DIY-made wearable sensing patch connected to clothing system via impermanent conductive ink pen on skin (mock-up)

natural extension of the wearer's skin and body (figure 23.2) and relies on the use of tactile nonwoven materials to provide comfort and natural interaction with devices. Emerging materials include flexible polymers and stretchable electronics from the medical field, such as the electronic fingertip cuff,[17] a flexible circuit that is worn on a surgeon's fingertip to enable greater sensitivity and precision during scans and surgery. These new generation wearables would follow a mono-materials design strategy, to ensure entire products can be recycled, or designed for disassembly to easily separate materials and components and recycle them independently.

Existing electronic consumer product disassembly technologies could provide inspiration for future disassembly of wearable technology, these include 'active disassembly' (Chiodo et al., 1999), 'end-of-life unzipping' of electronics (Wickham, 2013) and 'triggered degradation' (Scott, 2014). In addition, an emerging example from the textile and clothing sector is the wear2[18] technology, a process for microwave disassembly to de-brand clothing, remove labels or prepare textile-based products for recycling at end-of-life. Academic institutions and electronic consumer product companies have been working with design for recovery and recyclability since the mid-1990s; examples include Brunel University,[19] US company Dell Inc.[20] and Samsung,[21] and this movement was accelerated by the implementation of the original WEEE Directive in the UK in 2006, which outlined requirements for the recovery, reuse, recycling and treatment of WEEE.

Despite the on-going improvements regarding recyclability in the electronics industry and emerging recycling technologies for textiles and clothing (i.e. Evrnu cotton recycling[22] and Worn Wear chemical recycling for blended fibres[23]), by blending together electronics and textiles into one product, the recovery of raw materials becomes far more

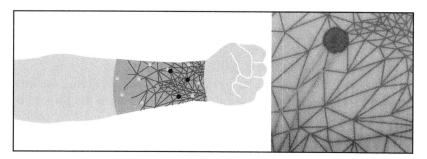

Figure 23.2 Second-skin sensing sleeve made with recyclable flexible polymer (mock-up)

complex and is only commercially viable if there is sufficient reuse or recycling value in the embedded materials and components. However, from an environmental perspective it is imperative that the industry develops technologies to separate electronic components from textiles, so they do not contaminate textile recycling or end up in landfill.

Design for biodegradability

In order to eliminate the use of fossil fuels and petroleum and discarded packaging going to landfill, we are seeing a significant influx of innovation around new biodegradable raw materials for short-lived products such as packaging. However, when considering this route for more durable products like clothing, designers must scrutinise their choices of materials and any colouration, treatment and finishing carefully, as these will have an impact on the products' safe and effective biodegradation. In addition, for biodegradability to work for clothing on a commercial scale, further research, development and implementation must be undertaken to provide access to efficient composting facilities and services for consumers around the globe.

As an alternative to the complex challenges of developing disassembly and recycling solutions for textile-based wearable technology, there could be compelling opportunities to develop entirely benign electronics, which can be dissolved or composted at end-of-life. This approach speaks to the shift in manufacturing science identified by Dr Carol Handwerker, a professor of materials engineering at Purdue University, who pointed out that in the context of wearable electronics, materials need to be engineered to be safe to be worn next-to-skin, and therefore must be harmless to the wearer's skin and organs.[24] Conceptually, this idea could also embrace the problem of technology obsolescence and fast-fashion by designing more transient wearables, worn for shorter periods of time, and this concept could take a more lo-tech approach to textile-based wearable technology design, to provide the user with more simple interaction, possibly without the need for complex on-body electronics. Natural or bio-based materials could be used to create wearable forms, which can provide basic non-electronic feedback, such as colour-change, through the use of thermo-chromic or other stimuli-responsive inks.

Textile substrates, which act as carriers for the enabling technology, could include include natural fibres such as wool (Figure 23.3), wood-based manufactured cellulose (i.e. Tencel or wearable paper), 3D spray-printed material made from latex and cotton (Cosyflex[25]), 'grown' materials utilising microbial cellulose (i.e. BioCouture[26]) or mycelium (MycoWorks[27]). A variety of emerging printed electronic and sensor technologies[28] could be temporarily attached to the substrate

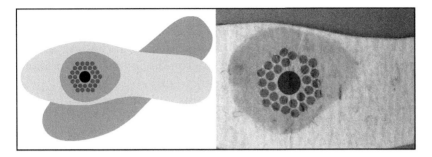

Figure 23.3 Felted wool sensing insole with biodegradable electronic transfer print (mock-up)

(i.e. biodegradable film or adhesive) to enable the wearable to provide interaction and feedback, while keeping the entire product biodegradable and compostable. Examples include transient electronics, which dissolve at a prescribed time;[29] biodegradable electronics, which utilise compostable semiconductive polymer;[30] or other biocompatible components, such as the diagnostic wax-printed paper sensor,[31] which does not require a power source. Power could also be generated from the wearer's sweat, as engineers at the University of San Diego have developed stretchable biofuel cells, capable of extracting energy from sweat, which can then power various electronics.[32] In addition, biodegradable batteries from wood pulp[33] or biodegradable batteries made from cuttlefish ink[34] could be utilised.

INDUSTRIAL APPLICATION OF CONCEPTUAL PROPOSALS AND DIRECTION FOR FUTURE WORK

As textile-based wearable technology is predicted to grow significantly over the next five to ten years, the need to develop effective and viable circular design proposals is extremely pressing. While repairable, recyclable and biodegradable electronics are at an early stage of innovation, these concepts illustrate that emerging materials and technologies such as bio-based and recycleable nonwovens, flexible polymers, transient and biodegradable electronics, biodegradable batteries and new manufacturing and disassembly technologies, could provide tangible inspiration for designing more resource-efficient wearable technology. However, in order to translate this type of conceptual work into an industrial context, we must develop methodologies to embed circular design thinking into the innovation, design, development and manufacture of commercial wearable technology products and services. Due to the complexity of the design and manufacture of wearable electronics and textile systems, it is vital to bring together and build on emerging research and developments from both the textile and clothing and the electronics industry, as well as enable cross-disciplinary collaboration between product, textile, user experience and service designers, product and material developers and scientists and engineers, in order to pioneer and implement new solutions.

Furthermore, textile-based wearable technology comprises a broad range of consumer product categories including fashion, sport, fitness and wellbeing, and health and medical, as well as a diverse product types including hardware, clothing, accessories and footwear. These products further differ in terms of the enabling technologies they utilise, such as sensors, electronic components and batteries. In addition, there are disparate levels of requirements across global markets; while the US and Canada have more specific state and federal certification regulations and standards regarding the user's health and safety, others may operate on a system of self-declaration or voluntary certification, offered by commercial global testing and certification services. According to testing and certification service company TÜV SÜD,[35] the problem goes deeper still, as even in regions where regulations and standards specific to wearable technology exist, these generally concern individual components, rather than the complete product or system. Although testing and certification companies outline comprehensive parameters to evaluate the reliability and safety of wearables during *consumer use*, and many companies comply with these voluntary certification standards already, the discussion of the *end-of-life* management of such products is far less advanced.

As previously mentioned, the European WEEE Directive does not cover textile-based wearable technology, such as sensor-enabled sportswear or fashion items with integrated lights or electronic displays. In the absence of any clear guidelines or regulations regarding end-of-life management of textile-based wearable technology, this makes for an extremely ambiguous scenario and the industry is therefore likely to continue the innovation of new materials, technologies and products without any consideration for disassembly and responsible recycling, or indeed alternatives such as biodegradability, at end-of-life.

It is hard to predict whether the European WEEE Directive or regulatory bodies in other regions will take steps to clarify and regulate producer responsibility regarding waste reduction, reuse and recyclability during the manufacture and end-of-life of textile-based wearable technology. However, this approach should be considered an essential step to accelerate the innovation agenda around circular design and manufacturing, before these types of devices become mass-market products. An important starting point would be to clearly define wearable technology consumer product categories in line with their specific end-use and materials, components and enabling technologies utilised. These should then be matched with globally applicable human and environmental health standards and requirements in terms of their design, use and end-of-life management, to prevent the market being flooded with irresponsibly designed products that will potentially cause harm to the wearer during use, as well as environmental damage at end-of-life.

NOTES

1 www.idtechex.com/research/reports/e-textiles-2016-2026-technologies-markets-players-000459.asp
2 http://endeavourpartners.net/assets/Endeavour-Partners-Wearables-White-Paper-20141.pdf
3 www.conformance.co.uk/adirectives/doku.php?id=weeeexemptions
4 http://www2.teijin-frontier.com/english/sozai/specifics/ecopet-plus.html
5 https://www.c-and-a.com/uk/en/corporate/company/sustainability/c2c/
6 www.rsc.org/chemistryworld/2012/06/electronic-skin-health-and-security-checks
7 www.newscientist.com/article/dn22162-fingertip-tingle-enhances-a-surgeons-sense-of-touch/
8 https://hpectechtrends.wordpress.com/category/6-smart-technology/page/3/
9 http://diymanufacturing.mit.edu/
10 http://lixpen.com/
11 www.bareconductive.com/
12 www.runnersworld.com/newswire/temporary-tattoos-could-be-the-new-heart-rate-monitor
13 http://advancedtextilessource.com/2014/03/22/synthetic-skin-is-self-healing-2/
14 www.chooseblocks.com/
15 www.recyclehealth.com/
16 www.fairphone.com/en/
17 www.newscientist.com/article/dn22162-fingertip-tingle-enhances-a-surgeons-sense-of-touch/
18 www.ctechinnovation.com/funded-projects/wear2-microwave-textile-disassembly/
19 www.brunel.ac.uk/research/Institutes/Institute-of-Materials-and-Manufacturing/Design-for-Sustainable-Manufacturing

20 www.dell.com/learn/us/en/uscorp1/corp-comm/designing-green-recycling
21 http://www.isri.org/news-publications/article/2016/04/07/samsung-elec tronics-america-receives-isri%27s-2016-design-for-recycling-award
22 www.evrnu.com/
23 http://wornagain.info/
24 www.triplepundit.com/special/circular-economy-and-green-electronics/ wearable-tech-goes-recycle-less/
25 www.tamicare.com/
26 www.dezeen.com/2014/02/12/movie-biocouture-microbes-clothing-wear able-futures/
27 www.mycoworks.com/
28 www.printedelectronicsworld.com/tag/32/sensors
29 http://discovermagazine.com/2013/september/12-stretchy-flexy-future
30 http://news.stanford.edu/2017/05/01/flexible-organic-biodegradable-new-wave-electronics/
31 www.laboratory-journal.com/news/scientific-news/origami-styled-sensor-technology-rapid-diagnostics
32 www.sciencedaily.com/releases/2017/08/170822092209.htm
33 www.sciencealert.com/scientists-have-made-soft-light-batteries-from-wood-pulp
34 www.technologyreview.com/s/522581/biodegradable-batteries-to-power-smart-medical-devices/
35 www.tuv-sud.com/activity/testing/wearable-technology-wearable-de vice-testing-and-certification

BIBLIOGRAPHY

Chiodo, J.D., Billet, E.H., and Harrison, D.J. (1999). Active disassembly using shape memory polymers for the mobile phone industry. *Proceeding of the 1999 IEEE International Symposium on Electronics and the Environment*, pp. 151–156 [Online]. Available at: http://ieeexplore.ieee.org/xpl/articleDetails.jsp?ar-number=765867 [Accessed 18 November 2011].

Ellen Mcarthur Foundation. (2015). *Towards the Circular Economy Vol. 1: An Economic and Business Rationale for an Accelerated Transition* [Online]. Available at: www.ellenmacarthurfoundation.org/publications/towards-the-circu-lar-economy-vol-1-an-economic-and-business-rationale-for-an-accelerated-transition [Accessed 26 June 2016].

Köhler, A. (2008). End-of-life implications of electronic textiles. Assessment of a converging technology [Online]. Master of Science Thesis, Lund University, Sweden. Available at: http://lup.lub.lu.se/student-papers/record/1480555/file/1480556.pdf [Accessed 10 October 2011].

Prahl, A. (2015). Designing wearable sensors for Preventative Health: An explo-ration of material, form and function [Online]. Ph.D. Thesis, University of the Arts London. Available at: http://ualresearchonline.arts.ac.uk/9077/ [Accessed 23 May 2016].

Scott, J.L. (2014). Skeleton-material for triggered disassembly and organs-recovery of high value materials. *CLEVER Symposium*, 20 May, London.

Wickham, M. (2013). *Reuse of Electronic Products* [Online]. Available at: www.npl.co.uk/upload/pdf/20130516_reuse_elec_prods.pdf   [Accessed   26 July 2016].

24 Makerspaces as free experimental zones

Cindy Kohtala

INTRODUCTION

In recent years, there has been notable interest in exploring Circular Economy (CE) issues in makerspaces, particularly in Europe. Makerspaces are shared community workshops filled with tools and machines for designing and making objects, from conventional tools for conventional materials to equipment such as milling machines and laser cutters. Makerspaces (including FabLabs,[1] hackerspaces[2] and increasingly even DIY-biology labs[3]) vary greatly, from commercial or fee-based services to open-access, self-organised peer spaces. They may be hosted in municipal libraries or museums, or even in someone's private garage. They are especially associated with digital fabrication communities and the 'maker movement', which tend to emphasise electronics projects and use of 3D printers and computer numerical controlled (CNC) equipment such as milling machines, but they offer space for do-it-yourself (DIY) activities of all kinds, as well as for courses, consulting, co-working and socialising. Makerspaces have mainly emerged and spread in the last 10 years, now numbering at least 5,000 worldwide (Ananse Group, 2015). In many regions (e.g. western and northern Europe, many South American countries), they are notably frequented by designers or design students or hosted by design schools (Kohtala, 2016).

Organisations such as non-profit associations, university research groups, professional design associations and municipal authorities have formed partnerships or collaborations with makerspaces – or have founded their own – particularly to explore designing for a CE.

Objectives for these activities range from awareness raising to hands-on material experiments. These actors see great potential in the DIY maker movement, and they hope to learn from and exploit several distinct characteristics of both makers and makerspaces:

(a) Makers' vast and deep knowledge of technologies, components and materials
(b) Makers' willingness and ability to share knowledge openly and collaborate on projects, even virtually
(c) Makers' willingness and ability to disassemble, reassemble, hack and modify even 'black-boxed' proprietary products
(d) Makerspaces' embeddedness in local neighbourhoods and civil society.

Simultaneously, some makerspaces explicitly pursue environmental sustainability-oriented issues, including CE issues, such as discussing material sources or reducing or repurposing waste. Makers are also forming grassroots, circular-oriented initiatives that use makerspaces for prototype development and discussions, such as Open-Source Circular Economy (OSCE) Days[4] and Fab City.[5]

TRANSITIONING TO A CIRCULAR ECONOMY (CE)?

Four key observations stand out as relevant with regard to makerspaces and the transition to a CE.

1. Neither sustainable design nor CE principles are addressed with any consistency or clear priority in makerspaces. The people organising and using makerspaces (at least in Europe) do not tend to be sustainability-literate; the actors who understand technologies, products and digital fabrication largely tend to be different groups from those who have sustainability and circularity expertise (see Kohtala and Hyysalo, 2015; Fleischmann et al., 2016).[6]
2. Makerspaces are by definition counter-culture, meaning they operate at a grassroots, peer-to-peer level and tend to be structurally and ideologically distinct from mainstream production and consumption. They are experimental zones where prosumers[7] are exploring new design and production capabilities. However, newcomers to the DIY maker movement easily underestimate the distance between the time-intensive, explorative, situated, often collaborative, one-off and batch production that occurs

in makerspaces and incumbent industrial manufacturing. If the intention is to learn how to make current mass production more circular, much time and effort must be invested to derive insights from makerspaces, test new ideas and have them implemented.

3. An observation related to the second, makerspaces are diverse with regard to objectives, activities, context and in-house expertise. This means not every makerspace is as amenable an experimental playground for exploring new, circular industrial models or circular product design. Stakeholders wanting to work with makerspaces should manage their expectations accordingly and clarify means and ends, whether the objective is awareness raising or exploring, e.g. design-for-disassembly.

4. Makerspace actors take initiative and act as 'user innovators': they do not wait for their needs to be answered by incumbent institutions nor lobby for it. They act directly, whether this means developing single products or tools for a maker's own use or contributing solutions for the larger maker community to tackle barriers to knowledge sharing and diffusion of solutions. Observing what makers focus on – and supporting and accelerating their work – can be one important strategy in fostering a transition to circularity, as these forerunners encounter barriers to new circular models before the mainstream is aware of them.

DESIGNING FOR A CIRCULAR ECONOMY (CE)

The potential for learning and practicing design for a CE in maker-spaces regarding the *technical* cycle,[8] especially with regard to complex products, is currently low, without involvement of other stakeholders. Makerspaces (particularly in the global North) are not marked by a concern with circularity and do not clearly or systematically prioritise waste *prevention, reuse, repair* or *refurbishment.* Additionally, makerspaces generally do not involve manufacturing or extensive complex product development, and stakeholders wanting to work with issues related to *remanufacturing* need to strategically select the makerspace that provides the setting and expertise desired (Stewart, 2017). This means bringing in outside expertise on circularity opportunities, as well as skills in ped-agogy, communications and public engagement. Makerspaces *are* con-cerned with material toxicity, as a general part of occupational health and safety, and this could provide one entry point to where wider sys-temic consequences of production are discussed.

Hackerspaces[9] often promote component reuse and repair, but, depending on the region, repair events do not generally appear to be connected to makerspaces; the more established repair groups (e.g. repair cafés) tend to differ from makerspace communities (for more on repair cafés and hackerspaces, see Charter and Keiller, 2014). There seem to be several reasons why reuse, repair and refurbishment are not activities prioritised in most makerspaces. For one, the 'cool' factor of the maker movement that emphasises technologies can lead makers to prioritise 'cool', explorative projects over utilitarian projects such as repair (Schor et al., 2016). In the author's own fieldwork, regular repair events organised by an artists' collective in a municipal library makerspace were eventually abandoned, despite achieving mainstream appeal. Members cited barriers such as lack of funding to pay expert fixers, a lack of expert fixers available in their networks and the lack of storage space for tools or longer repair projects in the makerspace.

Currently, the skills and knowledge needed in repair, particularly of electrical and electronic products, are not widespread. Moreover, there are particular design skills required in refurbishment and remanufacturing strategies that are not formally taught in most design schools (i.e. design for product integrity, as formulated by den Hollander et al., 2017.) In makerspaces, individuals become experts in these arenas on an ad hoc basis based on their own interests.

Of the hundreds of makerspaces in Europe, to the author's knowledge, the ones focusing on circularity activities number only a few. There is nascent interest in connecting makers, fixers and the general public in spaces called 'remakeries' (particularly in the UK [e.g. Al Jazeera, 2013]), and it is possible these types of spaces will grow. A designers' makerspace in France, for instance, collects waste materials for its members to use in furniture making and other projects. It also hosts competitions on material reuse for professional designers; the outcomes are publicised and then sold to neighbourhood residents in festivals. In the UK, the RSA's Great Recovery initiative collaborated with FabLab London in hosting teardown workshops to educate on the disassembly of complex products and where materials such as rare earths come from. The materiality of such efforts is as important as it is in repair workshops: people seem to need to feel materials and manipulate components to be able to understand their characteristics, potential and implications. These activities thus aim at raising awareness of the value of materials among the general public and provoking designers into designing for reuse, but they remain at the edges of the mainstream.

In the technical and *biological* cycles, *recycling* and *cascading*[10] in makerspaces appear to have stronger potential that could be leveraged. Several makerspaces have taken interest in developing and using solutions for recycling plastic, as well as developing and/or testing compostable or biodegradable bio-plastics. Researchers in Oxford University, for example, have developed an open-source 'Universal Testing Machine' for recycled plastics in makerspaces, to help them improve their results (Future Makespaces, 2016). Some makerspaces are developing bio-based materials for, for example, textiles or construction that may be amenable to multiple life cycles. As these experiments take place outside of corporate research and development (R&D) departments and university research labs, they are 'under the radar' and are invisible or easily dismissed as inefficient, non-scientific, or irrelevant.

For those makerspaces located in universities, designers and researchers use them as a free, open, cross-disciplinary zone for experimentation. The experiments may address makers' desire for non-fossil-fuel-based materials; for solutions to growing piles of plastic waste in the lab; or for scale-up of recycling systems for peer-production-based material flows (see e.g. Hunt et al., 2015). While marginal, they are noteworthy, as they indicate issues that industry and policymakers have not yet addressed, or perhaps even identified, as barriers to mainstreaming more sustainable, circular, localised and more consumer-centric production. Alone, these projects and initiatives will proceed at their own speeds with likely limited impact, but with appropriate and timely institutional support, particularly strategic design, they can contribute to more circular or spiral material flows with larger applicability (see e.g. Smith, 2017).

INNOVATING FOR A CIRCULAR ECONOMY

Developing new materials and related processes, as described in the previous section, is one way makerspaces can contribute to Circular Economy innovation. But there are also experiments with new business models around open design and with new ways citizens can engage in peer-to-peer prosumption, producing for their own households and community needs.

Many designers in Europe are joining grassroots initiatives around circularity and open design and using them to test consumer acceptance of circular solutions (for water conservation, food production, clothing reuse and many other applications). OSCE Days is a distributed, global annual event, focusing on open-source, circular solutions, peer challenges, discussions and self organisation, usually using local makerspaces to host activities. OSCE Days and related initiatives remain marginal and their impacts in environmental terms undetermined. But they appear to be useful for designers to test prototypes in co-design workshops, with other designers and the public, to trial open design business models and to try to self-organise peer-to-peer activities without hierarchical management. Indeed, how designers currently create a livelihood with such endeavours is unclear. Nevertheless, the shift to servitising, customising and end-user development is incentivising some businesses to reconsider their business models and incorporate citizens more profoundly in what is produced and how. Designers familiar with makerspace community building, peer production and the open design ethos can contribute their expertise in these new designer-user relations (van Abel et al., 2011).

The flagship Fab City project in Barcelona's Poblenou neighbourhood is experimenting with turning waste into nutrients for other projects, socially and economically revitalising the neighbourhood and re-localising some aspects of production. The aim is to use existing infrastructure in the neighbourhood, including its makerspaces, to turn the region into "a distributed FabLab" (Díez, 2017). During these important early stages, what comes out as products is less important than the challenge of designing an intervention with many actors and, particularly, how designers 'use these interventions to trigger a conversation' (Díez, 2017).

Fab City, OSCE Days and related initiatives have two functions. First, they indicate to citizens, the makerspace visitors, how production can be both local and circular. Second, they show industry and authorities that neither the market nor policy is recognising demand for more autonomous, local, circular production, and independent makerspaces are thus acting to meet their own needs. As Andrews has written,

> Designers cannot wait for the development of a remanufacturing, reuse and/or recycling infrastructure and other alternative business models (. . .) before they start to design for the Circular Economy; they must anticipate and prepare for the alternative economy particularly where there is a long product lead time from initial concept to shop floor.
>
> (Andrews, 2015, p. 312)

Several makerspaces in Europe have attempted to create new business models around local production networks: linking customers, designers, production infrastructure and local materials in virtuous and low- or no-waste loops. Achieving such networks, however, appears to require resources that time-pressed makerspace managers do not have, and these initiatives often drop in priority or ambition (Prendeville et al., 2017). Makerspaces are therefore heavily reliant on volunteers and sponsors, and/or they seek project partners. Fab City consists of makerspaces in particular cities forming strategic partnerships; the main makerspace actors rest on solid funding from universities, project funding (from the European Commission, for example) and sponsorship. The initiative involves both the public sector's planning operations and bottom-up, neighbourhood-based, purely explorative activities, in makerspaces and involving existing organisations.

In these initiatives, design for *innovating a Circular Economy* include

(a) Designing for sharing (open design), disseminating circular solutions
(b) Designing collaboration and dialogue with citizens, which spreads knowledge on and acceptance of circularity
(c) Designing operative local production networks of varied actors that circulate materials.

But there is yet another skill that can be added to the toolbox:

(d) Designing platforms for peer-to-peer projects, which enable new economic models for a CE. Decentralised, adaptable software and Internet-based tools do aid collaboration and communication in the maker movement. However, platforms and tools should foster equitable, transparent and goal-oriented peer-to-peer governance, in order to strengthen existing makerspaces' under-developed efforts to network in alternative recycling, reuse, refurbishment and repair ecosystems that differ significantly from today's linear and hierarchical business models.

CONCLUSIONS

Due to lack of time, awareness or knowledge, makerspaces are currently not using their full potential to drive sustainability, particularly issues relating to local, Circular Economies that appear to be so suited to distributed peer production. Even when they are linked (as in the FabLab network), makerspaces remain niche and fragmented and do not have the capacity on their own to drive larger scale positive change. Designers, developers and innovators therefore have an opportunity to work with makerspaces in strategically testing circular designs, business models and innovative new ways to engage citizens in closed-loop, local solutions. Because of their marginality and small material volumes, environmental impacts are currently small. Nevertheless, environmental impacts, positive or negative, can scale up if makerspace activities mainstream. The amount of waste in production, for example, can significantly diminish if it is already now considered a nutrient for other processes, through reuse or recycling. This increases even more if such thinking is expanded to the local level, of a neighbourhood or even city.

To the author's knowledge there is currently little explicit activity to *systematically* develop and *codify* knowledge in makerspaces on designing for a CE. At this nascent stage, it appears that makerspaces' biggest role is changing designers' and non-designers' perceptions about products and materials and bringing them together in collaboration and dialogue. Designers experiment with new circular solutions and materials, and non-designers learn how to realise their own ideas or hack and repair consumer products. This is a shift in agency that, in time, can help render obsolete the incumbent linear production model.

NOTES

1 www.fablabs.io
2 http://hackerspaces.org
3 e.g. https://diybio.org
4 https://oscedays.org
5 http://fab.city
6 CE issues are regarded here as one element of 'sustainability' and a concept that has reached discussion in European makerspaces quite recently, i.e. in only the past few years.
7 Prosumption refers to activities where consumption also involves consumers producing.
8 Circular activities in the technical cycle considered here include reuse, recycling, repair, refurbishment and remanufacturing, as well as waste prevention.
9 Hackerspaces have a distinct identity, history and ideology. They are often membership funded and member governed without hierarchical management (Maxigas, 2012). They are not easily accessible to the general public.
10 Circular activities in the biological cycle involve returning nutrients to the biosphere (through composting or biodegrading) or, before this, recycling them into new uses as many times as materially possible, i.e. cascading.

BIBLIOGRAPHY

Al Jazeera. (2 October 2013). *The Remakery: Rebuilding Products and Lives, Using Materials Previously Destined for Landfill* [Online]. Al Jazeera. Available at: www.aljazeera.com/programmes/earthrise/2013/09/remakery-2013927104415709115.html [Accessed 12 September 2017].

Ananse Group. (2015). *MAP: Mapping Collaborative Innovation Spaces* [Online]. Ananse Group website. Available at: http://anansegroup.com [Accessed 14 August 2017].

Andrews, D. (2015). The circular economy, design thinking and education for sustainability. *Local Economy* 30: 305–315.

Charter, M. and Keiller, S. (2014). *Grassroots Innovation and the Circular Economy: A Global Survey of Repair Cafés and Hackerspaces.* Farnham, UK: The Centre for Sustainable Design, University for the Creative Arts.

Díez, T. (2017). Presentation on Fab City at the FAB13 Santiago conference, 01.08.2017, Santiago, Chile.

Fleischmann, K., Hielscher, S., and Merritt, T. (2016). Making things in Fab Labs: A case study on sustainability and co-creation. *Digital Creativity* 27: 113–131.

Future Makespaces. (20 November 2016). *Material Makespace Update* [Online]. Future Makespaces [blog]. Available at: http://futuremakespaces.rca.ac.uk/material-makespace-update/ [Accessed 12 September 2017].

den Hollander, M.C., Bakker, C.A., and Hultink, E.J. (2017). Product design in a circular economy: Development of a typology of key concepts and terms. *Journal of Industrial Ecology* 21: 517–525.

Hunt, E.J., Zhang, C., Anzalone, N., and Pearce, J.M. (2015). Polymer recycling codes for distributed manufacturing with 3-D printers. *Resources, Conservation and Recycling* 97: 24–30.

Kohtala, C. (2016). Making Sustainability: How Fab Labs Address Environmental Issues. Doctoral Dissertation, Aalto University School of Arts, Design and Architecture, Department of Design, Helsinki, Finland.

Kohtala, C. and Hyysalo, S. (2015). Anticipated environmental sustainability of personal fabrication. *Journal of Cleaner Production* 99: 333–344.

Maxigas. (2012). Hacklabs and Hackerspaces: Tracing two genealogies. *Journal of Peer Production* 2 [Online]. Available at: http://peerproduction.net/issues/issue-2/peer-reviewed-papers/hacklabs-and-hackerspaces/ [Accessed 24 April 2018].

Prendeville, S., Hartung, G., Brass, C., Purvis, E., and Hall, A. (2017). Circular makerspaces: The founder's view. *International Journal of Sustainable Engineering* 1–17.

Schor, J.B., Fitzmaurice, C., Carfagna, L.B., Attwood-Charles, W., and Poteat, E.D. (2016). Paradoxes of openness and distinction in the sharing economy. *Poetics* 54: 66–81.

Smith, A. (2017). Social innovation, democracy and makerspaces (No. SWPS 2017–10 [June]), SPRU Working Paper Series. University of Sussex, Brighton, UK.

Stewart, H. (2017). Interview with the author, 04.07.2017. Topic: Future Makespaces for Redistributed Manufacturing project.

van Abel, B., Evers, L., Klaasen, R., and Troxler, P. (2011). *Open Design Now: Why Design Cannot Remain Exclusive.* Amsterdam, The Netherlands: BIS Publishers.

25 Repair cafés
Circular and social innovation

Martin Charter and Scott Keiller

BACKGROUND

Consumer culture fuelled by cheap credit and low cost products is driving the consumption of materials in developed economies. The prevailing Linear Industrial Model of 'take, make, and waste' is unsustainable. In Europe alone, of the 16 tonnes of material used by each person in a year, 6 tonnes becomes waste (European Commission, 2017). There is a growing acceptance of the need to move toward a more Circular Economy (CE), which is focused on 'closing (materials) loops' through the more efficient use of resources, in part through extending the lifetime of products. Research from the Oko-Insitute in Germany demonstrates that the product life spans of consumer electronics are getting progressively shorter due to faster replacement cycles and built-in product obsolescence (Ala-Kurikka, 2015).

A 'Fixer Movement' (part of a broader 'Maker, Modifier and Fixer' movement, Charter and Keiller, 2014) is starting to emerge around the world that is very diverse and includes a wide range of organisations. Examples include:

- Online fixing sites: for example, iFixit[1] an innovative WIKI based website that provides free online repair guides, solutions and 'how to' videos for a wide range of consumer electronics and other products, including clothing.
- Social enterprises: for example, The Restart Project,[2] a London-based social enterprise that encourages and empowers people to

use their electronics longer, by sharing repair and maintenance skills, through Restart events in communities and with companies in the UK.

- Repair cafés: "Repair Cafés are free 'community-centred workshops' for people to bring consumer products in need of repair where they can work together with volunteer fixers, to repair and maintain their broken or faulty products. In addition to repair, many Repair Cafés provide assistance with product modification, particularly to clothing to improve fit and appearance" (Charter and Keiller, 2016a).

The Repair Café Foundation, now named Repair Café International[3] (RCI), was founded by Martine Postma in the Netherlands in 2011 to enable people to come together to provide a free service to their community to help repair and, therefore, extend the lives of products that would otherwise end up as waste. The concept has grown rapidly and RCI now (13th April 2018) has a global network of 1,538 repair cafés in 34 countries. Repair cafés currently make up a small but growing part of the physical and virtual product 'repair ecosystem' in urban areas, along with commercial repairers, tool and parts retailers and online repair guidance.

INTRODUCTION

In 2014, The Centre for Sustainable Design® (CfSD) at the University for the Creative Arts (UCA) in the UK undertook the first global survey of volunteers at repair cafés, in collaboration with The Repair Café Foundation (Charter and Keiller, 2014). The aim was to understand the activities undertaken and importance of environmental, social and economic drivers as motivations for volunteer participation.

Since the 2014 survey, repair cafés around the world have more than doubled in number. This chapter presents a summary of the findings of a second global survey of repair café volunteers, undertaken in 2016 by CfSD in collaboration with RCI.

The work aims to understand whether there have been any changes in volunteer motivations and activities undertaken at repair cafés and introduced new questions on data collection and sources of repair guidance.

Additional questions were added to the 2016 survey as a result of CfSD's experience leading the development of Farnham Repair Café, UK that was established in February 2015.

METHODOLOGY

Members of repair cafés around the world were invited to complete a questionnaire hosted on an on-line[4] platform. The questionnaire was open to responses between 24th February and 20th March 2016.

The registered contact at each repair café was invited to participate via email direct from RCI. Access to the survey was provided in an embedded link in the body of the email.

RESULTS

Responses were received from 317 named repair cafés from 10 countries (Table 25.1), which at the time represented around 30 percent of those registered with RCI.

ABOUT RESPONDENTS

There are no significant differences in the key demographics of respondents compared to the 2014 survey.

- 90 percent describe themselves as founders and/or organisers
- 58-percent male, 42-percent female
- Most, 34 percent, aged between 56 and 65 with 20 percent aged over 65 years
- 75 percent of respondents are educated to at least Bachelor's degree level

Table 25.1 Number of survey responses from repair cafés in 10 countries

Country	Number of Repair Cafés that Submitted a Response
Netherlands	122
Germany	87
Belgium	44
France	25
United Kingdom	12
United States	9
Austria	9
Canada	4
Switzerland	3
Australia	2

ABOUT RESPONDENT'S REPAIR CAFÉS

- 75 percent always hold sessions at the same venue, this is exactly the same proportion as in the 2014 Survey
- 62 percent hold sessions once a month
- An average of 10 repair café volunteers attend each session, compared with 9 volunteers in the 2014 survey
- Repair café sessions have an average 29 visitors that bring an average of 19 products in need of repair. These questions were not asked in the 2014 Survey
- 72 percent of repair cafés have operated for two years or less compared with 95 percent in the 2014 survey, which demonstrates that a large proportion of repair cafés have continued to operate beyond two years

REASONS FOR PARTICIPATION AT THE REPAIR CAFÉ

Respondents were asked about their motivations for participation. The top four reasons (more than 90 percent strongly agree or agree) why respondents volunteer/participate at repair cafés (Figure 25.1) were:

- To encourage others to live more sustainably
- To encourage others to repair
- To provide a valuable service to the community
- To be a part of the movement to improve product reparability and longevity

In agreement with 2014 survey, the most common motivations for participation continue to be altruistic and supportive of sustainability and repair in the community. Indeed there have been increases in the proportions of those that participate to encourage others to live more sustainably (+4 percent) and to provide a valuable service to the community (+7 percent). Furthermore, an additional 7 percent of respondents strongly agree or agree that they participate to be part of the movement to improve product reparability and longevity.

ACTIVITIES UNDERTAKEN AT THE REPAIR CAFÉ

The five categories of items most frequently brought for repair (always or often) (Figure 25.2) include small kitchen appliances (94 percent

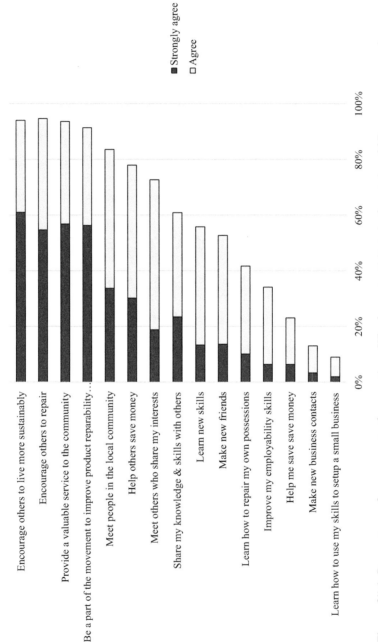

Figure 25.1 Percentage of responses to the question: *Why do you participate in the repair café?* Responses were given to a list of statements on a five-point scale from *Strongly agree* to *Strongly disagree*. Only Strongly agree or Agree are shown in figure.

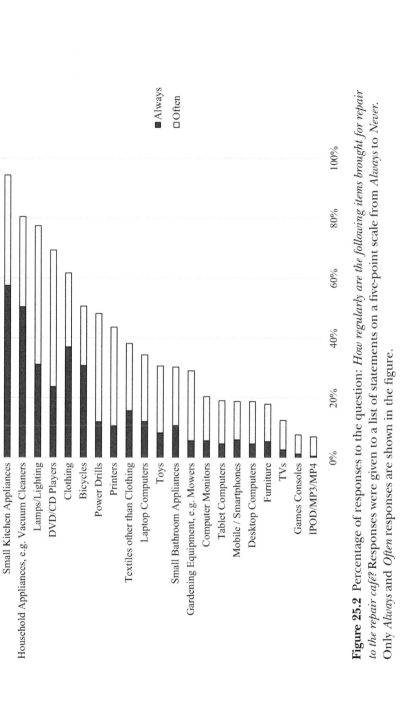

Figure 25.2 Percentage of responses to the question: *How regularly are the following items brought for repair to the repair café?* Responses were given to a list of statements on a five-point scale from *Always* to *Never*. Only *Always* and *Often* responses are shown in the figure.

of respondents, compared to 86 percent in the 2014 survey); household appliances, e.g. vacuum cleaners (81 percent, category was not included in the 2014 survey); lighting (78 percent, compared to 76 percent in the 2014 survey); DVD/CD players (70 percent, compared to 59 percent in the 2014 survey); and clothing (62 percent, compared to 69 percent in the 2104 survey). There has been a significant reduction in the proportion of repair cafés that frequently receive bicycles for repair; 51 percent compared with 65 percent in 2014. The proportion of electrical products has increased, while non-electrical items have reduced since 2014.

Compared with the 2014 survey, there has been a significant increase of over 8 percent in the proportion of repair cafés that always/often receive higher end micro-electronic products, including tablets, desktop and laptop computers.

PROPORTION OF ITEMS REPAIRED AT THE REPAIR CAFÉ

Repair cafés claim that an average of 63 percent of the products brought to them are successfully repaired. This is a significant finding that demonstrates the very real contribution that repair cafés can make in extending the useful life of consumer products and helping communities to reduce waste.

TYPES OF REPAIR RECORDS MAINTAINED BY REPAIR CAFÉS

Although 9 percent of repair cafés keep no records, the majority keep records on the overall number of repairs undertaken (78 percent), repairs by product category (63 percent) and the types of fault or repair carried out (56 percent).

These data are of use to repair cafés to monitor their effectiveness and impact and as a source of information to help with planning for future sessions.

A small proportion (8 percent) of repair cafés record the weight of products repaired, as a means of estimating the weight of products potentially diverted from the waste stream. As an example, Farnham Repair Café in the UK weighs all products that come in for repair and estimates that between February 2015 and October 2017 over 1 tonne has potentially been diverted from the waste stream through repair.

SOURCES OF INFORMATION USED AT REPAIR CAFÉ SESSIONS TO HELP GUIDE REPAIR

Access to information to guide repair is particularly relevant for many electrical and electro-mechanical products, where circuit diagrams and repair manuals are frequently essential. In addition, for many repairs, online access is required to search for availability and purchase of spare parts.

Seventy-seven percent of repair cafés access product manufacturer's websites during sessions and 71 percent search websites for the purchase of spare parts. However, most manufacturers do not provide access to repair guides or sell spare parts direct and so repairers frequently access information provided by others, for example iFixit, an organisation that provides free repair guides and videos. Half of repair cafés access online repair videos and 45 percent access online repair forums, where the public share tips on product repair.

MODIFICATION AND UPCYCLING ACTIVITIES AT REPAIR CAFÉS

In addition to repair, product modification and upcycling are under-taken at repair cafés (Figure 25.3). This is most common for clothing, where 60 percent of repair cafés (always, often or sometimes) modify clothing to improve fit and over 40 percent modify clothing to change its appearance, for example, by adding decoration.

VIEWS ON PLANNED OR IN-BUILT OBSOLESCENCE

Of the electrical/electronic items brought to repair cafés, printers and electrical tools are considered to be the most frequently in need of repair because of what respondents believe to be 'planned or in-built obsolescence' (Figure 25.4).

Over 35 percent of respondents believe that more than half of the printers and electrical tools require repair because of they are designed with in-built obsolescence.

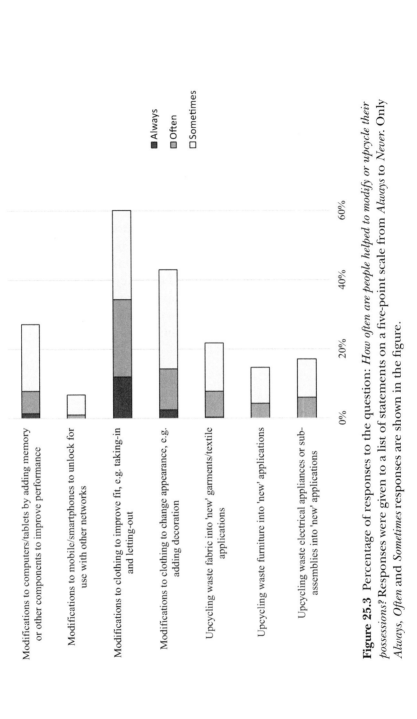

Figure 25.3 Percentage of responses to the question: *How often are people helped to modify or upcycle their possessions?* Responses were given to a list of statements on a five-point scale from *Always* to *Never*. Only *Always*, *Often* and *Sometimes* responses are shown in the figure.

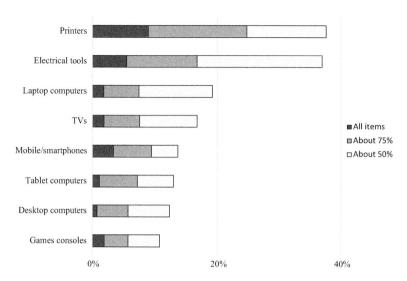

Figure 25.4 Percentage of responses to the question: *In your opinion, what proprtion of eletrical/electronic items are brought to the repair café because of what you believe to be planned or built-in obsolescence?* Responses were given to a list of statements.

EXPECTATIONS FOR THE FUTURE

In agreement with the 2014 survey, the top three expectations (more than 60 percent strongly agree or agree) of how repair cafés might change over the next five years (Figure 25.5) were:

- Greater links with other repair cafés to form more effective local repair networks
- Greater involvement with campaigning to improve product reparability/longevity
- More involvement with wider sustainability issues.

Compared to the 2014 survey, 10 percent more respondents disagree that repair cafés will introduce a charge for some repairs, which supports the repair café principle of free repair and advice.

Over 60 percent of respondents agreed that over the next five years (2017–2021) their repair café would have greater links with other repair cafés to form repair networks. Furthermore, almost 40 percent of respondents agreed that at their repair café the number of repairs undertaken will increase by ten-fold or more. The results also suggest that repair cafés will be more involved in campaigning to improve

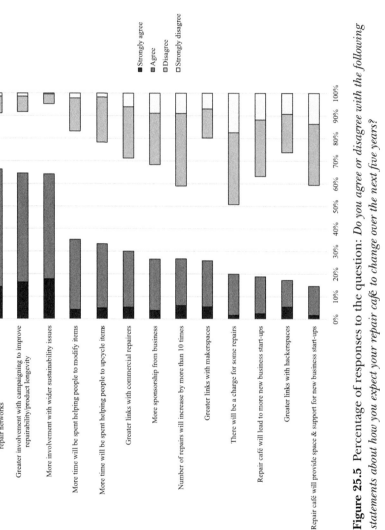

Figure 25.5 Percentage of responses to the question: *Do you agree or disagree with the following statements about how you expect your repair café to change over the next five years?*

product reparability and longevity and that their influence will continue to grow.

DISCUSSION

Repair cafés provide a place for people to socialise, share and learn new skills and address issues related to sustainable consumption in a 'hands-on' way. The founders, organisers and repairers at each repair café are normally volunteers who have elected to give up their time to offer this community service ('sharing economy'). As one might expect therefore, the most common reasons for participation at repair cafés are altruistic; *to encourage others to live more sustainably, to provide a valuable service to their community, to be a part of the movement to improve product reparability and longevity and to help others to learn how to fix their own products.* It follows that personal gain from participation is not important to most repair café volunteers. In particular, *making new business contacts, improving ones employability skills* or *learning how to use skills to set up a new business* are amongst the least important motivators. The high proportion of volunteer repairers either approaching retirement or retired might explain the low interest in personal gain regarding business opportunities and employment prospects.

Repair cafés do not just facilitate repair; product modification is also a common activity. Alteration is one way to extend the useful life of clothing and it is practised at least sometimes at 60 percent of respondent's repair cafés.

The notion that some products are designed and manufactured to fail prematurely – planned or built-in obsolescence – is widely believed by repair café volunteers. Compared to the 2014 survey an additional 7 percent of respondents strongly agree or agree that being part of the movement to improve product reparability and longevity is a motivation for participation. This is reflected in the finding that over 35 percent of respondents believe that at least half of the power tools and electronic printers that are brought to their repair cafés, have developed faults because of what they perceive to be 'in-built obsolescence'. The increased sharing of information on repair could influence manufacturers to change product designs for greater longevity and also inform policy to discourage design that is considered by many to have the intention of reducing product lifespan through perceived built-in obsolescence. It is noteworthy that over the next five years, almost 70 percent of respondents expect their repair café to be more involved in campaigning to improve product reparability and longevity.

Since 2014, RCI has become noticeably more engaged in lobbying the European Commission (EC) on these points. As part of a united effort to inform the development of the EC's new Circular Economy Package, in early 2015 RCI, iFixit and various European environmental advocacy organisations were signatories to a Joint Mission Statement: Sustainable consumption and production: improving product durability and reparability (RCI, 2015, and discussed in Keiller and Charter, 2015).

Repair cafés have more than tripled from an estimated 500 in June 2014 to 1,538 in April 2018. Despite the rapid growth of repair cafés, the key demographics of volunteers and their personal motivations for participation remain largely unchanged. Repair cafés still appear to attract slightly more men than women and volunteer age continues to be skewed toward older generations with the majority aged between 56 and 65, with 20 percent aged over 65 years. Volunteers are well educated, with 75 percent holding at least a first degree. Repair cafés appear to offer a place for people with a lifetime of repair skills and experience to work with other like-minded people to make a difference and give something back to their communities. Taking part in repair and seeing others repair products appears to be giving people the confidence to 'have a go' at repair themselves. According to a separate survey of visitors to Farnham Repair Café (FRC) (Charter and Keiller, 2016b), 60 percent of those attending FRC that had observed the repair process at a session had made them more likely to attempt to repair their own products in the future. Repair cafés are starting to spread a culture of repair by helping to empower people to develop a more active relationship with their possessions, which challenges the received wisdom that we live in a 'throw away society'.

The majority of repair cafés in the 2016 survey meet once a month at a fixed venue. There are an average of 10 volunteers at each session; a slight increase from nine in the 2014 survey. Each repair café session is attended by an average of 29 visitors who typically bring 19 products for repair. On average, 63 percent of products are repaired at each session and around 30 percent of repair cafés have a repair rate in excess of 71 percent.

While small household appliances continue to be the items most frequently brought to repair cafés, there have been some notable changes in the frequency that some product categories are brought for repair. There has been an increase compared to the 2014 survey in the proportion of repair cafés where electronic (DVD/CD players and desktop, laptop and tablet computing) are always/often brought for repair, while there have been decreases in non-electricals, like bicycles and clothing. This warrants further analysis, and could reflect changes in the repair offerings at repair cafés; for example, an increase in volunteers with electrical repair skills or conversely a decrease in those with the skills to repair bicycles and clothing. The increase in consumer electronics could also reflect an increased willingness amongst the public for non-professional repair of these items.

Repair café volunteers access a range of predominantly online information during repair café sessions to guide repair. The majority of manufacturers of electrical and electronics manufacturers do not provide repair manuals openly to the general public and without sites like iFixit and online repair forums, many electronics repairs could not realistically be attempted at repair cafés (Keiller and Charter, 2015).

If the number of repair cafés continues to grow at its current rate, roughly a doubling every two years, by 2021 there could be over 5,000 repair cafés around the world. Since each repair café has an average of 10 volunteers and 29 visitors, this suggests that by 2021 there could be 50,000 volunteers and 145,000 visitors attending repair cafés each month. It seems plausible; therefore, that repair cafés will have an increasingly significant impact and influence over the coming years and will play a far greater role in local 'repair ecosystems.'

CONCLUSIONS

- The number of repair cafés has tripled in number since May 2014 to over 1,500 in April 2018. Repair cafés present a real example of citizen-led grassroots social innovation that has developed predominantly without the involvement of mainstream business, government or institutions.
- Consistent with the 2014 survey, over 60 percent of respondents expect that over the next five years (2017–2021), their repair café will develop stronger links with other repair cafés to form repair networks and there will be greater involvement with campaigning to improve product reparability.
- Most repair cafés run sessions once a month at a fixed venue, with an average of 10 volunteers and 29 visitors who bring nineteen products for repair.
- Repair café volunteers continue to be motivated to participate through their desire to encourage others to live more sustainably, to encourage other to repair rather than discard of broken or faulty products and to be a part of the movement to improve the reparability and longevity of consumer products.
- Many repair café volunteers continue to hold the belief that some electrical products are designed with in-built obsolescence.

- Since 2014, there has been an increase in the proportion of repair cafés that frequently receive microelectronic products for repair, including; DVD/CD players and desktop, laptop and tablet computing while there has been a decrease in non-electrical items like bicycles and clothing.
- On average, 63 percent of the broken or faulty products brought to repair cafés are repaired.

NOTES

1 www.ifixit.com
2 www.restartproject.org
3 www.repaircafe.org/en
4 www.surveygizmo.com

BIBLIOGRAPHY

Ala-Kurikka, S. (2015). *ENDS Europe* [Online]. Available at: www.endseurope.com/article/39711/electronic-goods-life-spans-shrinking-study-indicates [Accessed 8 October 2015].

Charter, M. and Keiller, S. (2014). *Grassroots Innovation and the Circular Economy: A Global Survey of Repair Cafés and Hackerspaces* [Online]. Available at: http://cfsd.org.uk/site-pdfs/circular-economy-and-grassroots-innovation/Survey-of-Repair-Cafes-and-Hackerspaces.pdf [Accessed 6 May 2017].

Charter, M. and Keiller, S. (2016a). *The Repair Café WIKI* [Online]. Available at: http://repaircafe.shoutwiki.com/wiki/Main_Page [Accessed 9 May 2016].

Charter, M. and Keiller, S. (2016b). *Farnham Repair Café: Survey of Visitors and Volunteers* [Online]. Available at: http://cfsd.org.uk/site-pdfs/Farnham%20Repair%20Cafe%20Survey%202016.pdf [Accessed 6 May 2016].

European Commission. (2017). *Waste* [Online]. Available at: http://ec.europa.eu/environment/waste/ [Accessed 2 September 2017].

Keiller, S. and Charter, M. (2015). Repair Cafés: Implications for product developers and designers. *Proceedings of the 20th International Conference on Sustainable Innovation* pp. 140–147. ISBN 978-0-9543950-8-7.

Repair Café International. (2015). *Joint Mission Statement* [Online]. Available at: https://repaircafe.org/wp-content/uploads/2015/03/Mission_Statement_Reparability_and_Durability_of_Products.pdf [Accessed 24 April 2018].

26 Delivering a more Circular Economy for electrical goods in retail in the UK

Mark Hilton

CONTEXT – ELECTRICAL AND ELECTRONIC EQUIPMENT AND CIRCULAR ECONOMY

For decades, it has been appreciated that a far less linear approach to finite resource use is necessary to reduce global warming impacts and maintain quality of life for generations to come. While the concept of a Circular Economy (CE) is not new, making it happen remains difficult; overcoming economic, technical, institutional and policy barriers.

This chapter considers the UK retail environment for electrical and electronic equipment (EEE), and the issues around EEE 'customer returns', in particular related to low-cost, own-brand products. Often products now fail after just a few years (Umweltbundesamt, 2015) and it is cheaper to replace rather than repair, making waste electrical and electronic equipment (WEEE) one of the fastest-growing waste streams in the EU and most developed parts of the world. The European Union's (EU) producer responsibility regime, under the Waste Electrical and Electronic Equipment Directive,[1] focuses on recycling at end-of-life rather than reuse and preparing for reuse. The complimentary Eco-design Directive has been focused very much on energy efficiency, although, recently, design for improved durability and circularity has begun to creep into specific product legislation (e.g. vacuum cleaners).

A recent project "Countering WEEE Illegal Trade (CWIT)" (Huisman et al., 2015) offers the most accurate picture for WEEE management in the EU as a whole, noting that just 35 percent of used (but still functioning) and waste EEE, discarded by companies and consumers in 2012, ended up in official collection and recycling systems, and this is in an economic region with perhaps the best WEEE controls! This is of particular concern as EEE is generally very carbon intensive to make, contains hazardous substances and critical raw materials (CRMs) that are difficult to fully recover at end of life.

The CE business model options for EEE are essentially as follows:

- Design for durability, upgradability and reparability, to allow a long life without the need for significant refurbishment or remanufacture.
- Operational lease – where a third party owns the asset and rents it out several times so as to make a profit, with a vested interest to maintain the product and maximise its rental life and residual sale value.
- Commercial take-back for refurbishment and resale – a retailer, brand or third party takes the product back from the owner, pays something in exchange, but then refurbishes and sells the item in secondary markets.
- Not for profit reuse and refurbishment ('preparing for reuse') – where donated items have minor work done to allow them to be passed on to disadvantaged families.
- Commercial take-back and remanufacture – generally where a high value item is refurbished or re-built to 'as new' standard, making significant use of recovered components.

EEE 'LOSSES' IN RETAIL

While the issues associated with the formal EU WEEE producer responsibility systems are well known, what is perhaps less well known is the 'hidden' flow and lost value in the retail sector related to high rates of returns. For EEE, and in particular televisions (TVs), the return rates can be 10 percent of sales within the typical one-year warranty period and much of this occurs within the 30 day cool-off period.[2] This means that around 155,000 tonnes of EEE comes back through UK retailers, worth around £2.4 billion (WRAP, 2015). To make matters worse, return rates on electrical items are also growing due largely to:

- The complexity of products (e.g. Internet TVs with a wireless soundbar connection)
- The increase in online purchases,[3] where the ability to properly examine a product is very limited compared to an in-store experience with advice from a shop assistant.

In practice, over 60 percent of EEE returns have no fault found, in part because people haven't bought what they wanted in the first instance. In one project that the author was party to (2015), of 156 returned TVs to an asset recovery company, 66 percent had no fault found, 17 percent were damaged (either before return or in the reverse logistics process), and only 17 percent had technical faults.

Retailers are of course set up for forward distribution, and not reverse logistics and the return journey can be hazardous with many opportunities for damage (Figure 26.1). Often EEE items are returned without their original packaging and/or piled on top of each other in metal cages at the retail outlet for back hauling to assessment centres (e.g. at retailer distribution centres [DCs] or third-party sites). Even minor damage to the screen of a TV or tablet, for example, can make the

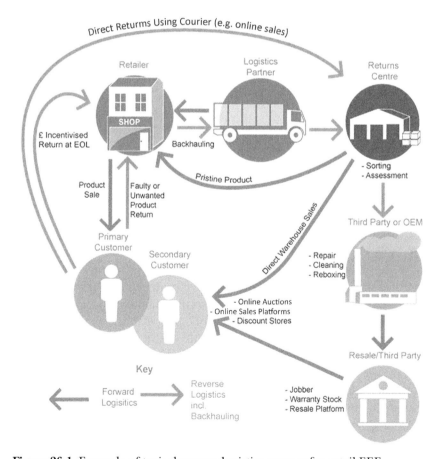

Figure 26.1 Example of typical reverse logistics process for retail EEE

Source: Zero waste Scotland. (2016). Reverse logistics and incentivised product return: an evidence synthesis and guide for Scottish businesses. Zero Waste Scotland Report.

product beyond economic repair and hence the product will be recycled as WEEE, despite the fact that many items start their journey in almost pristine condition. In general, only around 60 percent of the value of the items is recovered (iForce, n.d.); a serious problem where the item may only have a profit margin of 5 percent to 10 percent in the first instance. It is interesting to note that UK retailer ASDA recently stopped selling electrical items online, while Philip Clarke, when chief executive at the retailer Tesco, noted that electrical items 'take up a lot of space and don't make much money' (The GC Team, 2014).

While rates and standards of WEEE recovery have been much improved in the UK (the UK collects around 8 kg per annum per inhabitant; mid-table in EU terms), there is still a huge opportunity to keep EEE in use longer, in its first life and in subsequent lives, and hence reduce the wide range of environmental impacts.

Retailers can play a large part in this and better customer information (pre- and post-sale) is a critical aspect. Many retailers are now working hard to improve the situation by rewriting instruction manuals and working with manufacturers on simpler software to minimise set up problems. In addition, there is increased emphasis on better quality technical helpline support, where possible from the original equipment manufacturers (OEMs) rather than the retailers' own call centres. In many cases 'soft-fixes', e.g. software fixes, are possible over the phone where the right technical knowledge is available.

DURABILITY AND REPARABILITY

In WRAP survey work (WRAP, 2014), around half of all respondents said that they would be willing to pay extra for products that last longer, but this is not obvious; consumers only have cost, brand reputation and the length of the guarantee period as proxies for durability. In the absence of mandatory standards[4] and better product labelling on longevity,[5] it has been necessary to try and tackle the specification and choice-editing aspects of retail to improve the quality of 'budget' products which cause the majority of returns. One major area of the author's work has been on the WRAP Better Appliances project (WRAP, n.d.), with an initial focus on identifying the key reasons for return and the key failure modes. This has led to guidance and minimum specifications for the retailers to use to better inform buying trips to exhibitions and factory visits overseas.

Reparability is another key issue. Where faults do occur within the warranty period (or beyond) it is important that EEE can be repaired simply, locally and at a reasonable cost. Unfortunately not all products are made equal in this respect. iFixit for example, the DIY repairs website, undertakes teardowns and repair workshops and produces 'league tables' from the reparability perspective (Figure 26.2) (iFixit, n.d.). This is another aspect of specification and choice that also needs careful attention, and is addressed, alongside day-to-day maintenance, in the WRAP Better Appliances guidance.

It should be noted that while Apple may not do well in iFixit assessments, Apple recently made available specialist tools to third-party repair shops (Fingas, 2017), and reparability, while very desirable, isn't the whole story. *WHICH?* – the UK consumer magazine – produced data that shows, for example, that Apple products are amongst the most reliable and hence don't often need repair (Marshall, 2017). Some

Figure 26.2 Example of iFixit tablet reparability comparison

Source: iFixit. Tablet reparability scores. [ONLINE] Available at: www.ifixit.com/tablet-repairability. No Date [Accessed 16 September 2017]

manufacturers in fact argue that durability and reliability comes hand-in-hand with more integrated 'solid state' products that are less easy to take apart.

TAKE BACK FOR REPAIR

Store staff, generally, do not have the time or knowledge to assess EEE returns effectively and to assess the possibility of a relatively low cost repair via a local approved agent. Part of the problem resides with store till systems (electronic point of sale [EPOS]) which are focused on supporting sales rather than dealing with returns.

One interesting software solution in this regard is from an Australian company, Solvup (part of TIC Group) (Solvup, n.d.). The software (which can be downloaded on tablets or integrated with the EPOS), requires minimal staff training and offers a troubleshooting function making use of manufacturer information, allowing 'soft-fix' in store or the identification of a local repair option. In Australia, EEE return repairs have increased from around 1 in 10 to around 1 in 4 through use of the software, providing a huge economic and environmental benefit (Solvup, n.d.). The same software, accessing a standardised database, can be used in any call centre for technical support.

The system also allows efficiencies around the ordering of couriers (to ship to repairers), tracking of repairs and keeping customers informed and happy. It also allows central and granular data capture

Figure 26.3 Example of retail software trouble shooting from Solvup

Source: Solvup. (2016). Solvup presentation to Eunomia Research and Consulting Ltd.

(e.g. on return reasons) that then help to better inform the specification/buying and customer information processes, and to provide valuable feedback to manufacturers to allow design refinements.

LEASE AND INCENTIVISED RETURN

In recent times, lease has generally been limited to business to business (B2B) asset management, and mainly in the information technology (IT) space where suppliers have recognised that by incorporating leasing models, they can retain their client's business during these upgrade cycles, and often resell or reuse products on other contracts. Consumer electronics used to be the same in the 1970s and 1980s, when TVs and large appliances were far more expensive and less reliable that now (in relative terms), rental being common place.[6]

In these times of austerity, lease models have made a resurgence, with companies such as Hughes (2017) and Forbes-rentals (2017) offering rental in the UK, and indeed some retailers such as Euronics, offering very low-cost rentals on everything from laptops to washing machines, many of them refurbished. Increasingly this makes sense for the millennial 'generation rent' who may be living in smaller flats and moving more regularly. In the Netherlands, the company Bundles (2017) offers their appliances in partnership with Miele, the monthly subscription being more affordable than direct purchase.

Where products are not offered on an operational lease basis, it can still make sense to incentivise return, particularly for small consumer electronics that are likely to languish in drawers and cupboards, going beyond the point where they have a viable second life. WRAP's research (WRAP, 2014) shows that customers believe their laptops to be reaching the end of their useful/desirable life at two to three years of age, but don't realise that these items often have a gross resale value of over £100 each. Estimated collection and refurbishment costs are in the region of £25 to £40, therefore incentivising the return of these products, whilst making the reverse logistics process efficient, provides ample scope for a commercial margin. WRAP estimates the UK market value for trading in pre-owned products could be worth up to £3 billion per annum.

Two-thirds of UK consumers expressed a willingness to trade-in consumer electronic products and would prefer to do so with reputable high-street retailers (e.g. due to concerns over data security on ICT devices). Manufacturers such as Dell and Bosch (power-tools) already provide trade-in arrangements, however such approaches are unusual in mainstream retail. However, with support from WRAP, Argos recently introduced a scheme whereby they take back small electronic gadgets such as mobile phones and tablets in return for a gift voucher. Argos has used its retail presence to offer potentially more convenience and reassurance to their customers, whilst using it as an opportunity to drive more footfall through their stores and increase sales. A third-party asset recovery partner is used to handle the products and maximise value recovery.

REVERSE LOGISTICS AND ASSET RECOVERY

Where the return is unavoidable, and repair locally is not economic, the reverse logistics process (Figure 26.1) comes into play and needs to be efficient as possible. Once received at a sorting centre, the goal is to determine the greatest value that can be obtained from the returned asset. The business decision on whether to refurbish the product is based upon the product's residual value and the cost of refurbishment and further handling: low-value products are often not considered worth repairing (Philips Consumer Lifestyle consider anything under £70 as low value (Partridge, 2011)) as their value may turn negative when repairs, transport and sales overheads are considered. Products that are designed to be disassembled easily, or with modular components, may mitigate this somewhat, effectively bringing down the minimum value of the product deemed worth repairing.

Good practice here is around pushing the assessment and repair process as far upstream as possible to reduce further handling and potential damage. Ideally the assessment is done in store (e.g. using software as noted above) and repair locally to the store (e.g. by a network of authorised repair franchises), or next best, at a regional distribution centre where backhauling can be undertaken efficiently using delivery vehicles on return journeys. Most large retailers now use specialist third-party asset recovery companies who are able to maximise value recovery through smart tracking, comprehensive functionality and performance testing, refurbishment and repair and through utilising a wide range of resale channels, including online auction sites.

Exchange service models (sometimes called an Advanced Service Exchange) are another interesting and cost effective approach whereby the customer instigates a return of the product and at the same time a refurbished product is sent from a 'buffer stock' (i.e. of previously repaired products). Sony Entertainment Europe (SCEE) originally implemented the model with their PlayStation 2 and found that up to 50 percent cost savings could be generated per returned product compared with the traditional repair service model (King et al., 2011).

The key benefit of this approach is that it is less reactive and creates economy of scale savings; products with similar defects can be grouped together for repair, for example, rather than reacting on an ad hoc basis. Product movements and direct contact with the customer are also reduced, which saves costs and can generate goodwill and subsequent brand loyalty. Dell (n.d.), Lexmark (n.d.), and NEC (n.d.), all use this model in the form of a service package to their business customers. It also worth noting that 'box-on-demand' systems are also now available that allow bespoke re-boxing at the sorting centre, hence allowing the product to be put back in stock (Box-on-demand, n.d.).

THE WAY AHEAD

Online sales in the EU grew by over 18 percent from 2014 to 2015 and online EEE retail in the EU is now thought to be >30 percent of the market (OECD, forthcoming). The volume of EEE returns are therefore likely to increase in the UK and other developed countries, and retailers need to take action on several fronts to combat the growth and minimise costs. Various CE approaches offer the potential for retailers to increase profitability with less waste:

- Improved product specification and selection for durability and reparability
- Improved assessment software in stores to facilitate local repair and provide better returns data for the retailers, the asset recovery companies and the manufacturers
- Third-party reverse logistics, repair and refurbishment, ideally at distribution/returns centres to utilise backhaul efficiencies and minimise handling so as to maximise value recovery
- Lease and incentivising return models for the recovery of higher-value products.

NOTES

1 The original WEEE Directive 2002/95/EC became European Law in February 2003 while the revision, Directive 2012/19/EU, entered into force on 13 August 2012 and became effective on 14 February 2014.
2 Under the UK Consumer Rights Act, consumers only have the right to reject a faulty item and get a refund within 30 days of purchase. After 30 days, if an item is faulty, the retailer has to repair or replace the item even if the

warranty period has been exceeded (up to six years), but the onus is on the
consumer to prove a fault was present at the time of purchase.

3 Consumer electronics are now overtaking books as the second most popular
product category in Europe. Mintel estimated that in 2015 around 48 percent of all electrical and electronic good sales in the UK were made online.

4 The vacuum cleaner regulations are one of the few that have inherent durability requirements around motor and hose life. CENELEC continues work
on standards to measure durability and reparability.

5 Décret n° 2014–1482 in France obliges retailers to inform consumers about
the availability of spare parts for products, but not on expected lifetime.

6 At its peak, Radio Rentals had more than 2 million customers, over 500 shops
and employed 3,600 technicians.

BIBLIOGRAPHY

Box-on-demand. (No Date). *Box-on-Demand: About us* [Online]. Available at:
http://boxondemand.com/ [Accessed 16 September 2017].

Bundles. (2017). *It Is Our Goal to End the Throw-Away Society* [Online]. Available
at: www.bundles.nl/en/about-us/ [Accessed 16 September 2017].

Dell. (No Date). *3-Year Premium Panel Advanced Exchange Service.* [Online]
Available at: http://accessories.dell.com/sna/PopupProductDetail.aspx-
?c=us&l=en&cs=04&sku=986-4872&price=0.00&client=config [Accessed 16
September 2017].

Fingas, J. (2017). *Apple Offers Its iPhone Repair Tools to Third-Party Shops* [Online].
Available at: www.engadget.com/2017/06/05/apple-offers-iphone-repair-
tools-to-third-parties/ [Accessed 16 September 2017].

Forbes-rental. (2017). *Forbes-Rental* [Online]. Available at: www.forbes-rentals.
co.uk/ [Accessed 16 September 2017].

Hughes. (2017). *Hughes. Want It. Rent It* [Online]. Available at: www.hughesren-
tal.co.uk/ [Accessed 16 September 2017].

Huisman, J., Botezatu, I., Herreras, L., Liddane, M., Hintsa, J., Luda di Cor
temiglia, V., Leroy, P., Vermeersch, E., Mohanty, S., van den Brink, S., Ghen-
ciu, B., Dimitrova, D., Nash, E., Shryane, T., Wieting, M., Kehoe, J., Baldé,
C.P., Magalini, F., Zanasi, A., Ruini, F., Männistö, T., and Bonzio, A. (2015).
*Countering WEEE Illegal Trade (CWIT) Summary Report, Market Assessment,
Legal Analysis, Crime Analysis and Recommendations Roadmap.* Countering
WEEE Illegal Trade (CWIT) Project, Lyon, France, 30 August 2015.

iFixit. (No Date). *iFixit: The Free Repair Guide for Everything, Written by Everyone*
[Online] Available at: www.ifixit.com/ [Accessed 16 September 2017].

iForce. (No Date). *iForce Revive: What We Do* [Online]. Available at: http://
iforcegroup.com/About/WhatWeDo?iforce=Revive [Accessed 16 September 2017].

King, A., Mayers, K., and Barter, N. (2011). Closed-Loop Servicing of Sony Play-
Station: Report for Centre for Remanufacturing and Re-use. Oakdene Hollins, Aylesbury, UK

Lexmark. (No Date). *Advanced Exchange* [Online]. Available at: www.lexmark. com/en_ca/products/supplies-and-accessories/supplies-warranty/warranty-offerings/advanced-exchange.html [Accessed 10 August 2017].

Marshall, A. (2017). *Best Laptop Brands* [Online]. Available at: www.which.co.uk/reviews/laptops/article/best-laptop-brands/best-laptop-brands [Accessed 16 September 2017].

NEC. (No Date). *Advanced Exchange: Overnight Freight Service* [Online]. Available at: www.necdisplay.com/p/service/advexon2-mp [Accessed 16 September 2017].

OECD. (Forthcoming). Extended Producer Responsibility and the Impact of Online Sales. OECD Environment Directorate, Paris, France.

Partridge, A.R. (2011). *Full Circle: Reverse Logistics Keeps Products Green to the End* [Online]. Available at: www.inboundlogistics.com/cms/article/full-circle-reverse-logistics-keeps-products-green-to-the-end/ [Accessed 16 September 2017].

Solvup. (2016). Presentation: Australian retailer data. Presented to Eunomia Research & Consulting Ltd.

Solvup. (No Date). *Solvup: About us* [Online]. Available at: www.solvup.com/about-us/ [Accessed 16 September 2017].

The GC Team. (2014). *Asda Moves Away from Selling Electricals Online* [Online]. Available at: http://gcmagazine.co.uk/asda-moves-away-selling-electricals-online/ [Accessed 16 September 2017].

Umweltbundesamt. (2015). *Obsolescence Fact Check* [Online]. Available at: www. umweltbundesamt.de/en/press/pressinformation/obsolescence-fact-check [Accessed 15 September 2017].

WRAP. (2014). *Switched on to Value Summary Report: Why Extending Appliance and Consumer Electronic Product Lifetimes and Trading Used Products Can Benefit Consumers, Retailers, Suppliers and the Environment* [Online]. Available at: www. wrap.org.uk/sites/files/wrap/Switched%20on%20to%20Value%2012%20 2014.pdf [Accessed 15 September 2017].

WRAP. (2015). *Product Damage and Returns: Electrical and Electronic Products* [Online Document]. Available at: www.wrap.org.uk/sites/files/wrap/EEE%20 Product%20Damage%20&%20Returns%20Presentation%201Dec2015.pdf [Accessed 16 September 2017].

WRAP. (No Date). *WRAP Better Appliances Guidance* [Online]. Available at: http://eproducttechguide.wrap.org.uk/ [Accessed 16 September 2017].

Accelerating the Circular Economy @ HP

27

Kirstie McIntyre

BACKGROUND

In 2011, the global population passed 7 billion. And it's speeding up – the world's population is on pace to hit 9.4 billion by 2050 (U.S. Census Bureau, 2017). As the population grows, more people will be looking to move up the economic ladder, especially in developing and emerging economies. According to a paper by the Brookings Institution, there were about 3.2 billion people in the global middle class at the end of 2016 (Kharas, 2017). A bigger middle class means business growth, increasing prosperity and more economic opportunity than ever before.

At the same time, the number of technology consumers in the world is quickly accelerating, with approximately 3 billion new consumers expected by 2030. A younger generation of buyers recognise the environmental, health and social implications of 'throw away' societies that view products as disposable. 'Business as usual' isn't sustainable, because simultaneously, the world faces pressing challenges related to resource availability, climate change and inequality. Delivering the economic and social benefits of technology to billions more people must be done sustainably. This requires a profound shift from a traditional, linear production model of 'take, make, dispose', to a circular and low-carbon economy.

This new model is regenerative by design (Ellen MacArthur Foundation, 2017) and continually recovers and reuses materials. It decouples business growth from a reliance on increasingly scarce raw materials, benefiting the environment while advancing business success. Innovative new business models such as product-as-a-service offerings increase the value derived from resources while strengthening customer engagement and relationships. The shift from analog to digital printing and additive manufacturing (3D printing) holds the promise to transform whole supply chains. (Figure 27.1: HP, 2017a)

Figure 27.1 describes HP's strategy for applying Circular Economy (CE) to its business. It illustrates four 'loops' that contribute to 'circularity', with the inner loops being the most resource effective. HP has mapped its CE solutions and programmes onto each of the loops to demonstrate, both internally and externally, where it is developing and contributing to a CE. Closed-loop plastic recycling is an 'outer-loop play', recovering materials and introducing recycled content back into high value products. HP is also moving towards the 'inner-loops' and greater levels of circularity.

HP's priorities in this low carbon, CE are:

1.   Decouple business growth from consumption

   •   Keep materials in use at their highest state of value for as long as possible.

HP Circular Economy strategy

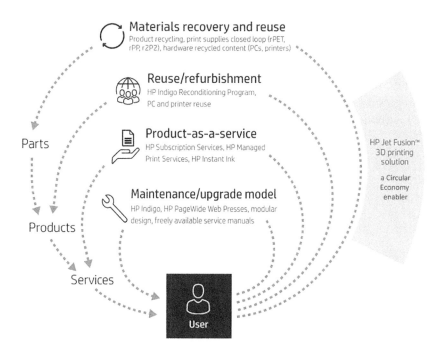

Figure 27.1 HP Circular Economy strategy

- Develop energy-efficient products that are designed for recyclability.
- Decrease the amount of materials required to make and use products.
- Create new technologies and products that enable customers to reduce their material usage.
- Repurpose products at end of service through repair, reuse and recycling.

2. Disrupt industry business models

- Reinvent how solutions are designed and delivered.
- Provide product-based services that help customers easily scale technology solutions while reducing costs and waste.
- Extend product life through design for repairability.
- Increase repair, reuse and recycling.

3. Digitise supply chains and production

- Transform how entire industries design, make and distribute products,
- Advance commercial print solutions to support the analog-to-digital shift.
- Progress 3D-printing technologies that streamline prototyping and improve the economics of short-run manufacturing.

Further to this, HP is building CE principles into its core corporate strategies as shown by the Figure 27.2. In this chapter, examples from HP's activities and programmes will be discussed.

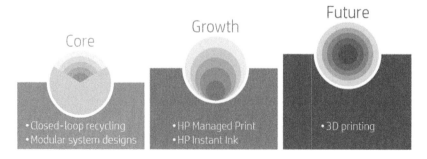

Figure 27.2 Circular Economy supports HP's strategy

CORE: CLOSED-LOOP RECYCLING

Through reinventing existing recycling activities, HP has innovated one of the largest and arguably most successful examples of CE applications with its closed-loop recycling process. The earliest closed-loop recycling activities began with creating HP toner cartridges with plastic recycled from the HP Planet Partners program in 2000 (HP, 2017a). This expanded in 2005 when the company started using recovered polyethylene terephthalate (PET) from ink cartridges as a material source for new cartridges. Over time, this programme has extended to include additional cartridges and polypropylene plastic. HP continues to scale this process. So far, 3.4 billion closed-loop HP ink and toner cartridges have been manufactured, using more than 88,900 tonnes of recycled plastic content derived from cartridges, apparel hangers and plastic bottles. Through this process, the company has kept 735 million cartridges, 70 million apparel hangers and 3.8 billion plastic bottles out of landfills (on average more than 1 million water bottles per day) (HP, 2017a). More than 80 percent of HP ink cartridges now contain 45- to 70-percent recycled content, and 100 percent of HP toner cartridges now contain 10- to 33-percent recycled content.

HP are collecting bottles from many countries and sources. For example, from 2016, HP has sourced recycled plastic collected from landfills in Haiti. By connecting CE principles to new market opportunities, this is generating a steady revenue stream and partnering to improve conditions for workers, creating jobs and more sustainable ink cartridges. Furthermore, this initiative helps prevent plastics from reaching the Caribbean Sea, combatting the ever-growing problem of ocean pollution (HP, 2017b).

This clearly demonstrates how an innovative approach to material reclamation can create new economic opportunities and drive a more inclusive CE. By connecting an 'outer-loop', CE solution to social responsibility programmes, HP has created positive *social* CE results. The inclusion of secondary materials in a high-volume, highly engineered, technical product is not always the easiest to achieve; there have been significant technical challenges along the way, such as materials qualification times and manufacturing limitations. However collaborating with supply chain partners has enabled HP to overcome these technical challenges.

GROWTH: PRODUCT AS A SERVICE

The next stage in HP's CE strategy illustrates the shift from selling a product to selling a service. Through HP's Instant Ink service, customers' Internet-connected printers recognise when ink cartridges are low

Figure 27.3 Cartridges and Circular Economy

and automatically ship new cartridges to their home or small office, pre-empting the frustration of running out of ink at inconvenient times. The new cartridges include return envelopes, which enables HP to close the loop by incorporating plastics from returned cartridges into the manufacturing of new cartridges. The Instant Ink service offers an opportunity to address customer pain points (such as running out of ink at inconvenient times) and design waste out of the system. Notably, Instant Ink is marketed as an easier and more affordable option for home/ small business users (customers can save up to 50 percent compared to purchasing ink from traditional outlets), and not as a CE initiative. Nonetheless, Instant Ink has resulted in some significant waste reduction benefits. The initiative's direct-to-consumer model has eliminated approximately 57 percent of materials used per printed page, primarily by eliminating the over-packaging retailers need for marketing and theft-prevention reasons. Since the costs of shipping cartridges to customers are now internalised, the product-as-a-service model incentivizes HP to maximize the amount of ink included in each cartridge, which also means Instant Ink cartridges need to be replaced less frequently.

The Instant Ink programme has yielded some clear business benefits for HP, as the service has about 2 million subscribers currently, across 12 countries and an extremely high customer retention rate. It was not originally envisaged as a circular product offering, but is now seen, internally and externally, as an excellent example of where technology megatrends (such Internet of Things (IoT) and 'Big Data') and product development can intersect to produce significant business value and environmental benefit. Customer loyalty and retention has increased, coupled with waste prevention and reductions.

IoT-enabled servitisation models are not a novel development at the enterprise level in the electronics sector. HP has been selling products as a service, e.g. Managed Print Services, for at least 15 years – the focus is to provide 'printing' as a bundled service: the hardware, paper, toner/ ink and any service requirements as a package. The associated software predicts service needs, re-supply and repair including monitoring energy and paper consumption. This experience with large corporate and public sector customers has informed thinking and business models at HP, such that developing alternative service solutions for other customer segments has not been a massive leap of faith. The foundation of an effective 'as-a-service' model is the use of Big Data analytics. This provides the insight necessary to ensure that devices are optimally utilised, from a cost, security and reliability perspective. Recent technological developments enable performance models to trickle down to small-and medium-sized enterprise (SME) customers where previously tracking and logistics were prohibitively expensive.

FUTURE: 3D PRINTING

According to PwC (2015), 67 percent of manufacturers are already using 3D printing (also known as 'additive manufacturing') in their production systems, and this is set to grow exponentially, with the global value of this technology predicted to reach $31.19 billion by 2022.

This transformation in manufacturing brings with it many opportunities to develop a more sustainable model, by helping to reduce CO_2 emissions, cut waste and allow businesses to develop more efficient processes and supply chains. As the technology develops, 3D printing is an increasingly viable option for a much broader range of industries. As a result, there is a potential revolution in the way products are made and how they are stored and distributed – transforming supply chains, distribution channels, business models and the use of resources.

A study published in the *Energy Policy Journal* (Gebler et al., 2014) suggests that the efficiency improvements provided by 3D printing could cut greenhouse gas (GHG) emissions by 130.5 and 525.5 megatons by 2025, which is the equivalent of taking about 105 million passenger vehicles off the road.

From the automotive, healthcare and aerospace sectors to consumer goods and advanced manufacturing, 3D printing is poised to revolutionise industry and commerce. 3D printing is ushering in what is being

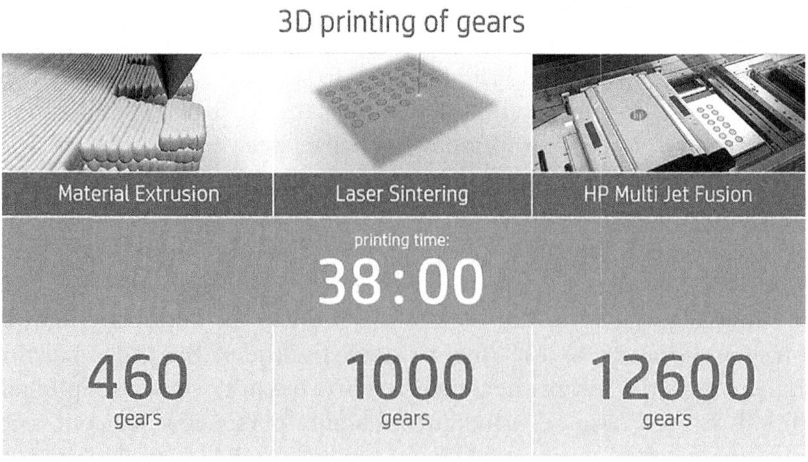

Figure 27.4 3D printing of gears

called the 'fourth industrial revolution' whereby mass digitization will reinvent how we design, manufacture, distribute and maintain products. HP launched its first commercial 3D printing solution in 2016, and the company is working with collaboration partners to deliver the speed, quality, reliability and cost improvements necessary for scalable production and widespread adoption.

This disruptive technology, which has the potential to enable localised, faster and more efficient manufacturing and prototyping than traditional processes, is a critical enabler of the CE. Key benefits include:

- Reduced environmental impact: 3D printing has the potential to reduce waste in manufacturing and distribution processes by enabling perfect matching of supply and demand and improving the cost-effectiveness of shorter production runs (analogous to enhancements HP has achieved by digitising commercial print production and enabling the analog-to-digital shift). Streamlined prototyping processes also support less wasteful and more rapid iteration in product design and development. Additionally, 3D printing will significantly reduce the amount of material needed to make some finished parts by realising complex shapes or redesigning complex assemblies into a single part, in some cases using a single material. These features can save money, decrease energy and resource consumption, lower GHG emissions and simplify materials capture at end of life.
- Reinvention of traditional supply chains: 3D printing has the ability to transform entire industry value chains – from design and manufacturing to distribution and service. With digital inventories and on-demand production, companies can print what they need, when and where they need it, reducing the need for inventories and transportation and packaging. 3D printing produces replacement parts locally and on-demand, which can extend the useful life of products for customers through just-in-time, localised delivery models. For example, in a traditional supply chain, a replacement part for an automobile might need to be shipped cross-country, or even overseas, to fulfil an order or repair, taking several days. With 3D printing, a customer will be able to pick up a replacement part locally, avoiding storage, excess transportation and waiting.
- Transformation of economies and societies: 3D printing can reduce barriers to market entry, expanding opportunities for emerging economies and small businesses, and accelerating adoption for new commercial users in industries such as automotive, healthcare, aerospace, consumer goods and advanced manufacturing.

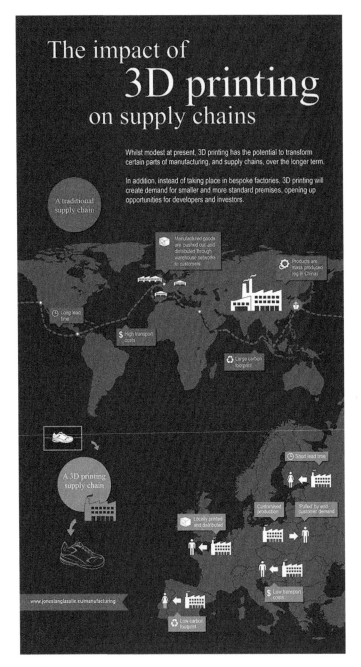

Figure 27.5 3D printing and supply chains

Source: Jones Lang LaSalle, 2017

3D printing is expected to transform how whole industries operate by helping to take ideas and turn them into finished products more efficiently and cost-effectively. While the true impact of 3D printing is yet to be fully realised, it is clear there are genuine, positive opportunities for it to improve manufacturing environmental performance by promoting efficiency to reduce waste and cut carbon emissions.

CONCLUSIONS AND LEARNING FROM HP'S CE JOURNEY (SO FAR)

The CE represents a markedly different way of doing business, forcing companies to rethink everything from the way they design and manufacture products to their relationships with customers. It requires a different approach across the value chain: leasing rather than selling products, remanufacturing goods, seeking ways to extend the life of products or their components and changing the behaviours of end-users. HP has reinvented its 25 year old recycling programmes and enterprise service solutions to create new customer value propositions. Some of the company's programmes are working at scale and are fully embedded into corporate strategy (Instant Ink/closed-loop plastic economy); others are still under development (3D printing). The concept of the CE is far from mainstream and there is still a need to educate and guide organisations in what opportunities the CE can bring – as a concept, it may seem a daunting challenge to embrace all aspects. A long-term vision is required, and organisations should look to their suppliers and customers for guidance in how to practically apply CE principles to their business.

RECOMMENDATIONS FOR PROGRESSING CE IN ORGANISATIONS

- If you sell a product, envision selling that product as a service. This is not only for CE reasons but also because competitors and others are likely already thinking about doing this. This is becoming especially common for large capital items.
- Just start. There is no need to think too hard about it all from an end-to-end process. For HP, one of the key advantages is that employees are allowed to experiment and they are allowed to fail.
- When you fail, make sure you fail fast. If you fail at something, move on and do something else. You have to be able to say to yourself: 'This is not working; let's work it in a different way.'

- Identify customer pain points. Understand how your customer uses your products and what their pain points are. Can you address those pain points by shifting to a product as a service model? Can you empower your customers to repair your products?
- You need passionate people. CE projects don't take off when people just think of them as a job. At HP, implementing CE initiatives is a small fraction of people's jobs, but they love it and they find it exciting. These initiatives give people a sense of purpose and a calling.

BIBLIOGRAPHY

Ellen MacArthur Foundation. (2017). *What Is a Circular Economy?* [Online] Available at: www.ellenmacarthurfoundation.org/circular-economy [Accessed 8 September 2017].

Gebler, M., Schoot Uiterkamp, A., and Visser, C. (2014). A global sustainability perspective on 3D printing technologies. *Energy Policy* [Online] 74: 158–167. Available at: www.sciencedirect.com/science/article/pii/S0301421514004868 [Accessed 8 September 2017].

HP. (2016). *HP 3D Printers and Printing Solution* [Online]. Available at: http://www8.hp.com/us/en/printers/3d-printers.html [Accessed 8 September 2017].

HP. (2017a). *HP 2016 Sustainability Report* [Online]. Available at: http://h20195.www2.hp.com/V2/GetDocument.aspx?docname=c05507473 [Accessed 8 September 2017].

HP. (2017b). *Rosette's Story* [Online]. Available at: www.youtube.com/watch?v=ibSkbHetqvY [Accessed 8 September 2017].

Jones Lang LaSalle (2017). *The Impact of 3D Printing on Supply Chains* [Image]. Available at: www.jll.eu/emea/en-gb/PublishingImages/Research/evolution-of-manufacturing-INFOGRAPHIC-2.png [Accessed 8 September 2017].

Kharas, H. (2017). *The Unprecedented Expansion of the Global Middle Class* [Online]. Brookings. Available at: www.brookings.edu/research/the-unprecedented-expansion-of-the-global-middle-class-2/ [Accessed 8 September 2017].

PwC. (2015). *3D Printing and the New Shape of Industrial Manufacturing* [Online]. Available at: www.pwc.com/us/en/industrial-products/3d-printing.html [Accessed 8 September 2017].

Singer, T. (2017). *Business Transformation and the Circular Economy: A Candid Look at Risks and Rewards* [Online]. Available at: www.conferenceboard.org.

"Vision 2050: The New Agenda for Business," World Business Council for Sustainable Development, February 2010.

U.S. Census Bureau. (2017). *International Database: Total Midyear Population for the World: 1950–2050* [Online]. Available at: www.census.gov/population/international/data/idb/worldpoptotal.php [Accessed 10 May 2017].

28 iFixit
A case study in repair

Kyle Wiens

INTRODUCTION

E-waste is reaching a global crisis point. Catalyzed by a take-waste-dispose model and continuous upgrade cycles, the market for consumer electronics is proliferating past the point of manageability. For such resource-intensive products, electronic devices have distressingly short life cycles – and they are getting shorter. Still, most manufacturers of consumer electronics have yet to embrace reuse options beyond shredding and recycling end-of-life devices.

Circular Economic (CE) models prioritize other forms of re-use – such as remanufacturing, refurbishment, resale and repair – over recycling. In the absence of more widespread reuse options, how can owners and other small businesses fill the gap? This case study explores how one company, iFixit, is working to reduce waste by teaching its community members how to repair devices. It explores why the company has focused on the repair as its mission, shows how providing free information to consumers can be a thriving business model, details some of the challenges of operating in the "aftermarket" space, and explains how iFixit has sought to overcome those challenges.

THE PROBLEM WITH E-WASTE

Consumers around the globe go through *a lot* of gadgets (McCue, 2013). In 2013, Americans alone owned 24 different electronic products per household. As technology evolves and manufacturers keep embedding computers and electronics into more and more things, that number keeps going up. And consumers toss away old devices as quickly as they buy new ones. In 2012, data gathered by the United Nations (UN) suggested that the world produced 49 million metric tons of e-waste in one year. By 2017, the UN also estimated that the world's citizens would produce 65 million metric tons of e-waste in a year – making e-waste one of the fastest growing waste streams in the world (Lewis, 2013). Imagine how much waste could be diverted if more people around the world repaired some of the electronics that are left in drawers, or sent away for recycling, or simply thrown away?

Repair and reuse are a key – often overlooked – pathway to a more sustainable electronics industry.

'Until now, the focus of the circular economy has been primarily on designing products for easier disassembling and recycling – the "outer circle" – which implies creating a closed loop of materials,' writes Janet Gunter of the Restart Project, a London-based social enterprise that empowers people to use their electronics longer in order to reduce waste (Gunter, 2013). 'In the case of electronics this means recovering metals in our gadgets, something only feasible at scale and something from which big companies can profit. The "inner circle" of repair and reuse, seems to have been fairly mute in public discussions on the circular economy but the inner circle is where we can transform our reality.'

Repair is remarkably effective at preserving resources – because it extends the lifespan of our products, offsetting the environmental impact of the device. In a 2015 report, the Green Alliance found that extending the lifetime of a mobile device by just one year can cut the carbon footprint of device usage by between 19 and 31 percent. Moreover, extending the life of smartphones and tablets to four years and laptops to seven years cuts their environmental impact by up to one half (Green Alliance, 2015).

EMBRACING THE INNER-CIRCLES

As the "inner-circle" of the circular economic model, repair should be a priority in the system. In comparison to recycling schemes, repair requires minimal infrastructure and processing. It's cheap and usually local – repairs happen at home, at corner stores and through local services. Also important: repaired products can be reintroduced to the market quickly, adding more value to the economy each time the product is sold.

For the past 14 years, iFixit – a small reuse company headquartered in California – has been working to tackle the e-waste problem head-on. The company has managed to build a successful business model by embracing what most business people would consider a counter-intuitive approach. iFixit teaches consumers, technicians, and reuse businesses how to repair electronics – for free.

iFixit is a massive, open-source encyclopedia of repair knowledge that can be accessed, shared and edited by anyone with Internet access. In 2016, some 94 million people came to iFixit for information about repair. That number grows every year. iFixit's aim is to be a complete repair solution – one that encompasses all the resources first-time do-it-yourselfers need to perform the repair: free repair information, quality replacement parts and precision repair tools.

IN A CIRCULAR ECONOMY, KNOWLEDGE IS POWER

iFixit's journey into the world of reuse has been unconventional, to say the least. In many respects, iFixit was born by accident in 2003 in a student bedroom at Cal Poly University. It started with one iBook laptop, broken and subsequently repaired by the company's founders: Luke Soules and Kyle Wiens.

Apple didn't provide information online about how to fix that laptop. Like most other modern electronics companies, Apple keeps that information for themselves. This is inherently problematic: at best, making repair information proprietary ensures that no one but the manufacturer can fix a device. At worst, it makes repair impractical or impossible for owners – forcing them to buy a new device.

It was harder than it should have been, but Luke and Kyle still fixed the laptop themselves. And they identified a gap in the market, which turned into a business idea: sell the parts people need to fix broken technology and give them the information they need to complete the repair on their own. So they wrote a few guides and posted them online – and iFixit was born.

For the first time, it was easy for someone with no technical background or experience to take apart an Apple Mac. Since then, the iFixit catalogue has swelled to roughly 30,000 guides for around 9,000 different devices. Those resources have been translated into a dozen different languages. The company has heard repair success stories from forensic detectives, field translators and even kids. From New York to Alaska, Tibet to Malawi, people all over the world have used iFixit's repair guides to fix their stuff. Those people saved money, they kept their stuff out of landfills, and they did it completely by themselves.

All of the information iFixit provides is free and open-source. It's also user-editable, so any member of iFixit's repair community can improve the guides or add their own repair guides to the site. Anyone can ask or answer a repair question on the online repair forums. iFixit's mission means that it will never charge for repair guides – or lock information behind a paywall. Simply put, the company believes that repair information is too important to be locked away.

There's a very famous quote from American writer Stewart Brand. It is widely referenced by technologists and netizens, but it holds a lot of truth for folks in the reuse industry:

> On the one hand information wants to be expensive, because it's so valuable. The right information in the right place just changes your life. On the other hand, information wants to be free, because the cost of getting it out is getting lower and lower all the time. So you have these two fighting against each other.[1]

iFixit believes that information about how to repair and reuse products is an environmental resource – and it should be widely circulated. The only way CE will ever scale is if information about how to reuse products is distributed, instead of centralised within individual companies.

It's not sustainable for Apple to be the only folks who know how to fix a broken iBook. Or Samsung to be the only company who knows how to fix a television. Or John Deere to be the only company who knows how to fix a tractor. Eventually, those products will end up in parts of the world where Apple, Samsung, and John Deere are not. It's imperative that there's a robust aftermarket in place where people can get those products repaired. That can only happen when information about how to reuse, repair and refurbish those products is as freely available as the products themselves. The Internet is a perfect vessel for that.

iFixit has been successful at creating a community around repair because the company is filling an information vacuum. iFixit reverse-engineers and writes its own repair instructions, instead of relying on technology companies to release the ones they already have. But there are too many new devices released every single year for iFixit's community to cover. Manufacturers have to step up and share repair information. Otherwise, CE activities – like reuse and repair – could become siloed in pockets of "authorised" parties, when really they need to be applied worldwide.

REVERSE-ENGINEERING CIRCULAR SYSTEMS FOR ELECTRONICS

It's difficult to apply circular systems to products that weren't designed with that in mind – especially electronics. Modern electronics are designed for speed, they're designed for aesthetics and they're designed to be sleek – but they're increasingly not designed to be reused or repaired. Often, with their glued-down li-ion batteries, modern electronics are barely even designed to be recyclable. Without the ability to change the battery, the entire device has a limited lifespan. That's a huge challenge for people in the business of reuse and a massive threat to the environment.

Electronics are ubiquitous, but they're not sustainable. They require a huge outlay of natural resources, energy and human effort. The laptop on someone's desk, the cell phone in someone's back pocket and the tablet on someone's nightstand are formed with materials wrested from the Earth – things like cobalt, cadmium, nickel, lead, copper and gold. A single cell phone, for example, is composed of between 500 to 1,000 different materials (Nokia, 2005) – some sourced from countries that aren't particularly well-known for safe practices, workers' rights or environmental standards.

According to Apple's own environmental reports, over its lifetime, a single 15-inch MacBook Pro Retina is responsible for 592 kg or 1,305 pounds of greenhouse gas emissions (Apple, 2015). Numbers that big are a little hard to conceptualise, so here are some other things that weigh roughly 592 kg (1,305 pounds):

- A well-fed Kodiak bear
- Half a Mini Cooper
- 290 15" MacBook Pro Retinas

The majority of those greenhouse gases (79 percent, by Apple's account) are emitted during the production phase – when the materials for your new computer are mined, refined, processed and assembled into a sleek final product (Apple, 2015). Choosing energy-efficient devices helps – but the biggest problem isn't how electronics are used, it's how electronics are made. Recycling devices is better than just tossing them away, but it's not a panacea. The material complexity of these sorts of devices makes them much more difficult to recycle than something like a glass bottle or a tin can. Many materials are lost in shredders and smelters. Reuse is a better environmental option – and it's more profitable.

'Reuse and parts harvesting are much more valuable than recycling,' writes the Green Alliance. In their 2015 study on repair and the CE, they found that the materials – the separated plastics and metals – in one second-hand phone were worth less than one US dollar. On the other hand, the components in the phone – like the screen, the camera module, or the motherboard – were worth $217. A working second-hand phone was worth as much as $372 (Green Alliance, 2015). There is vastly more value in a repaired product than there is in the recycled materials that come out that product.

And yet, despite the financial opportunity and the environmental imperative – many manufacturers of information technology (IT) equipment are actually making it *harder* to repair and reuse their equipment. In the chase for ever-sleeker devices, manufacturers have turned to strong adhesives instead of common fasteners like screws. More and more technology companies are even gluing down consumables like batteries, which artificially limits the life of the device. Even where repair is technically possible, many makers of electronic equipment have made it practically impossible to repair their goods by limiting access to replacement parts and specialty tools.

Over the years, iFixit has attempted to tackle those challenges by reverse-engineering solutions to the problems of unrepairable design and limited parts availability.

PROVIDING SPARE PARTS

> **Challenge:** Most manufacturers don't sell parts to the public or independent repair shops. At best, this limits the repair of the product to the manufacturer's authorised repair services. At worse, this makes repair either impossible or unaffordable for many owners. Also troubling is that "official" repair services aren't available in most rural communities and are non-existent in developing countries.
>
> **Solution**: iFixit and other reuse-focused companies offer electronics replacement parts to consumers and repair shops. iFixit relies on aftermarket parts-producers to meet the demand for spare parts. It's relatively easy to get aftermarket parts for high-value, popular devices – like Apple products. Though, as with all aftermarket products, quality can vary widely by supplier. iFixit imposes rigorous testing protocols to make sure that aftermarkets parts are safe and in good working order before a consumer uses them for a repair. They also offer a lifetime warranty on most parts and a year warranty on all batteries.

But the aftermarket can be very slow to react for parts that aren't quite as high-demand. At the same time, the variety of Android parts is incredibly varied and fragmented. Many smaller consumer electronics companies don't have any parts even for their own warranty programmes – let alone consumers. Those devices still break – and a consistent supply of parts for those devices is still needed.

In the absence of a steady supply from the aftermarket, iFixit has been partnering with Electronic Recyclers International (ERI) – the largest recycler of electronic waste in the United States – to make repair possible for gadgets of all kinds. From their eight facilities in the US, ERI processes over 250 million pounds (or nearly 113,400,000 kgs) of electronic waste for recycling each year – from tablets to digital cameras, laptops to flat-screen TVs. Many of these devices still work, some have broken screens but functional internals, and others have never even been used.

It doesn't make sense to shred functional electronic devices and components – especially when consumers and repair shops need wider, more reliable access to quality repair parts. That's why iFixit works with ERI to harvest components from electronics slated for recycling. In the process, they're helping consumers repair devices – like Kindles, GoPros, Microsoft Surfaces and Nexus devices – that have never before had a steady supply of replacement parts.

TOOLS TO ENABLE REUSE

Challenge: Manufacturers develop proprietary fasteners to keep third-parties out of devices. In other cases, certain product designs are secured not by screws, but by glues. Such adhesives need to be gently loosened before the glued-down component can be pried up and away. Without the proper tools for the job, repairers risk damaging the device further in the course of the repair.

Solution: iFixit reverse-engineers and sells tools that help consumers and repair shops open and repair their electronics. If tech companies continue not to release tools that enable consumers to repair their products, then the aftermarket has to fill the gap left behind.

iFixit's engineers are often the first repair specialists to encounter new fastener-types on new electronics devices. Every time iFixit's engineers find a new fastener, they reverse-engineer a tool for it. In 2011, Apple switched to a new type of tamper-resistant screw, called the pentalobe screw. Every new iPhone 4 came equipped with the new proprietary screws on the outside of the charging port. Every previous model phone that came in for service had their standard Phillips screws replaced with the proprietary screw by Apple. At the time, consumers and independent repair shops did not have a corresponding screwdriver, which effectively locked them out of iPhone repairs. So iFixit reverse-engineered a solution and sold its own screwdriver directly to consumers.

iFixit has also reversed engineered solutions to get around the increased use of adhesives in electronic devices. The internal components of electronics are delicate, and too much heat can destroy components on the inside. Repair professionals are adept at applying the just right levels of heat to soften adhesives without overheating the device, but consumers often require a more gentle approach. Inspired by massage heating pads, iFixit developed its very own tool, the iOpener, for softening the adhesive on electronics. The gel-filled pouch can be placed into the microwave, heated, and then placed over the adhesive on electronics. The gentle heat is enough to loosen the adhesive without destroying the component. The iOpener is especially helpful in removing screens from difficult-to-repair devices like iPads. As more and more consumer electronics – from laptops to smart speakers – are encumbered with glues, such tools, developed by the aftermarket for consumers, will play an important role in facilitating options for reuse.

REUSE IS THE FUTURE

iFixit's goal is to be the world's free, online repair manual. To help people fix things – all over the world. To empower users to rethink their relationship with their stuff. To move from consumerism to a more powerful position: ownership. Part of ownership is stewardship: maintaining and repairing. Increasingly, though, manufacturers of electronic equipment are eschewing the possibly of repair and reuse – not just for the owner, but for repair and reuse professionals, too.

The IT industry needs to change. A CE for electronics doesn't align with current design trends in the electronics industry. At the moment, the aftermarket fills in the gaps when it comes to reuse – but if reuse, repair and remanufacturing are to be truly institutionalized, if they are to scale worldwide, the tech industry is going to have to change its ways.

Consumers need access to repair information, they need devices that are designed to enable reuse, they need access to spare parts and they need to be able to buy the tools to do the job. Until then, actors in the CE are *at best* going to be reverse-engineering imperfect solutions to a massive, environmental problem.

It's going to take the coordinated effort of environmental organisations, of consumers, and of policymakers to force the most profitable companies in the world to make a change. The take-use-dispose economic model is broken. Mining for resources is destroying lives and ecosystems. E-waste is piling up all over the world. It's time to tackle the problem at its source – and fix it.

NOTE

1 This quote, or variations of it, has been repeated by Brand and others in too many places to cite. For an early reference, see www.edge.org/documents/archive/edge338.html

BIBLIOGRAPHY

Apple. (May 2015). *15-inch MacBook Pro with Retina Display Environmental Report.* Retrieved from: https://images.apple.com/environment/pdf/products/notebooks/15inchMBP_wRetinaDisplay_PER_2016.pdf.

Green Alliance. (2015). *A circular economy for smart devices.* Retrieved from: www.green-alliance.org.uk/resources/A%20circular%20economy%20for%20smart%20devices.pdf.

Gunter, J. (4 December 2013). Circular economy isn't just recycling products; repair and reuse are also vital. *The Guardian.* Retrieved from: www.theguardian.com/sustainable-business/circular-economy-recycling-repair-reuse.

Lewis, T. (15 December 2013). World's e-waste to grow 33% by 2017, says global report. *Live Science.* Retrieved from: www.livescience.com/41967-world-e-waste-to-grow-33-percent-2017.html.

McCue, T.J. (2 January 2013). 24 electronic products per household: Got recycling? *Forbes.* Retrieved from: www.forbes.com/sites/tjmccue/2013/01/02/24-electronic-products-per-household-got-recycling/#7ac21f842c2e.

Nokia. (April 2005). *Lifecycle Environmental Issues of Mobile Phones.* Retrieved from http://ec.europa.eu/environment/ipp/pdf/nokia_mobile_05_04.pdf.

29 Lessons learned from practice when developing a circular business model

Sigurd Sagen Vildåsen

INTRODUCTION

The Circular Economy (CE) is emerging as a solution to some of the core challenges our society is facing, and both business practitioners and academic scholars are embracing the concept (Kirchherr and Hekkert, 2017). This is creating a demand for new business models.

The company Plasto produces plastic components in the business-to-business (B2B) market, and decided in 2014 to investigate the strategic advantages of what the company calls 'circular material streams'. As of June 2017, it established the long-term goal of using 50-percent recycled materials in one of their product groups.

The case focuses on recycled plastic materials and implications for Plasto's supply chain. This reflects a circular business model (CBM) development process that aims to create value from waste by means of recycling. The remainder of this chapter describes the drivers and barriers to Plasto's CBM process and the lessons learned to overcome key challenges.

THE CASE OF PLASTO

Plasto is a small family-owned company that supplies plastic products to a variety of industries. It was founded in 1955 and is based in in the city of Åndalsnes in the west part of Norway. It is a company with around 40 employees. Most of the customers are based in Norway with several in the local area of Åndalsnes. However, through their customers' products, their high-end components are spread internationally.

Up until the early 2000s, Plasto was dependent on the automotive industry as a low-margin supplier to a car manufacturer. Financial difficulties resulted in a changed business model, going from standard components at low margins to innovative and customised products at higher prices. Today, Plasto's strategy is centered on research-based innovation with a special emphasis on networks and external collaboration. The company is renowned for its open attitude and willingness to commit resources to research and development (R&D) projects in collaboration with universities and research institutions.

Plasto's core business is to produce and deliver plastic components; the main product/market areas are aquaculture, maritime, oil and gas, furniture and automotive. Products are offered through advanced technology for injection moulding of thermoplastic polymers. See details in Table 29.1 on Plasto's core competence.

In 2016, approximately 50 percent of its market was in the aquaculture industry through the customer AKVA Group, which supplies equipment to fish farming operators. Figure 29.1 shows an example of brackets that hold cage pipes together, along with walkways on the top of the fish farm, which are Plasto's main products supplied to AKVA Group. The products are manufactured from high-density polyethylene (HDPE), which is a commonly recycled material.

The collaboration between Plasto and AKVA Group was established in 2008, and is described by both parties as a trust-based and long-term relationship. Representatives from both organizations work together to design moulds, the product and the production process, as these activities are dependent on each other to produce the desired output – e.g. a bracket with specific qualities and features. As of June 2017, AKVA

Table 29.1 Plasto's core competence

Core competence of Plasto
1. Knowing how to design the product so that it fulfils the customer's demands.
2. Knowing how to design the mould so that the final product acquires the required qualities, for example strength of the different parts of the product.
3. Knowing how to adjust the injection process of the production equipment so that these qualities are realised.

Figure 29.1 Brackets and walkways supplied to AKVA Group

Group has committed to contribute to Plasto's ongoing efforts of evaluating risks and opportunities of recycled materials, and how to develop a CBM in the longer run.

ABOUT THE PROCESS

The role of external stakeholders and collaboration is well established in the academic literature on CE business models (Bocken et al., 2016). However, implementing this takes time and reflects trial-and-error learning (Sosna et al., 2010). The case of Plasto indicates generic features of such a process, and especially the role of external networks in achieving internal commitment among managers and employees.

The development of Plasto's CBM has taken place in the context of the R&D project 'Sustainable Innovation and Shared Value Creation in Norwegian Industry' – SISVI.[1] The CBM process started as a conceptual idea of the CEO at a kick-off meeting in May 2014, when he was challenged by university researchers on how to change the company's business model in a way that could reduce the environmental impacts of its operations. As a follow up activity, a dedicated project manager became responsible for overseeing the CBM process in collaboration with the researchers. The project manager's main responsibility was to link R&D activities with marketing efforts and customer needs, and he is still Plasto's main contact point in the SISVI project as of June 2017.

Table 29.2 describes the main developments from May 2014 to June 2017. The first phase is represented by the two-year period from September 2014 – September 2016. SISVI researchers, along with master students, conducted several interviews with Plasto representatives to understand its context, challenges and strategic goals. In September 2015, the company hosted a two-day seminar with researchers, students and industry actors from the local community (SISVI, 2015). Moreover, a sub-project was initiated to conduct a Life Cycle Assessment (LCA) of Plasto's products delivered to AKVA Group (brackets and walkways), with the purpose of calculating the environmental impact of using recycled materials. In general, activities in the first phase were aimed at understanding the industrial context, and especially at identifying the challenges of developing a CBM.

September 2016 was the starting point for the second phase of the project, when external actors became involved in the process. At a CE conference, Plasto got to know two experienced companies in the industry: Nofir and Containerservice. Nofir specializes in recycling discarded fish farming equipment and Containerservice has unique technical capabilities related to the handling and cleaning of collected materials. In the same period, the Plasto project manager committed to an initiative regarding the application of the United Nations' Sustainable

Table 29.2 Main developments in the CBM process

- May 2014: Plasto's CEO presents the CBM idea to partners in the SISVI project.
- September 2014: A dedicated project manager begins to follow the CBM process.
- September 2015: Plasto hosts a two-day research seminar.
- September 2016: The project manager gets access to valuable networks.

    - The company Nofir provides valuable contacts and insights.
    - The company Containerservice becomes a potential supply chain partner.
    - The Polytechnic Society provides an arena for learning.

- March 2017: The project manager receives input from Interface and Ocean Cleanup.
- June 2017: The management group participates in a workshop on business model development.

Development Goals (SDGs) to the companies' strategies and operations (UN, 2016). This was organised by the Polytechnic Society Norway, a non-profit organization that facilitates multi-disciplinary and cross-sectoral activities for societal purposes. The project manager attended three interactive workshops between September 2016 – June 2017.

In March 2017, an academia-industry workshop was organized by the SISVI project in Utrecht, Netherlands (SISVI, 2017). Plasto, Interface and Ocean Cleanup were present as industry organizations. Interface is the world-leading producer of modular carpets and is well known for its corporate sustainability leadership (Bocken et al., 2016). Ocean Cleanup is a non-profit foundation developing advanced technology to clean the oceans of plastic waste. Follow-up activities were conducted with representatives from both organisations by the author to collect viewpoints on Plasto's CBM process.

The final activity to facilitate the CBM process was a one-day workshop in June 2017 with Plasto's management group facilitated by the aforementioned project manager along with the author. The 'value mapping tool' produced by Bocken et al. (2013) was applied explicitly in order to understand how environmental and social values are created or destroyed by the company's existing business model. Importantly, representatives from two external organizations, iKuben and ProtoMore, were given the task at the workshop of arguing environmental and social standpoints. These were actors from the local community that knew the company well and had good knowledge of CBMs and the SDGs.

To summarise, between the period of May 2014 to June 2017, Plasto became increasingly committed to a process of developing a CBM. More specifically, the company went from an internal focus on opportunity mapping to actively sharing experiences in external networks. Moreover, the company's management invested a considerable amount of time on the process from September 2016 and now have started to see the strategic relevance of a changed business model.

DRIVERS AND BARRIERS

An underlying driver and a motivation for Plasto's development of a CBM is the supply chain configuration. At present, Plasto relies on one single supplier to produce brackets and walkways to AKVA Group. Having the ability to use recycled materials means increased flexibility in supply due to access to multiple sources of raw materials. In addition, an estimation of the costs of recycled materials produced by

Cotainerservice show that Plasto will reduce their costs compared to procuring virgin materials.

Another driver is increasing expectations from external stakeholders in terms of sustainability and environmental responsibility. This is particularly the case when it comes to plastic waste in the oceans with the issue of micro plastics becoming more of a media issue (The Guardian, 2017). In April 2017, Plasto's CEO stated in the Norwegian *Financial Times*:

> We have identified new possibilities with a proactive approach. Sustainable utilisation of plastic materials is a prerequisite for further development within several industries. Micro plastic waste in the ocean is not a problem caused by our deliveries, but like any other company, we have a responsibility to utilise the raw material in a sustainable manner.
>
> (Finansavisen, 2017)

Responding to CBM drivers has led Plasto to encounter some barriers. First, the secondary materials need to be collected from coastal locations. For example, fish farming cages containing HDPE components must be collected, dismantled and then transported to production facilities. Second, the materials must be cleaned through a melt filter. Currently, this process needs an additional actor such as Containerservice because Plasto does not possess the technology needed,. A longer-term option is for Plasto to integrate a melt filter in its injection moulding machine, which enables the company to handle secondary materials directly. Third, and most important, the quality of the products must be assured in accordance with technical standards and customers' needs. These challenges require testing and experimentation with related competence development for the R&D engineers. Quality considerations are discussed in more detail below.

Typical quality features of plastic products are strength and stretching behaviour. According to Plasto's project manager, the quality of a product is inherently linked to the variation in raw material properties. As an example, the walkways depicted in Figure 29.1 demand less rigorous quality standards than the brackets holding the pipes together. The brackets ensure the stability of the fish farm and must endure the impact of heavy seas, which means that the plastic material must be reliable in rough conditions. Consequently, AKVA Group's main concern is that the brackets meet high quality standards and its technical staff have shown skepticism towards changing the raw materials used in established production processes. As a result, Plasto decided that the natural starting point for production of a product from recycled plastics is the walkways, rather than the brackets that must comply with stricter industry standards.

Working with recycled material also demands new competence among internal staff. Product engineers are used to working with virgin material that has well-known properties, leading to predictable behaviour during the production process. Recycled material, on the other hand, requires experimentation to understand the strength and stretching behaviour of the final product. This gives rise to psychological barriers since the engineers must think differently and change their routines and practices. However, according to the project manager, this can be reframed as something positive as the engineers will need to develop unique skills to tackle the more challenging material properties.

THE IMPORTANCE OF NETWORKS TO OVERCOME BARRIERS

The specialised knowledge and technical capabilities needed to develop a CBM do not emerge in a vacuum. One of the key learning points for Plasto is the importance of engaging external actors in the development process.

> Getting to know Nofir and Containerservice was a milestone. We had realised that setting up a supply chain would be the most complex element of the whole project, but as a first step we can use their existing chains, we can learn from them, and in the long run this can enable us to establish our own chain.
>
> (Plasto project manager, April 2017)

This statement points to an essential aspect, namely that CBMs demand new types of collaborative relationships and a willingness to interact and learn from external actors.

A similar experience happened when Plasto presented its CBM process at the workshop in Utrecht, Netherlands where Interface and Ocean Cleanup were represented. The other participants contributed with comments and suggestions for further work. Norbert Fraunholcz, the lead engineer for recycling at Ocean Cleanup and Jon Khoo, an innovation partner at Interface also provided written feedback on Plastos CBM process at a later stage.

A next step would be in my opinion to be able to make a statement that the parts made from recycled HDPE are just as good as those from virgin plastic, so for the customer there would be no difference in use.

(Norbert Fraunholcz, March 2017)

Norbert Fraunholcz from Ocean Cleanup stressed that achieving quality standards is crucial to establish confidence in the market. Moreover, he recommended that Plasto should dig deeper into the possible differences in technical properties of recycled and virgin materials and this should relate to a specific application, e.g. the production of the walkways. In this way, Plasto could show the customer that the final product meets the quality standards.

Jon Khoo from Interface emphasised different challenges Plasto was likely to encounter. This was based on his experience with NetWorks, a successful CBM development focused on the recycling of discarded fishing nets into carpet tiles (Luqmani et al., 2017). He argued that Plasto must overcome a conservative market that is used to virgin materials and is not motivated by environmental concerns. Moreover, the company must secure the right partners and make sure to have a 'plan B' if the situation changes. Lastly, there must be a business case that makes sense to the board of directors and benefits that customers understand. Plasto's project manager expressed that the workshop was both inspirational and practical. Interface's experience of working with CE at an operational level was particularly useful and provided practical insight that was transferable to Plasto.

Another input from external actors was through the Polytechnic Society Norway where Plasto indicated how the CBM process fits in the broader context of the SDGs framework. Plasto presented its experiences on two occasions within workshops where other company representatives were present.

The project manager highlighted that two working sessions in the Plasto management group had been assigned to the SDG framework and that they decided to prioritise four of the SDGs, while recognising that Plasto's operations were linked to all the goals. For example, goal number 14 is of specific strategic importance since it deals with the oceans and marine resources, and is therefore closely linked to Plasto's position in the aquaculture industry. Establishing a goal of 50-percent recycled materials within 2020 was a significant output of the process and the project manager has indicated that the SDG framework has in general facilitated internal communication over the CBM process.

CONCLUSIONS

Developing a CBM is a process of trial and error, which implies that companies will benefit from an incremental approach to minimise risks. The Plasto case illustrates how external activities and interaction with stakeholders speeds up the process.

The challenges of Plasto's CBM relates to product quality. The substitution of recycled from virgin materials increases the production complexity and creates potential skepticism among customers and internal stakeholders such as engineers. The case also shows the importance of technical testing in trust-based collaboration with the customer. This process also allows the company to invest in and to develop internal competencies based on solid experience.

Below are some lessons learned when developing a CBM based on the Plasto experience:

- The challenges of the CE represent opportunities for innovation and business development.
- Company management must commit to a process of learning and allow for technical testing and experimentation.
- Collaboration between industry actors and academia helps to develop internal competencies along with external networks.
- Sharing of early results and experiences to external actors has a motivating and accelerating effect on the development process.
- The commitment of top management is essential coupled with a willingness to allocate financial resources to R&D.
- The development process must be designed to include inspirational events with external stakeholders so that management is kept motivated and interested.
- The case study illustrates how R&D projects can play a facilitating role in promoting CBMs. Moreover, governmental agencies can help to move CE projects amongst small- and medium-sized enterprises (SMEs) by providing financial support that facilitates industry-academia collaboration.

ACKNOWLEDGEMENTS

This work was supported by the Research Council of Norway (grant number 236640). The author would like to thank Haley Knudson for help with the language and Malena Havenvid for providing parts of the empirical findings.

NOTE

1 The research findings presented are based on a four-year project called 'Sustainable Innovation and Shared Value Creation in Norwegian Industry' (SISVI), operating from May 2014 to May 2018, see www.sisvi.no/. Plasto is one of the core industrial partners in SISVI, which is owned and managed by the NTNU, the largest university in Norway.

BIBLIOGRAPHY

Bocken, N., Short, S., Rana, P., and Evans, S. (2013). A value mapping tool for sustainable business modelling. *Corporate Governance* 13(5): 482–497.

Bocken, N.M., de Pauw, I., Bakker, C., and van der Grinten, B. (2016). Product design and business model strategies for a circular economy. *Journal of Industrial and Production Engineering* 33(5): 308–320.

Finansavisen. (2017). Retrieved from: https://sisvi.no/2017/05/01/plasto-as-featured-in-finansavisen/

Kirchherr, J. and Hekkert, M. (2017). Conceptualizing the circular economy: An analysis of 114 definitions. *Resources, Conservation and Recycling* 127: 221–232.

Luqmani, A., Leach, M., and Jesson, D. (2017). Factors behind sustainable business innovation: The case of a global carpet manufacturing company. *Environmental Innovation and Societal Transitions* 24: 94–105.

SISVI. (2015). *Industry Seminar Hosted by Plasto*. Retrieved from: https://sisvi.no/2015/12/02/industry-seminar-at-andalsnes/

SISVI. (2017). *Creating Value from Marine Waste*. Retrieved from: https://sisvi.no/2017/03/28/seminar-in-utrecht-on-how-to-create-value-from-marine-plastic-waste/

Sosna, M., Trevinyo-Rodríguez, R.N., and Velamuri, S.R. (2010). Business model innovation through trial-and-error learning: The Naturhouse case. *Long Range Planning* 43(2): 383–407.

The Guardian. (2017). *The Eco Guide to Microplastics*. Retrieved from: www.theguardian.com/environment/2017/aug/06/the-eco-guide-to-microplastics

UN. (2016). *Sustainable Development Goals*. Retrieved from: www.un.org/sustainabledevelopment/

Interface

30 *Net-works* – lessons learnt turning nets into carpet

Jon Khoo

BACKGROUND

Interface Inc. is the world's leading manufacturer of modular carpet and has, for the last 24 years, embraced aspects of the Circular Economy (CE) to achieve its environmental goals whilst also growing its business.

Back in 1994, a customer asked Interface's late founder Ray Anderson to articulate the company's environmental stance. At the time, Ray did not have an answer, and he would discover that the company that he had created, for all its commercial success, had a huge environmental footprint – carpets back then were a dirty business – energy intensive, wasteful with resources and fossil-fuel dependent. A key influence on Ray was Paul Hawken and his book *The Ecology of Commerce*, which charged business and industry to be the major culprits in relation to damage to the biosphere and challenged them to take responsibility and use their influence and scale to protect our planet (Hawken, 1993).

Anderson decided things were going to change. He was inspired to look beyond environmental compliance and take a more positive and restorative stance. In 1995, he pledged that Interface would become the world's first wholly sustainable manufacturer, setting out the company's Mission Zero goal, a promise to eliminate any negative impact the company may have on the environment by the year 2020.

MATERIAL IMPACT

In the built environment, raw materials typically account for the largest percentage of a manufacturing company's environmental footprint – for Interface this figure was 68 percent (Arratia, 2013). The company has therefore focussed on reducing the amount of material necessary to create its products whilst achieving the required performance and aesthetic qualities. Interface has sought to switch from virgin to recycled or bio-based raw materials. As of 31 December 2016, 58 percent of the materials Interface uses across its whole portfolio are recycled or bio-based (Interface, Sustainability – Our progress, 2017).

Nylon yarn represents nearly two-thirds of the carbon footprint of the raw materials used in the production of Interface's carpet tiles. Interface has worked with its yarn suppliers to increase their level of recycled content and to reduce its products' footprint. For example, when using Aquafil's ECONYL® yarns, Interface can offer a yarn in many of its products that utilises 100-percent recycled post-industrial and post-consumer nylon content (Aquafil, 2017). For Aquafil's CEO Giulio Bonazzi, there was, at the outset in 1997, surprise at the audacity of Mission Zero, but this was followed by curiosity and a growing realisation that, 'it was possible, do-able and profitable' to become a sustainable company (Interface, 2012). Aquafil then looked to develop their own sustainability initiatives, including its ECONYL® Regeneration System. As a result, Aquafil is now one of the largest suppliers of 100-percent recycled nylon 6 to the carpet, fashion and automotive sectors.

Interface has also sought to develop its products and processes to take responsibility for its products at the end-of-life. The company's ambition is to close the loop by designing tiles to be reused and the constituent materials recycled, to reduce the need for virgin materials. To tackle this, the company invested in post-consumer recycling technology to separate carpet into face cloth and backing. The face-cloth is sent to suppliers and other companies for recycling and Interface turns the backing into new backing at its own manufacturing sites. Since 1995, the company has reclaimed over 140,160 metric tons of carpet through its ReEntry program, including products from its competitors and in broadloom carpet, material from another form of flooring (Interface, 2017).

In addition, Interface has been exploring bio-based options to create alternative and more sustainable yarns. The company has been researching bio-based yarns and launched a collection called *Fotosfera* in 2012 that featured a 63-percent bio-based nylon yarn derived from castor beans grown by small-scale farmers in India – in effect a carpet tile derived from plants (2degrees, 2012). Ultimately, *Fotosfera* was not a commercial success, as although the material and product were innovative and restorative, the cost of the material and the project could not be scaled across Interface's core product.

These innovations have allowed Interface to remain on track with its Mission Zero goal. Since the mid-2000s, Interface has also investigated how it might have a social impact through its supply chain.

SOCIALLY INCLUSIVE SUPPLY CHAINS

Interface's first foray into a more inclusive supply chain was *Fairworks*, a range of eco-friendly grass-woven tiles that sought to combine the use of sustainable materials with the protection of artisanal weaving skills and job creation in India. Again, by developing grass tiles, as with *Fotosfera*, this provided an opportunity to explore the feasibility and commercial aspects of bio-based alternatives for Interface's products.

Fairworks enabled Interface to better understand the different approaches needed to develop a social enterprise and to build a network within the developing world.

Despite early interest and enthusiasm from customers and a fair amount of market testing, once the fanfare over the *Fairworks* launches subsided, the sales of the products related to the collection did not perform well. The *Fairworks* tiles were too different to Interface's core products; from the customer's perspective they looked different and used an unusual material that could be perceived as less sturdy and more difficult to maintain. In contrast to the rest of Interface's portfolio, they were not tied to the main ingredient for Interface's products, Nylon 6.

SCALE, REPLICATION AND SELF-SUFFICIENCY

Scale, replication and self-sufficiency are key issues in developing innovative solutions in relation to the CE. Both *Fairworks* and *Fotosfera* had a limited ability to replicate or have a long-term impact, as the materials were not applicable across Interface's portfolio, the manufacturing costs were higher and did they not sell enough to prove their commercial value.

That said, both *Fairworks* and *Fotosfera* were very important in Interface's sustainability journey as they reinforced the benefit of offering permission to ideate, develop and explore within the company. They were in a way, successful failures. The next project, *Net-Works*, allowed

Interface to further develop some of the approaches lessons learnt from *Fairworks* and *Fotosfera* and learn some new lessons, too.

In 2011, a brief corridor conversation rekindled Interface's interest in a socially restorative supply chain. One of the company's sustainability directors highlighted that key yarn supplier, Aquafil, had found a new way to make its recycled yarn from old nylon fishing nets at both scale and to the high-performance standards required for heavy contract flooring.

It was a serendipitous moment, an opportunity for Interface again to explore the social impact of its carpet tiles and this revelation had the opportunity to link the worlds of conservation, community and carpet in a way that would this time make business sense and be tied to nylon, used in its core products across its portfolio. The result was *Net-Works*.

NET-WORKS – TURNING WASTE INTO OPPORTUNITY

Net-Works is a partnership between carpet tile manufacturer, Interface, and leading international conservation charity, the Zoological Society of London (ZSL). Together, they have created an inclusive business supply chain that empowers coastal communities in the Philippines and Cameroon to collect and sell used nylon fishing nets, which are regenerated into nylon yarn to make Interface carpet tiles.

Ghost fishing occurs when an abandoned fishing net continues to trap and kill marine life. Abandoned and discarded fishing nets impact the health of our oceans and seas and the livelihoods of the communities that live by them. Through *Net-Works*, coastal communities in the developing world are empowered to collect and sell discarded nylon fishing nets, removing these nets from the ocean where they would otherwise be a threat to marine life.

The nylon used in many of nets is the same nylon used in Interface's products – it is nylon 6 which can be created from 100-percent recycled sources. Under *Net-Works*, discarded nets are collected by the communities who are trained to identify nylon 6 nets, and to clean and process the nets to reach a commercial quality standard (set by yarn supplier Aquafil). The nets are then sold to *Net-Works*, who aggregate the nets into bales, which are then sold and shipped to Aquafil. The nets are then regenerated into yarn to make carpet tile. It is a CE solution as at the end-of-life; e.g. this yarn can be recycled again into more carpet or for use in the fashion or automotive industry. It is a restorative approach inspired by Interface's track record of designing sustainable products, a CE project that takes a dispersed waste material and reintroduce it into a mainstream supply chain where it can then be used, reused and recycled.

At a community level, *Net-Works* follows the principles of a social enterprise, so the aim is to pay as much of the profit back to the communities, through the price they receive for the nets they identify, collect and clean. When nets are sold to *Net-Works*, the proceeds become a credit for that individual in a local community bank established by *Net-Works*, based on a model of microfinance known as a Village Savings and Loan Association – administered by the communities themselves. These small community banks provide members with the opportunity to save and to take out small loans, which can be invested in alternative livelihoods such as seaweed farming – reducing dependence on fishing as a sole source of income.

Having started in 2012, *Net-Works* now operates in 37 communities in the Philippines and Cameroon. As of March 2018, *Net-Works* has collected nearly 167,000 kg of discarded nets, provided access to finance for 1,700 families and has contributed to a healthier local marine environment for 64,000 people (Net-Works, 2017).

Net-Works has been recognised as pioneering project winning awards including the US Secretary of State Award for Corporate Excellence (Sustainable Oceans Management) in 2016, the "Best Business/NGO partnership" at the Ethical Corporation's Responsible Business Awards 2014 and *Net-Works* has also been a finalist at the 2017 Buckminster Fuller Challenge.

NET-WORKS REFLECTION: REACH OUT TO YOUR NETWORK AND BEYOND

Few businesses have the resources or experience to tackle environmental and social challenges on their own. In developing *Net-Works*, Interface needed to look beyond its usual sustainability networks. A series of workshops was convened to look at the feasibility of a more inclusive supply chain for waste fishing nets that could do something for nylon akin to what the Fairtrade movement had achieved with coffee, cacao and cotton. Invitees included materials experts, marketing and communications specialists and sustainability consultants through to more unexpected collaborators – marine conservationists, social entrepreneurs, economists and international development professionals.

Choosing the attendees was about carefully cultivating a group that had a common interest in rethinking waste and empowering communities, who had credibility and experience, but also who had diverse and potentially contrasting viewpoints. It was about finding the right combination of people to explore a number of early concepts and to challenge them in terms of feasibility, impact, responsibility and legacy.

From these initial workshops, it was apparent that ZSL and Aquafil stood out in terms of shared strategic interests to Interface and the operational skills to develop *Net-Works.*

For Aquafil, its usual source of waste nylon material came from commercial fishing fleets and fish farms, so a community-level collection represented a new source of nets, one that could be found in many coastal regions across the developing world; and the opportunity to explore related social and environmental benefits that aligned with Aquafil's interests.

With ZSL, Interface found an organisation that had a longstanding record of working with communities on conservation in developing countries. In addition, ZSL had operations in a number of coastal communities in South East Asia where the proliferation of marine plastic waste was already evident. In the same way that Interface wanted to explore how its products could tackle poverty, ZSL were looking to work on more pro-poor solutions that empowered communities, improved livelihoods and incentivised communities to protect their local ecosystem.

Together Interface, ZSL and yarn partner Aquafil would make a formidable partnership with *Net-Works.*

NET-WORKS REFLECTION: CE SOLUTIONS REQUIRE WELL-DEFINED PROBLEMS

Defining the problem effectively is key to designing any CE solution. There is often a temptation to jump to considering ideas too soon, but that can be a dangerous path as it can lead to solutions that address only part of the issue or a miss an opportunity to have a more systemic impact.

Interface, ZSL and Aquafil sought to explore the issue fully. Assisted by 100% Open, an open innovation consultancy, the initial *Net-Works* workshops focussed on the following question:

> How could the attendees collaborate to create an inclusive business that aggregates, cleans, assures, cuts and packs nylon 6 fishing nets for shipping? An inclusive business being one that expands opportunities for poor and disadvantaged communities.

The workshops allowed the parties to explore diverse insights and explore varied approaches – including three geographies, with different maturities in relation to waste management and different benefits for fishing communities. It was an iterative process that embraced varied (and even contrasting) points of view. But through smart facilitation and a willingness to balance the diverse perspectives around shared values and ambitions, Interface, ZSL and Aquafil had agreed to a small-scale pilot between June and October 2012 to test if a community-based supply chain was feasible; within a few months 1,000 kg of discarded nets had been collected from five communities near the Danajon Bank, Philippines and the partners had started exploring how their joint project, *Net-Works*, could empower communities and replenish the ocean.

NET-WORKS REFLECTION: HUSTLE, BE SCRAPPY AND SEEK BUY-IN EARLY ON

A key challenge for *Net-Works* has been getting buy-in from the relevant key stakeholders, both internal and external. Whether the management team at Interface, or the communities in the Danajon Bank, Central Visayas, the Philippines, *Net-Works* represented something that was far from business as usual.

The more innovative an idea is, often the more removed it is from an organisation's day-to-day operations, and, as a result, you need to work hard on getting and maintaining buy-in to develop, prototype and prove that the idea makes business sense.

On *Net-Works*' journey, Miriam Turner, *Net-Works* Co-founder, now director of disruptive innovation at Friends of the Earth, and formerly assistant vice president co-innovation at Interface, reflected,

> Early on, some stakeholders struggled to get their heads around the fact that it wasn't the traditional corporate-NGO sponsorship arrangement: it was a partnership. We had to constantly reframe Interface and ZSL's relationship in this way. We had to demonstrate the value of *Net-Works*, presenting the business case in different ways to different people, depending on whether I was talking to the Chief Financial Officer or the Head of Marketing. That's what intrapreneurs do – hustle and make the case in different ways to different people.
>
> (Deignan, 2017)

Miriam and the team at Interface had had to hustle throughout *Net-Works'* development – always willing to explain the business benefits behind the partnership, to show how the idea would support Interface's sustainability and business goals and to pivot with respect to changes in Interface's market. This required resilience and the willingness to answer questions and challenges from within and outside the business.

Any sustainability or inclusive business project will benefit from internal and external scrutiny, and it is key to have a network that enables a critical dialogue. You will benefit from finding a group of critical friends both within and outside your organisation.

From a conservation angle, there was also an interesting challenge on getting buy-in at a community level in the Philippines and Cameroon. Whereas *Net-Works'* corporate and academic audiences wanted to focus on the social impact on household income or numbers of jobs, the communities themselves have an interest in what were initially less quantifiable elements such as empowerment, livelihood opportunities and risks. Dr. Nick Hill, Senior Technical Specialist (Conservation for Communities) at ZSL and co-founder of *Net-Works*, reflected,

> Achieving the right balance between clarity and detail in the communication is hard, especially because of the huge cultural differences between a Filipino-fishing community and audiences in the UK or US. Most people in these communities don't know the value of their incomes in dollar terms – they only know whether they have been able to put food on the table, repair their house, or pay the school fees. You have to strike a balance between data-based accountability and meeting communities' needs.

AN INTRAPRENEURIAL SPIRIT

Net-Works is a product of intrapreneurs driving change within organisations. A supply chain re-imagined – pivoting away from business as usual to reinvent a supply chain so that it was community-based and weaving in commercial, conservation and community elements. The driving force behind it has been a shared intrapreneurial spirit to. Here are 10 key lessons the *Net-Works* partners would like to share:

10 KEY LESSONS FOR CE INNOVATORS

- CE needs more innovators who can tackle social benefit alongside environmental impact.
- Innovating for the CE is a tough challenge and the more that an idea is removed from an organisation's day to day operations, the harder you will need to work to secure, maintain and renew buy-in.
- CE solutions should make business sense and reflect an organisation's sphere of influence.
- From the outset and through the idea's evolution, it's important to be considering the relative importance of scaling, replication and self-sufficiency.
- Collaboration will be key – for none of us is as smart as all of us.
- Find the right collaborators, look beyond your usual suspects and invite the challenge of critical friends.
- Defining the problem effectively is key to developing any successful CE solution.
- Hustle and be scrappy in your approach to innovation – perfect is the enemy of the good
- Empathy is key – be able to put yourself into the shoes of all your stakeholders.
- Embrace successful failures – collect experiences, maintain your network and apply your lessons in your next challenge.

BIBLIOGRAPHY

2degrees. (17 September 2012). *Interface Unveils Fotosfera, Its First Product Made from Bio-Based Nylon*. Retrieved from 2degrees: www.2degreesnetwork.com/groups/2degrees-community/resources/interface-unveils-fotosfera-its-first-product-made-bio-based-nylon/

Anderson, R. (9 February 2009). *The Business Logic of Sustainability*. Retrieved from TED: www.ted.com/talks/ray_anderson_on_the_business_logic_of_sustainability?language=en.

Aquafil. (2017). *Econyl*. Retrieved from: www.econyl.com/regeneration-system/

Arratia, R. (25 March 2013). *It's All About Products, Not Companies*. Retrieved from Cut The Fluff: www.interfacecutthefluff.com/2-its-all-about-products-not-companies/

Deignan, K. (25 September 2017). *Ethical Corporation and League of Intrapreneurs*. Retrieved from TBC: http://www.ethicalcorp.com/when-saving-world-your-day-job

Hawken, P. (1993). *The Ecology of Commerce: A Declaration of Sustainability*. New York: HarperCollins.

Interface. (2012). *Giulio Bonazzi, CEO of Aquafil on Interface*. Retrieved from You-Tube: https://youtu.be/OTblO22pWvQ.

Interface. (2013). *Learning from Nature*. Retrieved from Interface: http://interfaceinc.scene7.com/is/content/InterfaceInc/Interface/Americas/Website%20&%20Content%20Assets/Documents/Brochures/Biomimetic%20Brochure/wc_biomimicrybrochure2013spreads.pdf.

Interface. (2017a). *Interface*. Retrieved from: www.interface.com/EU/en-GB/homepage.

Interface. (2017b). *Interface Is Closing the Carpet Recycling Loop*. Retrieved from: www.interface.com/CA/en-CA/about/modular-carpet-tile/ReEntry-20-en_CA.

Interface. (October 2017). *Sustainability: Our Progress*. Retrieved from: www.interfaceglobal.com/Sustainability/Our-Progress/AllMetrics.aspx.

Kinkead, G. (24 May 1999). *In the Future, People Like Me Will Go to Jail Ray Anderson Is on a Mission to Clean Up American Businesses: Starting with His Own. Can a Georgia Carpet Mogul Save the Planet?* Retrieved from Fortune: http://archive.fortune.com/magazines/fortune/fortune_archive/1999/05/24/260285/index.htm.

Net-Works. (March 2018). *Net-Works*. Retrieved from Net-Works: http://net-works.com/

31 'Who is mining the Anthropocene?'

Duncan Baker-Brown

INTRODUCTION

In his essay from 2016 'Why wait for the future? There could be a present without waste', Herbert Kopnik[1] speculates about the launch of the iPhone 10.[2] He suggests that Apple Inc. CEO Tim Cook has changed the whole emphasis of Apple's modus operandi, from a company selling products, to a company selling services. Cook's justifies this massive corporate U-turn as a 'win-win-win situation'. 'Winner number one' is the consumer, as they will have a place to return their old Apple products instead of putting them in a drawer to deal with sometime in the future. 'Winner number two' is Apple itself who 'only have to buy the majority of the raw materials needed a single time rather than yearly. The third winner is of course the natural environment.

Obviously Apple Inc. has not yet acted on Kopnik's suggestion. However, if they did, then many people (Kopnik included) believe that there are a number of positive benefits for Apple as well as for planet Earth. Kopnik points out that 'Obtaining one tonne of gold by recycling 40 million used mobile phones is not only much easier and cheaper than getting one tonne of primary gold out of the earth; such a method is much less harmful to workers and to the environment.' Crucially he also states 'We have the technology to recycle over 95 percent of the 15 precious metals that are in a mobile phone!'

MATERIAL MEANINGS

Even within a scenario where a Circular Economy (CE) predominates human society, there will still be 'dumb' materials or 'dumb' products without an end of life plan that will need recycling (crushing/shredding/melting down, etc.) until they can be disposed of cleanly. The author describes this process in his book (*The Re-Use Atlas*[3]) as 'mining the Anthropocene', in other words, working with stuff that has already been mined and processed. This includes landfill sites, ocean waste plastic, whole cities and the communities sustaining them.

Many manufacturers, at different scales of operation, are now taking back their products or even actively sourcing formally discarded material as a valued resource and key part of their supply chain. This approach can often have a number of added benefits. For example, UK local authorities spend over £150 million a year removing chewing gum from pavements and other surfaces. Chewing gum is humankind's most common habit, with over 3.74 trillion sticks made every year. This equates to over 100,000 tonnes of gum manufactured annually. The negative outcome from this habit is that a considerable proportion of the gum ends up on our pavements. The removal of this waste is an expense most local authorities would rather not have and many cannot afford.

Anna Bullus is founder of Gum-tec.[4] While at university in Brighton in the UK, Bullus discovered that waste gum could be re-processed into a range of plastic-type compounds, which in turn could be a valuable resource for the rubber and plastics industry. It only took Anna eight months to prove her idea worked, although it took another five years to commercialise and scale up the process in order to produce marketable Gum-tec compounds that can be indefinitely reprocessed without losing their first-generation qualities. Gum-tec's first product was the Gumdrop Bin that is sold to local authorities across the UK. Designed for pedestrians to use to dispose of unwanted chewing gum, the bright pink bin is secured to lampposts for ease of use. When full up, the whole bin and its contents are removed and sent back to Gum-tec to be re-processed into more Gumdrop Bins. A brilliant mini-closed-loop system involving the recycling of a formerly environmentally burdensome material into the very bins that helps rid pavements of old chewing gum. Bullus is now marketing a whole range of products made from this seemingly endless material source.

For a many years, there have been a number of companies around the world selling products made from waste Polyethylene Terephthalate

(PET) often used to make plastic water bottles. However these initiatives have not been successful at capturing the attention of popular mass markets. Perhaps the alliance of brand developers Parley for the Oceans [5]with big multi-national brands like Adidas will begin to alter human behaviour when buying commodities such as shoes, clothes and other fashionable consumables? Parley was founded in 2012 by brand developer and designer Cyrill Gutsch. Since meeting environmental campaigner Paul Watson of The Sea Shepherd,[6] Gutsch has endeavored to raise awareness of the environmental problems associated with ocean waste by helping to develop products with Adidas made from this challenging material. This strategy recognises that the narratives and 'meanings' imbued within materials that have had a previous function are attractive to consumers. In effect, by investing in a pair of training shoes that claim to be using ocean waste plastic it may mean consumers feel like they are helping clean up an ocean that is choking on trillions of tonnes of waste plastic. The challenge will be to see if Adidas customers return the Parley products for reuse, or begin demonstrate environmentally conscious behavior change.

In addition to Adidas, there are plenty of smaller companies that have been creating less glamorous products made from recycled waste material. For example, in the construction supply chain a number of companies are starting to take the initiative. Re-worked[7] was set up in 2005 by Adam Fairweather as a non-profit business investing in green and social enterprise. In 2004 Fairweather developed a biodegradable polymer material made from waste coffee grounds. This material can be moulded into a robust and, crucially, reusable coffee cup to replace the ubiquitous paper/plastic throwaway cup. Re-worked received several grants to develop the material and subsequently to create a working supply chain model. Although the coffee cup was never commercialised, it led to a spate of interesting new products and collaborations.

Fairweather who has recently taken over recycling pioneer Smile Plastics Ltd.,[8] a producer of recycled plastic panels since 1994, explored additional ways that businesses could engage with the idea of reusing coffee through making flat-panel materials from recycled coffee and plastics. The finished product, Çurface,[9] is a dense and durable material originating from recycled coffee grounds. The panels have been used for a wide range of applications, including furniture. A key application for Çurface is within coffee shops, where the source material comes from in the first place. It is used as surfaces in furniture and countertops and has become a powerful way of engaging consumers and commerce with the sustainability. Google had its coffee collected and the grounds made into material used in furniture for its own self-service café, and

Sanremo included a variation of the Çurface material as panels on its green espresso machine, Verde.

Less romantic, perhaps, but no less challenging, Armstrong Ceilings [10] has opted for Cradle to Cradle Certification for a couple of its best-selling products, namely their Perla and Ultima+ suspended ceiling systems. Both products have Bronze Certification. This certification process was issued by the Cradle To Cradle Products Innovation Institute [11]established by William McDonough and Michael Braungart[12] in 2010. They are best known as the co-authors of a book entitled *Cradle to Cradle* (C2C) from 2002. This certification process promotes the idea of closed-loop systems in the production and manufacture of materials and products. At the point of writing, this certification process does not have third-party ratification. For many people, this could undermine its credibility.

Armstrong Ceilings are focussing on recycling material from old ceiling systems being stripped out of commercial buildings, which often occurs within five to seven years of installation as clients require up-to-the-moment interior fit outs. The company claims their two C2C Certified ceiling systems are selling well and profits are increasing, not least this relates to the fact that they incorporate waste material from old ceiling systems. The merit or not of having C2C Certification associated with one's product is a discussion for another essay. However, it is encouraging that large companies within the construction industry supply chain are seeing value in the collection and re-processing of material formerly considered as useless waste.

HOW ARE ARCHITECTS AND DESIGNERS APPROACHING THE CHALLENGE OF CLOSED-LOOP SYSTEMS?

Perhaps one of the areas where architects are having the biggest impact is around resource efficiency. A number of practices are questioning the way products, systems and buildings, are normally designed and assembled, and proposing innovative, 'circular' alternatives. The work of French architects Lacaton & Vassal [13]renovating un-loved residential towers in Paris and Bordeaux is an example of this approach. Their first tower block salvage project is situated in Paris. Originally built in the early 1960s and designed by architect Frédéric Druot, La Tour Bois le Prêtre as it is known, was in a poor state of repair. The mayor of Paris had decided to demolish the building and replace it with a new tower block. Lacaton & Vassal convinced the mayor to keep the existing building and wrap it in new 2-m deep fully glazed rooms (after unbolting and removing existing concrete cladding). The resultant building was upgraded without tenants moving out. It now has much more natural light, natural ventilation and hugely better insulation than the previous building. Tenant's utility bills have been reduced by over 40 percent, and quite unusually their apartments are substantially bigger than before. These benefits were provided at approximately 2/3 of the cost the mayor of Paris was prepared to pay for a new tower, and with hardly any material going to landfill.

A few years ago, Rau Architects based in the Netherlands set up a separate company called Turntoo.[14] Its purpose is to test new concepts and systems within the construction industry supply chain that could perhaps begin to enable a Circular Economy. Turntoo, working in partnership with Philips Lighting, famously invented the concept of 'Leasing Lux'[15] instead of buying light fittings. The idea being that Philips is paid for providing the appropriate level of lux in a particular room, and that to do this they regularly maintain the light fittings providing this service. The responsibility for removing redundant fittings, or elements of fittings, is entirely with Philips, who take back the material and are responsible for its disposal, or hopefully reuse in new light fittings. In addition to this, Turntoo are testing the idea of Material Passports,[16] a concept developed by MBDC[17] through the Environmental Protection Encouragement Agency in Hamburg (EPEA).[18] These concepts have been applied to a number of RAU Architects projects. For example, the new Brummel Town Hall extension and refurbished buildings for Alliander. The idea is that the owner of a particular building would have a detailed digital record of all materials that constitute the building. This data would allow design teams and contractors working on future additions or renovations to have a complete understanding of what they are working with, and therefore an understanding of the potential to reuse or recycle materials and components. The Material Passport concept works very well with the emerging world of BIM (Building Information Modeling). Buildings, old and new, are currently being completely digitally quantified with BIM. Additional digital information describing how a particular material or component can be efficiently taken apart for re-use is relatively straightforward to add to the BIM model.

In 2011 a group of architects working for the Danish practice Schmidt Hammer Lassen Architects enrolled on a weeklong course arranged by Vugge til Vugge Denmark, the Danish representative for EPEA.[19] EPEA was set up in Hamburg by Prof. Dr. Michael Braungart in 1987 to undertake scientific research, exploring the potential benefits of circular systems. The institute provides workshops and training for people who are interested in applying principles discussed in the aforementioned book *Cradle to Cradle*. Schmidt Hammer Lassen Architects were committed to exploring C2C principles further and then applying them to their own architectural projects. In 2012 Nordic Built Innovation [20]launched an open architectural design competition, The Nordic Built Challenge,[21] to develop innovative and sustainable building concepts for rehabilitating existing building stock. Schmidt Hammer Lassen Architects submission, known as Urban Mountain, won the competition. The concept was based on rehabilitating an existing 50,000 m^2 office tower in central Oslo. The design team proposed to recycle upwards of 80 percent of material stripped out of the existing tower as material for the extension and renovation. This strategy relies on the design team having very good relationships with the construction material supply chain. For example, aluminium from the original 1970s external cladding will be returned to the original curtain-walling supplier who will recycle the material, extruding it into modern thermally broken glazing sections. Recycling aluminium only requires 5 percent of the energy when compare to the manufacture of virgin material.

Another practice of architects, Rotor,[22] based in Brussels, is to literally dismantle the interiors of mainly commercial buildings one screw at a time and re-use the material again, often re-installing it back into the original site. They have set up a separate company, Rotor DC,[23] that deploys a team of 'de-constructors' to dismantle building interiors or whole buildings. They have their own digital platform selling the material and components. To facilitate this process, Rotor DC have their own warehouses to store the material they salvage until it is sold. However, they also partner local demolition contractors to work on projects. This allows Rotor to work efficiently and effectively with local authority departments already responsible for the disposal of material normally designated as waste.

Based in Rotterdam, Superuse Studios[24] has been developing the digital platforms (superuse.com) and the new working methods (Harvest Mapping[25]) with the ambition of enabling this new form of 'mining' for second-hand resources or 'material flows' as they call them. In contrast to Rotor DC, Superuse do not require warehouses to store the material they source. Instead, their networks locate waste material and flag it up on a number of digital platforms. One of these is known as a Harvest Map.[26] This digital platform uses geographic information to locate and prioritise waste materials near to a particular development site and highlights this opportunity to architects, planners, local authority officers, etc. Another digital platform known as a Cyclifier is designed to introduce disconnected material (and other) flows to one another.

Like Rotor, Superuse could not be described as a normal design practice. As a result of pursuing what their founder Jan Jongert calls a 'material-experimental design approach', it includes chemists and environmental scientists, supporting designers and architects dedicated to 'turning cities into a living web of connected material processes and flows'.

CONCLUSION

One theme that links the case studies discussed above is the depth to which the architects and designers have understood the supply chain associated with the projects. The case studies discussed above is extremely important, not least for cleaning up the natural world humans have polluted, and they are often closed-loop systems of sorts. However, a truly Circular Economy requires new intelligent materials with clean end-of-life strategies, as well as new products designed for perpetual remanufacture. The author believes that there is only one way to achieve this ambition, and that is by mobilising designers of all kinds to create the systems, materials, products and buildings that can be designed for perpetual re-use or the enrichment of our ecosystems.

Obviously this cannot be the sole responsibility of architects and designers, not least because it will be chemists and materials scientists who pioneer the production of new materials to replace plastics and other materials without an end-of-life strategy. However, it is architects who specify the material and systems that constitute the buildings they design. Architects literally construct their buildings one brick, beam, window, etc. at a time in their minds, their drawings, specifications and now in their BIM models. With this knowledge, they are best placed to unpack these same buildings one day for re-use. In short, architects have the knowledge. However, the author believes it can only happen if all designers rethink their own practices and design products, buildings, etc. that are able to be a genuine resource for the future. For these to be part of a Circular Economy, their constituent parts must have an end-of-life strategy that sits in either the 'bio-sphere' (re-use or compost) or 'tech-sphere' (perpetual re-use of toxic and synthetic materials). Meanwhile, humans need to test the concepts discussed in this chapter by completely *re-designing* new systems, new materials and new products that allow us to perform as the rest of the natural world does, i.e. where one system's waste, is food for another.

NOTES

1 Kopnick, H. (2016).p.33 'Why wait for the future? There could be a present without waste' from A future without waste? Edited by Christof Mauch. Germany. Published by Rachel Carson Center.

2 At the point of writing, Apple Inc. had launched their iPhone 8 & iPhone X

3 Baker-Brown, D. (2017). The re-use Atlas: A designer's guide towards a circular economy. Published by RIBA.

4 http://gumdropltd.com/gumtec/

5 www.parley.tv/#fortheoceans

6 www.seashepherd.org/

7 www.re-worked.co.uk/

8 www.smile-plastics.com/

9 www.rosaliemcmillan.com/materials/

10 www.armstrongceilings.com/commercial/en-gb/performance/sustainable-building-design/cradle-to-cradle-design.html

11 www.c2ccertified.org/

12 Joint authors of (2002). 'Cradle to cradle: Remaking the way we make things'. New York. Published by Farrar, Straus and Giroux.

13 www.lacatonvassal.com/index.php?idp=56

14 http://turntoo.com/en/

15 http://turntoo.com/en/circular-lighting/

16 http://turntoo.com/en/material-passport/

17 https://mbdc.com/about-mbdc/ set up by Braungart & McDonough.

18 Environmental Protection Encouragement Agency (EPEA) was set up in Hamburg by Prof. Dr. Michael Braungart in 1987 to undertake scientific research, exploring the potential benefits of circular systems.

19 www.epea.com Environment Protection Encouragement Agency founded in 1987 by Prof Dr Michael Braungart.

20 www.nordicinnovation.org/nordicbuilt/

21 http://nordicbuiltcities.org/thechallenge/

22 http://rotordb.org/

23 https://rotordc.com/

24 http://superuse-studios.com/

25 www.oogstkaart.nl/about/

26 http://superuse-studios.com/index.php/category/re-search/

32 Reversible building design

Elma Durmišević

INTRODUCTION

It is through buildings and cities that mankind is increasingly changing the environmental balance of the planet, through which various stocks and flows of environmental capital are shaped. The physical impact of the increasing building mass in industrial and developing parts of the world is undeniable. In Europe, the building sector accounts for 38 percent of the total waste production, 40 percent of the carbon dioxide (CO_2) emissions and 50 percent of all natural resources are used within construction (EIB, 2015).

In addition, real-estate developers warn that the existing building stock does not match the ever increasing changes in market demand. For example, in the Netherlands, 8.5 million m^2 of office space are vacant without a use value (PBL, 2013). Fifty percent of investments in building construction in the Netherlands are spent on partial demolition and adaptation of the existing buildings and 42 percent of new construction is due to the replacement of demolished buildings which do not have capacity to be modified to accommodate new needs.

In a time of diminishing of resources and increasing environmental problems, it has become crucial to understand the capacities of buildings to transform a negative environmental impact e.g. tonnes of degraded materials and CO_2 emissions to a positive one. The question is: How does one transform the current linear approach to the design of buildings that has one 'end-of-life' option (demolition) to a circular design solution that will guarantee multiple life options of the building, as well as its systems, products and materials? The switch is needed from a short-term focus on initial use requirements to a scenario which incorporates design visions for adaptability and reuse of buildings and materials. Such an approach brings focus to reversibility of buildings and their structures. It brings attention to disassembly, transformation and reuse as a mean to bring the construction closer to the continual use loops of resources in its systems, products and materials. A world where buildings and their materials are circulating in continual reuse loops with multiple value propositions form a base for Circular Economy (CE) in construction. This chapter will elaborate on barriers and opportunities of reversible (circular) buildings and a roadmap to reversible buildings will be discussed.

REVERSIBILITY OF BUILDINGS

This chapter addresses the state of reversibility of buildings, systems, products and materials. 'Reversibility' is defined as process of transforming buildings or dismantling its systems, products and materials without causing damage. Building design that can support such processes is reversible (circular) building design (RBD) and can be seen as key 'accelerant' of CE in construction. RBD is therefore seen as a design that takes into account all life cycle phases of the building and focuses on their future use scenarios. Design solutions that can guarantee high reuse potential of the building, systems, products and materials and that have high transformation capacity are described as reversible. A key element of RBD is design for disassembly, which allows for easy modifications of spatial typologies and disassembly of building parts.

Numerous researchers (Brand, 1995; Guy, 2006) as well as EU construction and demolition waste (CDW) reports, have indicated that there is a fundamental system error embodied in the building design and construction that has become clearer over the last 100 years. This is demonstrated through the CDW produced and the associated health and comfort issues.

In an ideal case, every molecule that enters a specific manufacturing process should leave as part of a saleable product; the materials and components in every product should be used to create another useful product at the end-of-life (Graedel and Allenby, 1996); the main structure of every building should accommodate different use patterns during its total life. Unlike car and product design where design for disassembly and design for reuse has been investigated and applied in the past, this approach is revolutionary to the building design.

Demolition in general can be defined as the process whereby the building is broken down, with little or no attempt to recover any of the constituent parts for reuse. Most buildings are designed for such an end-of-life scenario. They are designed for assembly but not for disassembly and recovery of building products, components and materials. Furthermore, building materials products and systems are integrated into one closed and dependent structure that does not allow alterations and disassembly. In addition, the materials used are often composites that pose a challenge to up/cycling processes. The inability to remove and exchange building systems and their products, components and materials results in: significant material consumption and waste; lack of spatial adaptability, e.g. modification of lay out of the building; and technical serviceability of the building, e.g. maintenance and replicability of worn out products, components and materials.

Buildings are made of thousands of materials that have technical life cycle form of 10 to 100 years. The *use* of these materials differs as well. The general static approach to building integration ignores that building systems, components and materials have different degrees of use and technical durability and demolition is considered as the only end-of-life option. (Figure 32.1)

In conventional building structures, faster-cycling components, e.g. space plan elements, are in conflict with slower-cycling components, such as the structure of the building, because of the permanent physical integration between different material layers which have different use or technical life expectations.

The ultimate durability of building is not only related to the durability of its materials but more importantly to the way that the materials are put together.

An example is the Fortis Bank Building in Amsterdam which became subject to redevelopment and demolition 18 years after construction.

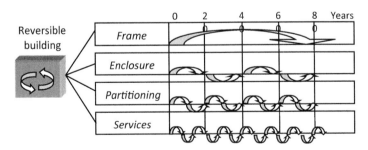

Figure 32.1 Different parts of a buildings have different life expectances

Source: E.*Durmisevic 2006*

This led to value degradation of the building, its components and materials as, for example, the granite façade was downcycled to a low-value material that was used in road construction.

The design and construction of future circular buildings should therefore integrate the factor of *time* that incorporates recovery and multiple use options of the building and its parts throughout the whole life cycle (Figure 32.2). Implementing life cycle design within building design will require a fundamentally new approach to design and construction in the future. Rather than destroying buildings while adapting them to fit new use requirements (being business as usual), it should be possible to transform buildings and recover their products, components and materials. Building design should guarantee high reversibility of buildings and their structures with multiple applications in the future.

TOWARDS REVERSIBLE BUILDING DESIGN

The world of tomorrow is upgradable with dynamic and reversible buildings that meet new requirements by transforming and upgrading structural and spatial typologies without loss of material and their value. In this world, building connections are standardised allowing for exchangeability of building units of different shapes and functions; and building products and components can be independently brought back to the factory for repair, upgrade, reconfiguration and remanufacturing. In this world, the concept of waste in construction is eliminated and circularity is implemented in building design. (Figure 32.2)

RBD can be seen as a new philosophy where demolition and waste is considered as a design error. The intention of such design is designing for circular value chains. This means that design should guarantee multiple reuse options of the building, its systems, products, and materials and provide incentives to retain or increase building value through reuse, repair, reconfiguration or remanufacturing. Different scenarios for reuse and transformation of buildings, systems, products and materials will result into different business/financial models which will reduce the risk of vacancy and poor technical performance in the future. Renting space is already well-known concept in real-estate, but as a result of RBD, renting building systems, products, and materials or their *performance* will introduce new business concepts (product service systems or take back systems).

When exploring the concept of RBD of buildings, products, materials, three dimensions of reversibility can be identified (1) spatial, (2) structural and (3) material reversibility. Reversibility of these dimensions is

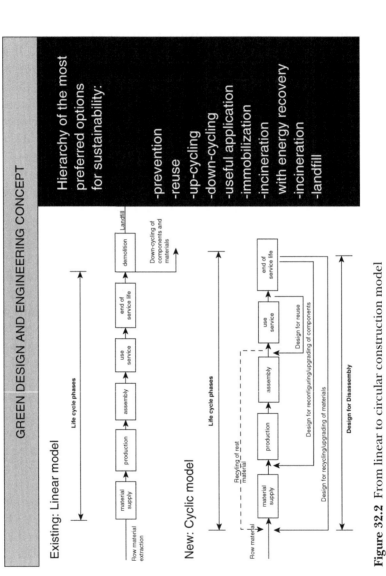

Figure 32.2 From linear to circular construction model

Source: Durmisevic 2006.

accommodated by transformative actions such as the capacity to separate, eliminate, add, relocate and substitute elements of the system without demolition (Durmisevic, 2006). As such these dimensions determine the level of space transformation (first dimension), structural transformation (second dimension) and material transformation (third dimension). Two key indicators of RBD are the transformation capacity and reuse potential of building and its structure. Both indicators depend on design for disassembly and together (transformation, reuse and disassembly) form the backbone/triangle of reversible building. (See Figure 32.3.)

The biggest circle of RBD is a circle of reuse which considers reuse on building, system and material levels. This means reuse of buildings, reuse of system or reuse of material in place of demolition the building, disposal of system and disposal of material. Reuse can take place through direct reuse, reuse by repair, reuse by transformation, reuse by remanufacturing. Reuse on a building level is the most beneficial in relation to reuse of systems and materials, from a social, economic and environmental point of view. Buildings are often part of a social infrastructure and provide cultural continuity; on the other hand reuse of buildings is the best prevention for material use and waste creation. The second circle of RBD involves transformation which again can be investigated on three levels. Completing transformation at the building level is the most beneficial from social, economic and environmental point of view for the same reason as described above. A high transformation potential for a building, its systems, products, and materials is indicated by flexibility of (i) space, (ii) systems and (iii) material and the ability to be adjusted and reused for a new purpose. On the other hand, high reuse potential of building and its parts gives an indication of their reuse options, e.g. direct reuse, reconfiguration, remanufacturing. Ultimately, RBD = high transformation capacity + high reuse potential (Figure 32.3).

REVERSIBLE BUILDING DESIGN

When analysing the three dimensions of RBD, (spatial, structural and material), (Figure 32.4) one realises that RBD needs to deal with defining a balance between spatial and technical reversibility since space with maximum flexibility does not exist; this is also true for maximum technical decomposition of building structure. If this is well balanced through design then the reuse and transformation potential of building can be

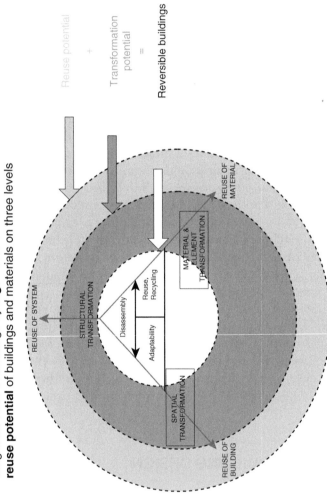

Figure 32.3 Three dimensions of building reversibility

Source: Durmisevic, 2006

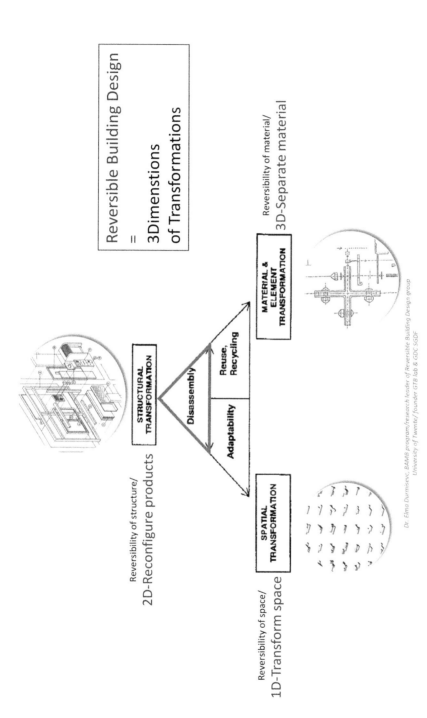

Figure 32.4 Three dimensions of building reversibility explained

kept at a high level. The next section will cover spatial reversibility and the one following that will cover structural/technical reversibility.

Spatial reversibility

It is a design task to ensure vitality and upgradability of buildings, their systems, products, components and materials throughout time. RBD therefore needs to integrate the requirements of all life cycle phases of a building addressing three design dimensions of reversible (circular) buildings as presented in Figure 32.5.

Neither maximum spatial flexibility or full technical decomposition of building, products, and materials for their direct reuse exists. For that reason, understanding of what reversible building and its structure should do after its initial use phase is an essential part of design process.

Every building is built with a basic purpose to accommodate human activities and provide shelter. These activities and needs change over time. The ideal reversible model, that can answer all use scenarios, does not exist. For example, an apartment block cannot answer requirements for differing typologies for schools or office at the same time. Therefore, it is important to understand spatial requirements for required use scenarios and define a set of compatible spatial configurations that will form one reversible and spatial transformation model per project.

Different use scenarios result in different spatial typologies which again require different building structures that will support transformation from one use scenario to another. The technical configuration of the building structure sets system boundaries and defines what a building structure can do to support reversibility throughout the life cycle

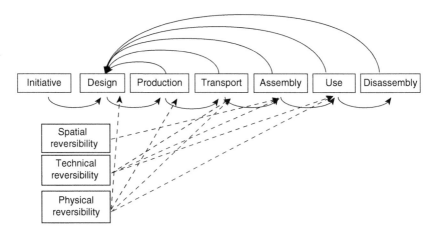

Figure 32.5 Life cycle design of reversible buildings

of the building. However, this has been predetermined by required use scenarios and associated spatial capacity. The balance between spatial capacity of the building and technical capacity of the structure as represented through (i) the dimension of space and position of durable parts on one hand and (ii) the hierarchy of systems, products, components and materials, their dependences and connections, on the other hand, will ultimately define the building's transformation and reuse potential in the future (Figure 32.5).

Once scenarios for spatial use have been determined the technical parameters that will facilitate spatial transformations and reversibility of building throughout its use phase need to be defined. The better these parameters are defined, the longer the building will be used. Two main technical parameters of spatial reversibility are (1) the base of the structure which needs to provide for stability of the structure and (2) facilitator of energy and climate solutions associated with spatial transformations. Together they form the technical core of a reversible building that aims at high transformation potential. When analysing these two parameters, the main question for designers is: what is the minimum number of fixed building elements (that form core of the reversible building) in order to provide for maximum number of spatial transformations within a reversible building?

One example of the above is presented in Figure 32.6 which covers design analyses of the development of Laboratory for Green Transformable Buildings (GTBLab) in the Netherlands.

The core design is optimised to accommodate different use scenarios (office spaces, housing units) is presented in the 3D model below (Figure 32.6, left). Besides vertical loadbearing elements, the core provides natural light and air to all spaces through two air ducts. Further to that, horizontal installation rings creates a horizontal installation network and possibility of plug-in of different functional units of the building which are presented in second and third 3D models.

After spatial configuration and the core of the reversible building has been set, the design will move to the next design phase where focus will gradually shift to parameters of structural and material reversibility. These phases will elaborate transformation and reuse options of building systems, products, components and materials. Design parameters for structural and material reversibility will be addressed in the next section.

Structural reversibility

Spatial reversibility sets up a framework for structural reversibility as presented in previous section. Reversibility of the building, systems, products, components configuration is measured by the level of functional,

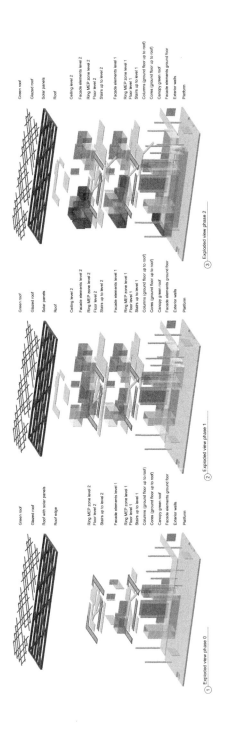

Figure 32.6 Three phases of transformation of GTB Lab

technical and physical dependencies within the their configurations. These dependences determine the state of structural reversibility and therefore the reuse potential of its parts.

The level of reversibility of a building structure is defined by three design domains that deal with above-mentioned dependences:

- Functional domain: deals with functional decomposition and allocation of functions into separate materials, which have different changing replacement rates; e.g. a building façade may have a changing rate of 20 years, a loadbearing structure of 70 years and partitioning walls of 10 years.
- Technical domain: deals with hierarchical arrangement of the building materials and relationships.
- Physical domain: deals with interfaces that define physical integrity and dependences of materials.

The design domains define dependencies that are created within the building and its structure.

During RBD, a designer allocates functions (as for example enclosure of buildings) to a set of elements (e.g. façade components, products and materials that can function as enclosure of a buildings) and conditions for their relationships. As a design activity, configuration design can be seen as an activity concerned with different relationships and interdependencies among building, systems, products, components and materials. Together building products and their relationships represent the physical structure of a building, which informs us how performance requirements of the building are translated into components, products, materials, and how such configuration can be transformed and its constituent parts reused. Ultimately this will determine the structure's reversibility (Durmisevic, 2006).

A structure can be reversed if its systems, products, components and materials are defined as independent parts of a building structure, and if their interfaces are designed for exchangeability. (Figure 32.7)

The benefits of reversible buildings are identified in Figure 32.8 which summarises the design indicators of reversible buildings and design aspects which lead to high reversibility of design solutions parameters for each dimension of transformation within a building.

During the use of a building, RBD can add to the quality of the building by improving the flexibility, and this can also reduce the risk of vacant buildings. Moreover, the users benefit from easier replacement of systems and from easy upgrading. This prevents vacancy and leads to lower life cycle costs.

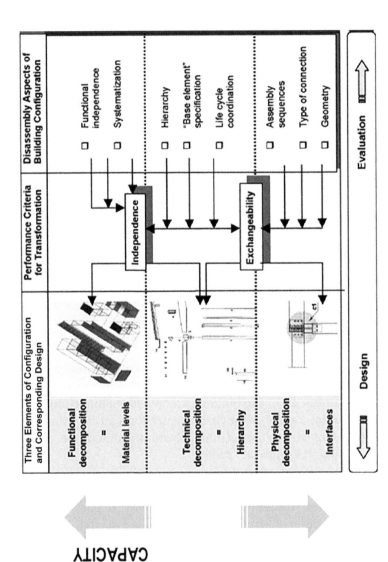

Figure 32.7 Performance criteria for reversible building structure

Source: Durmisevic, 2006

THREE DESIGN DIMENSIONS OF REVERSIBLE BUILDINGS

Dr. Elma Durmisevic

DESIGN PARAMETERS / ASPECTS OF REVERSIBLE BUILDING:

Project Brief definition: multiple scenarios for use of building if possible draft scheme of possible reuse options for the materials as well

PARAMETERS OF SPATIAL REVERSIBILITY/design aspects:

Transformation Model determines level of spatial reversibility. Parameters that determine Transformation Model are:

volume dimensions that are compatible with desired scenarios
position of the core elements that is not restricting number of use options,
core capacity to carry loads and provide space for services for desired upgradability and use scenarios

Core design: Core is integrated base element, a minimum needed to provide for structural stability and facilitate climate, energy and comfort for different use scenarios.

Core, this most fixed part of the building needs to have capacity to facilitate transformation form one use scenario to another without demolition and waste creation

PARAMETERS OF STRUCTURAL REVERSIBILITY/design aspects:

Functional independence
provided through separation of functions on building, system and component levels

Technical Independence
provided by minimization of relations between different functional modules and creation of structured and open hierarchy of elements within a structure that is supported by well defined base elements of the structure

PARAMETERS OF PHYSICAL REVERSIBILITY/design aspects:

Physical exchangeability
Provided by design of demountable connections that are preventing damages of elements by considering geometry and morphology of product edge, disassembly sequences, type of connection

Reversibility of space
Adapt space

Reversibility of structure/
Reconfigure /upgrade structure

Reversibility of material/
Separate elements/ material

1D

2D

3D

Figure 32.8 Reversible buildings

Design for ease of repair and maintenance also improves the quality of building and saves costs by reducing materials. Designing reversible buildings for easier upgrading/updating means that systems, products, components and materials can be removed in a non-destructive way and makes take back of parts easier. The non-destructive removal of systems, products, components and materials also means that they can be reused in the same or in other buildings (Bloemen, 2010). RBD also means that aesthetic preferences are easier to meet and that the service life of the building is extended (Crowther, 1999).

CONCLUSIONS

Buildings are characterised by their static rigid structures and are not designed to be transformed to meet changing requirements without demolition and waste generation. Systems, products, and materials within buildings are not designed to be recovered and reused and the major barriers can be summarised as:

- Lack of valid data about the technical composition of the building and quality of the elements
- Lack of instruments for certification of reusable elements
- Lack of protocols for design for reversibility
- Lack of reverse logistics strategies
- Lack of market strategies for second and nth use life
- Perceived risk of investment in reusable structures over longer period of time
- Lack of life cycle management strategy

However, understanding of decision-making and management strategies for reversible (circular) buildings can only start once we have full understanding of reversibility of building, reuse options of elements and how to increase the reuse potential of building, products, components and materials through RBD.

Central to RBD are two concepts: (1) capacity to transform building space and structure and (2) potential to reuse buildings, products, components and materials in new buildings systems, products and materials. The goal being to have (i) high transformation capacity and (ii) high reuse potential (through disassembly).

Many companies are struggling with reversible/circular building methods as there are a lack of take-back systems and reconfiguration processes which require a different approach to the manufacturing and construction. Reverse manufacturing and logistics are still not in place and design for Product Service Systems (PSS) is still in its initial phases in the construction sector. Industry 4.0 enabling technologies may provide an answer to the complexity of designing and servicing products for disassembly through the automation of production and introduction of automated re-assembly lines. For example, integrated façade modules could be disassembled and remanufactured on a robot reconfiguration line by adding new or replacing old components from the façade module and modifying it to meet new use requirements, e.g. more or less light, better insulation etc.

BIBLIOGRAPHY

Bloemen. (2010). *Design for Disassembly of Facades*. Delft University of Technology, Deflt, The Netherlands.

Brand, S. (1995). *How Buildings Learn, What Happens After They're Built,* Penguin Books, London.

Crowther, P. (1999). Conference proceedings on Durability of Building Materials and Components, Canada.

Durmisevic, E. (2006). *Transformable Building Structures: Design for Disassembly as a Way to Introduce Sustainable Engineering to Building Design & Construction*. Delft University of Technology, Delft, Netherlands.

EIB. (2015). *Investeren in Nederland*. Economisch Instituut voor de Bouw, Amsterdam, The Nertherlands.

Graedel, T. and Allenby, B. (1996). *Design for Environment*. Prentice Hall, Upper Saddle River, NJ.

Guy, B., Ciarimboli, N. Edited by Hendrickson, K. (2006). *Design for Disassembly in the Built Environment: A Guide to Closed-Loop Design and Building*. Hamer Center for Community Design, Seattle.

PBL 2013, Report of Duch National Environmental Assessment Agency, 2013, Planbureau Leefomgeving, Den Haag, The Netherlands

Design and the Circular Economy in the UK blinds and shutter industry

33

Deborah Andrews, Zoe De Grussa,
Andrew Chalk and Dave Bush

INTRODUCTION

Blinds and shutters are multi-functional products that have been used in residential and non-residential buildings around the world for hundreds of years. The component, ready-made and bespoke shading product industry is well-established in the UK and annual turnover exceeds £500 million, which equates to between 4 and 5 million products. The design and manufacture of shading products means that they lend themselves to activities associated with the Circular Economy (CE) such as repair, refurbishment and recycling, which are carried out by many manufacturers and installers. Despite this good practice, many blinds and shutters are disposed of by building occupants even though they still work and the majority of them end up as waste in landfill or are incinerated and as a result of which a considerable quantity of resources is lost every year.

This chapter discusses the various reasons why this happens, beginning with a brief history of blinds and shutters and the development of the shading product manufacturing industry. It also describes their various functions, user behaviour and the impact of motorisation and automation on users and the potential of these technologies as drivers of a more extensive CE. Despite the various positive activities and behaviours, there are a number of challenges to circularity but these are not unsurmountable and the chapter concludes with a series of design proposals that will help to overcome these challenges.

HISTORY AND CONTEXT

Blinds and shutters have been used around the world for hundreds of years to cover unglazed and glazed window openings, although the precise origin and date of invention is unknown. Early examples were made from natural materials including wooden slatted 'venetian' blinds, which were introduced from Persia to Europe and America. Since the middle of the eighteenth century there have been numerous patented and unpatented innovations, and currently there is a wide range of internal shading devices including venetian, roller, pleated, panel, vertical and mid-plane blinds, shutters, screens, and tensile structures. The range of external devices also includes roller and venetian blinds, both fixed and moveable louvre arrays, tensile structures, canopies and awnings. Like the structure of shading products, shading properties also vary and blinds may be opaque, dim-out, semi-transparent, sheer or perforated screen. Early blinds were all manual, but the market now includes motorised shading products that were initially developed because manual operation was difficult or impossible in some locations; motorisation is continually evolving and building façades can now include automated 'intelligent envelopes' that react and change in response to the exterior climate and position of the sun. Although the majority of interior shading products remain manually-operated mechanical products, the number of motorised and automated products is increasing in keeping with user interest in electric products.

THE FUNCTIONS AND BENEFITS OF BLIND USE

Blinds and shutters have various functions which can be divided into two main groups namely:

- Psychological: aesthetics, fashion, privacy and safety
- Practical: as contributors to thermal and visual comfort well-being and productivity, energy saving and security.

Aesthetics tend to be the main driver of choice for end users and specifiers (such as architects), even though the practical functions have a more significant long-term impact on the environment and building

occupants. If specified and used correctly, shading products attenu-
ate daylight and reduce thermal gain during the day and thermal loss
during the 'heating season' and at night. In fact theoretical models
show that they can save up to 15 percent energy when used with double glazed windows (Dolmans, 2006) and 25 percent energy when used
with single glazed windows (Hutchens, 2015). While temperature control and thermal comfort can improve productivity in the workplace, it
is essential for the wellbeing of very old and very young people, both
of whom can suffer from ill health and even death if exposed to low or
high temperatures for prolonged periods in the interior environment.

BLIND TECHNOLOGY AND USER BEHAVIOUR

Currently in the UK many blinds are incorrectly specified or underused
(i.e. they are raised and lowered infrequently) and therefore many of the
benefits listed above are not fully realised. This may be due to the fact
that the majority of blinds in residential properties are manually operated, although residents' behaviour and blind use may change if more
motorised blinds are installed as illustrated in a European study which
shows that motorisation encourages user engagement and residents raise
and lower motorised blinds more frequently than manual blinds (Paule
et al., 2015). Motorised products are either hardwired or battery operated and controlled with a hand-held or attached device. The installation of external and internal motorised and automated shading systems
is increasing in both residential and non-residential buildings; interest-
ingly in this setting users prefer motorised and semi-automated blinds to
fully automated blinds because they can control them to suit their personal preferences (Frontczak et al., 2012). The environmental impact of
this type of blind is higher of course than that of manual blinds because
they include electrical and electronic components. However, Life Cycle
Assessment studies show that the environmental benefits derived from
the energy savings associated with blind use outweigh the embodied
impact of manual blinds (Andrews et al., 2016) and outweigh the embodied and operational impact of motorised blinds (Andrews et al., 2016).

MARKET SIZE AND GROWTH

It is estimated that 50 million blinds are already installed in homes in
the UK where annual sales of blinds typically exceed £550 million (AMA
Research, 2014). This equates to between 4 and 5 million individual

products, about 80 percent of which are residential sales and 20 percent non-residential and, although some are replacement products, many are new sales. A number of factors indicate that both markets will increase: for example, the UK government plans to build 1 million new homes between 2015 and 2020. Sales will also increase as the functional benefits of blinds and shutters are becoming more widely recognised and new building performance guidelines that balance wellbeing and environmental factors are being developed. At present, average product life span varies from 5–20 years; length of life is influenced by quality and durability of components, the way in which blinds are used and maintained and frequency of decoration, which tends to be every five years on average; this activity may involve replacement of blinds for aesthetic reasons rather than because they no longer work and consequently many functioning products are wasted.

It is evident that millions of tonnes of materials and kilowatts of energy are embodied in this product sector and it is estimated that 3,000–5,000 tonnes of materials end up as waste every year in the UK alone because reprocessing is limited. We now discuss the various factors related to a Circular Economy (CE) for this sector.

THE DESIGN AND MANUFACTURE OF BLINDS

Many complete (readymade) blinds and components (including the majority of motors and batteries for motorised and automated blinds) are now imported from China, for example. Nevertheless, there are still a number of major component manufacturers in Europe and the UK where the blind and shutter industry is well-established and semi-industrialised. It evolved as a cottage industry alongside the interior furnishing industry, and although several companies employ 500+ workers, about 75 percent of businesses employ 1–5 people. Larger businesses either manufacture or buy in components and assembly is machine-based but in many small businesses components are bought in and products are assembled by hand (Experian, 2014). Both historical and current business practice have therefore influenced the design and manufacture of the three groups of blind components (operating, shading and fixing), the majority of which push or snap fit together.

Many of the mass-produced operating components are made from single polymers, but some are comprised of sub-components made from different materials; these include different types of polymer or polymers and metals. The shading components are also made from single materials (e.g. textile, aluminium and wood) and from composites (including polyester laminates and resin and glass fibre). Many are man-ufactured to standard dimensions while others cut to size for bespoke blinds; the majority of these components are then sewn by machine although some producers still sew by hand. Finally, when complete, the blinds are installed using mechanical fixings such as screws. The fact that the blind and shutter industry evolved alongside the furnishing industry has a major influence on perception of shading products and rather than being seen as building or architectural components, they are still frequently regarded as fixtures and fittings and, consequently, their perceived value is often relatively low.

These are all important considerations for the CE because they influ-ence overall product lifespan, final treatment at end-of-life and will influence any recommendations for changes in practice.

CURRENT BUSINESS PRACTICE AND THE CE

In addition to manufacture and installation a number of businesses in the UK and Europe specialise in the cleaning, maintenance, repair and refurbishment of blinds, all of which extend product life. These activi-ties are partly facilitated by current component design in that they have been developed for assembly by hand and/or machine and the majority push or snap fit together. As a result, disassembly of complete compo-nents can be relatively uncomplicated (although it can be time-con-suming). In some instances however, components are designed for one-way fit in which case they may be destroyed and replaced as part of the maintenance, repair and refurbishment procedure. Currently, the focus of service companies tends to be non-residential properties where maintenance contracts are commonplace. There are also a number of products on the market to aid cleaning and maintenance of domestic blinds, but this is not the case for repair and consequently many domes-tic blinds that could be repaired are replaced. The cost of professional maintenance and repair may also be higher than replacement, which also discourages repair of residential blinds.

Some manufacturers offer blind refurbishment services where oper-ating components are reused and shading components are changed to compliment new decorating schemes, for example. This service tends to apply to roller or Roman-type textile blinds because it is easier, quicker and more cost effective to replace textile panels than louvres or slats, for example. Product refurbishment can extend blind life by many years but eventually these products will reach end-of-life which is now discussed.

SHADING PRODUCTS AT END-OF-LIFE (EOL) AND THE CIRCULAR ECONOMY (CE)

Although there is no scientific data about treatment at end-of-life in the UK or Europe, anecdotal information indicates that the location where the blinds are installed (housing or otherwise) and type of installers (residents or businesses) influence treatment at end-of-life and that the predominant scenarios are the same as those for many other products:

- Being sent to landfill as waste – where all material value is lost
- Being incinerated as waste – where all material value is lost
- Being incinerated with energy recovery – where some value is recovered
- Partial recycling – where some material value is recovered

In the UK, many blinds from the residential sector end up in municipal waste sites if disposal is the responsibility of the homeowner/resident, in which case they are either sent to landfill or incinerated with energy recovery. There is some evidence of reuse when blinds are resold through second-hand or charity shops, but this is relatively infrequent. Whether this is typical in countries with comparatively high general recycling rates is unknown; it is possible that reuse and recycling rates are higher than the UK if special collection points or services have been established and/or there is a culture of disassembly and component separation among residents.

Blinds can end up as construction 'waste', although this is becoming less common because materials with economic value (especially metals) tend to be removed from buildings prior to the final demolition. If the blinds are not removed and become mixed with the other rubble to become hard core that is used in new construction projects, however, it could be argued that they have retained some value and have been downcycled.

When blinds are replaced by professional sales and installation companies (who service both the residential and non-residential markets) the redundant products tend to be recycled in part. The blinds are partly disassembled and components are separated; the major metal components are stripped out and recycled along with off-cuts from the manufacturing and assembly process while mixed-material, composite, polymeric and textile components are usually disposed of as general waste. In this context, recycling is incentivised by relatively high commercial waste disposal charges and the payment for metals; this is not the case for homeowners/residents who have no financial incentives to recycle. Recycling rates may increase as more motorised and automated blinds are installed because they include electric motors, batteries and other electronic components. Although these blinds have a higher environmental impact than manual blinds, they could encourage circular behaviour because owners are obliged to recycle at end of life to meet Waste Electrical and Electronic Equipment (WEEE) legislation.

WHAT CAN DESIGNERS DO TO ENCOURAGE A MORE CE FOR THIS SECTOR?

It is evident that activities associated with the CE are already well-established in the blind and shutter manufacturing and allied service industries, but there is potential to improve and extend these activities by redesigning products and services. These changes could also be economically beneficial to the industry and end-users, reduce environmental impact and conserve resources, although introduction will probably depend on economic viability. For example:

- Design components that enable damage-free disassembly: change one-way push fit parts, e.g. ensure they deform for separation.
- Design components that enable rapid disassembly.
- Reduce the number of components that are comprised of more than one material: component materials are selected for their specific properties, however, so if it is not possible to substitute material types then redesign the sub-components to ensure that they can be easily separated.
- Encourage repair at home: design and sell repair kits with easy-to-follow guides.
- Increase refurbishment services by manufacturers and at home to extend the life of operating components.
- Design guides to educate customers about maintenance, repair and refurbishment and include information (and possibly a tool) to encourage disassembly and separation of parts for recycling. Add the guides to all blind packages.
- Develop more comprehensive business service models where companies own blinds and 'sell shading'. Examples exist in the non-residential sector, but this could be extended to the residential sector: this model will encourage better management over product life which will aid maintenance and repair (which will extend product life) and treatment at end-of-life (which will increase recycling rates). Improved product management will also encourage

component harvesting and remanufacture where appropriate and component reuse. In this case, durability will have to be monitored but this can be carried out as part of regular maintenance services.

CONCLUSION

This chapter began by briefly describing the history of shading products, their functions and benefits arising from use. It then discussed user behaviour and the fact that these benefits are not fully realised at present; however, motorised blinds increase user interaction, which will reduce energy consumption for heating and cooling and increase thermal and visual comfort. Although motorised blinds have a higher environmental impact than manual blinds, LCA shows that the environmental benefits deriving from 'correct' use outweigh these impacts. LCA also shows that product refurbishment and recycling of some if not all components at end-of-life is environmentally beneficial.

The UK shading product market is already large and will increase concurrently with the construction of new buildings and the introduction of new standards for well buildings. The blind and shutter industry is also well-established and includes many examples of good practice that are integral to the CE, but there is room for improvement. The development of CE in the sector can be accelerated by several changes in component design and business practice which will extend product life and reduce waste of materials and embodied energy by facilitating repair, refurbishment, component harvesting, reuse and recycling at end-of-life. This will of course be dependent on the introduction of take-back schemes and manufacturers can encourage user participation through 'loyalty' discounts for replacement blinds, for example.

At present, the residential market is four times larger than the non-residential market, but there is little evidence of these circular activities in that sector and consequently a considerable quantity of materials and embodied energy are wasted. Furthermore, waste will increase concurrently with the predicted increase in sales. Some of the design proposals could encourage more circular behaviour by building occupants, but they must be supported by the introduction of comprehensive service-based business models that allow for professional management through all stages of the product life cycle. There are already examples of excellent practice in the blind and shutter industry, but they can be improved and extended through design and its importance in the development and implementation of a fully CE for this sector should not be underestimated.

BIBLIOGRAPHY

AMA. (2014). *Research Domestic Window Coverings Market Report: UK 2014–2018* [Online]. Analysis Available at: www.amaresearch.co.uk/Window_Cover ings.html [Accessed 20 July 2015].

Andrews, D., De Grussa, Z., Chalk, A., and Bush, D. (23–25 November 2015). *Using Life Cycle Assessment to Illustrate the Benefits of Blinds as Passive and Sustainable Energy Saving Products in the Domestic Environment in the UK Going North for Sustainability: Leveraging Knowledge and Innovation for Sustainable Construction and Development*. London: South Bank University.

Andrews, D., De Grussa, Z., Lowry, G., Newton, E., Chalk, A., and Bush, D. (7-9 November 2016). The challenges and benefits of developing a sustainable and circular business model for the blinds and shutter industry in the UK; Sustainable Innovation 2016: 'Circular Economy' Innovation and Design. University for the Creative Arts, Farnham.

Dolmans, D. (2006). *Energy Saving and CO_2 Reduction Potential from Solar Shading Systems and Shutters in the EU-25* [Online]. Available at: www.es-so. com/images/downloads/ESCORP-EU25%20volledig.pdf [Accessed 20 July 2015].

Experian Business Database. (2014). [Online]. Available at: www.experian. co.uk/assets/business-information/brochures/National_Business_Database_Guide.pdf [Accessed 20 July 2015].

Frontczak, M., Andersen, R.V., and Wargocki, P. (2012). Questionnaire survey on factors influencing comfort with indoor environmental quality in Danish housing. *Building and Environment* 50: 56–64 [Online]. Available at: http://orbit.dtu.dk/files/6325199/Frontczak%20et%20al%20Question naire%20survey%20on%20factors%20influencing%20comfort%20with%20 indoor%20environmental.pdf [Accessed 5 October 2016]. DOI: 10.1016/j. buildenv.2011.10.012.

Hutchens, M.G. (2015). *High Performance Dynamic Shading Solutions for Energy Efficiency in Buildings* [Online]. Available at: www.esso.com/images/down loads/Downloads%20presentations/ES-SO_RT-2015_Hutchins-M_V6_final. pdf [Accessed 20 July 2015].

Paule, B., Boutillier, J., and Pantet, S. (2015). *Global Lighting Performance, Annual Report 2013R2014. Project 81 0083: Swiss Federal Office for Energy* [Online], Lausanne. Available at: http://www.es-so.com/new/312-global-lighting-per formance-project-estia-swiss-study [Accessed 21July 2016].

Circularity information management for buildings

34 The example of materials passports

Lars Luscuere and Douglas Mulhall

INTRODUCTION

Demands are accelerating by policymakers,[1] the World Economic Forum[2] and municipalities[3] to have products and systems designed for the Circular Economy (CE).[4] These are being driven by newer CE-focused organisations like Ellen MacArthur Foundation,[5] and by an increasing number of European Commission (EC) funded projects focused on CE issues such as the Buildings as Materials Banks (BAMB)[6] project. As a result, manufacturers and their customers are looking for data to help them understand the CE potential of products, as well as their components and the chemical ingredients that make up their materials. This includes how to improve value through healthier use and subsequent re-use, and optimised recycling. Current environmental certificates like Environmental Product Declarations (EPDs) and Materials Safety Datasheets (MSDS) are less effective at supporting those improvements because they focus largely on evaluating hazards, toxicity and environmental impacts rather than improving resource productivity.

A new CE data collection, processing and reporting method is emerging to fill that gap. It is generally referred to as a materials passport (MP). It aims to catalogue and disseminate CE characteristics of products, their components and ingredients. In brief, a MP is a digital report containing CE-relevant data that is entered into and then extracted

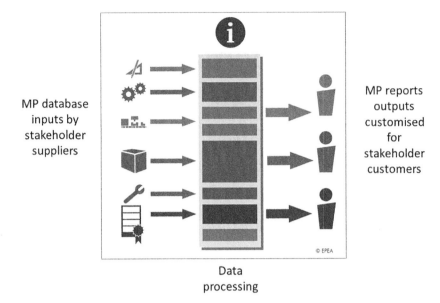

Data
processing

Figure 34.1 Schematic diagram of data collection from different sources, and the provision of information to different stakeholders. © EPEA

from a database in the form of reports customised to the needs of diverse users, see Figure 34.1. In the building sector, where this chapter focuses, the database is shared by a group of those users from across the supply chain, including, e.g. manufacturers and their suppliers, architects, building owners and operators, developers, contractors, demolishers and recyclers.

Tracking MP initiatives is a challenge as diverse companies and consortia are developing them.[7] As a result, this chapter provides an overview and selected insights into a moving target, rather than a comprehensive evaluation.

WHAT ARE MATERIALS PASSPORTS?

There is no commonly accepted definition of MPs. However, the building sector-focused BAMB project defines MPs as:

> Digital sets of data describing defined characteristics of materials and components in products and systems that give them value for present use, recovery and reuse.[8]

To achieve that, BAMB and other MP projects are being designed to have a similar structure consisting of a 'MP database', and data processing that generates datasets referred to here as 'MP reports'. Those reports are referred to in BAMB as 'materials passports'. The procedure for creating them generally works this way: data on products, components and their ingredients is entered into a MP database by users like manufacturers, installers and maintenance personnel. CE aspects are compiled from that data. (See 'MPs in buildings' for which aspects are addressed.) Reports are used by stakeholders to identify the CE aspects users want to focus on. The aim is to make the reports customisable for stakeholders across the supply chain. See Introduction for examples of those stakeholders.

Together, the database, processing and reports are being referred to as 'MP platforms'.

This chapter focuses on MP databases and reports rather than the data processing.

BRIEF HISTORY

Manufacturers often have database-generated reports for tracking changes to their products. These are sometimes also accessible to customers, but are generally held by one manufacturer rather than a consortium of users. The term 'passports' might not be applied to those datasets, but there are similarities. For example, a business-to-business (B2B) pump manufacturer might have a database describing each pump sold with a service contract and its maintenance history; the resulting record for each pump is a type of passport. These are well developed in vertically integrated industries like automotive, computing and aerospace. MPs emerged from those 'track and trace' mechanisms and today are being adapted for the CE.

Databases are less standardised in the building industry where products are often regionally focused.[9] MPs are designed in part for the sector to 'catch up' with other industries. Diverse MPs are emerging, where the term 'materials passports' overlaps with 'product passports' and 'circularity passports'. These terms refer to similar types of database reports. The following abbreviated chronology of the development of MPs demonstrates that the terminology is still developing and has to be standardised.

- The term 'building passport' was introduced by Eichstädt[10] in peer-reviewed literature in East Germany in 1982 to guide the modernisation of factories. Building passports are similar in some ways to building certifications like LEED and BREAAM where a building rather than its components gets the certificate. In 2016, 'building renovation passports[11]' were introduced in Europe for reasons similar to the 1982 initiative. Separately, a group in the Netherlands known as Madaster[12] also introduced a type of building passport.

- 'Product passports' for materials and products were introduced and described in 1990 by Turnbull[13] in a patent application.
- 'Recycling passport' for equipment was introduced and described in 2000 by Hesselbach et al.[14]
- 'Materials passports' for buildings was introduced in 2003 by Braungart & McDonough[15] and further described in 2012 by Hansen et al.[16]
- 'Resource passport' for ships was introduced in 2007 by De Brito et al.[17] In 2012 Damen[18]described the term for a range of products and materials.
- In 2011, the Maersk 'Cradle to Cradle passport' used with Maersk's new generation of container ships was developed with EPEA.[19] Based on that, in 2016 EPEA Nederland introduced the similar Circularity Passport (CP), where the name is aligned more closely with the CE.
- In 2015 the BAMB project was started with MPs for buildings as a focus. The greater part of this chapter is based on the experience so far with BAMB and the report Materials Passports Framework authored by EPEA and SundaHus.[8]

Products are the main focus

MPs in the building sector are being designed to accommodate diverse product types. The term 'product' refers in this chapter to products ranging from coatings, window blinds, carpet, and ceiling tiles to complex products (e.g. systems) like drainage, elevator, or façade systems. Products, components and the constituent ingredients – that make up their materials (see Figure 34.2) – are the focus of MP databases and reports, because products are often the most easily trackable units in the building industry. As well, the value of re-using products and components can be 20–25 times greater than if they are broken down to their constituent raw materials for recycling.[20] As a result, the priority for determining residual value is at the product and components level more than the raw materials level. For example, a chair is worth much more if it is refurbished than its components being re-used before being recycled. The 'cascade of uses' descending from reuse to repair, refurbishing then recycling is economically practical for users if they are able to see that cascade potential in a MP report.

MPS IN BUILDINGS

The following are highlights of MP databases and reports being developed in BAMB[21]:

MP databases and reports are designed to improve data sharing and support the use of CE-related data by stakeholders described in the Introduction. In particular, they are designed to provide insights into the potential of a building product or component for optimal use, recovery and re-use,[22] by storing data in a consistent way, which is a priority as regulations on materials content become stricter. See Figure 34.2 for how systems, products, components and ingredients fit together when storing data. The data is not always organised this way, so the following is to be taken as an example of best practice rather than standardised approach.

- Systems and products: Finished assembly installed in the building, e.g. lighting assembly.
- Components: Parts of the finished product, e.g. LED in a lighting assembly.
- Ingredients: Chemicals that make up products, components and their constituent materials, e.g. dozens chemicals are found in an LED.

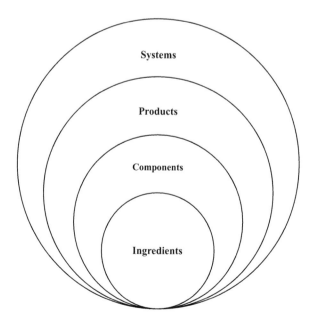

Figure 34.2 The Circular Economy hierarchy

Source: EPEA methodology and BAMB deliverable D5 2017.

If the hierarchy described here seems complicated, it's because products are complex. Due to this, if a too-simplistic approach is taken, e.g. totalling one type of material in a building like a metal, wood or plastic, without knowing which products or systems that material is found in, there is a risk of miscalculating residual value as well as recoverable content. This may lead to overlooking factors including the costs of recovering materials from each product, as well as what is in the products at an ingredient level. Together, these over-simplifications pose a systemic risk to the accuracy of CE methods and valuations. The risk seems substantially under-stated as MP platforms that promise easy use proliferate without accompanying standards for, e.g. design for disassembly.

However there are solutions. MP databases and reports in BAMB are designed to for example:

- Improve CE decision-making during building adaptions, e.g. demolition/ deconstruction, refurbishments and renovations, maintenance, repair and re-use of building products. For this, MP databases can hold data on:

  o Composition of products and components, e.g. expert assessments that go beyond traditional mechanisms. EPDs, MSDS and bills of materials often focus on environmental impacts and as a result often do not contain the full list of contents of products or the data required to determine optimal use, re-use and recycling that is necessary to improve resource productivity. Especially coatings, adhesives, and trace ingredients that add functionality but degrade the quality of recycling streams are considered only for their toxic characteristics but not their impacts on reusability and recyclability. The addition of expert assessments to the MP databases is designed to fill that gap.[23]

  o Modularity, de-mountability and re-mountability of a product like a room divider when a building is being repurposed, e.g. by displaying data on the type of connectors that fix the product to the building and hold it together, this can increase the speed of removal, repair and replacement.

  o Prefabrication versus requiring manufacturing or assembly on site. The approach identifies potential cost savings when prefabrication is used as it avoids waste removal costs on site.[24]

  o Designs for technical or biological cycles as described in CE literature.[25]

- Potentially improve the residual value of products. By describing designs that improve residual value, MP reports can support novel business models like materials banking,[26] where the materials are bankable assets, e.g. in a building. Assets include products like furniture, lighting, and portable room dividers that 'move' through the building during occupancy, repairs, renovations and repurposing.[27] These increase the potential for earlier value recovery by becoming available more often.
- Improve CE economics by describing how products contribute to improving productivity of building occupants.[28] Improved productivity is increasingly being recognised as a leading economic gain from healthier buildings, but is still an under-recognised part of CE economics.[29] For example, MP reports can describe the air-cleaning characteristics of microfibers in carpets that capture fine dust, a main indoor air pollutant[30] that affects the health of occupants.

Based on those aspects, a prototype MP platform for the building sector was launched by BAMB in September 2017.[31] At the time of publishing, about 200 MPs are being generated, for products ranging from sliding doors to lighting systems, and 300 MPs are expected to be launched during 2018. See Figure 34.3 for a screenshot of a form where information about a product is entered into the database to add a product to the system.

Who enters what types of data into the MP databases?

The data can be entered by different users at different stages of product and/or building development and use, starting from manufacture of the

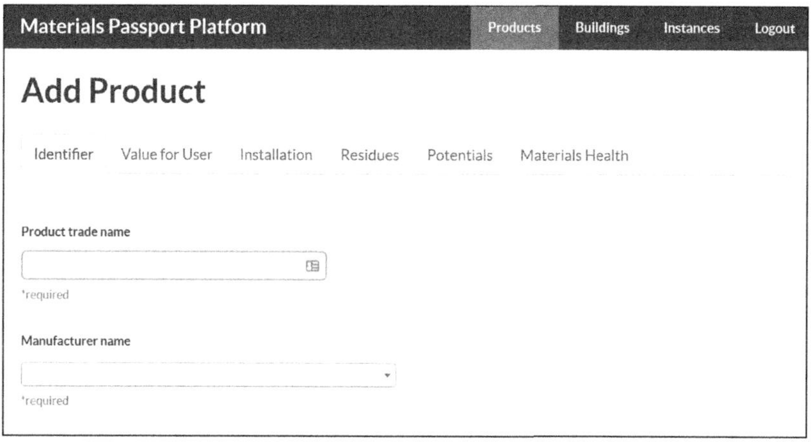

Figure 34.3 The recently launched BAMB Materials Passports Prototype software platform

product and progressing to its purchase, installation, maintenance and refurbishment. The prototype BAMB MP database is being designed so that data is entered by an authorised user at any time in the product's life cycle, e.g. by a manufacturer, installer or maintenance personnel. In this way, MP data development is dynamic. The type of data entered is dependent on the user. A manufacturer has data on its product, but the installer and maintenance personnel have data on the use phase of the product, its context, location and repair status. One challenge will be data integrity as the volume of data evolves. One approach to tackle this will be to assign authorisation levels to users as well as validation protocols, and this is a work in progress in most MP platforms.

Additional to CE characteristics described previously under 'MPs in buildings', the types of data entered can include:

- General information about the product, e.g. manufacturer and product name.
- Product functional description, how long it is designed to be used.
- Dynamic data like changes to ownership and adaptations that might occur during maintenance or the 2nd use of products.
- Context such as physical location, the method of attachment to the building and accessibility to the product in the building. The combination of manufacturer and installation-specific data is designed to provide building operators with customised information about products in buildings, allowing them to track changes affecting maintenance and residual value.
- Variations on a product or component when multiple installations exist in a building, e.g. if there are 20 pumps in a building but 5 models are a different generation from the others; e.g. which new parts might have been added over time.

MP databases also have fields with a capacity to incorporate existing documentation on products, e.g. PDF format, for example, maintenance instructions. These documents avoid the cost of duplicate entries and can be accessed by users clicking on the related field in the MP report.

Who owns and manages MPs and the associated platforms and data?

Ownership and management of MP-type platforms and their data will vary depending on who enters the data, who owns and governs the platform and if access to some data is restricted, e.g. by non-disclosure agreements. As with many database platforms, ownership of the software platform might be distinct from ownership of the data that is entered. The ownership structures are evolving rapidly and remain to be optimised for the platforms identified in this chapter.

Not certification or CE guarantee

MP databases and reports can incorporate existing product certifications, like for example the Blue Angel label or another environmental label. However MPs do not certify a product nor do they necessarily contain all information to improve circularity in buildings. The suitability of a product for the CE, as described in the section on 'MPs in buildings', is based on the completeness of data entered, not on whether the product has a MP report. As a result, a MP is more likely to be a starting point for CE decision-making rather than a guarantee of CE suitability. In a similar way, EPDs do not imply any environmental advantage of a product.[32]

VARIATIONS ON MPS AND LEARNING

Despite the intention described by BAMB consortia to consolidate CE data across the building supply chain, the MP 'universe' consists of diverging platforms and member-user groups. For example the C-passport by CIRMAR and the Materials Passport by Turntoo and Double Effect each has features that differ but are still variations on MPs as defined by the BAMB project.[33] As a forerunner to those, earlier-cited CPs were developed by EPEA Nederland B.V. as a commercial offering to manufacturers and building owners. CPs are dashboard-like documents derived from supplier data gathered by EPEA assessors, and are used, for example, in the recently built city hall of Venlo in the Netherlands, after being developed with manufacturers who provided products for that building.

A main learning from these diverse MPs is the importance of clear visual representations of the information in an easy-to-understand format. Another learning is the importance of protocols that let MP databases communicate with each other and with other databases like maintenance databases, to avoid duplicating data inputs. While common in other industries, they are not well established in the built environment, and considerable work remains to be done in this area.

CONCLUSIONS

MPs in the building sector are a response to demands for mechanisms to consistently describe CE attributes like reusability and residual value throughout the design, construction, use and decommissioning of buildings. MPs are designed to support circularity throughout that process with reliable and customisable reports for users on the composition, use and designs of products. There are a few MPs on the markets today but most are still being developed. As MP platforms grow, there will be increasing challenges related to data integrity and standardisation, communication between databases, and the avoidance of over-simplification of CE characteristics to prevent miscalculation of value and content.

ACKNOWLEDGEMENTS

The BAMB project has received funding from European Union's Horizon 2020 research and innovation programme under grant agreement no. 642384. For more information on the BAMB project and its partners, see www.bamb2020.eu

NOTES

1 http://ec.europa.eu/environment/circular-economy/index_en.htm Accessed 15.11.17.
2 www.weforum.org/projects/circular-economy Accessed 28.10.17.
3 For example, the cities of Amsterdam and Venlo in the Netherlands have CE specifications.
4 The abbreviation CE is not to be confused with the European CE mark.
5 http://reports.weforum.org/toward-the-circular-economy-accelerating-the-scale-up-across-global-supply-chains/leakages-due-to-materials-com plexity-and-proliferation/   www.ellenmacarthurfoundation.org/assets/downloads/Built-Env-Co.Project.pdf
6 See acknowledgement at end of this chapter.
7 For a list of these, refer to *D1 Synthesis of the state-of-the-art,* within the framework of H2020 BAMB project VITO (2016). www.bamb2020.eu/wp-content/uploads/2016/03/D1_Synthesis-report-on-State-of-the-art_20161129_FINAL.pdf
8 Framework for Materials Passports, EPEA and SundaHus. 2017.
9 *Impact of Fragmentation Issue in Construction Industry: An Overview,* Mohd Nasrun Mohd Nawi, Nazim Baluch, Ahmad Yusni Bahauddin, 2014, MATEC Web of Conferences 15 01009 (2014) DOI: 10.1051/matecconf/20141501009
10 Modernisation rationalisée des usines, Batiment International, Building Research and Practice, 10:3, 177–181, Joachim Eichstädt (1982).
11 Building Renovation Passports – Customised roadmaps towards deep renovation and better homes, http://bpie.eu/publication/renovation-passports/ Accessed 28.10.17.

12 www.madaster.com/nl Accessed 28.10.17.

13 Computer-based method and system for product development www.google. com/patents/US5208765 Accessed 28.10.17.

14 Approach of substance flow oriented closed-loop supply chain management in the electrical and electronic equipment industry. Hesselbach et al. Environmentally Conscious Design and Inverse Manufacturing, 2001. Proceedings EcoDesign 2001: Second International Symposium on. IEEE, 2001.

15 Towards a sustaining architecture for the 21st century: the promise of cradle-to-cradle design. William McDonough & Michael Braungart. UNEP Industry and Environment April–September 2003, p. 15.

16 Hansen, K., Braungart, M. and Mulhall, D. (2012). *Resource Re-Pletion. Role of Buildings. Introducing Nutrient Certificates A.K.A Materials Passports as a Counterpart to Emissions Trading Schemes,* The Springer Encyclopedia of Sustainability Science and Technology Meyers.

17 Extended producer responsibility in the aviation sector. De Brito, Marisa P., Erwin Van der Laan, and Brijan D. Irion. ERIM Report Series Reference No. ERS-2007–025-LIS (2007).

18 A Resources Passport For A Circular Economy, Master's Thesis, Maayke Aimée Damen, Utrecht University 2012

19 See www.youtube.com/watch?v=PRgp9tcOwaw for a short video on the Maersk Triple-E Cradle to Cradle passport

20 *Building a circular future,* 3XN Architects & Danish Environmental Protection Agency. 2016.

21 Annex 1. VITO, 2016.

22 The term 're-use' throughout this chapter encompasses direct re-use, refurbishment, remanufacturing and recycling.

23 For an example recognized by the U.S. EPA see www.c2ccertified.org

24 Prefabrication is widely used to reduce waste in the construction industry. See www.autodesk.com/redshift/using-bim-technology-for-prefabrication-to-remove-waste-and-save-money/

25 Biological and technical cycles form the basis for CE materials flows, are widely described in CE publications and were first described by EPEA www. epea.com

26 Hansen, K., Braungart, M. and Mulhall, D. (2012). *Resource Re-Pletion. Role of Buildings. Introducing Nutrient Certificates A.K.A Materials Passports as a Counterpart to Emissions Trading Schemes,* The Springer Encyclopedia of Sustainability Science and Technology Meyers.

27 Companies like Steelcase, Herman Miller, Orangebox and Ahrend recognized this by re-designing their furniture for reversibility.

28 The Impact of Ventilation on Productivity. Comparing worker productivity to physical conditions in the workplace environment. CBE (2007) www.cbe. berkeley.edu/research/briefs-ventilation.htm

29 Research shows if you improve the air quality at work, you improve productivity, May 31, 2017, Libby Sander, The Conversation, https://phys.org/news/2017-05-air-quality-productivity.html

30 www.desso-airmaster.com/en/home/ Accessed 28.10.17.
31 Materials Passports Platform prototype for materials banking now live www.bamb2020.eu/blog/2017/09/27/passports-platform/
32 www.environdec.com/en/Contact/FAQ/ Accessed 15.11.17.
33 VITO (2016).

Index

Note: Page numbers in **bold** and *italics* indicate tables and figures, respectively.

Printed and bound by CPI Group (UK) Ltd, Croydon, CR0 4YY

08/05/2025

01864486-0001